The Birth of a Nation

Rutgers Films in Print

Charles Affron, Mirella Jona Affron, and Robert Lyons, editors

My Darling Clementine, John Ford, director
edited by Robert Lyons

The Last Metro, François Truffaut, director
edited by Mirella Jona Affron and E. Rubinstein

Touch of Evil, Orson Welles, director
edited by Terry Comito

The Marriage of Maria Braun, Rainer Werner Fassbinder, director
edited by Joyce Rheuban

Letter from an Unknown Woman, Max Ophuls, director
edited by Virginia Wright Wexman with Karen Hollinger

Rashomon, Akira Kurosawa, director
edited by Donald Richie

8½, Federico Fellini, director
edited by Charles Affron

La Strada, Federico Fellini, director
edited by Peter Bondanella and Manuela Gieri

Breathless, Jean-Luc Godard, director
edited by Dudley Andrew

Bringing Up Baby, Howard Hawks, director
edited by Gerald Mast

Chimes at Midnight, Orson Welles, director
edited by Bridget Gellert Lyons

L'avventura, Michelangelo Antonioni, director
edited by Seymour Chatman and Guido Fink

Meet John Doe, Frank Capra, director
edited by Charles Wolfe

Invasion of the Body Snatchers, Don Siegel, director
edited by Al La Valley

Memories of Underdevelopment, Tomás Gutiérrez Alea, director
introduction by Michael Chanan

Imitation of Life, Douglas Sirk, director
edited by Lucy Fischer

Ugetsu, Kenji Mizoguchi, director
edited by Keiko I. McDonald

Shoot the Piano Player, François Truffaut, director
edited by Peter Brunette

My Night at Maud's, Eric Rohmer, director
edited by English Showalter

North by Northwest, Alfred Hitchcock, director
edited by James Naremore

The Birth of a Nation, D. W. Griffith, director
edited by Robert Lang

The Birth of a Nation

D. W. Griffith,
director

Robert Lang, editor

Rutgers University Press

New Brunswick, New Jersey

The Birth of a Nation is volume 21 in the Rutgers
Films in Print series

Copyright © 1994 by Rutgers, The State University

All rights reserved

Manufactured in the United States of America

Library of Congress Cataloging-in-Publication Data

The Birth of a nation: D. W. Griffith, director /
  Robert Lang, editor.
      p.   cm.—(Rutgers films in print; v. 21)
  Includes bibliographical references and filmography.
  ISBN 0-8135-2026-6 (cloth)
  ISBN 0-8135-2027-4 (pbk.)
    1. Birth of a nation (Motion picture)   2. Griffith,
  D. W. (David Wark), 1875–1948—Criticism and
  interpretation.   I. Lang, Robert, 1957–
  II. Series.
  PN1997.B553B57   1993
  791.43'72—dc20   93-1988
                                                        CIP

British Cataloging-in-Publication information available

  The illustrations on pages 52, 53, 67, 70 (bottom),
75 (top), 77, 79, 86, 89, 91, 92, 97, 139, and 154 (top)

courtesy of the Museum of Modern Art/Film Stills
Archive. Illustrations on pages 65, 69, 74, 76, 105, 115,
137, 146, 150, 151, and 156 courtesy of Photofest. All
other illustrations are from the author's collection.

  "*The Birth of a Nation*: Reconsidering Its Reception" by Janet Staiger, from *Interpreting Films:
Studies in the Historical Reception of American
Cinema* (Princeton: Princeton University Press,
1992). Reprinted by permission. "*The Birth of a Nation*: History as Pretext" by Mimi White, from
Enclitic 5, no. 2/6, no. 1 (Fall 1981/Spring 1982):
17–24. Reprinted by permission of the author. "The
Historical Novel Goes to Hollywood: Scott, Griffith,
and Film Epic Today" by James Chandler, from *The
Romantics and Us: Essays on Literature and Cul-
ture,* edited by Gene W. Ruoff (New Brunswick,
N.J.: Rutgers University Press, 1990). Copyright ©
1990 by Rutgers, The State University. Reprinted by
permission of the author and the publisher. "'The
Sword Became a Flashing Vision': D. W. Griffith's
The Birth of a Nation" by Michael Rogin, from
*Ronald Reagan, The Movie and Other Episodes in
Political Demonology* (Berkeley and Los Angeles:
University of California Press, 1987). Copyright © by
the Regents of the University of California.

Acknowledgments

I wrote part of this book during a happy year I spent at the City University of New York, The College of Staten Island, and I wish to salute my former colleagues in the Department of Performing and Creative Arts, and my ferry companions, Kent Greene and Jacob Levich. For assistance of various kinds, I should like to thank the following scholars and friends: Marta Balletbò-Coll, Eileen Bowser, Gerald Equi, Julian Halliday, Cora Harris, Karen Kelly Sandke, Leo Lerman, Anita Lowry, Peggy Roalf, Louis Schwartz, Charles Silver, Marge Sullivan, Thom Taylor, and my colleague in film studies at the University of Hartford, Michael Walsh. I am especially grateful to John Belton and Tom Gunning for their generous willingness, as Griffith scholars, to advise me in a number of ways during the preparation of this volume, and to Sandy Flitterman-Lewis for performing editorial miracles on an earlier draft of the introductory essay. My thanks to the Films in Print Series editors—Charles Affron, Mirella Affron, and Robert Lyons—for their encouragement and support; to Leslie Mitchner, Executive Editor at Rutgers University Press, who has been gracious and professional in seeing this project to completion; and to Marilyn Campbell, who has been an extraordinarily helpful and scrupulous copyeditor. To Paul Scovill, and to June, Vic, Lesli-Sharon, and Gordon Lang, I offer my love and gratitude.

Contents

Filmography and Bibliography

The Birth of a Nation

Introduction

The Birth of a Nation: History, Ideology, Narrative Form

Robert Lang

In filming *The Birth of a Nation,* I gave to my best knowledge the proven facts, and presented the known truth, about the Reconstruction period in the American South. These facts are based on an overwhelming compilation of authentic evidence and testimony. My picturisation of history as it happens requires, therefore, no apology, no defence, no "explanations."—D. W. Griffith, in a letter to *Sight & Sound,* 1947

Shortly after the Civil War, Robert E. Lee noted the importance of "the opinion which posterity may form of the motives which governed the South in their late struggle for the maintenance of the principles of the Constitution," adding that he hoped, "therefore, a true history [would] be written, and justice done them."[1] Nearly a hundred years later, Robert Penn Warren wrote that "the Civil War is, for the American imagination, the great single event of our history. Without too much wrenching, it may, in fact, be said to *be* American history."[2] In America, however, the Civil War is remembered not as history but as legend. The process of turning the bloody, traumatic reality into a Victorian melodrama began shortly after the fighting ceased. For Southerners and Northerners alike, it was a psychological necessity to make a legend out of the chaos and contradiction of the experience. In *The Birth of a Nation,* Griffith gave plastic reality to many of the images that dominated the historiographic Imaginary of the Civil War and its aftermath, and Griffith's narrative organization of history—his attempt to identify the causes of the Civil War and to explain Reconstruction to a people who needed romance, not realism—can perhaps be best described in terms of melodrama.

---

1. Quoted by Edmund Jenings Lee, M.D., "The Character of General Lee," in *Gen. Robert Edward Lee: Soldier, Citizen, and Christian Patriot,* ed. R. A. Brock (Richmond: Royal Publishing Co., 1897), 405.
2. Robert Penn Warren, *The Legacy of the Civil War: Meditations on the Centennial* (New York: Random House, 1961), 1.

Griffith's grasp of historiography was astonishingly naïve. In an article he wrote for a magazine called *The Editor* in 1915, he had this to say about the teaching of history:

> The time will come, and in less than ten years . . . when the children in the public schools will be taught practically everything by moving pictures. Certainly they will never be obliged to read history again.
>
> Imagine a public library of the near future, for instance. There will be long rows of boxes or pillars, properly classified and indexed, of course. At each box a push button and before each box a seat. Suppose you wish to "read up" on a certain episode in Napoleon's life. Instead of consulting all the authorities, wading laboriously through a host of books, and ending bewildered, without a clear idea of what exactly did happen and confused at every point by conflicting opinions about what did happen, you will merely seat yourself at a properly adjusted window, in a scientifically prepared room, press the button, and actually see what happened.
>
> There will be no opinions expressed. You will merely be present at the making of history. All the work of writing, revising, collating, and reproducing will have been carefully attended to by a corps of recognized experts, and you will have received a vivid and complete expression.[3]

From this quotation it is easy to see Griffith's inability to perceive the ideological encodings of the "natural." To "actually see what happened" is, of course, to actually see a construction; and the ideological underpinnings of Griffith's library of the future are implicit in his remark that "you will merely be present at the making of history." Griffith's complacent belief in "recognized experts" ignores the fact that experts have their own perspective on history.

In Andrew Sarris's words, "The best that could be said for Griffith was that he was not fully conscious of all the issues involved in his treatment of Reconstruction after the Civil War," and that "unlike Gance and Eisenstein, Griffith relied more on a theory of character than a theory of history."[4] The melodramatic move is toward character, and an example of how this process of characterization works is offered in Alan T. Nolan's observation that the Civil War "is defined in our

---

3. D. W. Griffith, "Five Dollar 'Movies' Prophesied," *The Editor*, April 24, 1915. Reprinted in *Focus on D. W. Griffith*, ed. Harry M. Geduld (Englewood Cliffs, N.J.: Prentice-Hall, 1971), 34–35.

4. Andrew Sarris, "*Birth of a Nation*, or White Power Back When," *The Village Voice*, July 17 and July 24, 1969. Reprinted in *Focus on "The Birth of a Nation*," ed. Fred Silva (Englewood Cliffs, N.J.: Prentice-Hall, 1971), 107–108. Gance, incidentally, described *The Birth of a Nation* as a *chanson de geste*. This is an apt description, considering the historical discrepancy in the earliest extant and most famous *chanson* of the Charlemagne cycle, *La Chanson de Roland*, which has Roland fighting the Muslim Saracens at Roncevaux, when in reality, Charlemagne and the Saracens were allies at Roncevaux, fighting against the Christian Basques. As in Griffith's film, legend rewrites history to conform to ideological imperatives.

consciousness by the clichés with which historians and the purveyors of popular culture have surrounded it: the troublesome abolitionists, the brothers' war, Scarlett and Tara, the faithful slave, the forlorn Confederate soldier, the brooding Lincoln, High Tide at Gettysburg, the bloody Grant, the Lost Cause, and the peerless Robert E. Lee. These images, each laden with emotion, are in our bones."[5]

Melodrama certainly cannot conceive of storytelling in anything other than these clichés that Nolan, the historian, deplores. However, my point here is not to establish where Griffith was inaccurate, or how he misplaced his emphases or distorted "the facts." What interests me here is Griffith's historiography as ideological practice, his shaping of history as fact and how that shaping itself is ideologically informed.

Since 1915, and certainly since the Civil War itself, much has changed in the historical landscape. Not only is the Civil War now remote in time, but there is a sense in which—thanks, partly, to the influences of film and television—we share a national culture. Some of the more extreme racial attitudes that underlie the

5. Alan T. Nolan, *Lee Considered: General Robert E. Lee and Civil War History* (Chapel Hill: University of North Carolina Press, 1991), 3.

clichés that dominated the discourse on the Civil War and Reconstruction have been dismantled or modified. But although these changes might shape our contemporary perspective, we need to understand that the Civil War was "the obsessive trauma of American politics and historiography of [Griffith]'s generation,"[6] and as a Southerner, Griffith presents a "Southern" point of view.

Historically, as Nolan points out, the South's contribution to the way in which the War and Reconstruction period were understood and represented had two elements: "The first concerned the role of slavery; the second involved the changing image of the slave and the freedman."[7] As in Griffith's film, it was not slavery but "liberty, independence, and especially states' rights [that] were advanced by countless southern spokesmen as the hallowed principles of the Lost Cause."[8] (Cf. intertitles 107, 146, and 507.)

Griffith was concerned to make sense of the defeat of the South by justifying the Southern effort and reclaiming its dignity. This discourse has come to be known as the Southern Legend, or Lost Cause. Although Russell Merritt has noted that "by 1914 most Southern writers considered the job finished and the legend dried up,"[9] Griffith was still greatly attracted to it. Like his Southern compatriot Thomas Dixon, upon whose book and play *The Clansman* much of *The Birth of a Nation* is based, he obviously still felt the need to redeem the defeat of the South. As we know, the result, in Everett Carter's words, is a record of a cultural illusion that is without equal.

Carter gives the essentials of this image of the South shared by Dixon and Griffith when he writes that the film became "a visualization of the whole set of irrational cultural assumptions which may be termed the 'Plantation Illusion.' The Illusion has many elements, but it is based primarily upon a belief in a golden age of the antebellum South, an age in which feudal agrarianism provided the good life for wealthy, leisured, kindly, aristocratic owner and loyal, happy, obedient slave."[10]

More importantly for some, Carter has noted how "the violation of the Southern illusion by the North" is translated by the film into sexual terms. Griffith's film, like Dixon's book, "incorporates one of the most vital of the forces underlying the illusion—the obscure, bewildering complex of sexual guilt and fear which the

6. Philip Rosen, "Securing the Historical: Historiography and the Classical Cinema," in *Cinema Histories, Cinema Practices,* ed. Patricia Mellencamp and Philip Rosen, American Film Institute Monograph Series, vol. 4 (Frederick, Md.: University Publications of America, 1984), 23.

7. Nolan, *Lee Considered,* 164.

8. Robert F. Durden, quoted by Nolan, *Lee Considered,* 164.

9. Russell Merritt, "Dixon, Griffith, and the Southern Legend: A Cultural Analysis of *The Birth of a Nation,*" in *Cinema Examined,* ed. Richard Dyer MacCann and Jack C. Ellis (New York: E. P. Dutton, 1982), 169.

10. Everett Carter, "Cultural History Written with Lightning: The Significance of *The Birth of a Nation,*" *American Quarterly* 12 (Fall 1960). Reprinted in Silva, *Focus on "Birth,"* 136.

ideal never overtly admits, but which are . . . deeply interwoven into the Southern sensibility."[11] Crises of narrative and sexuality—the mainstays of melodrama—become intertwined with Griffith's reconstruction of historical fact. It is precisely on the terrain of sexuality that history becomes legend and melodramatic myth.

Thomas Dixon's Historical Romance, *The Clansman*

In her autobiography, Lillian Gish insists that "Mr. Griffith didn't need the Dixon book. His intention was to tell his version of the War between the States. But he evidently lacked the confidence to start production on a twelve-reel film without an established book as a basis for his story."[12] Although this may have been so, a great deal of *The Birth of a Nation* (most of the second part, which deals with Reconstruction) closely follows Dixon's *The Clansman* and his play of the same title. While Dixon is remembered as an obsessed racist, and Griffith is not, both Dixon's novel and Griffith's film clearly share a narrative mode, and their subject matter bears the same distinctive relationship to history.[13]

The full title of Thomas Dixon's book is: *The Clansman: An Historical Romance of the Ku Klux Klan.*[14] In a preface, Dixon informs the reader that "*The Clansman* is the second book of a series of historical novels planned on the Race Conflict," and it "develops the true story of the 'Ku Klux Klan Conspiracy,' which overturned the Reconstruction régime." In a style that matches his measure of the events of the era, Dixon writes that "the chaos of blind passion that followed Lincoln's assassination is inconceivable to-day. The revolution it produced in our Government, and the bold attempt of Thaddeus Stevens to Africanize ten great States of the American Union, read now like tales from 'The Arabian Nights.'"

The term "historical romance" is something of an oxymoron—at least, as it can be used to describe *The Clansman*—despite Dixon's insistence that he has "sought to preserve in this romance both the letter and the spirit of this remarkable period." Dixon states that "the men who enact the drama of fierce revenge into which I have woven a double love story are historical figures. I have merely changed their names without taking a liberty with any essential historic fact."

More remarkable, surely, than anything that could be called "historical," is Dixon's description of the defeated South and the rise of the Ku Klux Klan:

---

11. Ibid., 138.

12. Lillian Gish, with Ann Pinchot, *Lillian Gish: The Movies, Mr. Griffith, and Me* (Englewood Cliffs, N.J.: Prentice-Hall, 1969), 132.

13. James Chandler discusses the influence of the historical romance as a literary form on Griffith in "The Historical Novel Goes to Hollywood: Scott, Griffith, and the Film Epic Today," reprinted in this volume, 225–249.

14. Thomas Dixon, *The Clansman: An Historical Romance of the Ku Klux Klan* (New York: Grosset & Dunlap Publishers, 1905).

In the darkest hour of the life of the South, when her wounded people lay helpless amid rags and ashes under the beak and talon of the Vulture, suddenly from the mists of the mountains appeared a white cloud the size of a man's hand. It grew until its mantle of mystery enfolded the stricken earth and sky. An "Invisible Empire" had risen from the field of Death and challenged the Visible to mortal combat.

How the young South, led by the reincarnated souls of the Clansmen of Old Scotland, went forth under this cover and against overwhelming odds, daring exile, imprisonment, and a felon's death, and saved the life of a people, forms one of the most dramatic chapters in the history of the Aryan race.[15]

Griffith emphatically claimed, as Dixon did with regard to his book, that he had not in his film taken a liberty with any essential historic fact. Yet what are we to make of such florid prose? Or of its "picturisation" in Griffith's film?

The historical romance—still popular in the early years of this century—is grounded in realism; but its highly charged emotionalism, driven by desire, pushes the form to the very limits of the plausible. Certainly, it feels no special allegiance to fact, and it freely modifies aspects of the past in accordance with current desires. The historical film melodrama works the same way. In Philip Rosen's words, Griffith's methods of narrative organization "involve a balance . . . between individual motives and traits on the one hand and general truths on the other. The balance is achieved through the mediation of family romance situations in historically significant settings. This method remained a staple of classical cinema."[16]

Melodrama

The Birth of a Nation announces the themes of its melodrama with its first title: "If in this work we have conveyed to the mind the ravages of war to the end that *war may be held in abhorrence,* this effort will not have been in vain." The kind of cinema that Griffith pioneered and consolidated, with its immediate origins in nineteenth-century stage melodrama, has always been concerned with articulating a moral ideology and demonstrating that the world is, finally, a coherent (and potentially benevolent) place. If human suffering is not to go unredeemed, the drama must, at the very least, offer a lesson, especially if the misfortunes represented have been brought about by human folly. *The Birth of a Nation,* like all melodramas, is a film with a message. But just what is that message?

15. The Nazi period in Germany is an even sadder and more gruesome chapter in "the history of the Aryan race"; and it is not surprising that members of the modern Ku Klux Klan have appropriated the specific ideological formulations and symbology of Hitler's fascism.
16. Rosen, "Securing the Historical," 23.

Griffith told a reporter, nearly thirty years after the release of *The Birth of a Nation,* that a good picture is "one that makes the public forget its troubles. Also, a good picture tends to make folks think a little, without letting them suspect that they are being inspired to think. In one respect, nearly all pictures are good in that they frequently show the triumph of good over evil."[17] These admirable sentiments continue to inform the American film melodrama to this day, giving it shape and ideological purpose—but the film melodrama is frequently unclear, and sometimes plainly wrong, about who or what the villain is. Human suffering is described and attempts are made to name causes, but more often than not the film melodrama as a form is inadequate to the business of figuring out why people suffer. For our purposes, it is equally inadequate to the task of analyzing why, for example, the American Civil War took place, or why, as Griffith understood it, the South had to suffer "degradation and ruin" (shot 913).

The second intertitle of *The Birth of a Nation* declares that "the bringing of the African to America planted the first seed of disunion." Already, even before the film's first image, Griffith attempts to identify evil with "the African" by implying that an America without Africans was a harmonious Eden. Although nowhere in the film does Griffith explicitly identify the institution of slavery as the root cause of the Civil War, the suggestion is insinuated immediately in this intertitle. It should be noted that Thomas Dixon was quite clear, but also irrational, about who the villains were. In 1905, he wrote that the South before the Civil War was ruled by an "aristocracy founded on brains, culture, and blood," the "old fashioned dream of the South" which "but for the Black curse . . . could be today the garden of the world."[18]

But Griffith was not the fanatic Dixon was, and his attitudes are not so stark, or so easy to dismiss. With his "spotty knowledge of history, his literary eccentricities, [and] his 'petit-bourgeois' morality,"[19] Griffith presents, paradoxically, a more insidious case than Dixon, who has been described as an "unasylumed maniac."[20] Like Lincoln (the historical figure, not the character portrayed by Joseph Henabery in the film), Griffith accepts the institution of slavery,[21] and with

17. Quoted by Sergei Eisenstein, *Film Form,* ed. and trans. Jay Leyda (New York: Harcourt Brace, 1949), 206.
18. Quoted by Carter, "Cultural History Written with Lightning," 136.
19. Richard Griffith, "Foreword," *D. W. Griffith: American Film Master* by Iris Barry, rev. Eileen Bowser (New York: The Museum of Modern Art/Doubleday, 1965), 5.
20. William Monroe Trotter, quoted by Richard Schickel, *D. W. Griffith: An American Life* (New York: Simon and Schuster, 1984), 299.
21. Frequently after 1854 Lincoln insisted that "all I have asked or desired anywhere is that [slavery] should be placed back again upon the basis that the fathers of our government originally placed it upon." By this, Lincoln meant that "as those fathers marked [slavery], so let it be again marked, as an evil not to be extended, but to be tolerated and protected only because of and only so far as its actual presence among us makes that toleration and protection a necessity." (Quoted by George B. Forgie, *Patricide in the House Divided: A Psychological Interpretation of Lincoln and His Age* [New York: Norton, 1979], 276.)

the third intertitle launches the notion that those who sought to end slavery, not the Africans themselves, were to blame for the troubles his film treats: "The Abolitionists of the Nineteenth Century demanding the freeing of the slaves" (shot 9). (In the second part of the film dealing with Reconstruction, Griffith is content to blame everything on scalawags and carpetbaggers.)

Griffith's attitude toward slavery can perhaps be clarified by briefly considering Robert E. Lee's position on the subject. Although Lee's role as a character in *Birth* is small and almost entirely iconic, he was, for Griffith, and appears to have remained for most Southern partisans, "the embodiment of all that was good and noble in the Old South. . . . the foremost Southern hero."[22] Lee's position on slavery more or less corresponds to Griffith's, as it can be inferred from *The Birth of a Nation.* As summed up by Nolan in *Lee Considered:*

1. Northerners' opposition to slavery, or to its expansion into the territories, was an "interference" with "the domestic institutions of the South," with which they had no appropriate concern.
2. In opposing slavery, Northerners were intolerant of the "Spiritual liberty" of the Southerners who supported slavery.
3. Although Northerners opposed to slavery had the right to proceed by "moral means and suasion," their opposition was somehow "unlawful," violated their duty as citizens, and predicted civil war.[23]

While the viewer's belief that war, as stated in the film's first title, should be "held in abhorrence" may or may not be reinforced by Griffith's film, this, surely, is not quite the point.[24] As a melodrama, the film is ostensibly committed to clarifying how to prevent future wars—not to persuading viewers that war is bad. The narrative enigma launched by the film's second intertitle—"The bringing of the African to America planted the first seed of disunion"—is resolved near the end of the film by asserting a way of eliminating the African threat: images of an election in which we see black voters intimidated by mounted Clansmen (1594–1599). This image of blacks being intimidated is the true *telos* of Griffith's vision—not the images of Margaret and Phil, and Ben and Elsie on their respective honeymoons, or the muddled intertitle that follows: "Dare we dream of a golden day when the bestial War shall rule no more. But instead—the gentle Prince in the Hall of Brotherly Love in the City of Peace" (1603). The very last intertitle reads: "*Liberty and union,* one and inseparable, *now and forever!*" (1609). Rather than offer a discourse against war, Griffith proposes the idea that the unity of the

---

22. Rod Gragg, *The Illustrated Confederate Reader* (New York: Harper & Row, 1989), 224.
23. Nolan, *Lee Considered,* 14.
24. Griffith articulated his melodramatic method by indicating his attitude toward war as a moral problem in relation to its value as spectacle when he remarked: "War is hideous, but it can be made the background for beauty, beauty of idea." (Quoted by Schickel, *D. W. Griffith,* 290.)

country is the most important thing, and this is to be bought at the price of subordinating the blacks.

A synopsis of the film submitted to the U.S. Copyright Office on February 8, 1915, describes the end of the film this way: "To Ben and Elsie, to Phil and Margaret, the sequel is a beautiful double honeymoon by the sea. To the American people, the outcome of four years of fratricidal strife, the nightmare of Reconstruction, and the establishment of the South in its rightful place, is the birth of a new nation."[25] That the film ends on images of the double honeymoon reveals not so much the melodrama's inability to come to grips with the real causes of the conflicts that structure the film, but Griffith's preference for the familial dimension of it, and perhaps, more important- ly, his unwillingness to examine his own racism.

A profound ambivalence underlies every aspect of the narrative characterized by a hypocritical stance of outward benevolence toward blacks and an underlying corrosive fear. An intertitle that appears late in the film succinctly expresses the controlling logic of the numerous oppositions in the narrative: "The former en- emies of North and South are united in common defense of their Aryan birthright," and it is duplicated in the mise-en-scène of the besieged cabin in which Dr. and Mrs. Cameron, their daughter Margaret, her suitor Phil Stoneman, and the Cam- erons' faithful servants Jake and Mammy are given refuge by two Union veterans. (The cabin is surrounded by black troops sent by Lynch to capture the elder Cameron.) The strand of the narrative involving the blacks does not end on shots of slaves being returned to Africa, as it is sometimes claimed was originally the case,[26] but on an image of their subordination. As the second of the two synopses submitted to the U.S. Copyright Office puts it, "At the next election the negroes dare not vote and the threat of a black empire is dissolved."[27] To the extent that the film tries to be plausible, this is realistic, for historically the war was lost over slavery and independence, but peace was waged—and won—for states' rights, white supremacy, and honor.

Griffith's feeling about the new relationship between whites and blacks in the South after the war—ambivalent, hypocritical—appears to be similar to Lee's;

---

25. Reprinted in full in John Cuniberti, *"The Birth of a Nation": A Formal Shot-by-Shot Analysis Together with Microfiche* (Woodbridge, Conn.: Research Publications, 1979), 196–198.

26. There is no hard evidence that the film ever actually included shots of a wholesale deportation of American blacks to Africa, although there is some indication that there may have been an intertitle referring to "Lincoln's solution," "Back to Liberia!" (see Cuniberti, *"The Birth of a Nation,"* 166–167). If this intertitle had once been in the film, there may have been an image to support it, as Seymour Stern claims to remember having seen. The synopsis submitted to the U.S. Copyright Office on February 8, 1915, includes the comment, "Lincoln's plan of restoring the negroes to Africa was dreamed of only, never carried out," which lends credence to the hypothesis that the film once included at least an intertitle to this effect.

27. This synopsis was printed in Clune's Program, 1915, and submitted to the U.S. Copyright Office, February 13, 1915. (Reprinted in Cuniberti, *"The Birth of a Nation,"* 180.)

and as Nolan notes, Lee's public and private assertions regarding the freedman were in conflict:

> Publicly, [Lee] was protective and benign. Everything would be all right if the North did not "stir up" the blacks. Dependent on their labor, the South would, of course, employ them. Privately, he was bitter toward the freedman and intervened personally to their detriment. In truth, Lee and his fellow Southerners were groping for a new method of white supremacy and exploitation of the blacks. With Northern complicity, the Southern effort was eventually to succeed; the outcome was a hundred years of near-slavery: disenfranchisement, Black Codes, Jim Crow, and suppression.[28]

If Griffith was at all ambivalent, confused, hypocritical, or self-deluding about what the "message" of his film was, Dixon was not. Rolfe Cobleigh, a newspaper editor who gained an interview with Thomas Dixon, wrote in a sworn deposition:

> I asked Mr. Dixon what his real purpose was in having *The Birth of a Nation* produced, what he hoped to accomplish by it. . . . [Dixon replied] that one purpose of his play was to create a feeling of abhorrence in white people, especially white women against colored men. Mr. Dixon said that his desire was to prevent the mixing of white and Negro blood by intermarriage. [. . .] Mr. Dixon said that the Ku Klux Klan was formed to protect the white women from Negro men, to restore order and to reclaim political control for the white people of the South. He said that the Ku Klux Klan was not only engaged in restoring law and order, but was of a religious nature.[29]

It is particularly important to note that Dixon's reference to the protection of white women is precisely what gets narrativized in the film, in accordance with melodramatic principles. It is, in fact, the film's core. Dixon's statements surely say it all—for the second part of Griffith's film bears out this ideological position with shocking conviction. Indeed, the "abhorrence in white people, especially white women against colored men" that Dixon speaks of exemplifies with more truth and force the film's real message than that other "abhorrence" for war that Griffith attempts to persuade us is his reason for making the film.

We are given to understand that, before the "seed of disunion" referred to in the film's second intertitle grows to disruptive proportions, there is a state of harmony and union in America—which is offered in the image of the Cameron family on their front porch at Cameron Hall (46). Every melodrama, as we have said, shows, or refers to, such an image—of the world before the villain enters it. As one intertitle puts it, with rather self-conscious simplicity and more than a little nostalgia, this is "the Southland. Piedmont, South Carolina, the home of the

28. Nolan, *Lee Considered*, 147.
29. Geduld, *Focus on D. W. Griffith*, 98–99.

Camerons, where life runs in a quaintly way that is to be no more" (33). This image of course will be shattered, and the whole effort of the film will be to restore it. Griffith's aim above all is to offer a "picturisation" of the Civil War and Reconstruction that will honor the Southern Legend, and its imagery necessarily lies in the iconography of melodrama.

Griffith prefigures the nature of the conflict that will be the motor of his narrative when he disrupts this tableau of the idealized and sentimentalized family by showing a kitten being dropped onto the puppy at Dr. Cameron's feet. "Hostilities" (53), announces the intertitle that follows; and the kitten and puppy start to fight. Griffith the narrator organizes his fictional world into binary oppositions (one puppy is white, and the other black), and puts them into conflict. We should perhaps not read too much into this little scene—by suggesting, for example, that the kitten be associated with the abolitionists, or with the scalawags and carpetbaggers who disrupt the happy relationship between Southern whites and blacks—but the scene makes it clear that Griffith is less concerned with analyzing *why* there is conflict, or with being (from our point of view) ideologically responsible, than with telling a good story and successfully controlling the dramatic rhythms of his narrative. The scene is also typical of Griffith's method of giving symbolic resonance to people, objects, and places, thus lending an allegorical dimension to his "history."

It is with considerable irony, but not surprising, that we discover that Woodrow Wilson—who was President of the United States when *The Birth of a Nation* was made, and from whose *History of the American People* Griffith quotes in *Birth* to help persuade us of the film's historical accuracy—was himself more concerned with impressing audiences with his style than with his ideas. While in the history department at The John Hopkins University in Baltimore, pursuing the doctorate he never completed, Wilson confessed to his fiancée:

> Style is not much studied here; *ideas* are supposed to be everything—their
> vehicle comparatively nothing. But you and I know that there can be no
> greater mistake; that, both in its amount and in its length of life, an author's in-
> fluence depends upon the power and the beauty of his style; upon the flawless
> mirror he holds up to nature; upon his facility in catching and holding, be-
> cause he pleases, the attention.[30]

It is worth noting—for the obvious reason that there are parallels between Griffith and the President; and because, in Lillian Gish's words, "Mr. Griffith had great respect for [Wilson's] erudition"[31]—that, when Wilson was a young professor, he wrote "a prodigious amount, almost all of it frankly inspirational and aimed at the widest public. His five-volume *History of the American People* was

---

30. Quoted by Garry Wills, "The Presbyterian Nietzsche," *The New York Review of Books,* January 16, 1992, 3.
31. Gish, *Lillian Gish,* 136.

composed in the 1890s in the form of lavishly illustrated articles for *Harper's*. He was paid $1,000 for each article, an unheard-of price at the time."[32]

In the writing of history, striking a proper balance between searching for what we call "truth" and reaching a popular audience is far from being a satisfactorily resolved matter. Consider the following remark made in 1991 by Simon Schama (author of *Citizens,* a best-selling [but anti-revolutionary] book about the French Revolution): The "pressing task," he writes, is to restore history "to the forms by which it can catch the public imagination. That form, as Ken Burns's stunning PBS series on the Civil War demonstrated, ought to be narrative; not to discard argument and analysis, but to lend it proper dramatic and poetic power."[33]

But the PBS series on the Civil War is not a commercial film (a Hollywood movie),[34] and it does not in the same way have the "dramatic and poetic power" of Griffith's film. Perhaps Edward Jay Epstein's remark about Oliver Stone's film, *JFK*—"When you mix fact and fiction you get fiction"[35]—is another way of saying: when you attempt a "picturisation of history," you get melodrama.

The Besieged House

Like Woodrow Wilson, Griffith understood that "an author's influence depends upon the power and the beauty of his style,"[36] and, like Abraham Lincoln before him, Griffith appealed to an audience with an essentially emotional solution. In 1861, Lincoln told an Indiana audience: "To the salvation of this Union, there needs but one single thing, the hearts of a people like yours."[37] Lincoln understood that the American people had to be emotionally involved if the Union were to be preserved, and his chosen metaphor of the besieged house was a conventional (but, as he knew, powerful) way of "figuratively expressing the Union." He called slavery "an element of division in the house."[38]

Before the war, Lincoln was not alone among American politicians who "increasingly tended verbally to structure the crisis according to the conventions of melodrama. Indeed, it is only a slight exaggeration to say that by the end of the

---

32. Wills, "The Presbyterian Nietzsche," 3.

33. Simon Schama, "Clio Has a Problem," *The New York Times Magazine,* September 8, 1991, 32.

34. *The Civil War.* A film by Ken Burns. Produced by Ken Burns and Ric Burns/Florentine Films and WETA-TV. Written by Geoffrey C. Ward, Ric Burns, and Ken Burns. Narrated by David McCullough. Edited by Paul Barnes, Bruce Shaw, and Tricia Reidy.

35. Quoted by Georgia Brown, "Patsies," *The Village Voice,* March 31, 1992, 58. Brown's article is mostly about a debate sponsored by *The Nation* at Town Hall (New York City) about Oliver Stone's film *JFK.*

36. Wilson, quoted by Wills, "The Presbyterian Nietzsche," 3.

37. Quoted by Forgie, *Patricide in the House Divided,* 271.

38. Quoted in ibid., 271.

1850s, the crisis of the Union not only imitated, but had become, a work of art, with the paradoxical result that as the crisis grew more serious its seriousness grew more difficult to measure."[39]

Fifty years later, Griffith's problem was one of organizing the war and the Reconstruction period into a commercially viable dramatic narrative; and according to the conventions of melodrama and his own definition of a "good picture," Griffith must attempt to "show the triumph of good over evil" in a way that is not simplistically reductive.

In the melodramatic tradition that figures evil as a rapist and virtue as a threatened virgin, Griffith organizes most of his narrative around images of women under threat.[40] Indeed, Lillian Gish writes in her autobiography about the audition that won her the part of Elsie Stoneman: "During the hysterical chase around the room, the hairpins flew out of my hair, which tumbled below my waist as Lynch held my fainting body in his arms. I was very blonde and fragile-looking. The contrast with the dark man evidently pleased Mr. Griffith."[41]

Such a scene, which of course appears in the film (1323 passim), describes very well the nature of Griffith's melodramatic imagination. The scene is emblematic of the sorts of contrasts that define melodrama and that give Griffith's films their undercurrents of perversity. Furthermore, it can be argued that such scenes of sexual aggression structure the narrative itself, rendering all discourses on history and politics somewhat ancillary. In Nick Browne's words,

> If there is a fantasy animating Griffith's narrative project, which cross-cutting and rape come to symbolize, it has to do, I think, with the seduction and at the same time the defense of the woman by his symbolic possession of her through his art. This scenario of rescue is essentially a chivalrous project couched in a kind of medieval and allegorical idiom, that has as its end the stabilization of the place and integrity of the bourgeois family against the threat of abandonment, dismemberment, homelessness or worse, that constitutes the clear and present danger in his films. It is in this role that the moralism of Griffith's vision as a director lies. The Griffith fantasy . . . is the protection or restoration of the holiness of the American family. It is the prerequisite of this vision that it be achieved in the mode of nostalgia.[42]

---

39. Ibid., 268.
40. Cf. the following: Rick Altman, "*The Lonely Villa* and Griffith's Paradigmatic Style," *Quarterly Review of Film Studies* 6, no. 2 (Spring 1981): 123–134; Nick Browne, "Griffith's Family Discourse: Griffith and Freud," *Quarterly Review of Film Studies* 6, no. 1 (Winter 1981): 67–80; Russell Merritt, "D. W. Griffith's *The Birth of a Nation:* Going After Little Sister," in *Close Viewings: An Anthology of New Film Criticism,* ed. Peter Lehman (Tallahassee: The Florida State University Press, 1990), 215–237.
41. Gish, *Lillian Gish,* 133.
42. Nick Browne, "Griffith's Family Discourse," 79.

One of Griffith's nostalgic images of the ideal relationship between white Southerners and their slaves (who have their place in a *familial* sense on the plantation) is offered early in *The Birth of a Nation*. Shortly after the Stoneman brothers arrive at Cameron Hall to visit their Southern friends, Ben, Margaret, Flora, and Phil take a walk "over the plantation to the cotton fields" (78). The scene describes the very conditions of property ownership in the South and the way in which the familial and romantic strands of Griffith's narrative are subtly intertwined with the economic discourse to suggest a "natural" order of things. As Margaret and Phil chat intimately, almost oblivious to their surroundings, Ben picks a cotton blossom and turns to beckon Phil. As the friends contemplate the blossom, two slaves can be seen in the background, industriously picking cotton. Ben and Phil are wearing top hats, and Margaret is twirling a parasol. Young Flora scampers about as if the field were a playground, and Margaret glances complacently at the slaves, confirming their status as scenery. When Ben notices the cameo in Phil's hand, he takes it from him and Phil explains that it is a likeness of his sister, Elsie. Ben smiles as he studies the portrait and in a playful gesture takes off his hat and bows to it.

Griffith thus effects a transfer of metaphors, or symbolisms—from the cotton blossom as "flower" of the South (shown in extreme close-up), to a close-up of the cameo of Elsie (the very flower of femininity; the linchpin of the chivalric code by which Southern gentlemen live). The close-up of the cotton blossom functions like a cameo. It is an overdetermined image which refers to the foundations of the economic system of the South—although, ironically, Ben contemplates it as an object of beauty, free of ideology. There is a sense in which we are being asked to see a natural connection or parallel in this visual zeugma. Ben dashes off, clutching the portrait of Elsie in which, an intertitle tells us, "he finds the ideal of his dreams" (93), thus condensing the pastoral, nostalgic scene in an image of love for the idealized woman. As Phil and Margaret depart, Phil (the Northerner) gives the slaves in the field a quick—perhaps self-conscious—wave. The scene is extended by shots 101–106, in which slaves are seen dancing to entertain the visitors. When the dancing comes to an end and Ben brings up the rear of the departing group, two old slaves approach Ben, who pauses to shake hands with one of them and put his hand paternalistically on the other slave's shoulder.

This extended image of the hierarchies of the Old South—so necessary to melodrama's method of showing, or referring to, a stable order that will be disrupted and then restored—is immediately followed by an intertitle that introduces the "historical" threat to this order: "The gathering storm. The power of the sovereign states, established when Lord Cornwallis surrendered to the individual colonies in 1781, is threatened by the new administration" (107); just as the earlier intertitle, "Hostilities" (53), announced the threat to the harmonious image of the two puppies playing at Dr. Cameron's feet. Later in the film, when the fortunes of the South are approaching their nadir, Flora will adorn her shabby dress with cotton wool, described in an intertitle as "Southern ermine" (515); and Ben will refuse the hand proffered by a black man (716). The order of things has been reversed; the "element of division in the house" has brought the house down. In this way, Griffith creates the symmetries on which his melodramatic vision is founded.

As a form, melodrama turns on the central need to keep alive the notions of symmetry and difference; and in this film, Griffith resolves the North-South opposition in the birth of a new nation, and the male-female difference in the marriages of Ben and Elsie, Phil and Margaret. But the film clearly has trouble with the difference between blacks and whites, and this is expressed in the figure of the mulatto.

Virtue and Villainy

The North-South opposition in *The Birth of a Nation* is expressed by the fact of the Civil War—two sides in opposition. Griffith tries to state this opposition in clear, melodramatic terms—indeed, before he shifts the focus of his film away from the war altogether, he attempts to propose it as a stark and Manichaean conflict—and he includes a shot of Ben showing Flora their state flag, on which we see the motto: "CONQUER WE MUST—VICTORY OR DEATH—FOR OUR CAUSE IS JUST" (198).

But the animating concern of the film is not really this conflict at all. As Dixon told Rolfe Cobleigh, one of the main reasons for making the film was to help "prevent the mixing of white and Negro blood by intermarriage." The film's obsession with miscegenation is the key to its structure and meaning as a melodrama. Throughout its history, the melodrama as a form has favored the image of the virgin as the representative of virtue—the principle around which the whole drama as a moral ordering turns[43]—and in *The Birth of a Nation,* it is above all Flora's death and Elsie's danger that symbolize the South's unhappy fate ("To escape with honor intact, [Flora] leaps . . . from a high cliff"[44]). Flora's death and Elsie's imperilment also provide the narrative with the revenge formula that is so serviceable to melodrama's requirement of an unassailably clear and simple logic: outrage begetting outrage. Flora's brother Ben, leading the Klan, vows to avenge her death: "Brethren, this flag bears the red stain of the life of a Southern woman, a priceless sacrifice on the altar of an outraged civilization" (1172). In 1913, only

---

43. "Virtue is almost inevitably represented by a young heroine, though in classical French melodrama (unlike later American melodrama) she need not be a virgin, for it is moral sentiment more than technical chastity that is at issue." (Peter Brooks, *The Melodramatic Imagination: Balzac, Henry James, Melodrama, and the Mode of Excess* [New Haven: Yale University Press, 1976], 32.)

44. Synopsis submitted to the U.S. Copyright Office, February 13, 1915. (Reprinted in Cuniberti, *"The Birth of a Nation,"* 180.)

months before Griffith began shooting *The Birth of a Nation,* Pitchfork Ben Tillman, governor of South Carolina (the home state of Griffith's fictitious Camerons), publicly supported the lynching of [black] rapists, claiming that "forty to a hundred Southern maidens were annually offered as a sacrifice to the African Minotaur, and no Theseus had arisen to rid the land of this terror."[45]

The villain who stands in opposition to Flora as a figure of virtue is, of course, Gus. While the threat of rape is repeatedly the melodramatic hook in the film's articulation of villainy, it is important to observe that Gus's villainy does not derive simply from his apparently rapacious intentions. Nor does it derive ultimately from the stark fact of his obvious *difference* from Flora—that is, his blackness, or his maleness—but rather from the fact that he has compromised his identity as a loyal slave. He is called a "renegade" because, after the Civil War, he betrays his white masters.

For a proper understanding of villainy as it functions in *The Birth of a Nation* as a melodrama, it must be observed that every villain in the film is in some way a *traitor,* confusing the clarity of a binary order in which identity is conceived of as being decisively one thing or another. Indeed, the war itself, as James Baldwin has observed, is represented as a "great betrayal by the Northern brethren" of "the gallant South."[46]

Silas Lynch is described as "a traitor to his white patron and a greater traitor to his own people" because he "plans to lead [his people] by an evil way to build himself a throne of vaulting power" (720). He also wants to marry Elsie, thus violating the taboo in the film on miscegenation. But his villainy originates in the fact that he is neither white nor black—that is, he is worse than black. Some of the complex and contradictory meanings of Lynch's character are suggested by Dixon's description of him, which Lillian Gish quotes in her autobiography: "A Negro of perhaps forty years, a man of charming features for a mulatto, who had evidently inherited the full physical characteristics of the Aryan, while his dark yellowish eyes beneath his heavy brows glowed with the brightness of the African jungle."[47]

The film's point is that if Gus had not become a traitor to his white masters and had remained true to his identity as a Southern black, he would be like Jake and Mammy, the "faithful souls" of the Cameron household. According to the dire logic of melodramatic symmetry, Gus is lynched for his ostensible intention to rape Flora.[48] Lynch, however, is one of the film's essentially villainous figures—as

45. Thomas F. Gossett, *Race: The History of an Idea in America* (New York: Schocken Books, 1965), 271.

46. James Baldwin, *The Devil Finds Work* (New York: The Dial Press, 1976), 45.

47. Gish, *Lillian Gish,* 134.

48. The essential elements of the film's ideological underpinnings are made starkly clear by Susan Brownmiller's observation that, "Rape is to women as lynching was to blacks: the ultimate physical threat by which all men keep all women in a state of psychological intimidation." (*Against Our Will: Men, Women, and Rape* [New York: Bantam Books, 1975], 281.)

a mulatto he is cast as a villain from birth, a demonized product of miscegenation—long before Stoneman turns him into a "Frankenstein" (*sic*).[49]

By similar logic, when the blacks who raid Piedmont in the film's first scenes of the town "scarred by war" break into Cameron Hall, they are led by a "scalawag white captain [who] influences the negro militia to follow his orders" (249). The raid is understood to be an aberration, a consequence of a betrayal—by a white man whose first allegiance should be to his whiteness (his "Aryan birthright").

The same goes for all carpetbaggers, white people who are so much motivated by profit that they become "as much enemies of the one race as of the other" (622). And the introductory intertitle of the second part of the film, "The blight of war does not end when hostilities cease" (620), is an echo of an earlier intertitle about Stoneman's desire for his mulatto housekeeper, Lydia Brown—described as "the great leader's weakness that is to blight a nation" (133). James Baldwin notes the false logic of the meanings Griffith attempts to assign to the figure of the mulatto when he writes that "the baleful effect of this carnal creature on the eminent Southern politician helps bring about the ruin of the South. I cannot tell you exactly *how* she brings about so devastating a fate, and I defy anyone to tell *me:* but she does."[50] Sex returns over treachery, and the consistent theme is of pure entities marred, compromised, misled, sullied—above all, betrayed—which results in evil.

Baldwin precisely identifies the film's logic of origins and causes, even as the film attempts to disguise the truth of its own logic. As he puts it, "*The Birth of a Nation* is really an elaborate justification of mass murder. The film cannot possibly admit this, which is why we are immediately placed at the mercy of a plot [that] is labyrinthine and preposterous."[51] The logic at the heart of the film's baroque structure is this:

> For the sake of the dignity of this temporarily defeated people [the Southern whites], and out of a vivid and loving concern for their betrayed and endangered slaves, the violated social order must, at all costs, be re-established. And it *is* re-established by the vision and heroism of the noblest among these noble. The disaster which they must overcome (and, in future, avert) has been brought about, not through any fault of their own, and not because of any defection among their slaves, but by the weak and misguided among them who have given the mulattoes ideas above their station.[52]

49. The synopsis printed in Clune's Program, 1915, and submitted to the U.S. Copyright Office, February 13, 1915, adverts to Lynch's supposedly *unnatural* character in this compressed description of the context of Lynch's supreme villainy: "In the meantime, Stoneman returns and Lynch tells him he is to marry Elsie. Stoneman now realizes the Frankenstein [*sic*] he has himself created, but is helpless until the Klan arrives, disarms all the negroes and rescues Elsie." (Reprinted in Cuniberti, "*The Birth of a Nation,*" 180.)

50. Baldwin, *The Devil Finds Work,* 45.

51. Ibid.

52. Ibid., 48.

Baldwin goes on to ask, "But how did so ungodly a creature as the mulatto enter this Eden, and where did he come from? The film cannot concern itself with this inconvenient and impertinent question."[53] At any rate, the South is "shamefully defeated—or, not so much defeated, it would appear, as betrayed: by the influence of the mulattoes."[54]

> The plot is entirely controlled by the image of the mulatto, and there are two of them, one male and one female. All of the energy of the film is siphoned off into these two dreadful and improbable creatures. It might have made sense . . . if these two mulattoes had been related to each other, or to the renegade politician, whose wards they are: but . . . they are related to each other only by their envy of white people.[55]

Neither white nor black, the mulatto is a living embodiment of a disturbance in the melodramatic field, in which one is *either* white *or* black. The order of things is confused by this merging of opposites, and *The Birth of a Nation* finds it convenient and logical to designate the mulatto as the villainous consequence of "the bringing of the African to America."

Lincoln, the "Great Heart"

While the Civil War made some sense of the political confusions of the 1850s, the war and Reconstruction in turn were structured by the simplifying terms of the melodrama, which characteristically converts complex problems into a struggle between virtue and vice. In the figure of Abraham Lincoln, however, Griffith achieves an extraordinary synthesis of potential incompatibilities. Lincoln's status in the film is unique. He is portrayed as an infinitely thoughtful and suffering man, rather in the manner of a father who must make unpopular decisions for the good of the entire family. Griffith aims for a proper solemnity in representing one of the first of those decisions Lincoln makes that will so affect the destinies of the Camerons and Stonemans: "Abraham Lincoln uses the Presidential office for the first time in history to call for volunteers to enforce the rule of the coming nation over the individual states" (146). When he has finished signing the proclamation, he is left alone in his office. He takes a handkerchief from his hat on the table and dabs his eyes with it, leans forward on the desk, and clasps his hands in prayer (147).

After the South has been defeated, Stoneman visits Lincoln to "protest against [his] policy of clemency for the South" (529). Lincoln responds to Stoneman's

---

53. Ibid., 48–49.
54. Ibid., 45.
55. Ibid., 47.

impassioned demand that the Southern leaders "be hanged and their states treated as conquered provinces" (531) by replying calmly: "I shall deal with them as though they had never been away" (533). Lincoln is thus also claimed by the South as a hero, and an intertitle announces that "the South under Lincoln's fostering hand goes to work to rebuild itself" (535).

Griffith offers only one brief and unconvincing image of the South rebuilding itself: Ben, rolling up his shirtsleeves, appears to be readying himself to direct Jake in some work in the garden, as Mrs. Cameron and Margaret attach a sign to one of the porch columns of Cameron Hall advertising that they will take in boarders (536). The melodramatic structure of the film, and the logic of Lincoln as a figure worthy of Southern hero-worship, depends entirely on the premise that if Lincoln had not been assassinated on "the fated night of April 14, 1865" (537), all the horrors of Reconstruction that we see in the second part of the film would never have occurred. Part One ends on Dr. Cameron's anguished cry: "Our best friend is gone. What is to become of us now!" (617).

Lincoln's untimely death provides the South with a convenient explanation for the failure of Reconstruction, and it establishes Lincoln's mythic status, which was historically—and in the film—so necessary to the South's attempt to find some dignity for themselves in their defeat. The Southern cause was not after all a dignified one, which explains why a mystique had to form around the idea of the "Lost Cause." The historical Lincoln understood, or was able to convey that he understood, that "the essence of what we call the crisis of the Union was not a conflict between one group that wanted to preserve a particular way of life or value and another group who wanted to destroy it. The conflict was one in which many groups competed—all of them conservatives who sought to preserve cherished values and traditions that had come into conflict with other cherished values and traditions."[56] This explains why even Dixon could be a "passionate admirer" of Lincoln, and in 1920, in a play called *A Man of the People,* could describe Lincoln as "the savior, if not the real creator, of the American Union of free Democratic states."[57] Richard Hofstadter has described the way in which

> Lincoln was able simultaneously to appeal to people who were hostile to slavery (he said it was wrong and must someday die) and to people who were hostile to blacks (he said he was opposed to their becoming socially or politically equal to whites) by insisting with regard to slavery and implying with regard to blacks that the territories not be ruined by either. Lincoln was similarly able to appeal to Young America types who wanted action and

---

56. Forgie, *Patricide in the House Divided,* 184–185.
57. Edward Wagenknecht and Anthony Slide, *The Films of D. W. Griffith* (New York: Crown Publishers, 1975), 60.

manhood, and to sentimentalists who wanted the restoration of, and regression to, a supposedly more secure past.[58]

With quintessentially melodramatic logic, Griffith portrays Lincoln as "the Great Heart." The intertitle that tells us Ben is to be hanged as a guerilla (476) is not necessary to the plot, but it reminds us that Ben is his "mother's gift to the cause" (201) and provides a scene in which Mrs. Cameron "will ask mercy from the Great Heart" (478)—described as "The mother's appeal" (480). We see a shot of Lincoln angrily denying the request of a demonstrative petitioner, who has to be led away by a White House official (483), and at first the President refuses Mrs. Cameron's plea that he intervene to save her son from hanging (487). But Elsie encourages Mrs. Cameron to appeal again, and the camera irises in on a shot of Ben in his hospital bed, demonstrating Lincoln's empathetic power to imagine the scene she has just described. Of course, he pardons her boy, as a father would pardon a son, and Mrs. Cameron is so moved with gratitude that, on a familial impulse, she nearly embraces the President (495). When she returns to the makeshift hospital, she tells Ben that "Mr. Lincoln has given back your life to me" (497), thus connecting in a single remark the apex of the public realm (the President of the United States) and the defining center of the personal realm (herself/the mother's bond with her child). Then, "Her son convalescent, Mrs. Cameron starts back for Piedmont to attend the failing father" (499). Thus, even politics becomes "familialized" in melodrama.

It is no coincidence that Dr. Cameron's health declines during the war in a direct correspondence to the deteriorating fortunes of the South. He is sickest when Ben is in the hospital, during the last days before "the surrender of Gen. Robt. E. Lee, C.S.A., to Gen. U. S. Grant, U.S.A." at Appomattox Courthouse (505). The film can be seen as an attempt by Griffith to resolve his own Oedipal conflicts;[59] and just as we can see Lincoln historically as having had a filial, or Oedipal, relation to George Washington and the "founding fathers," it can be said that Griffith, in turn, saw a parental figure in Lincoln.

In Part Two, the film's central metaphor—the birth of a nation-as-a-family—undergoes a troubled response to Lincoln's assassination. There are several vengeful assaults on actual or figurative fathers in the second part of the film: Dr. Cameron's humiliation and imprisonment by former slaves; the disenfranchisement of Piedmont's white-bearded city fathers; Lynch's manhandling of Stoneman—to list only a few of the film's coded enactments of filial hostility.

As a symbolic parricide, Lincoln's assassination in Ford's Theatre is the film's Oedipal climax. We see the father figure cut down by a son of the South,

---

58. Cited by Forgie, *Patricide in the House Divided*, 253–254.
59. See Michael Rogin's "'The Sword Became a Flashing Vision': D. W. Griffith's *The Birth of a Nation*," reprinted in this volume, 250–293.

John Wilkes Booth, who shouts, "Sic semper tyrannis!" (literally: "thus always to tyrants"); and when Booth leaps from the Presidential box to the stage, he breaks his leg, in what can only be described as an example of life imitating Freud. When Baldwin writes that he cannot tell us exactly how Lydia Brown's "baleful effect" on Stoneman "helps bring about the ruin of the South," he is only half serious, for the Oedipal logic becomes clear when the mulatto housekeeper informs Stoneman of the assassination and proclaims gleefully, "You are now the greatest power in America" (611). There are shades of *Macbeth* in her exultation, for there is a sense in which Stoneman himself, who is later described as the "uncrowned king" (625) of the Reconstruction state, is the author of this regicide/parricide.

Griffith's attempt to recuperate his drama in the mainstream terms of Oedipal logic shows some strain, for he represents Lincoln as an androgynous figure—a Northern *and* a Southern hero, the "Great Heart" that understands all Americans—and ends the film on an image of Jesus Christ. In the moment before Lincoln is shot, the President draws his shawl about his shoulders, as though in response to the chill of approaching death. It is a gesture coded culturally as feminine. Like Washington before him, the historical Lincoln also combined in his character and person both masculine and distinctively feminine qualities. "[Lincoln] was the masculine, rugged rail-splitter of the West and (to some people) he would become the bearded patriarch. But the beard was offset by the shawl, and [the] picture of Lincoln going to market wearing that garment, carrying a basket and with children in tow, casts up a domesticated image indeed."[60]

With the death of Lincoln, in the film, the nation/family loses both a mother and a father, resulting in "a veritable overthrow of civilization in the South" (623). The white South, impoverished by cynical carpetbaggers, mocked by buffoonish politicians, and threatened by the frenzy of unleashed black sexuality, resorts to violent repression in a desperate attempt to restore order. Historically, the Klan "sought to take the place of both the departed personal authority of the master and the labor control function the Reconstruction state had abandoned."[61] In *The Birth of a Nation,* the Klan is described as "the organization that saved the South from the anarchy of black rule" (925). In the end, however, neither the triumph of the Ku Klux Klan nor the couplings of the Stoneman and Cameron children is enough to achieve satisfactory closure.

Without a patriarch of Lincoln's stature to preside over the new nation, Griffith feels impelled to invoke the image of Jesus Christ himself. As Freud notes, regarding Christian doctrine, "In the same deed which offers the greatest possible expiation to the father, the son also attains the goal of his wishes against the father.

---

60. Forgie, *Patricide in the House Divided,* 254–255.
61. Eric Foner, *Reconstruction: America's Unfinished Revolution, 1863–1877* (New York: Harper & Row, 1988), 428.

He becomes a god himself beside or rather in place of his father."[62] This explains the logic of ending this melodrama as Oedipal drama on an image of Jesus: the contradictions of Oedipal desire are resolved in a figure who is both son and father.

While the apocalyptic style of the ending of *The Birth of a Nation* is a closing device used frequently by Griffith during this period, it signals nothing less than a tremendous, hysterical effort to assert that, though a great deal has been lost, something even greater has been gained. The nostalgic register of the film, which began with the intertitle that introduced an image of "the Southland. . . . where life runs in a quaintly way that is to be no more" (33), produces this intolerable fact: all that has been lost cannot be regained. The Oedipal tensions of *The Birth of a Nation*, also originating in a sense of something having been lost, are resolved, *après coup*, in the figure of Lincoln as a fantasy of the ideal father/mother/son— the "Great Heart." The resolution of *The Birth of a Nation*'s inherent narrative contradictions can only be achieved, therefore, in a fantasy of apocalypse and utopia.

62. Sigmund Freud, *Totem and Taboo* [1913], trans. A. A. Brill (New York: Vintage Books, 1946), 199.

D. W. Griffith:
A Biographical
Sketch

On January 22, 1875—not quite ten years after the end of the Civil War—David Wark Griffith was born to Mary Oglesby Griffith and Jacob Wark Griffith, on a farm near Crestwood, Kentucky, some twenty miles east of Louisville. He was the sixth of the seven Griffith children who survived childhood, and as he later observed in his unfinished autobiography, it was a childhood marked by "want and hunger," which was to shadow him all his life.

Griffith's father had been a surgeon and a farmer; but with the onset of the Civil War, he left the farm he had inherited from his father-in-law ten years before and enlisted to fight for the Confederacy, even though he was forty-two at the time and Kentucky was not a secessionist state. Jacob fought with a valor and skill that suggest he had found his true calling, and by March 1861 he had risen to the rank of colonel. During the course of the war, he was wounded at least twice; but when the war came to an end, his best years came to an end also, for he was never again able to deploy or channel usefully what the war had given him an opportunity to discover—his capacity for military leadership.

In 1877, when young David was two, his father was elected for the second time in twenty years to serve a term in the Kentucky General Assembly. Jacob's gift for oratory had earned him his monickers, "Roaring Jake," and "Thunder Jake." But during the nearly two decades that he lived after the end of the war, the economic fortunes of the Griffith family were increasingly strained, as Jake became a storyteller and something of a drinker, gambler, and braggart.

Although David was only ten when his father died in 1885, he would later claim that *The Birth of a Nation* "owes more to my father than it does to me." The many stories he had heard his father tell about wartime adventures "were burned right into my memory." In the meantime, however, the relative stability and comfort that David had known was rudely shattered as it was discovered that Jacob had heavily mortgaged the farm, Lofty Green, and left many debts behind him.

To settle all claims, Mary Griffith was forced to sell Lofty Green, and within a few months of Jacob's death, the Griffiths moved in with David's older brother

William and his bride, who lived on a farm in Shelby County, near Southville. While it was not an unhappy time, Griffith would remember the next five years as the hardest of his childhood. Then, in 1889, the family moved to Louisville, where David's adored older sister Mattie had gone to teach.

Louisville, with a population of close to 200,000, was at this time one of the most prosperous and interesting cities in the South. The Griffiths lived at no fewer than seven addresses in the downtown area during the nineties, and at each, they took in boarders. They lived in genteel poverty, and their difficulties were exacerbated when Mattie, who might have been able to ease their transition to city life, died of tuberculosis soon after they arrived. David took odd jobs at which he could work after school, and sometime in 1890 left high school to work full-time in the J. C. Lewis Dry Goods Store. He spent more than two years there, and then in 1893 took a job as a clerk at Flexner's Book Store, Louisville's leading book shop and a center of the city's intellectual life.

Griffith made the most of the fringe benefits his new job provided, indulging whenever he could his interest in books, art, music, and theater. What had come to interest him most was the melodramatic stage, and when the Flexners sold out, Griffith stayed on under the new owner for a short while, but by 1896 felt ready to leave, having decided to pursue his dream of a theatrical career. In the face of his mother's disapproval, he signed on with a touring company and spent the next year in a number of productions that played in small towns in Ohio, Michigan, Minnesota, and North Dakota.

In May of 1897, Griffith returned to Louisville and joined the Meffert Stock Company. Except for a summer tour of the small towns of Kentucky and Indiana with a company that called themselves the Twilight Revellers, and a season of summer stock at the Alhambra Theater in Chicago under the direction of Oscar Eagle, he would remain in the steady employ of the Meffert Stock Company for the next two years. His roles tended to be small, but the company was better than most, and it served as a good training school for the young man who had committed himself to a life in the theater. By September 1898, Griffith was again working in a touring company that took him through several midwestern states, and when the tour ended in Michigan in March 1899, he returned to Louisville. He worked again briefly for the Meffert Company. Then, late in 1899, he departed for New York.

For the next seven years, Griffith found acting jobs in New York and traveled widely in touring companies that more than once left him stranded in a remote place when the show folded. One of his better jobs, as the lead, "Happy Jack" Ferrers, in *London Life,* a popular melodrama of the day, took him to New York State, Ontario, Ohio, Michigan, Indiana, Illinois, Tennessee, Georgia, Alabama, Mississippi, Arkansas, Wisconsin, and Minnesota. When another tour ended suddenly in Tonawanda, New York, Griffith took a job shoveling iron ore in the steamers that crossed the Great Lakes. This was not the only time Griffith would take a job involving hard physical labor, but he appears never to have wavered in his ambition to realize a career in the theater.

Griffith decided in 1904 to move to San Francisco, which was then a theatrical capital second only to New York. He spent two seasons there and elsewhere on the West Coast employed as an actor, including six weeks of repertory with Melbourne MacDowell and his female star, Fanny Davenport, at the Grand Opera House on Mission Street in San Francisco, followed by five weeks with the company in Portland, Oregon. After the MacDowell company's run in Portland ended, Griffith joined the migrant laborers harvesting hops, and it was probably at this time that he started to gather material for a play he would write. His real ambition was to be a playwright, but when his play was eventually produced, *A Fool and a Girl* (1907), starring Fannie Ward, was a failure.

During his time at the Opera House, Griffith met a young local actress, Linda Arvidson, who would become his wife the following year. Their courtship was interrupted when Griffith traveled to Los Angeles to undertake a role in an adaptation of *Ramona*. It was interrupted again when, upon his return to San Francisco, Griffith was hired by Nance O'Neil, whose repertory during a long run in San Francisco and a cross-country tour of nearly four months included *Macbeth, Queen Elizabeth, Camille, Rosmersholm, Hedda Gabler, The Fires of St. John, Magda,* and, in San Francisco but not on tour, *Judith of Bethulia*—the last being the vehicle Griffith would choose a few years later for his transition from short to longer films.

Linda remained in San Francisco during the tour, which covered ten states and three Canadian provinces. Shortly after the great earthquake and fire struck San Francisco on April 18, 1906, Linda wrote to Griffith expressing her desire to join him, and they arranged to meet in Boston, where his tour would end on May 26. They married in Boston on May 14, and moved to New York, where they found a small apartment.

Griffith finished writing *A Fool and a Girl* late that summer, and he and his wife managed to get jobs in the same company, playing parts in *The One Woman,* written by Thomas Dixon, Jr. Griffith decided to approach the movie studios for work as a writer of scenarios, but his first work for the movies was as an actor, playing the leading role in the Edison Studio's *Rescued from an Eagle's Nest,* which was shot, on a four-day schedule, in early 1908. He called in at the studio of the American Mutoscope and Biograph Company at 11 East 14th Street, and started working there regularly as an actor and scenarist. The Biograph films in which he performed included *At the Crossroads of Life, The Music Matter,* and *When Knights Were Bold.*

Griffith spoke of his desire to direct, and when Biograph's only full-time director, George McCutcheon, fell ill, he was offered the job of directing a Stanner Taylor scenario, *The Adventures of Dollie,* about a child stolen by Gypsies. Griffith accepted the assignment and, on a typical schedule for one-reelers at Biograph, shot the film in two days, with Linda playing Dollie's anguished mother. He soon received other directing assignments, and in August signed a contract to direct films for Biograph, becoming, for the next few months, the studio's only director.

The Adventures of Dollie surpassed the house sales record, and whether he realized it or not, Griffith had found his métier. His cameraman on the film had been Arthur Marvin, but G. W. "Billy" Bitzer—Biograph's other photographer, who had joined the company in 1896 as an electrician—offered Griffith some useful advice on the art of direction, and would become his cameraman on nearly every film he made thereafter.

Over the next five years, Griffith was to make over four hundred films for Biograph—at the rate of one twelve-minute and one six-minute subject every week—during which time he established himself as the American cinema's leading director. He directed all Biograph films from June 1908 until December 1909, and all the important ones during the next four years. It was at Biograph, under Griffith's direction, that Mary Pickford got her start in motion pictures (in *Her First Biscuits,* 1909). So, too, did Dorothy and Lillian Gish, their first film—*An*

Unseen Enemy (1912)—being shot the day after Pickford introduced them to Griffith.

A handful of Griffith's films at Biograph had Civil War settings. These included *The Guerilla* (November 1908), *In Old Kentucky* (1909), *The Honor of His Family* (1910), *In the Border States, or A Little Heroine of the Civil War* (1910), *The House with Closed Shutters* (1910), *The Fugitive* (1910), *His Trust* and *His Trust Fulfilled* (1911), *Swords and Hearts* (1911), *The Battle* (1911), and *The Informer* (1912). Most of these films, not surprisingly, contain themes and scenes that would appear later in *The Birth of a Nation*.

There was resistance from the management of Biograph to making longer films, but Griffith recognized that longer films, while still the exception, would probably soon become the norm. *Judith of Bethulia,* which turned out to be Griffith's next-to-last film for the company, became the first American four-reel subject. Biograph had started sending Griffith to California for the winter months, and *Judith of Bethulia* was shot on location there, in conditions of great secrecy. The film cost more than double the $18,000 budgeted for it, which was a contributing factor in the strained relations Griffith was having with his Biograph bosses in New York. When Griffith returned to New York—to the new Biograph studio in the Bronx, built with the profits of Griffith's successes—it became clear to him that the time had come for him to leave Biograph.

Judith of Bethulia was edited down from six to four reels, and when it was released the following year (1914), was hailed as a great success. But Biograph had been irritated by Griffith's increasingly independent attitude, and while he was in California, they had negotiated a deal with the Broadway theatrical firm of Klaw and Erlanger to film some of its stage properties as feature-length specials of four to six reels. Griffith was informed that his job would be to supervise production, not direct.

Griffith rejected Biograph's terms, and after turning down an offer of $50,000 annually from Adolph Zukor's Famous Players, negotiated a contract with Harry and Roy Aitken. The Aitkens were agglomerators who operated thirty-five film exchanges in the Middle West and owned two major studios—Reliance in New York and Majestic in Los Angeles—and released under the name Mutual. Griffith was to direct two independent productions a year and to supervise a program of less costly films directed by others.

Griffith persuaded members of the Biograph company to follow him into the Aitken organization—among the actors: the Gish sisters, Blanche Sweet, Henry Walthall, Donald Crisp, Mae Marsh, Spottiswoode Aitken, Bobby Harron, and Jack Pickford. His story editor, Frank Woods, also went with him, as did Christy Cabanne, one of his principal directorial assistants. Before moving to Hollywood in February 1914, Griffith hurriedly directed two pictures for Reliance-Majestic, *The Battle of the Sexes* and *The Escape*. In California, he made two more—*Home, Sweet, Home* and *The Avenging Conscience*—before throwing himself full-time into preparations for an epic film based on *The Clansman,* Thomas Dixon's novel and play.

Frank Woods had written a script for the Kinemacolor company for a film version of *The Clansman* that had been started in 1912, then abandoned. Woods proposed a new version to Griffith, who immediately set about acquiring the film rights from Dixon. Dixon demanded the unusually high sum of $25,000, but eventually settled for $2,500 cash and a share of the profits. No script was ever actually written for the film that would become *The Birth of a Nation,* but with Woods's help, Griffith outlined a plot, and with four assistants started researching the Civil War and Reconstruction period for historical accuracy and details of dress, settings, and military and social customs.

The Clansman (as it was then called) went into production on July 4, 1914, and was completed on October 31. Harry Aitkin originally agreed to allocate $40,000 for the picture, but Griffith spent this sum on the battle scenes alone. The financing of the picture was fraught with crises, as Griffith brazenly went ahead with the fulfillment of his vision. The film eventually cost $110,000 and was twelve reels long. *The Clansman* opened on February 8, 1915, at Clune's Auditorium in Los Angeles, where it ran for seven months. (The title of the film was changed to *The Birth of a Nation* before its New York premiere in March.)

The Birth of a Nation at once became the most controversial and successful film in the history of cinema. It made Griffith a millionaire, although he lost much of his fortune on his next epic, *Intolerance,* which he made the following year. Griffith had almost finished making *The Mother and the Law* before the release of *The Birth of a Nation,* but after the great success of *Birth* decided that his new, seven-reel film about hard times in the big city was too small to follow his national saga, and so he decided to develop *The Mother and the Law* into something larger. The result was *Intolerance,* a four-story epic that was dominated by the original film (as the modern story) and by a visually stunning and expensively produced story Griffith called *The Fall of Babylon.*

Audiences found *Intolerance* confusing and exhausting, and despite its importance in film history (particularly its influence on the work of Soviet directors such as Eisenstein and Pudovkin), the film was a financial failure. Griffith was able, nevertheless, to hold his preeminent position within the burgeoning industry for the next five years.

In the spring of 1917, at the invitation of the British Government, Griffith sailed for Europe with Lillian and Mrs. Gish to make *Hearts of the World,* a propagandistic melodrama with a contemporary war setting. The film was shot partly in France and partly in England, and when Griffith returned to the United States in October, was completed in Hollywood and released in April 1918. Earlier in 1917, Griffith had agreed to do a series of films for Artcraft Pictures, to be distributed through Famous Players–Lasky, and the first of these, *The Great Love* (now "lost"), was released in August 1918. Another of the "lost" Artcraft pictures, *The Greatest Thing in Life,* was released in December, and contained—as perhaps a belated attempt by Griffith to refute the charges levelled against him of racism in *Birth*—a scene in which a selfish Southern snob, played by Bobby Harron, kisses the cheek of a dying black soldier.

The year 1919 was an extraordinary one for Griffith. On February 5, he formed a joint distributing company with Mary Pickford, Charlie Chaplin, and Douglas Fairbanks. They called their company United Artists, and Griffith's first film to be distributed by UA was *Broken Blossoms* (it premiered May 13, 1919, and was released October 20, 1920). In 1919, Griffith also released, through other companies, *A Romance of Happy Valley* (January 26), *The Girl Who Stayed at Home* (March 23), *True Heart Susie* (June 1), *The Greatest Question* (November 1), and *Scarlet Days* (November 30). He released *The Fall of Babylon* (July 21) and *The Mother and the Law* (August 18), both edited from *Intolerance,* and in October, Griffith moved his company from Hollywood to Mamaroneck, New York, where he had converted the Flagler estate into a studio.

On December 10, Griffith sailed for Nassau to do some location shooting in the Bahamas, but it was feared that he and his party had drowned at sea when their boat was reported missing for three days. It caused a tremendous sensation in the newspapers, but when they reappeared (they had put into a safe harbor because of a storm), Griffith resumed shooting the exteriors for *The Idol Dancer* and *The Love Flower,* both of which were released the following year, 1920.

In January, Griffith began work on *Way Down East.* He had paid $175,000 for the screen rights to it—more than the entire cost of *The Birth of a Nation.* As Lillian Gish later wrote, "We all thought privately that Mr. Griffith had lost his mind. *Way Down East* was a horse-and-buggy melodrama, familiar on the rural circuit for more than twenty years. We didn't believe it would ever succeed." But succeed it did, making more money than any other film of Griffith's after *The Birth of a Nation.*

The period between *Intolerance* and *Way Down East* marks the peak of Griffith's success. During the next decade, he continued to make films—most memorably, *Orphans of the Storm,* released in December 1921—but his best days were past. On the eve of the New York opening of *Way Down East,* Bobby Harron shot himself, dying a few days later. In January 1921, the Wark Producing Corporation (which had been formed to produce and distribute *Intolerance*) declared bankruptcy. Griffith filmed *Dream Street* with Carol Dempster, whom he hoped to make a star; and after *Orphans of the Storm,* Griffith let Lillian Gish go in an attempt to cut expenses.

One Exciting Night was released in December 1922, and *The White Rose,* starring Mae Marsh, was released the following August. Griffith began filming *America* at the Mamaroneck studio and other locations in Virginia, Massachusetts, and New York. In March, Griffith renewed his contract with United Artists for three more years, but later, as his business and financial problems grew increasingly complex, signed a contract with Famous Players–Lasky, prompting a dispute with UA. Griffith spent the summer of 1923 in Germany filming *Isn't Life Wonderful,* which opened in December. *America* opened in February 1924.

Sally of the Sawdust, produced by Famous Players–Lasky, was filmed at the Paramount studio on Long Island and released by UA in August 1925. Griffith's next two films, *That Royle Girl* (1925) and *The Sorrows of Satan* (1926) were produced by Famous Players–Lasky and distributed by Paramount. On January 2, 1925, he was forced to sell the Mamaroneck studio, and later in 1925, Griffith was released from United Artists. In 1927, Griffith returned to California and signed with Joseph Schenck's Art Cinema Corporation, for whom he made *Drums of Love* (1928), *The Battle of the Sexes* (1928), *Lady of the Pavements* (1929), and—his last film for Schenck—the "all-talkie" *Abraham Lincoln,* which premiered in October 1930.

The following year, 1931, Griffith filmed and released his last picture, *The Struggle* (distributed by UA), and in 1932 he resigned as president of D. W. Griffith, Inc., the production company he had formed in 1916. In 1933, increasingly beset by financial woes, Griffith sold his interest in United Artists.

In late December 1935, without his wife knowing about it, Griffith filed in Kentucky for divorce from Linda Arvidson Griffith, from whom he had been separated since 1911, and in March the following year married the twenty-six-year-old actress Evelyn Baldwin. He was honored by the Motion Picture Academy a week later by special citation for his contribution to the industry. Later in the year, the Griffith Corporation went into receivership, and in 1938 Griffith gave his films and business and personal papers to The Museum of Modern Art in New York.

Hal Roach hired Griffith in 1939 to "produce" and later to "direct" *One Million Years B.C.* Griffith collected his salary, but his services were not required, Roach no doubt only wanting Griffith's name for its publicity value.

In 1940–41, The Museum of Modern Art presented its first retrospective exhibit of Griffith's films, and in 1945, Griffith received an honorary doctoral degree from the University of Louisville.

Evelyn Baldwin Griffith filed for divorce in 1947, and on July 22, 1948, D. W. Griffith died in Los Angeles, where he had been living reclusively in the Knickerbocker Hotel. He was seventy-two. Griffith was buried in the family plot at Mount Tabor Methodist Church, Centerfield, Kentucky.

Sources

Aitken, Roy E., as told to Al P. Nelson. *The Birth of a Nation Story.* Middleburg, Va.: William W. Denlinger, 1965.

Barry, Iris. *D. W. Griffith: American Film Master.* Revised by Eileen Bowser. New York: The Museum of Modern Art/Doubleday, 1965.

Brown, Karl. *Adventures with D. W. Griffith.* 2nd ed. New York: Da Capo Press, 1976.

Gish, Lillian, with Ann Pinchot. *Lillian Gish: The Movies, Mr. Griffith, and Me.* Englewood Cliffs, N.J.: Prentice-Hall, 1969.

Henderson, Robert. *D. W. Griffith: His Life and Work.* New York: Oxford University Press, 1972.

O'Dell, Paul. *Griffith and the Rise of Hollywood*. New York: A. S. Barnes, 1970.

Schickel, Richard. *D. W. Griffith: An American Life*. New York: Simon and Schuster, 1984.

Spears, Jack. *The Civil War on the Screen, and Other Essays*. Cranbury, N.J.: A. S. Barnes, 1977.

Wagenknecht, Edward, and Anthony Slide. *The Films of D. W. Griffith*. New York: Crown Publishers, 1975.

Williams, Martin. *Griffith: First Artist of the Movies*. New York: Oxford University Press, 1980.

The Birth of a Nation

The Birth of a Nation

The Birth of a Nation premiered at Clune's Auditorium, Los Angeles, on February 8, 1915, but we shall never know exactly the composition of the film in its original exhibited state, for not only was Griffith bent on improving his film after every subsequent screening he attended ("I do not know of any work that could not be improved upon," he stated in a publicity release during the 1930 sound re-issue of the film), but official censorship, Epoch's careless preservation of the negative and primitive methods of assembling release prints, and inexpert on-the-spot repairing done by projectionists after film breakage during projection in theaters make it impossible to identify something that could be called a "true print" of The Birth of a Nation.

The version of the film used as the basis for this continuity script is the Museum of Modern Art's 16mm circulation print. This print has been transferred to videotape by Killiam Shows, Inc. (New York), with an original orchestral score by Fraser Mac-Donald and scene tints of sepia, amber, crimson, blue, and green. A detailed account of the general problems involved in determining a representative version of The Birth of a Nation and the fullest analysis of the differences among available prints can be found in John Cuniberti's "Introduction" to his book "The Birth of a Nation": A Formal Shot-by-Shot Analysis Together with Microfiche.

There is very little camera movement in The Birth of a Nation, and so we rarely encounter great changes of mise-en-scène or fluctuations of depth-of-field within shots. What we do find in the film, however, is an imaginative use of masking, of a kind almost never seen in the commercial cinema today. Many a shot, for example, is framed as a circle vignette, a side-arch vignette, or arch vignette. The effects of this sort of definition of the field within the frame are various and significant, and as the continuity script is not a substitute for the film, the indications of this cinematic figure, im-

precise as they are (see the abbre-
viations below), should be borne very
much in mind during any consultation
of the continuity script.

E L S	extreme long shot (landscape or other large spatial entity; human figures are subordinate to the total field)
L S	long shot (the human figure occupies approximately half the frame)
M L S	medium long shot (the whole human figure fills the frame)
M S	medium shot (the human figure from the knees up fills the frame)
M C U	medium close-up (the human figure from the waist up fills the frame)
C U	close-up (the human figure from about shoulder height fills the frame)
E C U	extreme close-up (section of face, other part of body or object)
P O V	point of view
A V	arch vignette
C V	circle vignette
S A V	side-arch vignette

Credits

Executive Producer
D. W. Griffith

Director
D. W. Griffith

Production Company
Epoch Producing Corporation

Screenplay
D. W. Griffith and Frank E. Woods,
from Rev. Thomas Dixon, Jr.'s
novels *The Clansman: An
Historical Romance of the Ku Klux
Klan* (New York, 1905) and *The
Leopard's Spots: A Romance of the
White Man's Burden, 1865–1900*
(New York, 1902), and the play,
The Clansman, which incorporates
material from both

Director of Photography
G. W. "Billy" Bitzer

Assistant Cameraman
Karl Brown

Assistant Director
George Siegmann

Editing
D. W. Griffith, assisted by Joseph
Henabery and Raoul Walsh

Cutters
James Edward "Jimmy" Smith
Rose Smith

Music
Compiled by D. W. Griffith and Joseph
Carl Breil, with original passages by
Breil

Sets
Frank "Huck" Wortman

Costumes
Robert Goldstein Costumes Company

Locations
Filmed at the Reliance-Majestic
Studio, Sunset Boulevard,
Los Angeles, California, and
various outdoor locations in the
area, principally in the San
Fernando and Big Bear valleys
and the open country by the Rio
Hondo

Shooting Schedule
July 4–October 31, 1914

Process
Black and white

Length
Approximately 159 minutes

Release Date
Previewed under the title *The
Clansman* January 1 and 2, 1915,
at the Loring Opera House,
Riverside, California. First shown
at Clune's Auditorium, Los
Angeles, February 8, 1915, under
the title *The Clansman;* world
premiere at the Liberty Theater,
New York City, March 3, 1915,
under its permanent title, *The Birth
of a Nation*

Cast

The cast list is based chiefly on the list in *"The Birth of a Nation"* by Cuniberti, which is a scrupulously researched compilation from a number of sources. Cuniberti's annotations address the inconsistencies of spelling of certain actors' names and the misidentification of the actors playing the roles of Wade and Duke Cameron (cf. the cast list transcribed in the continuity script).

Ben Cameron, "The Little Colonel"
Henry B. Walthall

Flora
Mae Marsh

Flora as a child
Violet Wilkey

Margaret, the older sister
Miriam Cooper

Mrs. Cameron
Josephine Crowell

Dr. Cameron
Spottiswoode Aitken

Wade Cameron, the second son
Maxfield Stanley

Duke Cameron, the youngest son
J. A. Beringer

Mammy
Jennie Lee

Jake
William de Vaull

The Hon. Austin Stoneman, Leader of the House
Ralph Lewis

Elsie Stoneman, his daughter
Lillian Gish

Phil Stoneman, his elder son
Elmer Clifton

Tod Stoneman, the younger son
Robert Harron

Lydia Brown, Stoneman's housekeeper
Mary Alden

Stoneman's servant
Tom Wilson

Silas Lynch
George Siegmann

Gus
Walter Long

Abraham Lincoln
Joseph Henabery

Mrs. Lincoln
Alberta Lee

Senator Charles Sumner
Sam de Grasse

Gen. Ulysses S. Grant
Donald Crisp

Gen. Robert E. Lee
Howard Gaye

The hospital sentry
William Freeman

Laura Keene
Olga Grey

John Wilkes Booth
Raoul Walsh

"White-Arm" Joe
Elmo Lincoln

Jeff, the blacksmith
Wallace Reid

Fallen Union soldier
Eugene Palette

Piedmont girl
Bessie Love

Man who reports Piedmont raid to Confederates
Charles Stevens

Man shot from roof
Erich von Stroheim

A black woman, Dr. Cameron's taunter
Madame Sul-Te-Wan

Elsie's maid
Lenore Cooper

Belles of 1861
Alma Rubens
Donna Montran

The Continuity Script

1. *Fade in.* TITLE: GRIFFITH FEATURE FILMS/Produced exclusively by D. W. Griffith
   Fade out.
2. TITLE: This is the trade mark of the Griffith feature films. All pictures made under the personal direction of D. W. Griffith have the name "Griffith" in the border line, with the initials "DG" at bottom of captions. There is <u>no exception</u> to this rule. D. W. Griffith [signature]
3. TITLE: A PLEA FOR THE ART OF THE MOTION PICTURE/We do not fear censorship, for we have no wish to offend with improprieties or obscenities, but we do demand, as a right, the liberty to show the dark side of wrong, that we may illuminate the bright side of virtue—the same liberty that is conceded to the art of the written word—the art to which we owe the Bible and the works of Shakespeare.
4. TITLE: D. W. GRIFFITH presents <u>The Birth of a Nation</u> or "The Clansman"/Adapted from Thomas Dixon's novel/Copyright 1915 David W. Griffith Corporation
5. *Fade in.* TITLE: The Players

Elsie, <u>Stoneman's daughter</u>	Lillian Gish
Flora Cameron, <u>the pet sister</u>	Mae Marsh
Col. Ben Cameron	Henry Walthall
Margaret Cameron, <u>elder sister</u>	Miriam Cooper
Lydia, <u>Stoneman's mulatto housekeeper</u>	Mary Alden
[shot begins to scroll]	
Hon. Austin Stoneman, <u>Leader of the House</u>	Ralph Lewis
Silas Lynch, <u>mulatto Lieut. Governor</u>	George Seigmann
Gus, <u>a renegade negro</u>	Walter Long
Tod, <u>Stoneman's younger son</u>	Robert Harron
Jeff, <u>the blacksmith</u>	Wallace Reed
Abraham Lincoln	Jos. Henabery
Phil, <u>Stoneman's elder son</u>	Elmer Clifton
Mrs. Cameron	Josephine Crowell
Dr. Cameron	Spottiswoode Aiken
Wade Cameron, <u>second son</u>	J. A. Beringer
Duke Cameron, <u>youngest son</u>	Maxfield Stanley
Mammy, <u>the faithful servant</u>	Jennie Lee
Gen. U. S. Grant	Donald Crisp
Gen. Robert E. Lee	Howard Gaye

6. TITLE: ¶If in this work we have conveyed to the mind the ravages of war to the end that <u>war may be held in abhorrence</u>, this effort will not have been in vain. *Fade out.*

7. *Fade in.* TITLE: ¶The bringing of the African to America planted the first seed of disunion.

8. MLS, CV: *tableau of a minister praying over manacled slaves to be auctioned in a town square. Fade out.*

9. *Fade in.* TITLE: ¶The Abolitionists of the Nineteenth Century demanding the freeing of the slaves.

10. MLS: *two women move away from the camera down the aisle of a crowded meetinghouse and seat themselves at the left, as the speaker in the background gestures toward a slave seated next to him on the dais.*

11. MS: *the speaker appeals to his audience and gestures toward the slave.*

12. MCU: *a stout woman seated in the audience.*

13. LS: *as in 10. The audience applauds as a black child is led up the aisle, toward the camera.*

14. MCU, CV: *the boy stands in front of the speaker, facing the camera. The man's hands are on the boy's shoulders.*

15. LS: *as in 13. A man walks toward the camera up the aisle with a plate, collecting money from the audience.*

16. TITLE: ¶In 1860 a great parliamentary leader, whom we shall call Austin Stoneman, was rising to power in the National House of representatives.

    ¶We find him with his young daughter, Elsie, in her apartments in Washington.

17. MLS: *Elsie moves behind her seated father in their parlor and assists him in mopping his brow and adjusting his wig. She kneels beside him.*

18. MCU, CV: *tableau of Elsie kneeling at her father's side and holding his right hand. They lean toward each other and converse intimately. Fade out.*

19. TITLE: ¶Some time later.

    ¶Elsie with her brothers at the Stoneman country home in Pennsylvania.

20. MLS: *pan right to Phil and Tod Stoneman seated in the garden. Tod asks Phil to read him a letter. Behind them Elsie comes out of the house and onto the porch.*

21. ECU *of the letter, which reads:*
    Dear Ben:-
    True to my promise brother and I are coming to visit you, arriving in Piedmont on Friday next. We are both just dying to see you again and to meet your Kith and Kin.

22. MLS: *as in 20. Phil unfolds the letter as the camera pans farther to the right.*

23. MLS, CV: *behind the curtain that screens the porch, Elsie is petting a cat.*
24. CU: *Elsie, mostly hidden behind the curtain, picks up the cat.*
25. MS: *as in 22. Phil reads the letter as Tod listens.*
26. CU: *as in 24. Elsie's feet can be seen moving in a little dance.*
27. MS: *as in 25. Phil returns the letter to its envelope. Tod gestures toward the porch, and Phil hails Elsie.*
28. MLS: *as in 23. Elsie emerges from behind the curtain, the cat in her arms, and looks in the direction of her brothers.*
29. MS: *as in 27. Phil beckons Elsie and points to the letter in his other hand.*
30. MS: *Elsie strokes the cat and starts to move toward her brothers.*
31. MLS: *as in 28. Elsie comes forward and leaves the frame at the left.*
32. MLS: *as in 29. Phil and Tod are seated in the foreground on the left; Elsie, in the center of the frame, skips toward them. She looks disappointed when they indicate that only they will be going to Piedmont. Phil runs back toward the house to give the letter to a servant for mailing, and then returns to Elsie and Tod, who has settled back in the chair and closed his eyes. Phil pulls him roughly from the chair and drags him into the house. With a skip of excitement, Elsie hops on a footstool, snuggling the cat, and follows her brothers indoors.*
33. TITLE: ¶In the Southland.
    ¶Piedmont, South Carolina, the home of the Camerons, where life runs in a quaintly way that is to be no more.
34. LS: *a street with the Camerons' columned house on the right. Margaret and Flora walk down the street, away from the camera, toward their mother, who is talking to two women in an open carriage. Margaret kisses her mother and greets the women.*
35. TITLE: ¶Bennie Cameron, the eldest son.
36. MLS: *Ben enters the frame on the right, wearing a top hat and morning suit. A picket fence is in the foreground. He pauses on the street as he opens the gate, looks back, and then turns toward the camera.*
37. LS: *as in 34. As a wagon pulls away down the street, two black children fall off. A black man rushes forward and picks them up. He puts one child under his arm and the other scampers off as the Cameron women and the ladies in the carriage look on.*
38. MLS: *as in 36. Ben smiles in amusement and enters the gate and leaves the frame left.*
39. LS: *as in 37. Ben enters on the right and the carriage moves forward toward the camera. He pauses and takes a puff on his cigar as he looks back down the street. He raises his hat to the ladies as they draw near in their carriage.*

40. MS: *Ben, with hat in hand, converses with the lady nearest him in the now stationary carriage.*

41. TITLE: ¶Margaret Cameron, a daughter of the South, trained in the manners of the old school.

42. LS: *Margaret leans her parasol against a couch in the hall of the Cameron house. She changes her mind and carries the parasol with her up the double staircase and out of the frame on the left.*

43. MS: *as in 40. Ben says goodbye and bows to the women in the carriage and the woman nearest him directs the carriage driver to move on.*

44. LS: *as in 39. The carriage pulls away at left, and Ben puts on his hat and walks toward the Camerons' house. A Negro servant opens the picket-fence gate for him.*

45. TITLE: ¶The mother, and the little pet sister.

46. MLS: *on the front porch of the house, Dr. Cameron, with a kitten in his lap, reads the paper. Flora, sitting on the step at her mother's feet, reads a book, and Mrs. Cameron is rocking in her chair. A little black girl peeks mischievously at Flora from behind one of the columns and runs off. Ben enters the frame on the left and kisses his mother as Flora darts behind the column. Pan left as Ben steps over to talk to his father. Ben glances back in the direction of the camera as he points in reference to something behind him.*

47. TITLE: ¶The kindly master of Cameron Hall.

48. *Fade in.* MCU: *Ben leans forward to see something Dr. Cameron is showing him in the newspaper. The camera tilts down to show two puppies (one black, one white) chewing on the rug at Dr. Cameron's feet.*

49. MS: *Ben takes a step toward the camera and puffs on his cigar as he leans on the column, pretending not to see Flora, who is trying to gain his attention. She tugs at his sleeve and then leaps at his neck and kisses him, as Mammy smiles and applauds. Ben and Flora sit on the step together.*

50. CU: *the puppies at Dr. Cameron's feet. Dr. Cameron reaches down to pet the white one.*

51. LS: *as in 42. Margaret comes down the stairs in the hall and sees a letter on the table.*

52. CU: *as in 50. Dr. Cameron drops the kitten onto the white puppy.*

53. TITLE: ¶Hostilities.

54. CU: *as in 52. The kitten and puppy start fighting.*

55. LS: *as in 51. Margaret runs forward excitedly with the letter, then stops to compose herself, before walking calmly out to the right.*

56. MLS: *as in 49. Margaret comes out onto the porch and gives the letter to Ben, who opens it and begins to read. Flora reads it with him.*

57. ECU *of Phil Stoneman's letter, which reads:*

Dear Ben:-

True to my promise brother and I are coming to visit you, arriving in Piedmont on Friday next. We are both just dying to see you again and to meet your Kith and Kin.

58. MLS: *as in 56. The girls become excited, and Flora scampers over to her father and jumps into his lap.*

59. TITLE: ¶The visit of the Stoneman boys to their Southern friends.

60. LS *of the street. A carriage pulls up in front of the Camerons' house, and the two Stoneman boys get out. Ben greets them.*

61. MLS: *Dr. and Mrs. Cameron and Margaret and Flora stand on the porch watching their arrival. Tod enters left, followed by Duke, who introduces him to Dr. and Mrs. Cameron, while Ben introduces Phil to the daughters. When Ben introduces Phil to his parents, the girls dash over to meet him again. Mrs. Cameron curtseys deeply for both introductions. The Cameron parents turn and lead everyone into the house, as Phil and Margaret move around a column and remain on the porch.*

62. MS: *Dr. and Mrs. Cameron enter right. At the center of the hall they pause, turn toward each other, and start talking.*

63. MS: *Phil and Margaret begin a conversation as she fiddles with her parasol. Ben, behind them, tries to get their attention, but they do not notice him. He comes forward, as Flora looks on, and puts himself bodily between them. They all laugh, and turn to follow him into the house.*

64. MLS: *as in 62. The group enters right. Phil and Dr. Cameron bow toward each other again.*

65. TITLE: ¶Chums—the younger sons.
            ¶North and South.

66. MS: *Duke Cameron points to Tod's derby.*

67. TITLE: ¶"Where did you get that hat?"

68. MLS: *as in 66. In response, Tod makes some comment about Duke's vest, and then gives him a playful punch and runs off. Duke chases him.*

69. LS: *as in 64. Dr. Cameron, hearing the commotion outside, starts toward the front door and out right.*

70. MS: *as in 68. Duke pursues Tod, who runs toward the camera, where they stop and wrestle each other.*

71. MS: *Dr. Cameron at the front door looks around and then sees the boys and exits left.*

72. MS: *as in 70. Dr. Cameron enters right and reprimands them gently. The boys respectfully agree to stop horsing around.*

73. LS: *as in 69. Margaret exits through a door at the right of the hall as Ben escorts Phil upstairs.*

74. MS: *as in 72. As Dr. Cameron turns and exits right and Duke attempts to follow, Tod pulls him back by the hair.*

75. M S : *as in 73. Dr. Cameron enters the hall right and turns to see if the boys are following him.*
76. M S : *as in 74. Tod raises his finger at Duke in a mock reproach, then they embrace affectionately and enter the house right.*
77. L S : *as in 75. As Tod and Duke enter the hall right, Dr. Cameron exits through a door right. Phil and Ben appear momentarily on the stair landing and then go back upstairs. Wade enters at right and is introduced to Tod. The three of them start to go up the stairs. Tod dashes up first, in the wrong direction, before Duke and Wade call him to go left.*
78. T I T L E : ¶Over the plantation to the cotton fields.
79. M L S : *Ben and Flora and a small boy, led by a black servant, enter left.*
80. M L S : *Phil and Margaret talk. The picket fence is in the foreground. They respond to a call and move out of the frame on the right.*
81. *Iris/fade in.* L S , C V : *Phil and Margaret stroll about in a pastoral setting of trees, cows, and lakeside. Iris/fade out.*
82. T I T L E : ¶By Way of Love Valley.
83. *Iris/fade in.* L S , C V : *as in 81. The couple move out left. Iris/fade out.*
84. *Fade in.* L S : *two slaves working in a cotton field.*
85. M C U : *two slaves picking cotton.*
86. C U : *a slave's hands tending a cotton bush.*
87. L S : *as in 84. Ben, Flora, and the boy enter left. Ben beckons Margaret and Phil offscreen to the left and picks a cotton blossom, holding it aloft. Phil and Margaret enter left; Phil is holding a picture in his hand. Ben turns to show Phil the blossom.*
88. M S : *Ben shows Phil the blossom.*
89. E C U : *Ben turns the blossom slowly in his hand.*
90. M S : *as in 88. Phil takes the blossom and shows it to Margaret. Ben notices the picture in Phil's hand and takes it from him. Phil explains that it is a likeness of his sister, Elsie. Ben smiles as he studies the portrait, and in a playful gesture takes off his hat and bows to it. Phil tries to regain the portrait, but Ben exits right.*
91. *Fade in.* M C U : *Ben enters left, grinning back at Phil and clutching the portrait with both hands, indicating that he plans to keep it. Flora and the boy amuse themselves in the background.*
92. M S : *as in 90. Phil turns questioningly to Margaret, who looks slightly doubtful.*
93. T I T L E : ¶He finds the ideal of his dreams in the picture of Elsie Stoneman, his friend's sister, whom he has never seen.
94. M C U : *as in 91. Ben looks at the portrait again, this time intently.*
95. E C U , C V : *a photograph of Elsie, elaborately framed.*
96. M C U : *as in 94. Ben brings the picture toward his lips and is about to kiss it, when he decides instead to tuck it into his breast pocket. He looks back at Margaret and Phil and calls to them.*

97. MS: *as in 92. Phil looks over to Ben and makes a gesture of mock accusation.*

98. MCU: *as in 96. Ben turns and exits right. Fade out.*

99. MS: *as in 97. Phil says goodbye to the slaves and exits with Margaret right. The camera lingers for a moment on the working slaves.*

100. TITLE: ¶In the slave quarters.
>¶The two-hour interval given for dinner, out of their working day from six till six.

101. LS: *the party (Ben, Phil, Margaret, Flora, Flora's young friend, Tod, Duke, and a black servant) in a crowd of slaves in front of cabins in the background. Ben shakes hands with an old, stooped slave, who offers Ben his seat. Ben refuses. Margaret takes a seat at left, as slaves begin to dance at right. Other slaves join in the merriment, clapping their hands and stomping their feet.*

102. MS: *the group of whites, with Margaret seated in the center, watch the slaves dancing.*

103. MLS: *slaves dancing.*

104. MS: *as in 102. Phil looks down at Margaret.*

105. MLS: *as in 103. Some slaves wave their hats in the air and others clap rhythmically.*

106. LS: *as in 101. Margaret rises, and the party leaves at left. Ben, bringing up the rear, is approached by two old slaves. He pauses to shake hands with one of them, his hand on the other one's shoulder, and then follows the party out left. The two old slaves nod approvingly in Ben's direction.*

107. TITLE: ¶The gathering storm.
>¶The power of the sovereign states, established when Lord Cornwallis surrendered to the individual colonies in 1781, is threatened by the new administration.

108. MLS: *Dr. and Mrs. Cameron are on the porch of their house, reading a newspaper, as Margaret and Phil enter on the left. Margaret kneels at her father's side; Tod and Duke, with their arms around each other's shoulders, enter and cross to the right, followed by Flora and the boy. Tod and Duke reappear behind the Cameron parents, as Ben enters on the left, and Dr. Cameron points to an item in the newspaper.*

109. ECU, CV: *the headline, which reads:* If the North carries the election, the South will secede.

110. MLS: *as in 108. In an impassioned gesture of disapproval, Dr. Cameron shakes his finger violently at Ben. Ben and Phil try to make light of the headline, while Tod and Duke indicate to each other that nothing will come between them. Fade out.*

111. TITLE: ¶The Stoneman library in Washington, where his daughter never visits.
>¶Charles Sumner, leader of the Senate, confers with the master of Congress.

112. *Fade in.* L S :   *Sumner, seated across from Stoneman at his desk, is speaking.*
113. M C U :   *Stoneman leans forward to make a persuasive reply.*
114. M C U :   *Sumner, in a circle-vignette at left of screen, disagrees vigorously.*
115. T I T L E :   ¶Lydia Brown, Stoneman's housekeeper.
116. M L S :   *Lydia, in the foreground on the right, holds out a dustcloth at arm's length, as if she were too good to do such work; then she flings the cloth at the other servant woman who has come forward, cringing at Lydia's command.*
117. M C U :   *as in 113. Stoneman heatedly makes a point as he crudely scratches his bald head under his wig.*
118. M C U :   *as in 114. Sumner shakes his head.*
119. M C U :   *as in 117. Stoneman thumps the table violently with his fist.*
120. T I T L E :   ¶The mulatto aroused from ambitious dreamings by Sumner's curt orders.
121. L S :   *as in 112. Standing, the two men shake hands, and Stoneman, limping on his clubfoot, escorts Sumner to the door. He slaps Sumner on the back, as the senator exits at right.*
122. M L S :   *as in 116. Sumner enters left as Lydia is parading about, pretending to be a grand lady. When she notices him, she bows with exaggerated servility. He asks for his hat, and she goes to fetch it, exiting at left.*

123. LS: *as in 121. Stoneman returns to his desk, adjusts his wig, and strikes a contemplative pose.*

124. MLS: *as in 122. Lydia holds out Sumner's hat in an insolent manner, and drops it just before he is able to take it from her. She pretends to be dismayed at her clumsiness, and reaches down to pick it up. When she hands the hat to him, he snatches it from her impatiently. She offers to dust it off, but he pushes her away. Lydia opens the door and Sumner exits at right. She mimics a servile bow, and then, with clenched fists and breathing heavily, looks out the door.*

125. MCU: *Lydia spits twice through the doorway after the departed senator.*

126. LS: *as in 124. Lydia slams the door shut, and starts tearing at her blouse in a fit of distress. She falls to the floor, then rises to her knees and spits twice more, then collapses.*

127. MCU: *Lydia tears at her blouse, sobbing in frustration and anger. Suddenly, she sits up, her eyes flashing with some idea that has come to her, and she looks left, in the direction of Stoneman in his library.*

128. LS: *as in 123. Stoneman, standing at his desk, picks up a newspaper and starts to read it.*

129. MCU: *as in 127. Lydia looks in the direction of the library door on the left, and then at the door through which Sumner has departed, and she draws the back of her hand across her mouth.*

130. LS: *as in 128. Stoneman picks up the newspaper again, and walks to the door on the right.*

131. MS: *Lydia staggers forward with a faint smile on her lips.*

132. LS: *as in 130. Stoneman opens the door and exits right.*

133. TITLE: ¶The great leader's weakness that is to blight a nation.

134. MS: *as in 131. Stoneman enters at left. Lydia is on the floor in the foreground. As Stoneman comes forward, Lydia starts to fake sobs. She rises and turns toward him. When he asks her what is the matter, she describes how Sumner treated her roughly. Stoneman puts his hand on her bare shoulder, and at first she draws away with false modesty. She starts to smile and turns back to look at him as he puts his arms around her.*

135. TITLE: ¶The visitors called back to their northern home.
¶The chums promise to meet again.

136. MS: *Duke and Tod emerge from the house. A servant is ironing on the porch in the background. They stop and shake hands.*

137. TITLE: ¶Young Stoneman vows the old vow that his only dreams shall be of her till they meet again.

138. MS: *Phil speaking to Margaret in the hall. Ben enters right and, on seeing them, stops. He leads them out right.*

139. MS: *as in 136. Tod and Duke are saying goodbye to each other on the porch. The rest of the family joins in bidding the Stoneman boys farewell when Ben, Margaret, and Phil emerge from the house. Ben, looking at*

his watch, reassures Phil of the time. Phil and Margaret shake hands, and then he, Ben, Tod, and Duke exit right. The Camerons wave from the porch.

140. MLS: *Ben and Phil shake hands in front of the carriage; Tod and Duke indulge in a last-minute bit of horseplay, which Ben pretends to stop, before Tod jumps into the carriage. Ben shakes Phil's hand once more, and the carriage pulls away. Slaves wave goodbye also, as three black children and the elderly slave run after the departing carriage.*

141. MS: *as in 139. The family waves from the porch, turns, and enters the house, leaving Margaret for a moment by herself, looking forlorn.*

142. MLS: *as in 140. With his arm around Duke's shoulders, Ben waves one more time as the two brothers turn and enter the gate.*

143. MS: *as in 141. Margaret, alone on the porch, and with eyes downcast, turns and enters the house. Ben and Duke enter right. Duke goes in while Ben pauses on the porch looking after the departed carriage. He leans against a column in a contemplative pose. He seems worried. Fade out.*

144. TITLE: ¶The First Call for 75,000 Volunteers. President Lincoln signing the proclamation.

AN HISTORICAL FACSIMILE of the President's Executive Office on that occasion, after Nicolay and Hay in "Lincoln, a History."

145. *Fade in.* MLS: *tableau of Lincoln seated in foreground at a desk, with several gentlemen standing in the background. He listens while an official reads the proclamation. Lincoln takes the proclamation as he rises, examines it for a moment, and turns back to the desk. He sits down, puts on his glasses, takes a quill from an official, and signs.*

146. *Fade/iris in.* TITLE: ¶Abraham Lincoln uses the Presidential office for the first time in history to call for volunteers to enforce the rule of the coming nation over the individual states. *Fade out.*

147. MLS: *as in 145. Lincoln finishes signing the proclamation and dries the ink with powder. He turns and hands the document to the official behind him, who takes it and exits through the door at right. As the others exit at the rear, Lincoln takes off his glasses and returns them to his inside coat pocket. He is left alone. He takes a handkerchief from his hat on the table and dabs his eyes with it, leans forward on the desk, and clasps his hands in prayer. Fade out.*

148. TITLE: ¶The Stoneman brothers departing to join their regiment.

149. MLS: *Tod and Phil are saying goodbye to their weeping aunt on the porch of the house. As they run forward with Elsie, they turn back and wave excitedly. They pause, as Elsie shakes her head in mock despair at the sight of Tod in his uniform. While she is embracing Phil, Tod attempts to steal away without a sisterly hug from Elsie. She stops him, shakes a finger at him, and they embrace tenderly as Phil puts on his hat and exits right.*

150. MLS: *Phil jumps over the vine-covered fence onto the road, turns and calls back.*

151. MS: *as in 149. Elsie and Tod say goodbye.*

152. MLS: *as in 150. Phil sighs, turns, and walks out at right.*

153. MS: *as in 151. Tod leaves Elsie and exits right as Elsie holds out her arms.*

154. MLS: *as in 152. Tod jumps over the fence and turns to look back.*

155. MS: *as in 153. Elsie mimes a soldier shooting a gun, holds up two fingers, then points to herself, as if to say "Do it for me."*

156. MLS: *as in 154. Tod holds up two fingers and leans forward over the fence with reckless, youthful energy.*

157. MS: *as in 155. Elsie makes the shooting gesture in an emotionally ambivalent register.*

158. MLS: *as in 156. Tod waves and runs out at right.*

159. MS: *as in 157. Elsie brings her hand up to her mouth in a stifled sob, turns, and runs back toward the house and falls on the porch steps at her aunt's feet. Fade out.*

160. TITLE: ¶After the first battle of Bull Run.
   ¶Piedmont's farewell ball on the eve of the departure of its quota of troops for the front.

161. LS: *the ballroom of Cameron Hall crowded with dancers. Ben can be seen among them. The camera dollies back slowly. Fade out.*

162. TITLE: ¶Bonfire celebrations in the streets.

163. LS: *night. A large crowd of people, in silhouette, waving their hats and dancing around fires in front of Cameron Hall.*

164. LS: *Ben chats with a young lady and his mother in the foreground of the ballroom. He takes his leave of them and exits left.*

165. LS: *Ben enters the hall from the right, greets a couple seated on the couch, and walks forward.*

166. LS: *as in 163. The bonfire celebrations in the street.*

167. MLS: *the picket fence in the foreground and couples sitting or walking about on the other side of it. Smoke wafts through the air from the bonfires.*

168. LS: *as in 165. Ben, standing in the hall, looks outside, smiles, and turns back toward the staircase.*

169. MLS: *as in 167. Couples walk about as men move among them with flaming torches. Fade out.*

170. TITLE: ¶While youth dances the night away, childhood and old age slumber.

171. MLS: *Ben tiptoes into a room through a door on the right, and looks down at Flora sleeping on a couch, then glances up at Dr. Cameron dozing in a chair.*

172. *Fade in.* LS: *as in 164. The dancing in the ballroom continues.*

173. MS: *as in 171. Ben tickles his sister's face playfully with a Confederate flag, then drops it over her head. She sits up, turns to him with her arms outstretched, and they embrace. She falls to sleep, and Ben, smiling tenderly, covers her with the flag and kisses her. Fade out.*

174. TITLE: ¶The first flag of the Confederacy baptized in glory at Bull Run.

175. LS: *as in 172. Cheers go up as Ben and a young lady, carrying the outspread flag, make their way forward through the dancers.*

176. MCU: *glasses are lifted to the flag, which forms a backdrop to the shot. A young woman on the right waves her handkerchief excitedly.*

177. LS: *as in 175. With his back to the camera, Ben holds up the flag to the cheering crowd. Two men in the foreground at right embrace.*

178. LS: *as in 166. The bonfire celebrations continue in the street.*

179. MLS: *as in 169. Couples within the picket fence walk about amid the wafting smoke.*

180. LS: *as in 177. Ben and a young lady carry the flag back through the excited, cheering crowd.*

181. TITLE: ¶Daybreak.
      ¶The time set for the troops' departure.

182. L S : *a soldier on horseback gallops down the street lined with cheering, waving people, and stops in front of Cameron Hall, which is draped festively in bunting.*

183. M L S : *as in 168. Ben leaves Duke and Wade and others gathered in the hall and walks forward and exits right.*

184. L S : *as in 182. Ben walks from the house on the right to the horseman in the street. He gives the horseman some instructions and the horseman gallops off in a cloud of dust as the crowd cheers and waves after him.*

185. T I T L E : ¶The assembly call.

186. L S : *a horseman gallops out of the crowded square at right as another moves into the crowd in the rear. Two more horsemen enter left and pull up in the clearing at the center. A bugler on the left is ordered to sound a call.*

187. *Iris in.* M C U , C V : *the bugler sounding the call.*

188. L S : *as in 180. The dancers in the ballroom stop dancing when they hear the bugle call.*

189. *Iris in.* M C U : *as in 187. The bugler calling. Iris out.*

190. L S : *as in 188. The dancing comes to an end.*

191. L S : *as in 186. The two horsemen and the bugler begin to cross the square to the rear and are followed by several soldiers running.*

192. L S : *as in 190. The men in the ballroom start to bid the ladies farewell.*

193. L S : *as in 184. Three soldiers run through Cameron gate into the street crowded with cheering people.*

194. M L S : *Dr. Cameron awakens from his nap in the chair and walks to the rear of the room and out at left, as Flora rouses herself on the couch.*

195. L S : *as in 192. General commotion as the ball breaks up and men begin to leave at left. Two women in the foreground look disconsolate.*

196. T I T L E : ¶Their state flag.
      ¶The spirit of the South.

197. M L S : *as in 194. Ben enters the room and picks up Flora and carries her aloft on one shoulder and starts to exit at rear. They pause at the door, where Ben points to the flag draped above it. Flora tugs on it.*

198. E C U *of the motto in circular motif on the state flag, which reads:* CONQUER WE MUST—VICTORY OR DEATH—FOR OUR CAUSE IS JUST

199. M L S : *as in 197. Ben carries Flora back to the couch in the foreground on the right and returns the small Confederate flag to her, as Dr. and Mrs. Cameron, Wade, Duke, and Margaret enter through the door in the rear. Ben and Flora exit through the door in the rear as Wade and Duke bid their parents and sister farewell.*

200. L S : *as in 191. Townspeople, including slaves, cheer the departing soldiers.*

201. T I T L E : ¶A mother's gift to the cause—three sons off for the war.

202. MLS: *as in 199. Duke embraces Flora and Ben embraces Margaret. Duke and Wade begin to leave through the door on the right as their parents say goodbye.*
203. MLS: *as in 183. Duke and Wade come forward through the hall. Duke steals a kiss from a girl who blushingly throws her hands up to her face and turns to her giggling friends. The boys exit right.*
204. MLS: *as in 202. Ben releases himself from his father's embrace to pick up Flora, who throws her arms around her brother's neck. He puts her down, and as he opens the door on the right, she holds up her little Confederate flag. He places his arm around his mother as they all leave the room to the right.*
205. LS: *as in 200. A fife and drum band leads mounted officers, flagbearers, and a battalion of foot soldiers forward through the crowded square and out at left. Teams of horses in harness bring up the rear.*
206. MS: *Flora and Margaret skip excitedly out onto the porch, followed by Ben and his parents, as Mammy and other women look on.*
207. LS: *crowds on the street in front of Cameron House wave and cheer as the parade approaches. An elderly slave on the left gets down on his knees and throws his arms up in the air.*
208. MS: *as in 206. Ben kisses his mother.*
209. LS: *as in 207. The crowds move to the curb and the old slave gets up off his knees and doffs his hat to the mounted officer who calls the parade to a halt in front of Cameron Hall.*
210. MS: *as in 208. Ben leaves his parents on the porch and exits right, followed by Mammy.*
211. LS: *as in 209. The excited crowd on the street continues to wave at the halted parade. A man on his knees leads a small group of children in song.*
212. MS: *Ben mounts his horse as Flora waves her handkerchief and Margaret, Mammy, and others wave in farewell. Ben draws his sword in salute, shouts "Forward march!" and rides off to the right.*
213. LS: *as in 211. Ben leads the troops forward and out.*
214. LS: *as in 205. Foot soldiers march across the square and out to the left.*
215. LS: *as in 213. Troops march past Cameron Hall and cheering townsfolk, followed by three jubilant slaves. Fade out.*
216. MS: *as in 210. Dr. and Mrs. Cameron watch the departing troops from their porch. Mrs. Cameron wipes a tear from her eye as her husband puts a solicitous arm around her and holds her hand.*
217. LS: *as in 215. The crowd continues to cheer wildly as it closes in behind a covered supply wagon that brings up the rear of the parade.*
218. MS: *as in 216. Flora and Margaret run in from the right to their parents standing on the porch. Mrs. Cameron takes a sobbing Flora under one arm and a subdued Margaret under the other, and they turn and enter the house.*

With an impatient gesture of his hand, Dr. Cameron waves them in, while he lingers for a moment to look one last time down the street. Fade out.

219. MLS: *Mrs. Cameron, followed by Dr. Cameron, Margaret, and Flora enter the parlor slowly from the right. Each takes a separate seat, and Dr. Cameron smokes contemplatively. Margaret, seated at the spinet on the left, begins to play. Flora, sitting on the couch on the right, holds up her small Confederate flag, clutches it to her chest, then buries her face in the couch. Fade out.*

220. TITLE: ¶Elsie on her return to her aunt's home in Washington tells her father of her brothers' leaving for the front.

221. MLS: *a servant enters the Stoneman parlor through a door on the right and ushers in an excited Elsie and her maid. Stoneman is in the extreme foreground on the left. The servant points to Stoneman and exits to the rear left. Elsie rushes forward to her father, who rises to greet her. She kisses him, and her expression becomes serious as she tells him the news of her brothers. She puts her arm around her father and they turn to move to the rear.*

222. TITLE: ¶Two and a half years later.
¶Ben Cameron in the field has a letter from home.

223. *Iris in.* MLS: *a battlefield with men in the background—some seated, some standing—discussing strategy. Ben enters from the right, reading a letter. He stops at the entrance to a tent on the left.*

224. E C U : *the letter, which reads:*
—and you have really grown a moustache—oh my! I'm just dying, dying to see you. Well, I'm growing up too—they say I'm such a big girl now you wouldn't know me.

X X X X X X (Kisses)

Your ~~little~~ big

Sis

225. M L S : *as in 223. Ben enters the tent at left as an officer walks past from the right. Iris out.*

226. T I T L E : ¶News from the front.

¶Little sister wears her last good dress as a ceremonial to the reading of her brother's letter.

227. M L S : *Flora, wearing a tartan dress, emerges from the front door of Cameron Hall, reading the letter and twitching with supressed excitement. She folds it, kisses it, and places it inside her dress, and then turns to go back in. The door is jammed.*

228. M L S : *in the hall, Margaret puts on her hat and Mrs. Cameron hands her a parasol.*

229. M L S : *as in 227. Flora at the front door calls and knocks.*

230. M L S : *as in 228. Margaret moves forward and out at right as her mother watches admiringly after her.*

231. M L S : *as in 229. Margaret opens the door and asks what the trouble is; Flora indicates that the door was jammed. The two sisters open their parasols and walk off to the right.*

232. T I T L E : ¶Piedmont scarred by the war.

¶An irregular force of guerillas raids the town.

¶The first negro regiments of the war were raised in South Carolina.

233. L S : *a man, followed by two horsemen, runs forward across the town square waving a paper. Other figures run toward them to see what the excitement is about.*

234. M L S : *Margaret and Flora come through the gate and walk along the street in front of Cameron Hall and out at right.*

235. L S : *the two girls hear some commotion on the street behind them. They turn and see the two horsemen and several people scattering and running toward them, and they run back into the yard.*

236. M L S : *as in 231. The girls dash up onto the porch, looking terrified as they glance back at the street and try to open the jammed door.*

237. L S : *as in 233. In the town square Union guerillas are swarming in different directions.*

238. L S : *as in 230. Dr. Cameron enters from the left, walking quickly forward across the hall with a pistol in his hand.*

239. MLS: *as in 236. Margaret and Flora manage to get the door open, and they hurry in and close the door behind them.*

240. LS: *as in 238. The girls rush toward their father and cling to him in fright.*

241. LS: *as in 237. Black guerillas in the square are gathered about a supply wagon; others run out to the right, carrying rifles.*

242. LS: *as in 235. The street in front of Cameron Hall is swarming with people. An elderly man in civilian clothes is shot by a raider, and a soldier signals to the guerillas down the street to follow him.*

243. LS: *as in 240. Dr. Cameron motions his daughters toward the door at left rear.*

244. MLS: *the girls burst into the parlor from the right. Mrs. Cameron rushes to help them lock the door.*

245. LS: *as in 242. Guerillas climb over the picket fence and pour through the gate. A black woman and a soldier jeer at a dead man.*

246. MS: *as in 239. Three guerillas enter from the left. Two of them look about wildly while the third tries to force open the jammed door.*

247. MLS: *as in 243. Dr. Cameron, pistol in hand, comes forward.*

248. MS: *as in 246. The door is forced open and the three guerillas enter.*

249. TITLE: ¶The scalawag white captain influences the negro militia to follow his orders.

250. MLS: *as in 247. Dr. Cameron holds up his hand to stop the soldiers, who enter from the right, but they push him aside as the white captain enters from the left and tries to wrest the pistol from Dr. Cameron's grip.*

251. MLS: *as in 244. Margaret at the center of the room, and Flora and Mrs. Cameron at the door, recoil at the sounds in the hall.*

252. MLS: *as in 250. As the white captain and Dr. Cameron struggle, the pistol discharges. The captain knocks Dr. Cameron to the floor as more soldiers swarm in from the right; one of them kicks over the table in the center of the hall.*

253. MS: *as Flora turns the key in the lock, Margaret and Mrs. Cameron rush toward her.*

254. MLS: *as in 252. The white captain picks up a rifle from the floor and turns to join the other guerillas who are beginning to mount the stairs.*

255. MLS: *as in 251. The women retreat in fright through the door in the rear, and Flora closes it behind them.*

256. MLS: *the door on the right opens and the women enter the kitchen. Mrs. Cameron starts toward a trap in the floor.*

257. MLS: *as in 254. The soldiers swarm about the hall destructively. Some batter the door to the parlor at left.*

258. MLS: *as in 256. Flora, Mrs. Cameron, and Margaret step down through the trapdoor.*

259. MCU, CV: *Margaret and Flora in the cellar. Flora clasps her hands in nervous excitement and giggles. Margaret reproaches her.*

260. LS: *soldiers force a mother and her three children from their house and into the yard. When a man comes into the yard and sees what is happening, he is shot by a soldier on the porch. In the background, guerillas are running about among the houses and jumping over the picket fences.*

261. MLS: *as in 257. The hall of the Camerons' house is crowded with soldiers looting and destroying.*

262. MCU, CV: *as in 259. Margaret is unconsciously posed in an attitude of prayer, as Flora wrings her hands and giggles with the terrifying thrill of it all.*

263. MLS: *as in 261. The looting and destroying continues in the hall as soldiers batter down the parlor door on the right.*

264. MCU, CV: *as in 262. Margaret and Flora embrace each other in fright.*

265. MLS: *as in 255. The white captain tumbles into the parlor through the door on the right, followed closely by four soldiers. One of them searches the couch as the others make their way through the door to the kitchen in the rear.*

266. MCU, CV: *as in 264. Margaret and Flora are still holding each other tightly.*

267. TITLE: ¶A company of Confederate state troops informed of the raid.

268. LS: *as a company of Confederate troops approaches, three men run in from the left to inform them of the raid. The officer draws his sword and leads his troops at a run out at left.*

269. MLS: *as in 265. In the parlor, the white officer smashes a vase with his rifle and grabs a vase with flowers off the spinet and throws it violently to the floor, while the four black soldiers continue searching.*

270. MCU: *as in 266. Margaret and Flora start in alarm.*

271. LS: *a man on a roof shoots with a pistol at a Union soldier on the ground at right. He kills the soldier, but another soldier runs in from behind the house at left and fires up at him with a rifle, and the man falls from the roof.*

272. MLS: *as in 269. The white captain comes forward and pauses in center of the parlor and listens, then he and the others exit through the door on the right.*

273. LS: *the company of Confederate troops, urged on by the officer, moves out left.*

274. LS: *as in 260. A Union guerilla sets fire to a house.*

275. TITLE: ¶The Confederates to the rescue.

276. LS: *as in 241. Union soldiers are crowded around a horse and wagon in the square as Confederate troops enter rear right. They exchange fire.*

277. MLS: *as in 263. The white captain stops in mid-gesture in the center of the hall and listens in alarm, then turns to retreat to the rear. A piece of furniture is on fire at right.*

278. LS: *as in 276. In the square, the wagon pulls away to the right as Union
and Confederate troops continue to exchange shots. The Unionists begin
staggering back.*
279. MLS: *as in 277. In the hall, Union guerillas prepare to leave the house.*
280. LS: *as in 278. In the square, Confederate troops move to the left through thick
smoke as a mounted officer, waving his sword aloft, urges them forward.*
281. MLS: *as in 279. The white captain and guerillas in the hall rush forward and out to the right in hasty retreat.*
282. MCU: *as in 270. Flora and Margaret, hearing the soldiers retreating,
turn to follow their mother up the steps to the trapdoor.*
283. LS: *as in 245. The Union raiders, shot at by Confederate troops in front
of Cameron Hall, retreat across the street and out left.*
284. MLS: *as in 258. Flora unlocks the kitchen door and the women exit right.*
285. LS: *as in 281. Mammy, followed by Mrs. Cameron and Flora, rushes
into the hall from the left carrying buckets of water, which they throw on
the flames at right, while Dr. Cameron, on the floor in the foreground on
the right, sits up.*
286. MS: *Dr. Cameron enters right and staggers past the burning walls.*
287. LS: *as in 285. Mrs. Cameron helps her husband out left, while Mammy,
Margaret, Flora, and two servants fight the fire.*

288. L S : *as in 283. Confederate troops advance down the street and out left as smoke billows from Cameron Hall on the right.*

289. L S : *as in 287. Confederate soldiers, entering from the right, help put out the fire in the smoke-filled hall.*

290. T I T L E : ¶After the rescue.

291. M S : *as in 289. In a flurry of excitement, Flora thanks the soldiers as they exit to the right. Before Margaret can thank the last soldier, Mammy, still carrying a bucket in each hand, throws her arms around him. Margaret brings her hands to her mouth in shock, then shakes the soldier's hand and goes over to her parents who are resting on the couch on the right. Mammy turns, puts down the buckets, and brings her apron up to her face as the girls embrace their parents. Fade out.*

292. T I T L E : ¶Letters from home revive tender reveries for "the little Colonel."

293. M C U : *in the tent, Ben strokes his moustache and smiles as he reads the letter. He kisses the letter, and as he places it inside his coat, he feels the portrait of Elsie there. He retrieves it slowly and begins to look at it.*

294. E C U : *the portrait of Elsie Stoneman in circle-vignette.*

295. M C U : *as in 293. Ben is about to throw the portrait to the ground as being unimportant to him, when he changes his mind and with a smile looks at it again and prayerfully closes the hinged frame with two hands.*

296. T I T L E : ¶On the battlefield.
         ¶War claims its bitter, useless, sacrifice.
         ¶True to their promise, the chums meet again.

297. M L S : *Confederate soldiers crouch under a bush on the left, while in the background a line of soldiers shoot at the enemy. A group of Confederates enter on the right and run toward the left on the far side of the bush.*

298. M C U : *Duke Cameron, one of the soldiers under the cover of the bush, looks to the left and then leads a charge out to the right.*

299. M L S : *as in 297. The soldiers rush out into the open. Most are hit by enemy fire, and they fall out of frame to the right. Duke is also hit, and he collapses to the ground just as a Union soldier—Tod Stoneman—rushes toward him wielding a bayonet.*

300. M C U : *Tod raises his bayonet to stab the fallen man.*

301. M C U : *Duke, flat on his back, raises his head a little and holds out his hands in a small gesture of appeal as he calls out Tod's name. Tod's feet are visible at his side.*

302. M C U : *as in 300. Tod, on the point of stabbing Duke with his bayonet, recognizes his friend, and a look of shock comes over his face. The look of shock gives way to a smile.*

303. M C U : *as in 301. Duke's body slumps and he is still.*

304. M C U : *as in 302. A shot is fired from the bushes behind Tod, and he is hit. He drops his gun.*

305. M L S : *as in 299. Tod twists in pain and falls.*

306. M C U : *as in 303. Tod drops beside Duke, his hand falling across Duke's chest. He looks at Duke for a second, smiling, and then closes his eyes in pain.*

307. M L S : *as in 305. Tod and Duke are in the foreground, as men continue to fight in the thick smoke in the background.*

308. M C U : *as in 306. Tod slowly brings his arm around Duke's neck in an embrace, and dies. The grass moves in the breeze. Fade out.*

309. T I T L E : ¶News of the death of the youngest Cameron.

310. M S : *Dr. Cameron is reading a letter as Margaret, on the left, clutches her black shawl in grief. Mrs. Cameron and Flora enter the hall at left, and Mrs. Cameron insists on taking the letter from her husband, to read the news for herself. As he tries to comfort her, she turns away, her eyes wide with shock and disbelief. Flora comes forward and holds her sister's hand. Mrs. Cameron collapses on the couch to the right, and her husband rushes over to her, followed by Margaret and Flora. Fade out.*

311. T I T L E : ¶Others also read <u>war's sad page.</u>

312. *Iris/fade in.* M L S : *Stoneman is seated, reading a letter. Elsie, kneeling at his side, suddenly bursts into tears, and he puts his arms around her. He looks up grimly. Iris/fade out.*

313. T I T L E : ¶The last of their dearest possessions to be sold for the failing cause.

314. M S : *Margaret hands the soldier a shawl and Flora contributes her tartan dress as Dr. and Mrs. Cameron look on proudly. The soldier tips his hat and exits right. As her parents turn and exit to the rear on the left, and Margaret sits pensively on the couch on the right, Flora steps forward, tugging at her poor dress and looking subdued. Suddenly, she brightens with a new resolve and turns to parade her plain dress in front of an amused Margaret, then skips over to her sister and jumps on the couch. They embrace.*

315. T I T L E : ¶Elsie Stoneman goes as a nurse in the military hospitals.

316. M L S : *Elsie comes forward, fastening her cape, as her father and aunt enter left. She and her father walk back toward the door on the right, Elsie kisses her aunt goodbye as he opens the door, and they exit.*

317. T I T L E : ¶While the women and children weep, a great conqueror marches to the sea.

318. *Iris/fade in.* M C U , C V : *a mother comforts her three weeping children huddled in an outdoor space. The camera pans slowly to the right as the iris opens fully to reveal an army moving to the left in the valley far below.*

319. M C U , C V : *the mother and children beside the charred remains of their house.*

320. ELS: *as in 318. The army continues to move across the valley out left.*
321. *Fade in.* MCU: *as in 319. The mother and children remain huddled together.*
322. ELS, AV: *the Union army swarms up from lower left and forward across the valley. Smoke from a burning house billows wildly.*
323. TITLE: ¶The torch of war against the breast of Atlanta.
¶The bombardment and flight.
324. LS: *a chaotic night scene of people on foot and on horseback running through the smoke-filled streets. In the distance the burning buildings of Atlanta are visible in silhouette.*
325. LS: *as in 320. The camera pans left from the army in the valley and comes to rest on the mother huddled with her children on the hillside. Iris/fade out.*
326. LS, AV: *A high-angle shot of refugees struggling uphill. Wade Cameron, supported by a comrade, is visible in the foreground.*
327. LS: *as in 324. Panicked citizens rush through the smoke-filled streets.*
328. LS: *as in 326. Refugees continue uphill. The upper third of the split screen shows Atlanta burning in the distance.*
329. LS: *as in 327. Men on horseback and people in silhouette swarm through the smoky streets as Atlanta burns ferociously in the distance.*

330. L S :   *as in 328. Upper border of the frame masked. The refugees, with Wade Cameron in the foreground, make their way up the hill.*

331. L S :   *as in 329. The street is now almost completely obscured by thick, white smoke.*

332. M S :   *Wade is dragged in from the right by his comrade, an older, bearded soldier, and laid down beside a wooden fence, behind which people flee to the left.*

333. T I T L E :   ¶The death of the second Cameron son.

334. M C U :   *the soldier cradles Wade in his arms, but lays him down when Wade's head falls back.*

335. L S :   *as in 331. People continue to flee through the fire- and smoke-ravaged streets.*

336. L S :   *as in 330. The refugees making their way up the hill and out to the left. Atlanta still burning fiercely in the split screen above.*

337. L S :   *as in 335. The streets of the burning city, with people fleeing through the smoke.*

338. L S :   *as in 336. Refugees climb the hill; some of them look back at the burning city.*

339. T I T L E :   ¶The last grey days of the Confederacy.
¶On the battle lines before Petersburg, parched corn their only rations.

340. M L S :   *Confederate soldiers lined up in a trench as one of them distributes parched corn.*

341. E C U :   *the dried corn being portioned out of a skillet with a twig. A soldier asks for more and is given a few more kernels.*

342. M S :   *the soldier distributing the corn moves down the line as others begin to eat; two men are roasting their share over an open fire.*

343. M L S :   *as in 340. One of the men roasting his corn tries a kernel prematurely and burns his tongue. The soldier with the skillet moves farther down the line.*

344. T I T L E :   ¶A sorely needed food train of the Confederates is misled on the wrong road and cut off on the other side of the Union lines.

345. L S :   *two men on horseback come up to the head of the food train and deliver a message to the lead officer. As they gallop off to the right, a third horseman pulls up and does the same.*

346. M S :   *two soldiers standing by a covered wagon filled with food supplies.*

347. E C U :   *cured hams and other foodstuffs in the wagon.*

348. M S :   *as in 346. The two soldiers stand guard by the wagon.*

349. L S :   *as in 345. Two horsemen gallop in from the right and pull up beside the officer leading the food train. The officer hands the first horseman a paper and directs him off left.*

350. T I T L E :   ¶General Lee orders an attempt to break through and rescue the food train.

¶A bombardment and a flanking movement are started to cover the charge.

351. MLS: *as Lee writes an order, a horseman turns and moves away. A second horseman arrives and Lee hands him the letter.*

352. TITLE: ¶The action before daybreak with artillery duel in distance.

353. ELS: *Confederate troops charge from the left and Union troops from the right, as the darkened sky flashes with artillery fire, illuminating clouds of smoke.*

354. LS: *as in 349. The food train at a standstill. Soldiers begin to reach for their rifles (stacked to the right).*

355. ELS: *as in 353. The predawn battle continues. The Confederates are pushed back.*

356. TITLE: ¶"The little Colonel" receives his orders to charge at an appointed moment.

357. MS: *a courier enters the Confederate trench and hands a message to Ben in the foreground. In thick smoke, the soldiers are firing furiously at the enemy off to the right. The courier leaves to the left; Ben draws his sword and waves it above his head, shouting a command as he charges out to the right.*

358. TITLE: ¶The intrenchments of the opposing armies separated by only a few hundred feet.

359. ELS: *as in 355. High-angle shot of a valley in which two ribbons of sol-
     diers—the Union line of infantry on the right, and the Confederate line
     on the left—exchange fire as the wind blows huge clouds of smoke off to
     the left.*

360. LS, AV: *the Union line waving flags and shooting out to the left from
     behind sandbags.*

361. ELS: *as in 359. Great clouds of white smoke drift left across the
     battlefield.*

362. TITLE: ¶The masked batteries.

363. LS, CV: *cannon fire coming from a group of trees at the foot of a hill.*

364. ELS: *as in 361. The two lines continue to exchange fire. Fade out.*

365. LS: *Ben, in the foreground of the Confederate trench on the left, is rally-
     ing his fellow soldiers.*

366. LS, AV: *as in 364. Union soldiers advancing left toward the intrenched
     Confederates.*

367. LS: *as in 365. In the thick smoke, a Union flag and a few Northern sol-
     diers can be seen just a few yards from the intrenched Confederates on
     the left. Ben runs behind his men to get closer to the center of the line.*

368. LS, AV: *as in 366. The Union forces start retreating to their trenches.*

369. LS: *under their waving flag, Union troops fire to the left.*

370. LS: *as in 367. Ben removes his hat and continues, with sword in hand, to rally his men in their trench.*
371. ELS: *as in 368. The camera pans slowly right, showing the Union troops running for cover and returning to their trenches. Thick, black smoke churns into the sky behind the gun carriages entering from the right.*
372. TITLE: ¶The field artillery.
373. LS: *cavalry troops gallop to the rear, behind the line of artillery facing left.*
374. LS, CV: *as in 363. The hidden batteries fire from the hills.*
375. LS: *as in 373. Union cannons fire left, as a cannon is wheeled in from the right.*
376. ELS: *as in 371. The camera pans left across the Union position. A man is shot from his horse.*
377. LS: *as in 375. The Union cannons fire left.*
378. TITLE: ¶The mortars.
379. LS: *the mortars fire and the pit fills with smoke.*
380. LS: *as in 377. An enemy shell explodes spectacularly behind the Union cannons.*
381. LS: *as in 379. The mortar pit filled with smoke.*
382. ELS: *as in 376. A Union standard-bearer advances left to the midway point between the two lines.*
383. LS: *as in 381. The pit shrouded in smoke as the mortars prepare to fire again.*

384. ELS: *as in 382. The camera pans slightly right and then left across the Union trenches.*
385. TITLE: ¶"The little Colonel" leads the final desperate assault against the Union command of Capt. Phil Stoneman.
386. MS: *as in 357. Ben Cameron in the foreground, waving his hat and his sword, shouts a command to his troops in the trench and then charges forward and out to the right.*
387. LS, AV: *the Confederate line about to attack. Ben jumps up, his sword high in the air, and gives the command to advance. The troops scramble out of the trench and charge to the right.*
388. MLS, CV: *the Confederates charge to the right, with Ben Cameron in the middle, urging them on.*
389. ELS, AV: *as in 384. The Confederates advance from the left under fire from the Union line.*
390. LS, AV: *as in 360. Under their waving standards, the Union troops fire.*
391. LS: *Confederate soldiers dash back to their trench. Two standard-bearers fall and are helped back to the trench.*
392. ELS, AV: *as in 389. Confederate soldiers can be seen advancing right.*
393. LS, AV: *as in 390. The Union trench continues to fire.*
394. MCU: *"the little Colonel" leads the charge toward the rapidly back-tracking camera.*
395. LS, AV: *as in 393. A cannon fires from the Union trench.*
396. MLS, SAV: *the intrenched Union troops fire in unison and begin to reload.*
397. ELS, AV: *as in 392. Confederate troops advance to the right against a backdrop of white smoke. Fade out.*
398. *Fade in.* MS: *tableau of Dr. Cameron seated at a table praying over an open Bible, with his wife at his side and daughters kneeling at her feet.*
399. ELS, AV: *as in 397. The battlefield under a pall of white smoke. The two sides engage.*
400. MS: *as in 398. Dr. Cameron prays and Mrs. Cameron, Margaret, and Flora listen. Fade out.*
401. MLS, CV: *as in 395. The Union line, its flag waving prominently. Ben Cameron and his troops enter from the left and the two sides engage in hand-to-hand combat.*
402. MS: *the enemies fight hand-to-hand in the trench.*
403. LS, AV: *in the face of enemy fire, the Confederates stream in from the left and engage in combat with the Union soldiers.*
404. MCU: *the frenzied fighting in the trench continues, as a Union soldier bayonets one Confederate soldier, and then another.*
405. MLS, CV: *as in 401. A Confederate standard-bearer waves his flag wildly as the fighting in the Union trench continues.*
406. LS: *Union soldiers retreat to a trench farther back.*

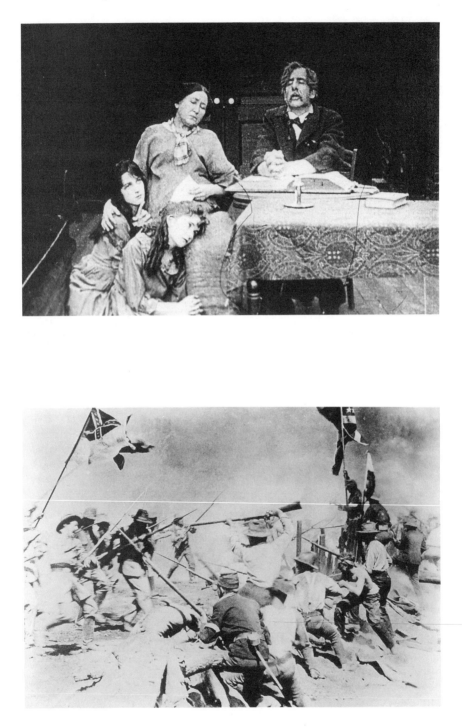

407. TITLE: ¶Two lines of intrenchments taken, but only a remnant of his regiment remains to continue the advance.
408. LS, AV: *as in 405. The remnant of the Confederate force crouches behind the Union trench just taken.*
409. MLS: *Capt. Phil Stoneman stands among his men in the second Union trench, facing left.*
410. TITLE: ¶All hope gone, "the little Colonel" pauses before the last charge to succor a fallen foe.
411. MLS, CV: *entering from the left, Ben leaps up onto a sandbag stacked against the trench, holding his sword aloft.*
412. MCU: *a wounded Union soldier writhes in pain on the ground.*
413. MLS: *as in 411. Ben sees the man.*
414. MCU: *as in 412. The wounded soldier clutches at his chest.*
415. MLS, CV: *as in 413. Ben drops down from the edge of the trench, picking up a water bottle as he exits right.*
416. MCU: *as in 414. Ben enters from the right and crouches beside the man as he uncaps the water bottle.*
417. TITLE: ¶The Unionists cheer the heroic deed.
418. MLS: *as in 409. Capt. Phil Stoneman and his men cheer and wave their hats wildly.*

419. MCU: *as in 416. Ben brings the water bottle to the man's lips and props his head.*

420. MLS: *as in 418. The Union soldiers continue to cheer.*

421. MCU: *as in 419. The wounded soldier drinks, and Ben smiles challengingly in the direction of the Unionists, even as he ducks a bullet.*

422. MLS, CV: *as in 415. The Confederate remnant crouching behind the Union trench.*

423. MCU: *as in 421. Ben lays the man back down, looks up to choose his moment, and dashes out to the right.*

424. MLS, CV: *as in 422. Ben runs back up to the top of the trench and turns, grinning, toward the Northerners.*

425. LS, AV: *as in 408. The Confederate remnant follows Ben in the final charge out to the right.*

426. LS, AV: *as in 406. At Phil Stoneman's signal, the Unionists fire.*

427. LS: *the Confederate remnant follows "the little Colonel" across the open field in the final charge. As Ben runs out to the right, one of his men is shot and falls.*

428. LS, AV: *as in 426. The Unionists fire.*

429. MLS: *several of the Southerners are hit, including the standard-bearer and Ben, who clutches at his right shoulder as he staggers toward the fallen flag.*

430. LS, AV: *as in 428. The Union trench continues to fire.*
431. MLS: *as in 429. Ben picks up the flag and lurches forward out to the right.*
432. LS, AV: *as in 430. Phil Stoneman sees his friend and orders his men to hold their fire.*
433. MLS: *as in 420. The guns fall silent as Ben enters carrying the Confederate flag. With both arms in the air, Phil Stoneman watches Ben approaching a few feet away.*
434. MS: *Ben enters right and rams the standard decisively into the cannon's mouth. He looks up and grins, before falling.*
435. MLS: *as in 433. Phil raises his arms, ordering his men again to hold their fire, and begins to climb over the sandbags toward Ben. He reaches forward and strokes his friend's head.*
436. MCU: *Phil jumps down next to Ben, cradles him in his arms, and lifts him up.*
437. MLS: *as in 435. With some difficulty, assisted by a soldier, Phil drags Ben's limp body over the barricade into the trench.*
438. TITLE: ¶In the red lane of death others take their places and the battle goes on into the night.

439. ELS: *as in 399. Ghost figures mingle with real on the smoky battlefield.*
440. TITLE: ¶War's peace.
441. *Fade in.* MS, AV: *as in 396. Dead soldiers lie in the trench. The soldier in the foreground is clutching a bugle. Fade out.*
442. ELS: *as in 439. The battlefield, still exploding in clouds of smoke, grows dark. Fade out.*
443. *Fade in.* MCU: *a chaotic heap of dead bodies, one of them half-dressed, others upside-down. Fade out.*
444. ELS: as in 442. On the smoky battlefield, ghostly figures and real advance and engage as the scene grows very dark, lighted only by gunfire and exploding shells.
445. TITLE: ¶The North victorious.
446. LS, AV: *as in 444. A Union flag waves in the foreground on the left over the quiet battlefield. A few distant figures run left.*
447. LS, CV: *as in 446. The empty battlefield, as the Union flag waves in the foreground. Iris out.*
448. TITLE: ¶News of the death of their second son and of the eldest being near death in a Washington hospital.
449. MS: *in the hall of Camerons' house, Margaret and Mrs. Cameron immediately get up from the couch on the right and Flora comes forward as a soldier with a letter enters right. The soldier hands the letter to Dr. Cameron, who has entered left, and points to a name on it. The soldier speaks to Dr. Cameron, salutes, and limps out to the right. Mrs. Cameron*

takes the letter from her stunned husband's hand, reads it, and slowly turns toward Flora, who takes it from her. As Flora reads it, Dr. and Mrs. Cameron turn to the rear and exit left.

450. TITLE: ¶War, the breeder of hate.

451. MS: *as in 449. Flora turns in the direction of the departed messenger, her eyes flashing, then she throws down the letter and clenches her fists. She turns to Margaret and grabs at her shoulders in anger and frustration, then she holds out her arms in helpless despair. She turns, her arms still held out, and stares sightlessly in front of her. Margaret reaches out to touch her sister.*

452. TITLE: ¶The woman's part.

453. MCU: *Flora is seated on the couch and Margaret is kneeling beside her. They embrace, as Flora stares widely ahead and shakes her head slowly.*

454. TITLE: ¶"The little Colonel" in the military hospital set up in the Patents Office where Elsie Stoneman is a nurse.

455. MLS: *a doctor enters right and stops briefly to look down at Ben Cameron who is on a bed in the foreground on the left. As the doctor makes his way back into the room full of wounded men, he bows to Elsie, who is coming forward, playing a banjo. She sits on a stool next to Ben's bed and begins to sing.*

456. CU, CV: *Elsie singing.*

457. CU, CV: *Ben, whose head is bandaged, opens his eyes in wonder at the sound.*

458. CU, CV: *as in 456. Elsie singing.*

459. CU, CV: *as in 457. Ben moves his head to look up.*

460. CU, CV: *as in 458. Elsie still singing, looks kindly down at Ben.*

461. CU, CV: *as in 459. Ben is gazing up at Elsie. Iris/fade out.*

462. MLS: *as in 455. Elsie finishes her song, puts down the banjo, and takes out a letter, which she starts to read to Ben.*

463. ECU: *The letter, which reads:*

and remember above all my request that you use your influence in any way possible for the welfare of my old boarding school friend Col. Ben Cameron, who has been committed to your hospital.

Lovingly your brother

Phil

464. MLS: *as in 462. Still holding the letter, Elsie looks at Phil. He speaks.*

465. TITLE: ¶"Though we had never met, I have carried you about with me for a long, long time."

466. MLS: *as in 464. As Ben speaks, Elsie motions him to be quiet, and she takes up the banjo again. He reaches under his pillow and hands her the tiny portrait, which she takes and opens.*

467. ECU, CV: *Elsie's portrait.*

468. MLS: *as in 466. Elsie, surprised, asks Ben how the portrait came into his possession, and he explains. She looks pensively ahead.*
469. TITLE: ¶Mother Cameron comes from Piedmont to visit her stricken eldest boy.
470. MS: *a soldier enters right and stops to glance at a young nurse who has just passed through the door and out to the right. Mrs. Cameron comes forward, but her way is barred by a sentry standing at the door on the right.*
471. MLS: *as in 468. Elsie has stood up and is holding Ben's hand. With his eyes closed, he murmurs something to her.*
472. MS: *as in 470. Mrs. Cameron confronts the sentry.*
473. TITLE: ¶"I am going into that room to my boy. You may shoot if you want to."
474. MS: *as in 472. Her chest heaving with emotion, Mrs. Cameron pleads with the sentry as he looks over to the right. The moment he turns to signal his covert assent, she hurries past him and out to the right.*
475. MLS: *as in 471. Elsie and Ben are in the foreground as Mrs. Cameron enters left. When Mrs. Cameron peers around a partition in the room, she sees a sobbing, grief-stricken woman approaching, and she draws back in alarm. The camera pans left and tilts down as the woman is led away and*

*Mrs. Cameron turns and sees Elsie. She comes forward and asks if Elsie
has seen her son, Ben Cameron, and as Elsie is about to tell her, Mrs.
Cameron recognizes Ben propped up against the pillows. She falls to her
knees and brings her hand to his bandaged head as Elsie looks on. Ben
squirms with discomfort, then opens his eyes, to behold his mother.*

476. TITLE: ¶The army surgeon tells of a secret influence that has condemned Col. Cameron to be hanged as a guerilla.

477. MS: *as in 475. The doctor, standing to the right of the bed, makes a motion with his hand at his neck. Mrs. Cameron rises and goes to the doctor,
but he indicates there is nothing he can do, and walks off. Elsie and Mrs.
Cameron look stunned. As Mrs. Cameron returns to the bedside and
hangs her head, Elsie indicates that she has an idea.*

478. TITLE: ¶"We will ask mercy from the Great Heart."

479. MS: *as in 477. Elsie dashes off right, and a moment later returns wearing her cloak. As she and Mrs. Cameron exit left, Elsie directs the young
nurse to watch Ben.*

480. TITLE: ¶The mother's appeal.

481. MLS: *three uniformed dignitaries bow before Lincoln, and as they move
to the rear, he turns and sits at his desk. Several visitors, Elsie and Mrs.
Cameron among them, enter on the right. Two men approach the Presi-*

dent; the first shakes his hand and moves to the rear, and the second man begins a lively exchange with Lincoln.

482. MCU, CV: *Elsie and Mrs. Cameron, looking apprehensive, glance over to the left.*

483. MS, SAV: *as in 481. Lincoln gestures angrily at the man to leave, and a White House official comes forward and leads the man away.*

484. MCU, CV: *as in 482. Elsie turns to Mrs. Cameron to indicate that they are next.*

485. MLS: *as in 483. Elsie and Mrs. Cameron approach the President and Elsie shakes his hand as she introduces Mrs. Cameron. Lincoln rises and shakes Mrs. Cameron's hand. As Mrs. Cameron speaks, Lincoln indicates a refusal.*

486. MCU, CV: *Elsie looks on intently.*

487. MS: *as in 485. Again, Lincoln shakes his head and makes a gesture of refusal. Mrs. Cameron looks dejected, and she turns to Elsie.*

488. MCU, CV: *as in 486. Elsie encourages Mrs. Cameron to appeal again.*

489. MS: *as in 487. Mrs. Cameron turns toward the President.*

490. *Iris in.* MCU: *as in 479. Ben in the hospital bed. Iris/fade out.*

491. MS: *as in 489. Mrs. Cameron concludes her appeal and, with hanging head, turns to leave. As she takes a step toward the right, Lincoln puts out his hand and places it on her shoulder.*

492. M C U , C V : *as in 488. Elsie looks encouraged.*

493. M S , S A V : *as in 491. Lincoln brings his arm down and nods, and then turns and sits at his desk. Mrs. Cameron falls to her knees at Lincoln's side as he puts on his glasses and begins to write.*

494. M C U , C V : *as in 492. Elsie breaks into a smile and suppresses a little jump of excitement as she brings her clasped hands to her mouth.*

495. M L S : *as in 493. Lincoln folds the pardon and gives it to Mrs. Cameron. As he stands, he shakes her hand, and she turns and moves toward Elsie. As she embraces Elsie, Lincoln takes off his glasses and sits again at his desk. Mrs. Cameron moves forward on an impulse to embrace the President, but stops herself at the last moment. As she and Elsie turn and leave to the rear, an aide enters through the door on the right, announces another visitor, and returns to open the door. Fade out.*

496. M S : *the young nurse is leaning over Ben as he opens his eyes, expecting to see Elsie. He falls back slightly into his pillows in disappointment. The nurse rises as Elsie and Mrs. Cameron come rushing in from the right, and departs to the rear. The women both seat themselves close to Ben as Mrs. Cameron holds up the pardon.*

497. T I T L E : ¶"Mr. Lincoln has given back your life to me."

498. M S : *as in 496. Ben brings his hand up to the pardon and touches it as he looks into Elsie's eyes.*

499. T I T L E : ¶Her son convalescent, Mrs. Cameron starts back for Piedmont to attend the failing father.

500. M S : *as in 498. Ben, now sitting up and smiling, kisses his mother good-bye, then turns to watch Elsie lead Mrs. Cameron out to the left.*

501. M S : *as Elsie and Mrs. Cameron embrace, the sentry looks on. Mrs. Cameron exits to the rear left, and Elsie follows her for a few steps. The sentry continues to gaze at her as she turns, comes forward, and pauses in front of him, lost in thought. She becomes aware that he is looking at her and involuntarily takes a step back, then exits right. The sentry sighs, turns to look in her direction, and sighs again.*

502. M S : *as in 500. Elsie sits beside Ben and begins to speak. Then, fidgeting self-consciously, she turns, gets up to leave, and shakes a finger at him with mock sternness. He smiles.*

503. T I T L E : ¶Back at home with the good news.

504. M S : *Dr. Cameron, wrapped in a blanket, is dozing in a chair in the Cameron parlor when Mrs. Cameron hurries in excitedly through the door on the right. She embraces Margaret and comes forward to kiss her husband as Mammy comes through the door and closes it behind her. Flora comes in from the left rear and goes to her mother to hear the news. As Mrs. Cameron takes off her hat and tells Flora, Margaret talks to her father, and Mammy gesticulates with excitement in the rear. Flora hugs her mother and then turns and hugs Margaret.*

505. TITLE: ¶Appomattox Courthouse, on the afternoon of April 9, 1865, the surrender of Gen. Robt. E. Lee, C.S.A., to Gen. U. S. Grant, U.S.A.

> AN HISTORICAL FACSIMILE of the Wilmer McLean home as on that occasion, and the principals and their staffs, after Col. Horace Porter in "Campaigning with Grant."

506. *Fade in.* MLS: *Lee, looking woodenly ahead, is seated at a table on the left. Grant, smoking a cigar, is seated at a small table on the right. Behind the two generals stand several aides. Two aides come forward, each with a document. Grant signs at once and hands the document back to the aide. Lee, continuing to stare, is prompted by the aide, then he leans forward, looks at the paper for a moment, and signs. Fade out.*

507. *Fade in.* TITLE:

> ¶The end of state sovereignty.
> ¶The soul of Daniel Webster calling to America: "Liberty and union, one and inseparable, now and forever." *Fade out.*

508. MLS: *as in 506. The aides exchange documents and Grant rises. With the cigar in his mouth and a hand in his pocket, Grant comes to the center. Lee rises stiffly, approaches Grant, and the two generals shake hands. Fade out.*

509. TITLE: ¶The same day, Col. Cameron is discharged and leaves for home.

510. MS: *Ben and Elsie enter from the right and pause in front of the sentry at the door of the hospital. As they shake hands, a soldier enters briskly from the left and relieves the guard on duty. Ben tries to kiss Elsie, but she holds up her hand to restrain him. He lifts her hand and brings it to his lips, then places his hand over his heart, smiles, and turns to exit left. Elsie runs after him a short distance, stops, turns, and walks back pensively to a spot near the sentry, who is staring at her. She exits right and the sentry shakes his head and sighs.*

511. TITLE: ¶The feast for the returning brother.
     ¶Parched corn and sweet potato coffee.

512. *Fade in.* MS: *Flora, standing in the kitchen, sifts through a plate of parched corn with her hand.*

513. ECU: *Flora's fingers checking the kernels individually on the plate.*

514. MS: *as in 512. As Flora puts the plate on the table and picks up a sweet potato, Mammy comes up to her from the rear and places a small piece of cloth decoratively on her shoulder. Flora hops up and down with delight.*

515. TITLE: ¶"Southern ermine," from raw cotton, for the grand occasion.

516. MCU: *Flora arranges little strips of cotton wool on her dress and admires herself in the mirror on the right. Fade out.*

517. MCU: *Flora reaches down into the fireplace, and with a sooty finger dabs little black smudges onto the cotton wool on her dress. Fade out.*
518. MCU: *as in 516. Flora rises from the fireplace on the left and runs forward to the mirror on the right, in which she admires herself. She suddenly grows pensive, and looks down sadly as she brings a hand to her mouth.*
519. TITLE: ¶The homecoming.
520. LS: *Ben enters the empty street from the left, looks back down the street and at the houses lining it, and walks slowly toward the picket fence in front of Cameron Hall.*
521. MCU: *as in 518. Margaret and Mrs. Cameron enter the parlor from the rear right and come up to Flora, who is still admiring her handiwork. Margaret exclaims with enthusiasm, and Flora shows her mother her skirt and then skips over to the door and looks out to check for Ben. She runs back and indicates excitedly that Ben is wearing a moustache, and the sisters run arm in arm out through the door on the right, followed by their mother.*
522. MLS: *the women hurry forward into the hall from the left rear, and they pause, as Dr. Cameron comes up slowly behind them.*
523. MS: *as in 520. Ben stares directly at the camera for a long moment, then turns to open the gate. He leans on the gate for support as he enters the yard and makes his way toward the front door of the house.*

524. MS: *as in 522. Margaret and Mrs. Cameron push Flora forward.*

525. MS: *as in 523. Ben pauses in the yard, looking at the front door. He brings his hand to his chin.*

526. MS: *as in 524. Flora adjusts her "ermine," walks forward smiling, and exits right.*

527. MCU: *Ben enters right as Flora bursts through the front door. She remarks on his clothing, and he on hers, as he plucks a piece of cotton wool off her shoulder and rubs it between his fingers. He smiles when she explains what it is, and then she points to his worn and tattered hat. He looks down and she looks away sadly. Then, tearfully, she throws her arms around his neck and they embrace. They move toward the door, smile at each other, and embrace again.*

528. MCU: *as they reach the threshold, Mrs. Cameron's arm reaches out in an embrace, and draws her son into the house. Fade out.*

529. TITLE: ¶The Radical leader's protest against Lincoln's policy of clemency for the South.

530. MLS: *as Stoneman is ushered into Lincoln's office through the door on the right, other visitors are led out to the rear. Stoneman hands his hat to the aide as Lincoln rises and turns to greet Stoneman, who comes forward to shake the President's hand. The aide brings forward a chair, and the two gentlemen sit. Stoneman makes an impassioned statement, and Lincoln responds by calmly shaking his head. Stoneman thumps his cane on the floor and rises.*

531. TITLE: ¶"Their leaders must be hanged and their states treated as conquered provinces."

532. MLS: *as in 530. Stoneman continues to protest violently and thrash the air with his clenched fist, and Lincoln rises and responds mildly.*

533. TITLE: ¶"I shall deal with them as though they had never been away."

534. MLS: *as in 532. Stoneman turns, picks up his hat, and exits scowling and muttering. Lincoln continues to stand, looking down reflectively. Fade out.*

535. TITLE: ¶The South under Lincoln's fostering hand goes to work to rebuild itself.

536. MLS: *Ben emerges from the house wearing a hat and rolling up his sleeves. He is followed into the garden by the servant Jake, Flora, Margaret, and Mrs. Cameron. As Ben and Jake exit right, Flora runs back to her mother and Margaret, says something, then skips out to the right. Mrs. Cameron and Margaret put up a* BOARDING *sign on one of the porch columns.*

537. TITLE: ¶"And then, when the terrible days were over and a healing time of peace was at hand" . . . came the fated night of April 14, 1865.

538. *Fade in.* MLS: *Stoneman sits grimly in the foreground on the left, smoking a cigar, as Elsie comes twirling in left rear, showing her dress to her admiring aunt and servant.*

539. M L S :   *a servant shows Phil through the hall to the door on the left.*
540. M L S :   *as in 538. Elsie shows Phil her dress as he comes through the door on the right. He pauses to admire it, then walks over to his father, who shakes his head when asked if he will come with them.*
541. T I T L E :   ¶To the theatre.
542. M L S :   *as in 539. Elsie and Phil cross the hall and exit right, followed by the servant.*
543. M L S :   *as in 540. Stoneman walks to the door on the right, says good night to his sister, and exits.*
544. T I T L E :   ¶A gala performance to celebrate the surrender of Lee, attended by the President and staff.
        ¶The young Stonemans present.
                    AN HISTORICAL FACSIMILE of Ford's theatre as on that night, exact in size and detail, with the recorded incidents, after Nicolay and Hay in "Lincoln, a History."
545. *Iris in.* L S :   *Phil takes off Elsie's cloak and then his own, and they take their seats. The iris opens fully to reveal the crowded theater, the stage visible on the left.*
546. M C U :   *Phil hands Elsie opera glasses, which she tries.*
547. T I T L E :   ¶The play: "Our American Cousin," starring Laura Keene.
548. L S :   *as in 545. As latecomers take their seats, the painted curtain rolls up and the play begins to the audience's applause. On the stage two maids are dusting furniture, a manservant is standing, and another is seated.*
549. L S :   *the leading lady, Laura Keene, makes an extravagant entrance.*
550. L S :   *as in 548. Laura Keene acknowledges the audience's applause with a curtsey and turns to resume her performance in the play.*
551. M C U :   *as in 546. Elsie, fanning herself, breaks into applause. Her brother, with his arms folded, smiles.*
552. L S :   *as in 549. Laura Keene comes downstage with her arms out-stretched.*
553. L S :   *as in 550. As the audience applauds, Laura Keene walks to the apron and receives bouquets from the conductor.*
554. T I T L E :   ¶Time, 8:30.
        ¶The arrival of the President, Mrs. Lincoln, and party.
555. M S :   *preceded by a bodyguard, an officer, and a young woman, Mrs. Lincoln and the President climb the steps to the Presidential box.*
556. M L S :   *in the box, the bodyguard arranges the chairs and the officer looks about.*
557. M S :   *as in 555. Lincoln hands his hat and coat to a man before entering the box.*

558. MLS: *as in 556. In the box, the officer and the young woman are standing on the left as Lincoln comes forward and looks out into the theater.*

559. MCU: *as in 551. Elsie and Phil spot the President, and they rise with the audience in applause.*

560. LS: *as in 553. The audience stands and applauds.*

561. MLS: *as in 558. The President and Mrs. Lincoln nod their acknowledgment of the applause.*

562. LS: *as in 560. The audience continues to wave and applaud.*

563. MLS: *as in 561. The President and his party sit.*

564. TITLE: ¶Mr. Lincoln's personal bodyguard takes his post outside the Presidential box.

565. MS: *the bodyguard emerges from the box, closes the door behind him, and places a chair next to it. He checks that the door is properly closed and sits on the chair.*

566. LS: *as in 562. The ovation continues.*

567. MLS: *as in 563. Lincoln nods to the audience and draws his wife over by the hand.*

568. LS: *the audience is still applauding wildly and waving white handkerchiefs at the spotlit President and his wife.*

569. MLS: *on the stage the leading lady exits with a man to the rear as another couple enter from the rear.*

570. TITLE: ¶To get a view of the play, the bodyguard leaves his post.
571. MLS: *as in 565. The bodyguard glances back twice at the closed door of the Presidential box.*
572. MLS: *as in 569. On the stage the man shows off his clothes to the woman.*
573. MLS: *as in 571. The bodyguard rises, checks the door of the Presidential box, picks up his chair, opens the gallery door next to it, and enters.*
574. LS: *as in 566. The performance continues. The bodyguard can be seen bringing his chair to the railing in the gallery at upper right. The camera begins to iris out.*
575. MLS: *the bodyguard arranges his chair and sits down, leaning forward for the best view of the stage.*
576. TITLE: ¶Time, 10:13.
             ¶Act III, Scene 2.
577. LS: *as in 574. An iris at the upper right corner of the frame isolates the gallery. The bodyguard watches the play.*
578. MCU: *as in 559. Elsie and Phil are enjoying the play, when suddenly Elsie notices something off to the left. She leans over to her brother and points with her fan.*
579. TITLE: ¶John Wilkes Booth.
580. MCU, CV: *Booth motionless, his eyes looking left, and his right hand tucked inside his coat.*
581. MCU: *as in 578. Phil hands Elsie the opera glasses. Amused, but curious, she puts down her fan and looks through the opera glasses out left.*
582. MCU, CV: *as in 580. Booth, not moving, looking right.*
583. LS: *as in 568. The bodyguard sits in the gallery, and behind him, in the shadows, stands Booth.*
584. MCU, CV: *as in 582. Booth looking intently out right.*
585. MLS: *as in 572. On the stage a male character is gesturing with his hat as he speaks to a woman.*
586. MLS: *as in 567. Lincoln smiles, then suddenly he feels a chill and reaches back for his shawl.*
587. MCU, CV: *as in 584. Booth raises his head.*
588. MLS: *as in 586. Lincoln gathers the shawl about his shoulders.*
589. *Iris at upper right,* LS: *as in 577. Booth moves behind the bodyguard and to the gallery door at left. Iris opens left.*
590. MLS: *as in 575. Booth moves behind the bodyguard and exits left.*
591. MLS: *as in 573. The gallery door opens and Booth comes forward into the hallway. He closes and locks the gallery door behind him, then crouches to look through the keyhole of the door to the Presidential box. He rises and steps back, pulling a pistol from his vest.*
592. ECU, CV: *Booth cocks the pistol.*

593. MLS: *as in 591. Booth steps toward the box door on the right, with a little difficulty turns the knob, and enters.*
594. MLS: *as in 588. Booth moves behind the President and pulls the pistol from his vest.*
595. MLS: *as in 585. On the stage, the woman exits to the rear, with the man yelling after her.*
596. MLS: *as in 594. Booth fires at the President, who slumps in his chair. The officer leaps to his feet, as Booth stabs him and vaults from the box at the left.*
597. LS: *as in 589. Booth lands on the stage, bringing a piece of bunting down with him. He staggers to the center of the stage and raises the knife in his clenched fist at the audience.*
598. TITLE: ¶"Sic semper tyrannis!"
599. MLS: *as in 595. Holding the knife aloft in his left fist, Booth shouts to the audience, and then limps quickly to the rear of the stage.*
600. MLS: *as in 596. Mrs. Lincoln waves frantically toward the audience for help as the young woman in the Presidential party attends to the stabbed officer.*
601. MCU: *as in 581. Phil and Elsie look stunned. They rise from their seats.*

602. LS: *as in 597. The performers crowd the stage as a man is assisted into the Presidential box from the stage. In the foreground, Elsie faints and is caught by her brother.*

603. MLS: *as in 600. The man climbs into the box and rushes over to the President on the right.*

604. LS: *as in 583. On the stage and in the audience there is general confusion.*

605. LS: *as in 602. As the audience continues to clamor in distress, in the foreground Phil helps his sister out to the right. Fade out.*

606. MLS: *as in 603. Lincoln is carried out of the box and the others follow. Fade out.*

607. TITLE: ¶Stoneman told of the assassination.

608. MLS: *Stoneman is seated in his library, in the middle of a vigorous exchange with a servant and Lydia, when a man bursts in through the door on the right and hurries forward to tell him the news. As Stoneman rises, three more men enter. After the men leave to the right, Stoneman directs his servant to turn away any other visitors. Stoneman ponders the meaning of the news as the servant at the door prevents two more men from entering.*

609. MLS: *in the parlor, Elsie, still wearing her cape, excitedly describes the evening's events to her aunt, as Phil closes the door on the right.*

610. MLS: *as in 608. As Stoneman stands with his eyes closed, lost in thought, Lydia rubs her hands together.*
611. TITLE: ¶"You are now the greatest power in America."
612. MLS: *as in 610. Lydia takes hold of Stoneman's arm and closes her eyes as she presses her cheek against his shoulder and smiles dreamily. Fade out.*
613. TITLE: ¶The news is received in the South.
614. MS: *Dr. Cameron is seated on the porch, reading a newspaper, as Margaret kneels at his side and Mrs. Cameron reads over his shoulder. Ben and Flora, arm in arm, come dashing in happily from the left rear, followed by Mammy. As Dr. Cameron shows the newspaper to Ben, who takes it gravely, Mrs. Cameron puts her hand over her heart and looks up in a silent prayer.*
615. ECU: *the headline on the front page of* The New South, *Saturday, April 22, 1865:* Assassination of President Lincoln and attempt to take the life of Secretary Seward.
616. MS: *as in 614. Ben continues to read, as Dr. Cameron says:*
617. TITLE: ¶"Our best friend is gone. What is to become of us now!"
618. MS: *as in 616. Ben looks up grimly as his father crosses his legs, puts a hand over his eyes, and bows his head. Fade out.*

619. TITLE: ¶End of the first part.
620. *Fade in.* TITLE: <u>The Birth of a Nation</u>
    ¶<u>Second part—Reconstruction.</u>
    ¶The agony which the South endured that a nation might be born.
    ¶The blight of war does not end when hostilities cease.
    Fade out.
621. TITLE: ¶This is an historical presentation of the Civil War and Reconstruction Period, and is not meant to reflect on any race or people of today.
622. TITLE: ¶Excerpts from Woodrow Wilson's "History of the American People":
    ¶" . . . Adventurers swarmed out of the North, as much enemies of the one race as of the other, to cozen, beguile, and use the negroes. . . . In the villages the negroes were the office holders, men who knew none of the uses of authority, except its insolences."
623. TITLE: ¶" . . . The policy of the congressional leaders wrought . . . a veritable overthrow of civilization in the South . . . in their determination to 'put <u>the white South under the heel of the black South.</u>'"
    WOODROW WILSON
624. TITLE: ¶"The white men were roused by a mere instinct of self-preservation . . . until at last there had sprung into existence a great Ku Klux Klan, a veritable empire of the South, to protect the Southern country."
    WOODROW WILSON
625. TITLE: ¶The uncrowned king.
    ¶The Executive Mansion of the Nation has shifted from the White House to this strange house on the Capitol Hill.
626. *Iris in left.* MLS: *Stoneman, seated in his library filled with visitors, is surrounded by four men with whom he is engaged in a discussion. His cane drops to the floor, and all four men lunge to pick it up. As he takes a drink, Lydia ushers in another visitor and walks forward, yawning, to the table on the right, where she picks up her fan. A man standing next to Stoneman rushes forward to her, and they walk together to the rear.*
627. TITLE: ¶Stoneman's protege, Silas Lynch, mulatto leader of the blacks.
628. MS: *in the parlor, Lydia rises from a chair in the foreground on the right as Lynch enters through the door on the right and hands his hat to a servant. He waits for the servant to exit and close the door behind him, then, as Lydia fidgets with her fan nervously, he comes forward, bows, and kisses her proffered hand. He indicates that he would like to speak with Stoneman.*
629. MLS: *as in 626. Stoneman is still talking to the visitor.*

630. M S : *as in 628. Lydia indicates that Lynch should wait, and she exits rear left, as Lynch bows.*
631. M L S : *as in 629. A servant approaches the door on the right.*
632. M S : *as in 630. Lydia gestures to Lynch with her fan, and Lynch bows again.*
633. M L S : *as in 631. Lydia pokes the man Stoneman is speaking to in the back with her fan, and he steps aside. She goes up to Stoneman and indicates that Lynch is waiting to see him. Fade out.*
634. M S : *as in 632. Lynch smiles to himself.*
635. M L S : *as in 633. Lydia leaves Stoneman and exits to the right.*
636. M S : *as in 634. Lydia enters from the left and indicates to Lynch that he may go in to see Stoneman. Before Lynch reaches the door, Lydia calls to him, and he touches her hand, then exits left.*
637. M L S : *as in 635. Lynch enters the library and comes forward to Stoneman, who immediately rises and extends his hand. Lynch bows and is about to kiss Stoneman's hand, when he checks himself as Stoneman speaks. Stoneman raises his cane in his left hand in a dramatic gesture.*
638. M C U , C V : *Stoneman, his eyes flashing, turns to the man on the left and points to him as he speaks.*
639. M C U , C V : *Lynch, clutching his hat with both hands, bows vigorously.*
640. M C U , C V : *as in 638. Stoneman looks at Lynch and speaks.*
641. T I T L E : ¶"Don't scrape to me. You are the equal of any man here."
642. M C U , C V : *as in 640. Stoneman, speaking to Lynch, raises his right hand in a grand manner.*
643. M C U , C V : *as in 639. Lynch looks up and smiles.*
644. T I T L E : ¶The great Radical delivers his edict that the blacks shall be raised to full equality with the whites.
645. M L S : *as in 637. Stoneman places his right hand firmly on Lynch's shoulder as all the visitors in the room look on.*
646. M S : *as in 636. Lydia, who has been listening at the door, runs into the center of the outer room and flings her hands in the air in triumph. She throws her fan to the floor and pounds her fists on the books lying on the table, then brings her right hand to her chest, smiling.*
647. M L S : *as in 645. With his hand on Lynch's shoulder, Stoneman continues his speech.*
648. T I T L E : ¶Senator Sumner calls.
 ¶Forced to recognize the mulatto's position.
649. M S : *as in 646. Sumner comes forward and indicates that Lydia, who is fanning herself, should announce his arrival.*
650. M L S : *as in 647. As Stoneman walks to the rear of his library, a man on the left extends his hand to Lynch.*
651. M S : *as in 649. Lydia stalls Sumner with chatter and holds out her hand in an ambiguous manner. He is about to take her hand, when she withdraws it. Fade out.*

652. MLS: *as in 650. Lynch is in conversation with the man on the left. Stoneman, looking through the door to the outer room, laughs.*
653. MS: *as in 651. Sumner appears embarrassed and annoyed as Lydia bows in a servile manner.*
654. MLS: *as in 652. Stoneman closes the door and begins to come forward, shaking his head in amusement.*
655. MS: *as in 653. Sumner scowls, as Lydia, behind him, bows and sticks out her lower jaw in anger before exiting left.*
656. TITLE: ¶The Senator urges a less dangerous policy in the extension of power to the freed race.
657. MLS: *as in 654. As Sumner enters through the door on the right and comes forward, the men in the room bow and Stoneman turns toward him and bows slightly.*
658. MCU: *Lydia, by the door to the library, leans forward on a small table and looks up in an ecstasy of private glee.*
659. MLS: *as in 657. Standing between the two men, Stoneman shakes a finger first at Lynch, then at Sumner.*
660. MCU: *as in 658. Lydia clasps her hands to her chest and presses against the table, talking to herself.*

661. MLS: *as in 659. The two men take a step forward as Stoneman listens to Sumner.*

662. MCU: *as in 660. Lydia turns away from the door, her face beginning to cloud at what she hears, and hovers over the small tabletop.*

663. MLS: *as in 661. Stoneman gestures emphatically at Lynch as he speaks to Sumner, then makes a point by pounding his cane on the floor. Lynch is grinning.*

664. TITLE: ¶"I shall make this man, Silas Lynch, as a symbol of his race, the peer of any white man living."

665. MLS: *as in 663. Stoneman, facing Sumner, raises his hand in a sweeping gesture toward Lynch.*

666. MCU: *as in 662. Lydia, listening at the door, gasps with excitement.*

667. MLS: *as in 665. Stoneman pats Sumner on the back and Sumner nods. Stoneman then turns to the smiling Lynch and puts his hands on Lynch's shoulders. Fade out.*

668. TITLE: ¶Sowing the wind.

¶Stoneman, ill at his daughter's apartments, sends Lynch South to aid the carpetbaggers in organizing and wielding the power of the negro vote.

669. *Fade in.* MLS: *Stoneman, wrapped in a blanket and seated in the foreground on the left, instructs Lynch, who nods and walks to the door on the right. Stoneman slumps in his chair and closes his eyes as Elsie enters left, carrying a vase of flowers. Lynch turns and bows to Elsie as she greets him.*

670. MCU, CV: *Lynch stares at Elsie.*

671. MCU: *as Elsie arranges the flowers, she becomes aware that Lynch is gazing at her.*

672. MCU, CV: *as in 670. Lynch continues to stare.*

673. MCU: *as in 671. Elsie makes a remark to Lynch.*

674. MCU, CV: *as in 672. Lynch smiles and bows slightly as he replies.*

675. MCU: *as in 673. Elsie returns to arranging the flowers.*

676. MCU: *as in 669. Lynch bows and takes his leave, as Elsie finishes arranging the flowers and puts them on the table in the rear. Stoneman, in obvious pain, calls to his daughter, and she come running forward and puts her arms around him. Fade out.*

677. TITLE: ¶Lynch makes Piedmont his headquarters.

678. MLS: *Lynch steps out of a carriage and enters a house.*

679. MLS: *Lynch enters a bare room from the rear, followed by a black captain carrying a carpetbag and another man rubbing his hands together.*

680. TITLE: ¶Starting the ferment.
¶The black party celebration.
¶Inducing the negroes to quit work.

681. MLS: *on a wide path, Lynch attempts to take a pitchfork from a worker. The worker resists and walks off to the left.*

682. MLS: *two blacks are working in a cornfield.*

683. MLS: *as in 681. Lynch, seeing the workers, instructs two of the men with him to go into the field. The third man follows Lynch toward the rear, where people can be seen dancing.*

684. MLS: *blacks are dancing in bare feet and others are drinking or clapping their hands to banjo music. Two men are eating watermelon.*

685. MLS: *as in 682. Lynch's men approach the workers in the field and talk to them, pointing left toward the celebrants.*

686. MLS: *as in 684. The dancing continues.*

687. MLS: *as in 685. The workers in the field stop what they are doing and follow the two men out left.*

688. MLS: *as in 683. As the two workers from the field are led in from the right, Lynch and his companion come forward from the party and welcome them to join in the celebration. As they all move to the rear, a man runs toward them with watermelon. The camera tilts up slightly. A portion of a billboard on which, in the largest letters, are painted the words, "Forty Acres and a Mule," is visible in the upper left corner of the frame.*

689. TITLE: ¶The Freedman's Bureau.
    ¶The negroes getting free supplies.
    ¶The charity of a generous North misused to delude the ignorant.
690. MLS: *blacks clamor outside the Freedman's Bureau to receive supplies.*
    A man picks up his bundle and places the hat he has received on top of
    his own. He tips it at the white supervisor and walks out right.
691. *Fade in.* MS: *Lynch enters left on the street in front of Cameron Hall. He*
    glances back and continues toward the rear as a group of soldiers mar-
    ches forward and Ben and Flora approach their gate on the right. As Ben
    and Flora are about to pass through the gate, the squad stops in front of
    them and they are prevented from passing into the street. The squad
    leader sharply reprimands Ben and the frightened Flora, and then leads
    his soldiers out right. Lynch walks forward to the affronted couple and
    speaks to them.
692. TITLE: ¶"This sidewalk belongs to us as much as it does to you,
    'Colonel' Cameron."
693. MS: *as in 691. Lynch tips his hat and walks out right as Ben looks after*
    him, scowling with anger. The Camerons then turn and walk down the
    street to the rear. Fade out.

694. TITLE: ¶Stoneman, advised by his physician to seek a milder climate and desiring to see his policies carried out at first hand, leaves for South Carolina.

695. MS: *Elsie adjusts her father's shawl and then she and Phil walk with him to the door on the right. As her aunt and maid look on, Elsie kisses her father and then turns to them as Phil and Stoneman pass through the door.*

696. MLS: *Stoneman, Phil, and Elsie proceed through the hall to the right as a servant follows carrying Stoneman's luggage, which includes a carpetbag. Fade out.*

697. TITLE: ¶Their arrival in Piedmont.
    ¶Influenced by his children he has selected the home town of the Camerons for his sojourn.

698. MLS: *the carriage stops on the left in front of Cameron Hall as Ben comes through the gate on the right. Phil steps from the carriage and Ben helps Elsie out. As Stoneman is assisted from the carriage by a servant entering left, Phil shakes Ben's hand. Mammy waits by the porch.*

699. MLS: *Flora comes hurtling through the front door and onto the porch. She realizes she has a dustcloth in her hand, and dashes back inside.*

700. MS: *Mammy enters the neighboring house and is followed by Stoneman, the servant assisting him, and Phil. Ben and Elsie enter from the right. Ben indicates that he will wait outside, and Elsie and a servant go in.*

701. MLS: *Stoneman, the servant, Phil, and Elsie go through the hall to a door Mammy indicates on the right. Another servant enters right carrying bags.*

702. MLS: *Stoneman enters the parlor at left, followed by Phil, the servant, and Elsie. He pauses in the center of the room and looks around.*

703. MLS: *as in 701. The servant carrying the bags attempts to hand them to Mammy, who refuses to take them, pointing to a room in the rear.*

704. TITLE: ¶"Yo' northern lown down black trash, don't try no airs on me."

705. MLS: *as in 703. Mammy clenches her fist and points to the door behind the staircase. She then kicks the servant in the pants and pushes him toward the door in the rear.*

706. MLS: *as in 699. Flora comes through the front door of Cameron Hall onto the porch and looks left as Mrs. Cameron goes in.*

707. MCU: *Ben and Elsie are talking on the steps of the porch of the neighboring house. Ben points to the right.*

708. MLS: *as in 706. Flora sees Ben and Elsie and runs toward them, exiting left.*

709. MCU: *as in 707. Ben and Elsie are talking when Flora comes dashing in from the right and smothers Elsie in an avalanche of kisses. Elsie looks startled and she appeals to Ben, asking him who the girl is. Ben explains*

laughingly that Flora is his sister, and they embrace once more, with
scarcely less enthusiasm, as Ben tugs at Elsie's shawl.

710. MLS: *as in 705. Stoneman comes forward through the hall, scowling,*
followed by a servant. As Stoneman exits right, Mammy comes through
the door on the right. She greets the servant and then they circle each
other as he wiggles his brow at her.

711. TITLE: ¶"Dem free-niggers f'um de N'of am sho' crazy."

712. MLS: *as in 710. The servant exits through the door on the right and*
Mammy turns and tiptoes to the door to look after him.

713. MCU: *as in 709. Flora releases herself from her embrace with Elsie and*
dashes out to the right. Elsie notices that Ben is holding onto the hem of
her shawl.

714. MLS: *as in 708. Flora enters left, and, on the porch, swings around to*
look at Ben and Elsie again before turning and scampering in.

715. TITLE: ¶Lynch's second meeting with "the little Colonel."
¶The black's condescension.

716. MCU: *as in 713. Elsie and Ben are still talking on the steps of the porch*
when Stoneman appears behind them. Lynch enters left and he and
Stoneman shake hands enthusiastically. Lynch then takes off his hat and
extends his hand toward Elsie, as Stoneman pats him on the back. Elsie

*shakes his hand quickly and somewhat reluctantly when she notices that
Ben is grimly avoiding Lynch's gaze. Stoneman leans forward between
Lynch and his daughter and introduces the two men. When Lynch extends
his hand, Ben pointedly folds his arms and glares at Lynch and then turns
and looks out right. Stoneman is about to intercede angrily, when Elsie
prevents him. Lynch says something and bows with false humility and
then follows Stoneman into the house.*

717. MS: *as in 702. In a room to the rear, Phil can be seen instructing a maid
about the luggage. Stoneman marches in angrily from the right, followed
by Lynch. At the center of the room, Stoneman throws off his shawl and
turns to Lynch, who hands him a piece of paper. Stoneman takes the
paper and seats himself to read it.*

718. MCU: *as in 716. Smiling, Ben leads Elsie out right.*

719. MS: *as in 717. Stoneman says something to Lynch, who turns angrily
toward the front door on the left and exits.*

720. TITLE: ¶Lynch a traitor to his white patron and a greater traitor to his
own people, whom he plans to lead by an evil way to build himself a
throne of vaulting power.

721. MLS: *as in 712. Lynch backs out through the door from Stoneman's
room into the hall. He bows as he closes the door, then shakes his fist at it*

in a defiant gesture. He thumps his chest and smiles grimly as he comes forward and exits right.

722. TITLE: ¶The Southern Union League rally before the election.

723. LS: *in a crowded meeting hall, white men explain the rally signs to blacks. One sign reads:*

EQUALITY
Equal rights
Equal politics
Equal marriage

Another sign reads:

40 ACRES AND A MULE

for every colored citizen

724. MCU: *a black speaker is delivering an impassioned speech to the crowd, while a few feet from him a white man is making a point vigorously with his clenched fist to another white man.*

725. LS: *as in 723. The commotion continues.*

726. MS: *another gesticulating speaker is addressing an excited group in a different corner of the hall.*

727. MLS: *as Lynch, Stoneman, and Phil approach the door, Phil decides not to accompany them. He turns and exits right, as Lynch knocks.*

728. CU: *Lynch knocks. An eye appears at the peephole.*

729. ECU: *the eye at the peephole looks out.*

730. MLS: *as in 727. The door opens and a man appears. Lynch whispers to him and so does Stoneman. The man goes back in.*

731. LS: *as in 725. The general commotion in the meeting hall continues.*

732. MLS: *as in 730. The man has reappeared at the door, and he invites Lynch and Stoneman in.*

733. LS: *as in 731. The man escorts Stoneman and Lynch down the aisle of the meeting hall, which is now calmer. The man seated on the dais rises.*

734. TITLE: ¶Stoneman the guest of honor.

735. MS: *with his arm raised high, Lynch speaks to the crowd from the dais. He brings his hand down hard on the lectern in front of him. Stoneman is seated next to Lynch on the right.*

736. MS: *the enthusiastic crowd listens.*

737. MS: *as in 735. Lynch continues to speak, gesturing emphatically.*

738. LS: *as in 736. The crowd grows more demonstrative in its response.*

739. MS: *as in 737. Lynch continues his address.*

740. LS: *as in 733. The excited crowd rises as Lynch concludes his harangue.*

741. TITLE: ¶Enrolling the negro vote.
    ¶The franchise for all blacks.

742. MS: *outside the Freedman's Bureau, an elderly black man shakes his head at a white official.*

743. TITLE: ¶"Ef I doan' get 'nuf franchise to fill mah bucket, I doan' want it nohow."
744. MS: *as in 742. The old man, shaking his head, moves out right as the official tries to persuade him to register. Fade out.*
745. *Iris in.* MLS: *Lynch, standing under a tree in the woods, shakes a dog violently by the neck and then throws it toward two men looking on.*
746. TITLE: ¶The love strain is still heard above the land's miserere.
747. *Fade in.* MLS: *Ben and Elsie walk in from the right. They pause in a clearing between two trees.*
748. MLS: *as in 745. The two men pick up the dog and walk off to the rear as Lynch comes forward and, seeing Ben and Elsie, stands partly hidden behind a tree.*
749. MLS: *as in 747. Ben leaves Elsie and exits left. She takes a step toward the trees, stops, and runs back into the sunlit clearing.*
750. MS: *as in 748. Lynch steps behind the tree to avoid being seen.*
751. MLS: *as in 749. Elsie skips forward and then leaps behind the tree on the right as Ben enters from the right carrying a cage and a dove. He puts down the cage and Elsie steps toward him. He kisses the dove.*

752. C U : *Ben holds the dove as Elsie kisses it. Ben also kisses the bird and then attempts to steal a kiss from Elsie, who pulls back and shakes her finger playfully at him.*

753. M L S : *as in 751. Ben tries again to kiss Elsie, and she pulls back. He hands the dove to her and picks up the cage. They walk off to the right. Fade out.*

754. M L S , C V : *as in 750. Lynch comes out from behind the tree and walks off left.*

755. T I T L E : ¶The love token.

756. M L S : *Elsie enters her bedroom from the rear right holding the dove close to her heart. She comes forward, puts down the cage, and sits on the love seat on the left.*

757. C U : *Elsie caresses and kisses the dove. Fade out.*

758. T I T L E : ¶Bitter memories will not allow the poor bruised heart of the South to forget.

759. *Fade in.* M C U : *Margaret sits forlornly in a garden with a basket of flowers in her lap, rose petals falling through her fingers.*

760. M C U : *Phil, on the other side of the fence and surrounded by bushes, is looking at Margaret.*

761. M C U : *as in 759. Margaret looks down at the rose in her hand.*

762. M C U : *as in 760. Phil smiles and moves out to the right.*

763. MCU: *as in 761. Phil enters left and leans over the fence and speaks to Margaret, offering to hold the basket. She draws back, looks at him scornfully, and walks off proudly to the left.*
764. MCU: *Margaret enters right, pauses, and stares ahead.*
765. MCU: *as in 763. Phil holds out his hand.*
766. MCU: *as in 764. Margaret's eyes widen as she crushes the flower in her hand. Fade out.*
767. MCU, CV: *as in 334. Margaret's brother Wade lies dead in a comrade's arms.*
768. *Fade in.* MCU: *as in 766. Margaret stares ahead, her breast heaving.*
769. MCU: *as in 765. Phil straightens up and withdraws his hand.*
770. MCU: *as in 768. Margaret turns to leave left. Fade out.*
771. TITLE: ¶Still a North and a South.
      ¶Pride battles with love for the heart's conquest.
772. MCU: *Elsie and Ben are walking forward together beside a stream. Ben speaks, and they stop. They begin to embrace, when Elsie suddenly pulls back. She withdraws from the embrace and walks off to the left.*
773. *Fade in.* MS: *Elsie enters right, looking back at Ben. She stops, then breaks into a sob as she brings her hands up to her face and totters back toward a log and sits down. Ben rushes in from the right and sits next to her. He consoles her; they embrace and kiss. Fade out.*
774. TITLE: ¶"I'll watch you safely home."
775. *Fade in.* MLS: *Ben and Elsie enter left and come forward to the fence. As Elsie tries to leave, Ben pulls her back and steals a kiss. She then dashes off to the left.*
776. TITLE: ¶Love's rhapsodies and love's tears.
777. MLS: *Elsie runs into her room from the door in the rear and pauses. She hops about, waving her arms in a flutter of excitement, glances at herself in the mirror on the right, then dashes over to the dove in its cage on the left.*
778. MLS: *as in 775. Ben, still standing by the fence, smiles, turns, and walks off toward the woods in the rear.*
779. MLS: *as in 777. Elsie dashes about in her room, blows kisses to the dove, jumps on her bed, and kisses the bedpost.*
780. CU, CV: *with her cheek pressed against the bedpost, Elsie gazes ecstatically upward.*
781. MS, CV: *Ben enters right, pauses on the porch of his house and sighs, looking out to the left, and goes in.*
782. CU, CV: *as in 780. Elsie wipes a tear from her cheek and brings the back of her hand to her mouth. She kisses the bedpost and looks down.*
783. MLS: *as in 779. Elsie hops down from her bed, runs over to the window on the left, runs back, and hugs the bedpost.*
784. TITLE: ¶Election day.

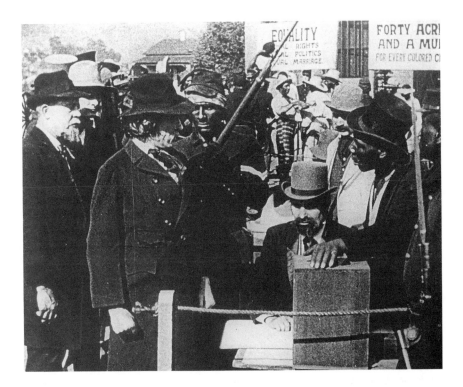

¶All blacks are given the ballot, while the leading whites are
   disfranchised.

785. M S : *a black man places a ballot in the box, and while the white official
   is preoccupied with registering the vote in a book, the voter slips a
   second ballot in the box and exits left. Two white men approach the box
   to place their ballots, but the official shakes his head at them. One of the
   men leaves in disgust, and the other is pushed away violently by an
   armed guard.*

786. M L S : *Dr. Cameron, Ben, and another man come through the gate of
   Cameron Hall and pause for a moment, discussing something, then they
   exit left. Fade out.*

787. *Fade in.* M S : *two white men attempting to place their ballots are pushed
   back by the guard. Dr. Cameron sees this, but steps forward and reaches
   out boldly to place his ballot in the box. A black man puts his hand over
   the box and Dr. Cameron looks to the official for an explanation. The official shakes his head, and the guard steps forward and shoves Dr.
   Cameron out left.*

788. T I T L E : ¶Receiving the returns.
   ¶The negroes and carpetbaggers sweep the state.

789. MS: *Lynch, seated at a desk in his office, impatiently pushes a man away, and the man falls to the floor. Another man comes forward and hands Lynch a piece of paper.*

790. MS: *in the Stoneman parlor in Piedmont, Stoneman and Phil come forward, reading a newspaper Phil is holding. Stoneman nods and Phil turns, signals to a servant, and walks to the rear.*

791. TITLE: ¶Silas Lynch is elected Lieut. Governor.

792. MS: *as in 789. Clutching a piece of paper, Lynch and an official raise their arms and whoop in triumph. Lynch picks up his hat and turns to exit with the official and the jubilant group of men in the rear.*

793. MS: *as in 790. Lynch enters the parlor at left, followed by the official, and hurries over to Stoneman seated on the right. He hands Stoneman the results, and Stoneman congratulates him heartily. Elsie enters from the left and comes over to her father. Lynch immediately takes off his hat. Elsie, perhaps not realizing precisely what the fuss is about, congratulates her father excitedly and hugs him. She points to the paper in her father's hand and he gestures toward Lynch, and she offers him her subdued and modest congratulations.*

794. TITLE: ¶Celebrating their victory at the polls.

795. LS: *a large crowd lines the street in front of Cameron Hall as a formation of black soldiers marches forward. They come to a stop as the crowd waves and cheers.*

796. MLS: *Mrs. Cameron and Margaret are huddled in the center of their parlor when Flora walks in from the right, stands behind them, and gestures to the right.*

797. LS: *as in 795. The soldiers in the street fire their rifles into the air.*

798. MLS: *as in 796. Flora crouches at Margaret's feet and Mrs. Cameron comforts her two daughters.*

799. TITLE: ¶Encouraged by Stoneman's radical doctrines, Lynch's love looks high.

800. MS: *as in 793. As Stoneman looks at the paper, shaking his head and smiling, Elsie runs back to the desk in the rear. Lynch moves a few steps to the left and stares at her.*

801. MCU: *Lynch stands with his hat in his hands, looking at Elsie off to the right.*

802. MCU: *Elsie takes a paper from the desk, looks at it, and puts it back.*

803. MCU: *as in 801. Lynch continues to stare.*

804. MCU: *as in 802. Elsie retrieves more papers from the desk and examines them.*

805. MS: *as in 800. Lynch comes forward and takes a note from Stoneman, who is clearly very pleased. He replaces his hat, bows, and exits through the door on the left. Elsie comes forward and hands the paper to her father.*

806. MLS: *a crowd waiting at the gate cheers Lynch as he approaches, and men lift him up onto their shoulders.*

807. MCU: *Stoneman goes to the window on the left, looks out, and laughs.*

808. MS: *as in 805. Phil exits to the rear, and Elsie stands alone in the center of the room, looking mildly perturbed.*

809. MLS: *as in 806. Lynch is carried down the street by his cheering supporters.*

810. MCU: *as in 807. Stoneman, still looking out the window, smiles.*

811. TITLE: ¶"The little Colonel" relates a series of outrages that have occurred.

812. MLS: *in the Camerons' hall, Ben points to a paper and speaks, as his father and three other men sit listening to him.*

813. TITLE: ¶"The case was tried before a negro magistrate and the verdict rendered against the whites by the negro jury."

814. MLS: *as in 812. Ben reads from the newspaper in his hand.*

815. LS: *in a courtroom, a black magistrate is addressing a black jury.*

816. CU, CV: *a black man sits with hunched shoulders in the witness chair.*

817. MS: *the black jury listens.*

818. MCU, CV: *the magistrate addresses the jury off to the right.*

819. MS: *a white family sit listening. The father pulls his small daughter close to him.*

820. LS: *as in 815. The jury bows to the magistrate, who tells the accused black man that he is acquitted. The man slaps his knee with excitement and leaves the witness stand to shake hands with members of the audience and the jury. Mammy rises and turns to the men behind her to protest the verdict.*

821. MLS: *as in 814. Ben concludes his account. Fade out.*

822. MLS: *four black men in military uniform push a white man and his two small children off the sidewalk into the street.*

823. MS: *a white family is being dispossessed, and as they walk forward and out left, a black officer violently pushes the lame old man, as one of the black soldiers looking on laughs.*

824. TITLE: ¶Even while he talks, their own faithful family servant is punished for not voting with the Union League and Carpetbaggers.

825. MS: *two black men persuade Jake to go with them, and they lead him off to the right.*

826. MLS: *as the two men enter with Jake from the left and stop under a tree, several black men in uniform surround Jake and start to tie him up as he shakes his head vigorously in response to their accusations.*

827. MS: *as in 825. An elderly black man enters left and goes through the door to the servants' quarters from which Jake has just been abducted.*

828. MLS: *as in 826. Jake is flogged under the tree by the black officer as the others look on. Fade out.*

829. MS: *as in 827. The elderly black man emerges from the servants' quarters and looks up the street to the right.*

830. MLS: *as in 828. The officer continues to flog Jake, then hands the whip to another man who starts to laugh.*

831. MS: *as in 829. The elderly man looking for Jake rushes out to the right.*

832. MLS: *as in 830. The elderly man enters left and tries to grab the whip from the man lashing Jake. The officer pushes the would-be rescuer and pulls out a gun and fires two shots at him. As the man falls, the soldiers run off behind the tree to the left, and Jake also falls to the ground.*

833. MS: *as in 821. As the men in the hall listen, Ben rises slowly, clutching the paper in one hand and clenching his other hand into a fist. Iris closes left.*

834. MLS: *as in 832. Jake is bending over his dead friend. He rises and staggers out to the right, holding his head and his back.*

835. MS: *as in 833. Ben and one of the men embrace as Dr. Cameron and the others rise and take a step toward them.*

836. TITLE: ¶The faithful soul enlists Dr. Cameron's sympathy.

837. MLS: *as in 834. Standing under the tree, with his dead friend at his feet, Jake describes to Dr. Cameron what happened. On the point of collapse, Jake brings his hand up to his head, and Dr. Cameron assists him out to the right.*

838. MS: *as in 835. Dr. Cameron and Jake enter right and Jake describes the incident to Ben and the other men.*

839. TITLE: ¶The riot in the Master's Hall.

¶The negro party in control in the State House of representatives, 101 blacks against 23 whites, session of 1871.

AN HISTORICAL FACSIMILE of the State House of Representatives of South Carolina as it was in 1870. After photograph by "The Columbia State."

840. *Fade in.* LS: *the State House of Representatives stands empty, showing desks, speaker's platform, and visitors' gallery above.*

841. *Fade in/lap dissolve.* LS: *as in 840. The House members sit at or walk among the desks as visitors stand in the gallery.*

842. TITLE: ¶Historic incidents from the first legislative session under Reconstruction.

843. MLS: *a man standing below the Speaker of the House reads a bill. The Speaker raps his gavel and points toward the right.*

844. MCU: *a man eats peanuts from a bag as another in a top hat talks to him. The man in the top hat helps himself to a peanut.*

845. TITLE: ¶The honorable member for Ulster.

846. MS: *as other House members look on, a representative furtively takes a bottle of liquor from beneath a book and steals a mouthful. He replaces the bottle and, looking straight ahead, suppresses a smile.*

847. M S : *a representative with his feet on his desk takes off a shoe, as another, standing in front of him eating a joint of meat, turns.*
848. M S : *a man in a check suit is making a point with emphatic movements of his arms, when he stops in mid-gesture and looks out left.*
849. M S : *as in 847. The legislator eating the joint of meat waves a document in one hand and with his other hand gestures toward the man with his feet on the desk. Nearby, another man stands and addresses the Speaker.*
850. M S : *as in 848. The man in the check suit brings a handkerchief to his nose and gestures vigorously toward the left.*
851. M S : *as in 849. The man with the joint of meat continues to eat, as the man with his feet on the desk twirls his toes.*
852. T I T L E : ¶The speaker rules that all members must wear shoes.
853. M L S : *as in 843. The Speaker pounds his gavel and gestures broadly to the left.*
854. M S : *as in 851. The representative with his feet on the desk puts on his shoe as others look on.*
855. M S : *as in 850. The man in the check suit continues to speak, and turns left again.*
856. T I T L E : ¶It is moved and carried that all whites must salute negro officers on the streets.
857. M L S : *as in 853. The officer standing in front of the Speaker reads the bill, and the Speaker brings down his gavel.*
858. L S : *as in 841. There is a general uproar among the representatives at their desks and the visitors in the gallery.*
859. T I T L E : ¶The helpless white minority.
860. M L S : *in the foreground, white representatives sit quietly, as black representatives debate heatedly in the background and black pageboys run up the aisle.*
861. T I T L E : ¶White visitors in the gallery.
862. L S : *as in 858. Iris closes to the right where the visitors are standing in the gallery.*
863. M L S : *the visitors look down from the gallery. Two white women among them burst out laughing.*
864. M S : *as in 846. Representatives at their seats turn and look up left in an affronted manner.*
865. M L S : *the white man in the gallery gestures to the two women to start leaving to the right.*
866. T I T L E : ¶Passage of a bill, providing for the intermarriage of blacks and whites.
867. M S : *as in 864. The representatives continue to look up to the left, then suddenly rise, smiling.*
868. M L S : *as in 865. The two women and the man make their way out to the right as others in the gallery watch them depart.*

869. LS: *as in 862. The legislators on the floor of the assembly and visitors in the gallery cheer wildly.*

870. MLS: *as in 868. The blacks in the gallery wave their hats and cheer.*

871. MCU: *Silas Lynch grins as members of the House surround him and boistrously offer their congratulations.*

872. LS: *as in 869. The jubilant commotion continues on the floor of the assembly and in the gallery. Lynch can be seen in the foreground accepting the congratulations of the legislators. Iris closes to the right.*

873. MLS: *as in 870. In the gallery, the happy visitors wave their arms and lift their knees.*

874. *Iris opens from the right.* LS: *as in 872. Lynch is still visible in the foreground amid the cheering legislators. Fade out.*

875. TITLE: ¶Later.
¶The grim reaping begins.

876. MS: *Flora comes out onto the Cameron porch, where she meets Elsie. With their arms around each other, they come forward and go out to the right.**

877. MLS: *the girls go through the gate and Flora leads to the right.*

878. MS: *hand in hand, Flora and Elsie run in from the right behind two trees and come around to the front. Flora points up, Elsie agrees, and they seat themselves under the trees on the right.*

879. TITLE: ¶Gus, the renegade, a product of the vicious doctrines spread by the carpetbaggers.

880. MLS: *as in 877. Gus enters left with his hands in his pockets and pauses in front of the picket fence.*

881. MS: *as in 878. Flora and Elsie, sitting under the trees, embrace each other.*

882. MLS: *as in 880. With a scowl on his face, Gus looks off to the left and then walks off right.*

883. MS: *as in 881. As Flora and Elsie embrace, Gus enters from the right in the background on the other side of the picket fence. He pauses and looks about.*

884. ECU, CV: *Gus stares off to the right.*

885. MS: *as in 883. As Gus moves off left, Flora and Elsie get up, circle behind the trees and exit right. Gus reappears from the left and runs to the spot where he can peer between the two trees from the far side of the picket fence. He pauses there and then walks off right.*

886. MLS: *as in 882. Flora and Elsie run in from the right, the picket fence in the foreground, and they enter the gate on the left.*

*This shot (876) and the shot that follows it (877) do not appear in the Museum of Modern Art print, but do appear in the 35mm tinted nitrate print that is preserved in the National Film Collection at the Library of Congress.

887. MS: *as in 885. Gus is just visible on the far side of the fence before exiting right.*

888. MLS: *as in 886. Gus enters from the right, on the near side of the fence.*

889. MS: *as Elsie and Flora come forward from the left, Lynch appears on the right and lifts his hat and extends his hand in greeting. Elsie shakes his hand, and Flora's mouth drops open in shock.*

890. MLS: *as in 888. Gus quickly picks up a stalk of grass and begins to chew on it as he shuffles off to the left.*

891. MS: *as in 889. As Lynch shakes Elsie's hand, Flora turns indignantly away. Elsie is about to follow her, when Lynch calls her back. Ben can be glimpsed in the background, coming toward them.*

892. MCU: *Ben draws back in dismay at what he sees.*

893. MS: *as in 891. Elsie tries to take her leave of Lynch.*

894. MCU: *as in 892. Ben glares with indignation.*

895. MS: *as in 893. Elsie is able to pull herself away from Lynch and exits left. Lynch puts on his hat as Ben comes forward, staring at him angrily. Lynch notices Ben, who has paused a few feet from him, and he glares back.*

896. MS: *as in 876. Flora enters right and stands in front of her porch, her arms rigidly at her sides.*

897. MS: *as in 895. Lynch's glare turns into a gloating smile and, as Ben exits right, Lynch turns and walks away to the rear. Fade out.*

898. MS: *as in 896. As Elsie joins Flora, Flora points left and asks angrily about Lynch. Elsie lightly and briefly explains, and the two women kiss. Elsie exits left, and Flora looks after her, then she turns to enter the house, but pauses, looking disturbed.*

899. *Fade in.* MS: Gus *walks forward along the fence, looking at Cameron Hall.*

900. MS: as in 898. Flora stands on the porch looking out, then turns and quickly enters the house.

901. MS: *as in 899. Gus has stopped in front of Cameron Hall and is looking intently toward it. Ben enters left behind Gus and goes through the gate. The two men look at each other.*

902. TITLE: ¶The "little Colonel" orders Gus to keep away.

903. MCU: *Ben gestures to the right with his hand as he speaks.*

904. MCU: *Gus replies indignantly.*

905. MCU: *Lynch, entering from the right, mounts the steps to his house, and is about to open the front door, when he turns and looks out to the right at Ben and Gus.*

906. MS: *as in 901. Gus continues speaking, and in a surly manner puts his hands in his pockets.*

907. MCU: *as in 905. Lynch clenches his jaw in a manner of resolve and exits right.*

908. M S : *as in 906. Lynch comes forward quickly and demands to know what is going on. Gus gives an account.*
909. M C U : *as in 903. Ben glares with outrage.*
910. M C U : *as in 904. Lynch speaks and points angrily at Ben.*
911. M C U : *as in 909. Ben looks at the two men disdainfully.*
912. M S : *as in 908. Without replying, Ben flashes a last look of scorn, turns, and walks back to the front porch of his house. Lynch tells Gus to report any further incidents of this kind to him, then turns and walks back toward his house. Gus stares at Cameron Hall as he puts his hands in his pockets and walks out to the right. Fade out.*
913. T I T L E : ¶In agony of soul over the degradation and ruin of his people.
914. M S : *Ben enters left and stands on the riverbank looking out across the valley. He takes off his hat and sits on a rock, holds his clenched fists out in a gesture of helplessness, then gestures sweepingly with his left hand and bows his head.*
915. M L S : *two white children, a boy and a girl, come forward carrying a sheet. They glance behind them.*
916. M S : *as in 914. Ben looks up, seeing them.*
917. M L S : *as in 915. The two children sit on the ground and cover themselves with the sheet. Two pairs of black children come forward along the same path and stop in front of the sheet-covered pair.*
918. M S : *as in 916. Ben leans forward, watching them.*
919. M S : *the black children giggle.*
920. M C U : *the sheet begins to move.*
921. M S : *as in 919. The black children become frightened, turn, and flee back down the path.*
922. M L S : *as in 917. As the black children run off, the two white children under the sheet rise and take a few steps after them.*
923. T I T L E : ¶The inspiration.
924. M S : *as in 918. Ben rises and points toward the children and smiles. Fade out.*
925. T I T L E : ¶The result.
            ¶The Ku Klux Klan, the organization that saved the South from the anarchy of black rule, but not without the shedding of more blood than at Gettysburg, according to Judge Tourgee of the carpet-baggers [*sic*].
926. M L S , C V : *two hooded Clansmen sit astride their horses. The one on the left raises, then lowers his rifle. Iris/fade out.*
927. T I T L E : ¶Their first visit to terrorize a negro disturber and barn burner.
928. *Fade in.* M S : *two blacks emerge from a cabin door on the right and exit left.*
929. *Fade/iris in.* M L S , C V : *as the two black enter right and come to the gate, they stop at the sight of two hooded Clansmen on horseback and a third standing on the ground. The Clansman on the ground slowly lifts a bucket.*

930. MS, CV: *the Clansman on the ground lifts the bucket to his mouth and slowly drinks, as the mounted Clansmen wave their arms slowly from side to side.*

931. MCU, CV: *the two blacks turn to each other in fear.*

932. MS, CV: *as in 930. The one Clansman continues to drink while the mounted one behind him lifts his arm high.*

933. MCU, CV: *as in 931. The two terrified blacks begin to shake.*

934. MS, CV: *as in 932. The mounted Clansmen motion with their hands held high and the one on the ground continues to drink.*

935. MLS: *as in 929. As the Clansman lowers the bucket, the blacks flee to the right.*

936. MS: *as in 928. The blacks run in from the left. The one stumbles on the step of the cabin, and the other helps him in through the door.*

937. MLS: *as in 926. The three mounted Clansmen turn and ride off into the woods to the rear.*

938. TITLE: ¶Lynch's supporters score first blood against the Ku Klux.

939. MS: *a man rushes in from the right and speaks excitedly to Lynch as the soldiers accompanying Lynch turn to listen. Gus joins the messenger and points toward the rear.*

940. L S : *the three mounted Clansmen come galloping forward through the woods.*
941. M S : *as in 939. Gus and the soldiers fire to the left through the bushes as Lynch urges them on.*
942. L S : *as in 940. The Clansmen return fire, but the first two are hit and fall from their horses.*
943. M S : *as in 941. Gus directs the soldiers, who continue to fire.*
944. L S : *as in 942. The third Clansman and his horse fall.*
945. M S : *as in 943. Gus and a soldier run out to the left as Lynch looks on.*
946. T I T L E : ¶The new rebellion of the South.
947. M S : *Stoneman is seated in his study examining papers, when Lynch and Gus burst in from the left carrying Clan costumes. Lynch shows Stoneman a Clansman's tunic and describes the incident. Stoneman pounds his cane on the floor.*
948. T I T L E : ¶"We shall crush the white South under the heel of the black South."
949. M S : *as in 947. Stoneman points to the door, and as Lynch turns to leave, Stoneman grabs the costumes from him. As Lynch and Gus go through the door, Stoneman flings the costumes onto his desk.*
950. T I T L E : ¶"Your lover belongs to this murderous band of outlaws."
951. M S : *as in 949. Elsie comes running in from the left and approaches her father, who holds up the Clan tunic and shows it to her. As he explains, she becomes subdued, and he shows her a note. She reads it and puts her arm around her father, and they both look out to the left.*
952. T I T L E : ¶The tryst.
      ¶Confirmed in her suspicions, in loyalty to her father she breaks off the engagement.
953. *Fade in.* M S : *Ben enters left and walks forward to the gate. Elsie runs in from foreground left and meets him. She speaks to him, pointing off left as they walk forward together.*
954. C U : *a bundle wrapped in paper falls to the ground at their feet.*
955. M S : *as in 953. Elsie stops in mid-sentence, looks down, and points to the bundle.*
956. C U : *as in 954. A Clan costume is visible through the torn paper.*
957. M S : *as in 955. Elsie stares at the fallen parcel for a moment, then looks up at Ben. He looks around, then bends down to pick it up.*
958. C U : *as in 956. Ben reaches for the costume.*
959. M S : *as in 957. Looking around, Ben rolls up the costume and quickly conceals it beneath his coat, as Elsie stares ahead rigidly. Ben takes off his hat and turns to offer Elsie a kiss, when he notices her accusing look. He tries to take her hand, but she pushes him away. He begins to speak, but she pulls away sharply and exits left.*
960. M S : *Elsie enters right, her eyes flashing. She stops and looks back.*
961. M S : *as in 959. Ben calls her name.*
962. M S : *as in 960. Elsie turns back toward Ben and exits right.*

963. MS: *as in 961. Elsie enters left and approaches Ben. She puts her finger to her lips as she speaks.*

964. TITLE: ¶"But you need not fear that I will betray you."

965. MS: *as in 963. Ben tries to explain, but Elsie will not hear it, and she exits left.*

966. MS: *as in 962. Elsie comes forward from the right, looking back at Ben. She pauses briefly, then walks off to the left.*

967. MS: *as in 965. Ben looks after her for a moment, then turns and walks off to the right.*

968. MLS, SAV: *Elsie enters her bedroom from the rear and comes forward. She stands in the middle of her room and stares pensively.*

969. MS: *Ben enters the Cameron parlor through the door on the right, locks it behind him, and comes forward to Flora, who is standing in the foreground on the left.*

970. TITLE: ¶Over four hundred thousand Ku Klux costumes made by the women of the South and not one trust betrayed.

971. MS: *as in 969. Ben opens out the Clan costume and shows it to Flora. He leans toward her and in a conspiratorial manner gives her instructions. She nods, and they walk back to the rear where Margaret and Mrs. Cameron are seated on the left. The women rise as Ben shows them the tunic and they discuss the insignia. Mrs. Cameron takes the costume from*

her son, and he walks forward with Flora, who claps her hands in excite-
ment. Ben takes her hand and tries to impress her with the need for
secrecy. Flora exits left and returns, carrying her small Confederate flag,
which she places diagonally across her chest and over her right shoulder
as she raises her right hand and vows secrecy. Ben smiles, they embrace,
and she runs back to her mother and sister.

972. MCU, SAV: *in her room, Elsie stares sightlessly at her dove cage.*

973. MS: *as in 971. Flora skips forward to Ben, who is staring sadly toward*
the left. She asks him what the matter is.

974. MCU: *as in 972. Elsie continues to stare. Fade out.*

975. MS: *as in 973. Flora embraces her brother and tries to cheer him up,*
and he responds by making her promise not to go outside alone. Flora
skips after Ben as he turns and goes toward the door. He takes a paper
from his coat pocket, picks up his hat, and exits right.

976. MLS: *Ben enters the hall from the left and comes forward slowly, read-*
ing the paper in his hand. He stops in the middle of the room.

977. MS: *as in 975. Flora opens the door to the hall on the right and looks*
out.

978. TITLE: ¶Little sister consoles the disconsolate lover.

979. MLS: *as in 976. Flora skips stealthily in from the left and comes up be-*
hind Ben. She surprises him with a little pounce at his arm, and he turns
toward her.

980. MLS: *as in 977. Margaret rushes over to the door Flora has just left*
ajar and closes it, turning the key in the lock.

981. MS: *as in 979. Flora kisses her brother playfully half a dozen times on*
both cheeks and scampers off to the rear. Ben smiles and blows her a kiss.
She exits left, and he walks off right.

982. Fade in. MLS: *as in 968. Elsie falls at the foot of her bed, sobbing.*

983. MS: *Flora finishes folding a Clan costume, rises, and goes to the table.*
She and Margaret put costumes in a pillowcase as Mrs. Cameron sews.

984. TITLE: ¶Against the brother's warning, she goes alone to the spring.

985. Fade in. MS: *as Flora rocks back and forth on the arm of the couch,*
Mrs. Cameron pours herself a glass of water, takes a sip, and declares it
stale. Flora jumps up and offers to fetch fresh water from the spring. She
exits left and returns with a bucket. Mrs. Cameron tries to dissuade her,
but Flora insists, and exits through the door on the right.

986. MLS: *Flora comes through the front door, pauses on the porch with the*
bucket in her hand, and skips happily out to the right.

987. MLS: *Flora comes through the gate and stops to admire the roses.**

---

*Shots 987 through 991 do not appear in the Museum of Modern Art print, but they are in the 35mm
tinted nitrate print that is preserved in the National Film Collection at the Library of Congress.

988. *Fade in.* MLS: *Flora comes running forward between the trees and stops to pick up a stone.*

989. MLS: *as in 987. Gus stoops down and sneaks along the garden fence. He picks a flower and looks back.*

990. MLS: *as in 988. Flora continues out right.*

991. MLS: *as in 989. Gus sneaks along the picket fence.*

992. *Fade in.* MLS: *in the woods Flora enters left, comes forward and picks up another stone.*

993. MLS: *as in 990. Gus comes forward carrying his coat and pauses.*

994. MLS: *as in 992. Flora tosses the stone to the left. She skips forward and goes out left.*

995. MLS: *as in 993. Gus looks intently out to the right, turns and starts to go back, pauses, looks over his shoulder, and exits left.*

996. MLS: *Flora enters left and stops at the spring. She puts her left foot on the edge of the spring and leans forward with the bucket.*

997. CU: *the bucket is dipped in the spring and lifted up.*

998. MLS: *as in 996. Flora straightens up and looks at her soiled hands.*

999. MLS: *as in 994. Gus comes in left from behind the bushes, pauses, and cranes his neck looking ahead.*

1000. MLS: *as in 998. Flora notices something offscreen left and points to it smiling, then, leaving the bucket at the spring, goes out left.*

1001. MLS: *as in 999. Gus stoops to gain a better view, then runs left behind a bush.*

1002. *Fade in.* MLS: *Flora skips in from the right, kneels on a log in the foreground, and looks up into the tree above.*

1003. CU, CV: *a squirrel hops onto a branch.*

1004. MLS: *as in 1002. Flora calls to the squirrel and tosses something at it.*

1005. CU, CV: *as in 1003. The squirrel picks up a nut and begins to chew on it.*

1006. MLS: *as in 1004. Flora responds with delight, readjusts herself on the log, and looks up to the left.*

1007. MS: *Gus creeps forward under overhanging, dead branches.*

1008. MS: *Flora rocks back and forth on the log, smiling, and glances up to the right.*

1009. CU, CV: *as in 1005. The squirrel rubs its nose on the branch.*

1010. MS: *as in 1008. Flora, twitching her feet, looks up at the squirrel and talks to it.*

1011. CU: *from the shadows, among the dead branches, Gus watches intently.*

1012. MS: *as in 1010. Flora continues talking to the squirrel.*

1013. CU, CV: *as in 1009. The squirrel looks about.*

1014. MS: *as in 1012. Flora blows the creature a kiss.*

1015. CU: *as in 1013. The squirrel hops off the branch and out of sight.*

1016. MS: *as in 1014. Flora clasps her hands together in delight.*

1017. MLS: *Mrs. Cameron enters left, crosses the hall, and looks out the window on the right.*

1018. MS: *as in 986. Ben mounts the porch steps and goes through the front door.*

1019. MLS: *as in 1017. As Ben enters right, his mother comes forward. He asks about Flora, and she tells him. He looks alarmed and comes forward a few steps, his mother clinging anxiously to his arm.*

1020. MLS: *as in 1016. Flora climbs down off the log, says goodbye to the squirrel, and goes out to the right.*

1021. MS: *as in 1019. Ben tries to reassure his worried mother, but with a look of extreme alarm on his face, exits right..*

1022. MS: *as in 1018. Ben comes through the front door and exits right.*

1023. MS: *as in 1021. Mrs. Cameron walks back to the center of the hall and pauses. She turns, brings a hand to her mouth in a nervous gesture, and goes out to the left.*

1024. MLS: *as Flora enters left and stoops behind the log to pick up something, Gus rushes forward, grabs her elbow to stop her, then touches his cap.*

1025. MS: *Flora draws back slightly as Gus tips his hat.*

1026. TITLE: ¶"You see, I'm a Captain now—and I want to marry—"

1027. MS: *as in 1025. Gus leans forward earnestly as he speaks.*

1028. MCU, CV: *Flora rubs her hands nervously and glances out left and then right.*

1029. CU, CV: *his eyes wide in appeal, Gus speaks. [He seems to be saying "I love you."]*

1030. MS, CV: *as in 1028. Flora twists her fingers and replies.*

1031. MS: *as in 1027. Flora attempts to leave, but Gus holds out his arm to prevent her and continues to speak, pointing to himself and to her. Flora draws back, looking frightened.*

1032. MLS: *as in 1024. Flora strikes Gus and leaps forward over the log and out to the right. Gus jumps over the log, dropping his coat as he falls.*

1033. LS: *Flora looks back as she stumbles forward, flings her arms up in the air, and cries out as she exits right.*

1034. MLS: *as in 1032. Gus picks himself up off the ground and, clutching his knee, goes out to the right.*

1035. MS: *Flora comes forward through the bushes, throws her arms up in the air, and calls for help, then runs out right.*

1036. LS: *as in 1033. Gus runs forward from the left, stops, and calls out.*

1037. TITLE: ¶"Wait, missie, I won't hurt yeh."

1038. LS: *as in 1036. Gus calls after Flora, then dashes out to the right.*

1039. MLS: *as in 995. Ben enters left and hurries forward along the fence and exits right.*

1040. MLS: *Flora jumps over the trunk of a fallen tree and comes forward to a tree on the left, which she clings to as she looks back.*

1041. LS: *Gus runs forward, jumps over a fallen trunk, and looks left.*

1042. MLS: *as in 1040. Flora hides behind the tree, her eyes flashing in terror.*

1043. LS: *as in 1041. Gus sees Flora and runs off left.*

1044. MLS: *as in 1042. Flora pulls away from the tree and runs out right.*

1045. MLS: *as in 1001. Ben runs in left behind the bushes, comes forward through a space between them, and rushes out left.*

1046. LS: *Flora enters left and runs through the forest. She turns and starts to come forward, when Gus enters from the left in the foreground. She sees him and, waving her arms about in fright, retreats to the rear and out left. He runs after her, calling and gesturing to her to stop. Fade out.*

1047. MLS: *as in 998. Ben enters left and approaches the spring. He sees the bucket, leans forward, and touches it. He straightens up and calls Flora's name, then looks around on the ground for clues and exits left.*

1048. MLS: *Flora bursts in left and hides under a bush.*

1049. MCU: *Flora crouches under the foliage and glances about, terrified.*

1050. MS: *as in 1035. Gus comes forward, parting a way between two small pine trees, and holds up his hand and calls.*

1051. MCU: *as in 1049. Flora cries out in fear.*

1052. MS: *as in 1050. Gus hears her and comes forward and out to the right.*

1053. MCU: *as in 1048. Flora leaves her hiding place and runs off to the right.*

1054. MLS, AV: *as in 1034. Ben runs in from the right, stops behind the log, and calls out Flora's name, then exits left. He returns, jumps over the log, and finds Gus's coat. He drops the coat and calls, "Flora!" then runs out to the right.*

1055. LS: *Flora appears from behind an enormous fallen tree, flings her arms up in distress, and runs back behind the tree to the left.*

1056. LS: *as in 1046. Ben runs in from the left through the forest and pauses in a clearing. He looks around, then throws up his hands and starts to run to the left.*

1057. MLS: *Flora climbs forward up a rocky slope and stumbles out to the right.*

1058. MLS: *as in 1055. Gus runs to the left behind the fallen tree.*

1059. *Fade in.* MCU: *Flora climbs forward and out to the right.*

1060. MLS: *Flora reaches the top of the hill.*

1061. MLS: *as in 1057. Gus runs up the rocky slope from the rear and loses his cap, then exits right.*

1062. MS: *as in 1060. Flora, looking behind her to the left, gestures and calls out to Gus to stay away.*

1063. MS: *as in 1059. Gus appears from below, crawling up over the rocks.*

1064. MLS: *as in 1062. As Gus approaches from the left a few feet farther down the slope, Flora motions wildly to him to stay away and raises her arms, preparing to jump.*

1065. M S :   *as in 1052. Ben comes forward through the pine trees, calls out Flora's name, and exits right.*
1066. M L S :   *as in 1064. Flora gestures to Gus to keep back.*
1067. M S :   *as in 1066. Flora gestures toward the drop and threatens to jump.*
1068. T I T L E :   ¶"Stay away or I'll jump!"
1069. M S :   *as in 1067. Flora's eyes are wide with fear as she looks back toward Gus and motions him to keep back.*
1070. M C U :   *as in 1063. Gus is foaming at the mouth as he falls back a step and urges Flora to come away from the edge.*
1071. M C U :   *she motions him to stay back, then points to the drop and cries out, "I'll jump!"*
1072. E L S :   *Gus approaches Flora at the rocky summit.*
1073. M L S :   *Ben runs in from the right and pauses in a clearing in the forest. He sees something out to the left, calls out Flora's name and runs out left.*
1074. M C U :   *as in 1071. With her arms in the air, Flora cries out, "Ben!" She looks down over the edge and back toward Gus.*
1075. M L S :   *as in 1069. She motions Gus back and stands up.*
1076. M C U :   *as in 1070. Gus comes forward, foaming at the mouth.*
1077. E L S :   *as in 1072. Flora with her arms in the air is about to jump, as Gus motions to her to step back from the edge.*
1078. M L S :   *as in 1075. Flora jumps over the edge and out of sight.*
1079. E L S :   *as in 1077. Flora falls from the promontory to the rocks below.*
1080. M L S :   *Flora's body rolls in from the right and comes to rest at the base.*
1081. M L S :   *as in 1078. Gus climbs to the edge of the precipice to look down.*
1082. M L S :   *as in 1080. Flora lies still.*
1083. E L S :   *as in 1079. Gus stands at the top of the promontory, his arms held high.*
1084. M L S :   *as in 1081. Gus turns and goes out left.*
1085. M L S :   *as in 1061. Ben runs up the hill and stops when he finds Gus's cap. He picks it up.*
1086. L S :   *Gus jumps down from a large rock and disappears behind another.*
1087. M L S :   *as in 1085. Ben cries out and comes forward and out to the right.*
1088. M L S :   *as in 1084. Ben reaches the summit from the left and looks down.*
1089. *Fade in.* M L S :   *as in 1082. Flora moves slightly.*
1090. M L S :   *as in 1088. Ben leans forward, sees Flora, and rushes out to the left.*
1091. *Fade in.* M L S :   *as in 1089. Ben clambers down the rocks on the left and runs forward. He kneels beside Flora and raises her.*
1092. M S :   *holding her, Ben wipes the blood from Flora's mouth with the Confederate flag she had worn about her waist. She looks up at him and murmurs something. He asks her who did it, and she says, "Gus." He reacts as if he has been shot. With a faint smile, she whispers something else to him, then slumps forward in his arms, dead. He bends*

over her body in his arms, then looks up and stares out fiercely, then embraces her.

1093. TITLE: ¶For her who had learned the stern lesson of honor we should not grieve that she found sweeter the opal gates of death.

1094. *Fade/iris in.* MLS: *as in 1022. Ben enters from the left carrying Flora's body and goes through his front door. Fade/iris out.*

1095. *Fade in.* MS: *Ben comes into the parlor through the door on the right and lays Flora's body on the couch. Mrs. Cameron enters from the rear and hurries forward as Ben attempts to stay her advance. She sees Flora and exclaims in shock, then comes forward and falls to her knees beside her dead daughter. Margaret rushes in from the right and Ben holds her back a moment. Half embracing Ben, she comes forward and kneels next to her sister and weeping mother. The scene darkens as Ben goes to his father who has come in from the rear.*

1096. TITLE: ¶And none grieved more than these.

1097. MS: *in the kitchen, Mammy weeps and Jake sits morosely with his elbows on his knees. Fade out.*

1098. TITLE: ¶The son's plea against his father's radical policy.

1099. MS: *Phil stands next to his seated father, arguing and gesturing emphatically. Stoneman replies angrily but pats his son on the shoulder.*

1100. M S : *as Dr. Cameron sits motionless in a daze of grief, with his right hand over his heart, Ben asks Margaret for a Clan costume. She tries to dissuade him, but relents, and they carefully take the pillow supporting Flora's head. He hides the bundle under his coat and exits right as Margaret pleads with him.*

1101. T I T L E :   ¶Gus hides in "white-arm" Joe's ginmill.

1102. M L S :   *Gus comes forward from behind the saloon and glances off to the right before entering.*

1103. M S :   *Gus comes in through the door on the right and runs forward to a group in the foreground. He asks them to hide him, and they all move to the rear of the saloon. Gus closes the door again, which had swung open.*

1104. M S :   *Jeff, the smith, enters right carrying an anvil. As he speaks to a wainwright on the left, Ben and two companions enter from the left. Ben talks to Jeff and the wainwright and they follow him and his companions into the workshop, where Jeff puts down his anvil.*

1105. T I T L E :   ¶Townsmen enlisted in the search for the accused Gus, that he may be given a fair trial in the dim halls of the Invisible Empire.

1106. M S :   *as in 1104. In the doorway of the workshop, Ben instructs Jeff, then he walks off to the right with his two companions. Jeff speaks to his assistant, the wainwright, and they both take off their aprons. Jeff walks forward and out to the right and his helper exits left.*

1107. M S :   *Jeff's assistant enters right, glances back, and hides around a corner.*

1108. M L S :   *as in 1103. In the saloon, Gus goes over to the door and closes it again.*

1109. M S :   *as in 1102. Jeff enters from the right and approaches the saloon door. With his hand on the knob, he pauses and looks right.*

1110. M L S :   *as in 1108. "White-arm" Joe points to the left and Gus quickly hides under the bar on the left.*

1111. M S :   *as in 1109. Jeff pushes open the door and peers in before entering.*

1112. M L S :   *as in 1110. Jeff enters the saloon, comes forward, and speaks to Joe. Joe rises from his chair, and as Jeff speaks to him, he shakes his head. As Jeff turns to walk over to the bar, Joe pulls him back by his shirt, and Jeff clenches his fists.*

1113. M S :   *Jeff and Joe stare at each other in a menacing fashion.*

1114. *Fade in.* M C U : *Jeff slowly lifts his right hand.*

1115. M C U : *Gus looks up from his hiding place and scowls.*

1116. M C U : *as in 1114. Jeff slowly lowers his clenched fist.*

1117. M C U , C V : *"White-arm" Joe smiles as he makes a reply.*

1118. M L S : *as in 1112. Jeff turns and starts to cross left.*

1119. M C U : *as in 1115. Gus, hiding under the bar, smiles.*

1120. M L S : *as in 1118. Joe pulls Jeff back by his shirt and speaks angrily to him. Jeff smiles, but the moment Joe stops speaking, he punches Joe in the jaw. One of the men in the saloon leaps at Jeff, and Jeff hurls the man to the floor. Another man comes forward, and Jeff knocks him to the floor.*

1121. MS: *Ben questions two blacks, and as they exit to the left, they smile. Ben and his companion move on toward the rear.*

1122. MLS: *as in 1120. Jeff throws a man bodily at Joe and the others, and they all land in a heap on the floor. Gus comes forward from behind the bar and attacks Jeff, who knocks him to the floor. Gus leaps up and lunges again at the smith.*

1123. MS: *as in 1121. Ben and his friend come forward along the path and out to the right.*

1124. MS: *Jeff continues to fight off his attackers, one of whom he lifts and throws out the window to the right.*

1125. MS: *as in 1111. Outside, the man comes flying through the window and lands at the feet of a group of startled blacks. Another man stumbles out the door.*

1126. MS: *as in 1124. In the saloon, the fighting continues as chairs are thrown about and bodies collide.*

1127. MS: *as in 1125. Outside, the man who was thrown through the window and the man who came through the door run off.*

1128. MLS: *as in 1126. Jeff throws a man to the floor. The man leaps up and throws a chair at the smith. Jeff ducks to avoid the chair, and hits the man on the head with a bottle. Gus charges at Jeff, and Jeff picks him up, kicking violently, and exits right.*

1129. MS: *as in 1127. Jeff comes through the door carrying Gus and throws him to the ground.*

1130. MLS: *as in 1128. Inside the saloon, a man by the bar fires a pistol out to the right.*

1131. MS: *as in 1129. Jeff, standing outside in front of the open door, is hit.*

1132. MLS: *as in 1130. The man with the gun goes over to the door.*

1133. MS: *as in 1131. Gus takes the gun and shoots Jeff again. Jeff falls to the ground, and Gus shakes his fist over the body.*

1134. MS: *as in 1107. Jeff's assistant comes around the corner of the saloon and looks right.*

1135. MS: *as in 1133. Gus looks up to the left, rushes over to the door of the saloon, then runs out to the right.*

1136. MS: *as in 1134. Jeff's assistant runs forward and out to the right.*

1137. MLS: *Gus runs in from the left and goes over to a horse tied to a fence.*

1138. MS: *as in 1135. Jeff's assistant rushes forward from the corner of the saloon and kneels beside Jeff.*

1139. MLS: *as in 1137. Gus mounts the horse and rides off left.*

1140. MS: *as in 1138. The assistant gets up and runs off to the right.*

1141. MLS: *as in 1139. The assistant runs in from the left to the fence, as a man enters from the right. As the man draws a pistol from the holster at his hip, Jeff's assistant grabs it and the two men run out to the left.*
1142. MS: *a man approaches Ben and his companion, shaking his head.*
1143. MLS: *Gus rides forward and shoots at the two men who run in from the right. As he gallops off to the left, the two men run forward, shooting at him.*
1144. LS: *Gus gallops forward along the fence.*
1145. MLS: *as in 1143. Jeff's assistant stands at the gate with the man and fires straight ahead.*
1146. LS: *as in 1144. The horse falls and Gus is thrown to the ground.*
1147. LS: *Ben and the two men with him look and rush out left.*
1148. LS: *as in 1146. Gus is running forward as Ben enters right and lunges at him. Ben's companions rush in and help him catch Gus, and they lead Gus out to the right.*
1149. TITLE: ¶The trial.
1150. MLS: *a group of hooded Clansmen stand in the foreground with their heads bowed as a Clansman on the left holds his arms up high. Clansmen on horseback are lined up in the rear, and a cross can be seen burning in*

the rear on the right. The Clansman on the left motions with his arm, and a terrified Gus is dragged in from the left and brought forward. A Clansman holds out Gus's cap as evidence, and then he and one of his hooded comrades point to the Clansman on the right. Gus looks up at the Clansman on the right, who takes a step toward him and begins to remove his hood. Fade out.

1151. *Fade/iris in.* M S , C V : *in the parlor, Flora lies on a bier heaped with flowers, as Dr. and Mrs. Cameron and Margaret watch over her.*

1152. M L S : *as in 1150. The Clansman on the right is Ben, who points to Gus and then to the rear, as Gus is dragged away. Fade out.*

1153. T I T L E : ¶Guilty.

1154. M L S : *as in 1152. Gus is thrown across a Clansman's horse and ridden out to the rear.*

1155. T I T L E :   ¶On the steps of the Lieut. Governor's house.
¶The answer to the blacks and carpetbaggers.

1156. *Fade in.* L S : *a group of five Clansmen rides up to the front steps of Lynch's house.*

1157. M L S : *the horseman carrying Gus's body goes up to the porch and roughly drops the dead man on the doorstep.*

1158. M S : *Gus's body lies on its side in front of the doors to Lynch's house. On his shoulder is pinned a piece of paper bearing the letters "K K K" and a depiction of a skull and crossbones.*

1159. M L S : *as in 1156. The Clansmen turn and gallop off.*

1160. M L S : *as in 1100. Ben comes slowly into the Cameron parlor and Margaret closes the door behind him. Dr. Cameron sits on the left with a large Bible open on his knees. Ben puts the bundle on the couch and walks over to the bier on the left. He looks sorrowfully at his dead sister, and as Margaret comes forward, he puts his arm around her.*

1161. T I T L E : ¶Morning.

1162. M L S : *a servant and Lynch emerge from their front door and see Gus's body. Lynch reaches down and takes the paper pinned to Gus's shoulder. As he reads, he gasps, "Oh, no!"*

1163. M S : *from across the street, Stoneman's servant and two other men see, and run out left.*

1164. M L S : *as in 1162. Stoneman's servant and the two men rush in from the right. Lynch gives an order, and the men pick up the dead man and follow Lynch out right.*

1165. T I T L E : ¶Lynch accepts the challenge by ordering negro militia reinforcements to fill the streets.

1166. M L S : *Stoneman looks down at Gus's body lying on the floor of his study. As Lynch puts on his hat and exits left, Stoneman orders the body to be removed.*

1167. MLS: *as in 1164. Lynch enters right, and on his porch he turns, with clenched fists, and curses, "Son of a bitch!" He goes in.*

1168. TITLE: ¶Having embroiled Lynch in the uprising, Stoneman takes his temporary departure to avoid the consequences.

1169. MLS: *Stoneman comes through the gate on the right, followed by a servant carrying bags. Stoneman glances to his left and right before entering the waiting carriage. They drive off as the camera pans slightly to the left.*

1170. TITLE: ¶The Clans prepare for action.

1171. *Fade in.* MS: *Ben holds up Flora's little Confederate flag and looks away as he dips it twice in a basin of water held by a fellow Clansman. He wrings it out and holds it aloft again.*

1172. TITLE: ¶"Brethren, this flag bears the red stain of the life of a Southern woman, a priceless sacrifice on the altar of an outraged civilization."

1173. MS: *as in 1171. Ben takes a burning cross from a Clansman behind him and holds it and the flag aloft as the Clansmen and a man in a dark coat and hat look on.*

1174. TITLE: ¶"Here I raise the ancient symbol of an unconquered race of men, the fiery cross of old Scotland's hills . . . I quench its flames in the sweetest blood that ever stained the sands of Time!"

1175. M S: *as in 1173. Ben quenches the fiery cross in the basin and hands it to the man in street clothes. The man listens to Ben's instructions, puts the cross under his coat, runs back to his horse, and rides off.*

1176. L S: *the man rides forward along a tree-lined road and out left.*

1177. M S: *as in 1175. Ben looks down, overcome by emotion, as a fellow Clansman turns and puts his arms around him. Fade out.*

1178. T I T L E: ¶The summons delivered to the Titan of the adjoining county to disarm all blacks that night.

1179. L S: *the rider comes forward, stops by a signal flare and blows a whistle.*

1180. Fade in. M L S: *behind the foliage, crouching Clansmen rise.*

1181. M L S: *the rider continues to blow the whistle.*

1182. M L S: *as in 1180. The hiding Clansmen start to move toward the left behind the foliage.*

1183. L S: *as in 1179. Clansmen emerge from the foliage on the right, and the rider hands over the cross. He delivers his message and rides off.*

1184. T I T L E: ¶Spies dispatched to hunt out whites in possession of the costume of the Ku Klux.
¶The penalty—death.

1185. M S: *Lynch, in his office, instructs two men, and they exit to the rear. He thrusts his hands in his pockets and starts to pace about angrily.*

1186. M L S: *Margaret enters the Cameron parlor from the rear and comes forward, as Dr. Cameron enters from the right and exits left. Margaret takes a Clan costume from beneath her skirt and stuffs it into a pillowcase, which she hides under a cushion on the couch. In the rear, the back door opens, and a spy crawling on his hands and knees can be seen peering in.*

1187. M C U: *the spy looks in from under the curtain in front of the door.*

1188. M L S: *as in 1186. Margaret stuffs the costume under the cushion on the couch and the spy departs. As she turns, Margaret gasps, realizing that the double doors to the parlor are open. She hastens to the back door and bends down to check under the curtain, then looks forward to the couch to check the sightline, in case anyone had been spying on her.*

1189. M S: *as in 1185. Lynch enters his office from the left with a glass in his hand. He drinks from the glass and reels slightly as he puts down the glass and looks left.*

1190. M L S: *as in 1188. Margaret closes the double doors and comes forward, shaking her hands anxiously. She glances back toward the doors, checks the hiding place of the Clan costume once more, and decides to stop worrying about it.*

1191. T I T L E: ¶Lynch happy at last to wreak vengeance on Cameron House.

1192. M S: *as in 1189. Lynch starts toward the rear of his office, when two men burst in and deliver a message. Lynch pushes them out and turns, clenching his fist and looking pleased. He calls in a soldier standing out in the hall, comes forward to his desk, and writes an order.*

1193. TITLE: ¶The bitterness of ideals crushed.
1194. MS: *Elsie sits at her vanity table, fixing her hair. She brings her hand up to her face and looks up unhappily.*
1195. *Fade in.* MS: *as in 1190. Mrs. Cameron enters the parlor left, followed by Dr. Cameron and Margaret. She sits down, and her husband and daughter comfort her.*
1196. TITLE: ¶The scalawag white Captain, in accordance with the Carpetbaggers' policy, makes the arrest.
1197. MS: *the Captain and soldiers enter right and approach the front door of Cameron Hall. The Captain sends men to the left and right and then knocks.*
1198. MS: *as in 1195. Mrs. Cameron rises and approaches the door on the right.*
1199. MS: *as in 1197. The Captain and two soldiers wait at the front door.*
1200. MS: *as in 1198. Mrs. Cameron goes through the parlor door on the right.*
1201. MLS: *from the rear left of the hall, Mrs. Cameron looks forward anxiously.*
1202. MS: *as in 1199. The Captain and soldiers go through the front door.*
1203. MLS: *as in 1201. The Captain and soldiers enter the hall right and go toward Mrs. Cameron.*
1204. MS: *as in 1200. Mrs. Cameron and Margaret quickly shut the parlor door.*
1205. MLS: *as in 1203. The soldiers start to beat down the door on the left.*
1206. MS: *as in 1204. Dr. Cameron tells his wife and daughter to open the door.*
1207. MLS: *as in 1205. The soldier continues to smash at the door with his rifle.*
1208. MS: *as in 1206. The Captain and two soldiers burst into the parlor, and Dr. Cameron is placed under arrest. The spy/soldier points to the couch and the Captain lifts up the cushion and looks it over. He digs under another cushion and withdraws a Clan costume, which Margaret tries to take from him. As they struggle, Dr. Cameron steps forward and tries to assist Margaret, but he is pulled back. The Captain pushes Margaret away, and when Dr. Cameron resists arrest, he is thrown onto the couch. He is lifted from the couch and led through the door to the hall.*
1209. MS: *as in 1202. Dr. Cameron is led, struggling, through the front door onto the porch and out to the right. The Captain follows, carrying the Clan costume, as Mrs. Cameron, Margaret, and Mammy look on in help-less distress.*
1210. MCU: *Lynch comes forward on his porch and looks out to the right.*
1211. MS: *Dr. Cameron is pushed through the gate and brought forward. The group pauses as the Captain comes to the front to speak to Dr. Cameron.*
1212. MCU: *as in 1210. Lynch looks on from his porch and smiles.*
1213. MS: *as in 1211. As the Captain speaks, Dr. Cameron clenches his fists in impotent rage, before he is pushed forward and out to the right. An on-looker in the background laughs hard.*

1214. MS: *as in 1209. On the porch, Mrs. Cameron struggles with Margaret and Mammy, then collapses on a chair as Margaret rushes out to the left.*
1215. MLS: *Margaret runs in from the right and enters the Stoneman house.*
1216. TITLE: ¶Appealing to Elsie Stoneman to have her father intervene.
1217. MS: *as in 1194. Elsie is sitting at her vanity table when Margaret rushes in from the rear. Margaret is hysterically incoherent, but when Elsie shakes her, she begins to explain.*
1218. MS: *as in 1214. On the porch, Mammy tries to comfort Mrs. Cameron. She leaves Mrs. Cameron and turns to face the street.*
1219. MS: *as in 1217. As Margaret explains, Elsie brings her hand to her mouth in shock, and Margaret begins to sob on her shoulder.*
1220. MS: *as in 1218. Mammy starts down the porch steps, wailing and rubbing her eyes.*
1221. MS: *as in 1213. On the street, the amused onlooker is doubled over in helpless laughter.*
1222. MS: *as in 1220. Mammy is infuriated, and she rolls up her sleeves and exits right.*
1223. MS: *as in 1221. The laughing man does not see Mammy coming through the gate behind him. She comes forward to face him and then knocks him to the ground with a single blow, steps over his body, and goes back through the gate and out right.*
1224. TITLE: ¶The faithful souls take a hand.
1225. MS: *as in 1222. Jake comes onto the porch from the right and Mrs. Cameron explains to him what has happened. Mammy enters right, pushes Jake forward, and follows him out to the right.*
1226. MS: *as in 1223. The man who was laughing is staggering to his feet as Mammy pushes Jake through the gate. As Jake goes out to the right, Mammy knocks the man down again and, shaking her fist, follows Jake out.*
1227. MS: *as in 1219. Elsie embraces Margaret and sends her out the door, then hurries forward and starts to dress.*
1228. MLS: *Margaret comes forward quickly in the hall, pauses and pulls back her hair, and exits right.*
1229. MLS: *as in 1226. Mrs. Cameron comes through the gate onto the street, followed by Margaret, who tries to restrain her. They exit right.*
1230. MLS: *Elsie dashes into her father's room from the left and looks about frantically. She sees a servant in the hall, and asks her father's whereabouts. When the servant is unable to help, Elsie runs out to the left.*
1231. TITLE: ¶The master in chains paraded before his former slaves.
1232. MLS: *the Captain leads Dr. Cameron into the slave quarters and stops near a group to show off his captive. A woman spits at Dr. Cameron's feet and leads the others in berating him. The Captain takes Dr. Cameron off to the rear, and the slaves follow, jeering and taunting the handcuffed man.*

1233. TITLE: ¶Hoping to effect a rescue, the faithful souls pretend to join the mockers.

1234. *Fade in.* MLS: *Jake and Mammy come forward and talk to a man standing on a wagon. Jake points to the right.*

1235. MLS: *as in 1229. Phil enters from the left and comes forward quickly along the sidewalk in front of Cameron Hall. He looks anxiously ahead as he exits right.*

1236. MLS: *as in 1234. Jake and Mammy continue to talk to the wagoner, who agrees to help them.*

1237. MLS: *as in 1232. The rowdy group of slaves taunts Dr. Cameron and pulls at his hair. The Captain pulls him out to the right.*

1238. MS: *the Captain drags Dr. Cameron in from the right. They stop, the Captain laughs, and they exit left as Dr. Cameron is pushed by a guard.*

1239. MLS: *as in 1236. Dr. Cameron is yanked in from the right by the Captain, and they stop next to the wagon as Jake comes forward.*

1240. TITLE: ¶"Is I yo' equal, cap'n —jes like any white man?"

1241. MLS: *as in 1239. Jake gestures to the Captain.*

1242. MCU: *Mammy has her arms around the two soldiers, who are laughing. She steals a glance back.*

1243. MS: *Jake laughs uproariously with the Captain.*

1244. MCU: *as in 1242. Mammy, laughing hard, turns and puts her arms around the two soldiers. She glances back.*

1245. MLS: *as in 1238. Mrs. Cameron and Margaret rush in from the right, followed by Phil. They stop suddenly when they see what is happening, and Margaret puts her arms around her mother.*

1246. MLS: *as in 1241. Jake continues to laugh ostentatiously.*

1247. MLS: *as in 1243. Jake jabs at Dr. Cameron's shoulder.*

1248. MLS: *Mammy looks back and then pushes the two soldiers to the ground with the weight of her whole body.*

1249. MLS: *as in 1246. Jake punches the Captain in the face and he falls to the ground, as Mammy pummels the two soldiers pinned under her. Jake quickly assists Dr. Cameron onto the wagon.*

1250. MS: *the soldiers kick their legs and flail their arms in an effort to wrestle free of Mammy.*

1251. MLS: *as in 1249. Jake goes over to Mammy.*

1252. MS: *as in 1245. Phil pulls out a pistol and rushes out left as Mrs. Cameron and Margaret look on in distress.*

1253. MLS: *as in 1251. Phil punches the Captain in the face as he attempts to rise.*

1254. *Fade in.* MS: *Elsie enters left and sees what is happening. She involuntarily points to the right and raises her hand to her mouth in shock.*

1255. MS: *Phil fires a shot and one of the soldiers falls at his feet. He kneels beside the dead man.*

1256. MS: *as in 1252. Mrs. Cameron and Margaret bring their hands up to their mouths in fright and rush out to the left.*

1257. MLS: *as in 1253. Margaret and her mother run in from the right and Mrs. Cameron quickly gets onto the wagon.*

1258. MS: *as in 1254. Elsie looks on anxiously for a moment and rushes out to the right.*

1259. MS: *the excited group in the wagon call to Phil.*

1260. MLS: *as in 1257. Phil hops onto the wagon as it pulls away, and the Captain staggers after the fleeing group for a few yards before turning and running back and out to the right.*

1261. TITLE: ¶Elsie learns her brother has slain a negro in the rescue of Dr. Cameron.

1262. MS: *as in 1258. Elsie and the Captain walk in backwards from the right, gesturing in the direction of the scene of the crime. He explains what happened, and exits left. Elsie looks bewildered as she comes forward a few steps, pauses, and runs out to the right.*

1263. MLS: *Iris of the departing wagon.*

1264. TITLE: ¶Awaiting her father's expected arrival.

1265. MLS: *as in 1230. Elsie rushes into her father's study, looks about anxiously, clasping her hands, and falls exhausted into a chair. Suddenly, she sits up and turns.*

1266. MLS: *the Captain runs in from the lower left, stops to blow a whistle, and enters a building on the right.*

1267. LS: *the wagon moves away down a country road as Jake urges the wagoner to go faster.*

1268. MLS: *a squad of black soldiers runs forward and out left.*

1269. TITLE: ¶The social lion of the new aristocracy.

1270. MS: *in Lynch's dining room, two elegantly dressed mulatto women remove their shawls, as Lynch, their escorts, and two servants assist them and position the chairs.*

1271. MLS: *as in 1260. The squad of soldiers runs in from the right and goes down the street toward the rear. The leader comes back and orders one of his men to stay with the man Phil shot. The soldier comes forward and kneels beside the dead man.*

1272. MCU: *Elsie sits, waiting patiently. Fade out.*

1273. MS: *as in 1270. As Lynch's guests drink and laugh, he stares ahead.*

1274. MLS: *as the wagon enters left and goes down a small bank, a wheel comes off, and the escaping party scrambles out.*

1275. TITLE: ¶The little cabin occupied by two Union veterans becomes their refuge.

1276. *Fade in.* LS: *a small cabin sits isolated in an open space.*

1277. MLS: *the cabin.*

1278. *Fade in.* M L S : *inside the cabin, a man is cooking at the fireplace, while another man and a small girl look on.*

1279. M S : *the man, leaning forward, adjusts the position of the frying pan on the fire.*

1280. E C U : *with a long-handled fork, the bacon is turned in the pan.*

1281. M S : *as in 1279. As the man cooks, the young girl and the other man continue to look on intently.*

1282. L S : *as in 1276. Iris opens completely. The fugitive group enters left and makes its way across the open space toward the cabin.*

1283. M L S : *as in 1277. Phil runs in from the left, followed by the Camerons. They go to the front door.*

1284. M L S : *as in 1278. The man puts down the cooking fork and rises. He comes forward, picks up a lantern, and exits through a door on the right.*

1285. M S : *the man enters left and sets down the lantern. He walks to the front door on the right and opens it.*

1286. M L S : *as in 1283. The veteran appears on the threshold of his cabin, and the fugitive party crowds around him.*

1287. T I T L E :   ¶The former enemies of North and South are united again in common defence of their Aryan birthright.

1288. M S : *as in 1285. The Camerons come forward, and as Dr. Cameron explains, the man holds his lantern up to Dr. Cameron's face. He smiles and heartily shakes Dr. Cameron's hand.*

1289. M L S : *as in 1284. The young girl, who has been looking through the door on the right, climbs into bed and pulls up the covers, as the veteran seated by the fireplace looks on.*

1290. L S : *the leader of the search party calls his men, who are fording a stream in the rear. They come forward and follow him out to the left.*

1291. M S : *as in 1288. The veteran leads the Camerons through the door on the left.*

1292. M L S : *as in 1289. The veteran holds open the door, and Mrs. Cameron enters and sits by the fire. Margaret and her father come in, and when Phil enters, he closes the door behind him. The veteran introduces his friend.*

1293. T I T L E :   ¶Her father failing to return, and ignorant of Lynch's designs on her, Elsie goes to the mulatto leader for help.

1294. *Fade in.* M S : *as in 1265. Elsie rises suddenly from her chair with an idea, and dashes out to the left.*

1295. L S : *as in 1274. Two black men on horseback examine the broken wagon, and start riding off toward the right.*

1296. M S : *Elsie dashes in from the right, past a group of laughing sentries. She tries the door on the left and, finding it locked, asks a sentry to open it for her. He obliges, and they enter.*

1297. M S : *Elsie and the sentry come forward quickly. He exits left as she urges him to hurry.*

1298. M S : *in the inner room, Lynch is hosting a party. The sentry enters through the door in the rear and comes forward, through the drinking and laughing guests, to Lynch.*

1299. M S : *as in 1297. Elsie waits impatiently in Lynch's office.*

1300. M S : *as in 1298. The sentry salutes Lynch and exits through the door at the rear. Lynch puts down his drink, quickly excuses himself, and follows.*

1301. M C U, C V : *Lynch peers through the door on the left, and upon seeing Elsie, smiles to himself.*

1302. M S : *as in 1299. With her hand to her head in a distracted gesture, Elsie asks the sentry if he has delivered her message, and he nods.*

1303. M S, C V : *as in 1301. Lynch, still smiling, withdraws into the room.*

1304. M S : *as in 1300. Lynch comes through the door at the rear and orders a servant to clear the room. The servant asks the guests to leave.*

1305. M S, C V : *as in 1303. Lynch comes through the door, closes it behind him, and exits right.*

1306. M S : *as in 1302. Lynch enters his office from the left and indicates to Elsie that he will be with her in a moment. He goes toward the rear and tells the sentry to leave and close the door behind him. He comes forward and listens to Elsie's appeal. He shows surprise, and abruptly calls to the sentry, who opens the double doors and comes forward. As the sentry salutes, Lynch sits at his desk and begins to write.*

1307. M S : *as in 1304. Lynch's servants usher the guests out at the rear right. Fade out.*

1308. M S : *as in 1306. Lynch rises and gives the letter to the sentry, who leaves. Elsie picks up her cloak and prepares to go, but Lynch comes forward and detains her.*

1309. T I T L E : ¶Lynch's proposal of marriage.

1310. M S : *as in 1308. Elsie takes a step toward the door, but Lynch recalls her. He speaks to her, and she backs away from him slightly.*

1311. M C U, C V : *Lynch speaks, bringing his hands up to his heart.*

1312. M C U, C V : *Elsie stares at him.*

1313. M S, C V : *as in 1311. Lynch mutters something and juts out his lower lip.*

1314. M C U, C V : *as in 1312. Elsie opens her mouth, as if to speak, and draws back.*

1315. M S : *as in 1310. Elsie points to him angrily and threatens to have him horsewhipped. She turns and goes toward the door in the rear, but Lynch runs back, locks the door, and pockets the key. They both come forward, Lynch speaking and gesturing with agitation, and Elsie trying to calm him down.*

1316. T I T L E : ¶Lynch's reply to her threat of a horsewhipping for his insolence.

1317. MS: *as in 1315. Lynch steps to the window, flings aside the shade, and points out toward the street.*

1318. LS: *black soldiers jostle whites on the sidewalk and fire their rifles into the air.*

1319. MS: *as in 1317. Lynch points to himself and says to Elsie, "Those are my people!"*

1320. LS: *as in 1318. The black soldiers, now lined up in the street, discharge their guns in unison, as townsfolk on the sidewalk wave and cheer wildly.*

1321. MS: *as in 1319. Lynch lets the shade drop against the window as he turns toward Elsie and gestures with both hands.*

1322. TITLE: ¶"See! My people fill the streets. With them I will build a Black Empire and you as a Queen shall sit by my side."

1323. MS: *as in 1321. Lynch gestures widely with his arms as Elsie sinks into a chair. He kneels down and takes the hem of her blouse and brings it to his lips. Elsie draws back in horror, then rises, throws her hands in the air, and runs to the door. She pounds at the door and presses herself against it, as Lynch sits in a chair and grins.*

1324. MCU, CV: *Elsie turns, with her back pressed against the door, and draws her hands across her face.*

1325. MCU, CV: *as he speaks, Lynch gestures left toward the street and then points to himself and to Elsie.*

1326. MCU, CV: *as in 1324. Elsie pleads with him and holds out her arms.*

1327. MCU, CV: *as in 1325. Lynch smiles and rubs his hands against his thighs.*

1328. MCU, CV: *as in 1326. Elsie's eyes widen, she turns her body away from Lynch and screams.*

1329. *Fade in.* LS: *two Clansmen on horseback ride in from the right and pull up in front of a barn. One of them holds aloft a burning cross.*

1330. *Fade in.* LS: *a Clansman gallops in from the right and stops at a crossroads.*

1331. TITLE: ¶Summoning the Clans.

1332. MCU: *in front of the barn, one of the hooded horsemen holds up the burning cross and the other blows a whistle.*

1333. LS: *as in 1329. The two Clansmen ride forward and out left.*

1334. LS: *as in 1330. The horseman at the crossroads comes forward and goes out left.*

1335. *Fade in.* LS: *as in 1333. Five mounted Clansmen gallop in from the left in front of the barn and come forward and out left.*

1336. MS: *as in 1323. Elsie dashes from the door over to the window, but Lynch gets up off his knees, grabs her, and pushes her to the center of the room. He pleads with her as she turns away from him and clutches at her face in distress.*

1337. MLS: *two Clansmen—one of them carrying the fiery cross—gallop forward along a tree-shaded road and out left.*

1338. MS: *as in 1336. Lynch shakes a fist at Elsie and pounds his chest.*

1339. *Fade in.* LS: *the two Clansmen enter right and ride toward the rear down the center of the stream. Fade out.*

1340. MS: *as in 1338. Lynch, shouting, raises his fist and gestures toward the window.*

1341. MS: *as in 1307. In the parlor, the three startled servants hear.*

1342. MS: *as in 1340. Lynch calls out as Elsie cowers in fright.*

1343. MS: *as in 1341. One servant rushes to the door in the rear and opens it, as the other two look on in fright.*

1344. MCU, CV: *as in 1305. The servant comes through the door and exits right.*

1345. MS: *as in 1342. The servant enters left and Lynch speaks to him.*

1346. TITLE: ¶Lynch, drunk with wine and power, orders his henchmen to hurry preparations for a forced marriage.

1347. MS: *as in 1345. The servant exits to the left and Lynch turns to Elsie. He points to her and to himself, as she brings a hand up to her mouth in horror.*

1348. MCU, CV: *as in 1344. The servant dashes left through the door.*
1349. MS: *as in 1343. The servant comes through the door and immediately in-structs a fellow servant and sends him out to the right. He comes back into the room and begins to instruct the maid.*
1350. MS: *as in 1347. Elsie gestures helplessly as Lynch grins and tells her what he plans to do. She makes a dash out left toward the door.*
1351. MS, CV: *as in 1348. Elsie comes in right, flings herself against the door and tries to open it, struggling with the doorknob.*
1352. MS: *as in 1350. Lynch gestures to her to move away from the door and come back to him.*
1353. MS, CV: *as in 1351. Elsie turns to face Lynch. Her eyes are wide with fear.*
1354. *Fade in.* LS: *Clansmen ride in from the left, cross a shallow stream, and go out right.*
1355. MS: *as in 1352. Lynch beckons Elsie forward.*
1356. MS, CV: *as in 1353. As if hypnotized, Elsie walks toward him, out to the right.*
1357. MS: *as in 1355. Elsie enters left, goes to Lynch, and pleads with him.*
1358. *Fade in.* LS: *two Clansmen ride in from the right carrying a burning cross. They pause to give a signal, then ride out rear right.*

1359. MS: *as in 1357. Elsie pushes Lynch and makes a dash for the double doors in the rear. He chases after her, and she runs forward and pulls a chair to one side in an attempt to obstruct him.*

1360. *Fade in.* LS: *an army of Clansmen assembles in a large field. Ben is in the foreground.*

1361. MCU, CV: *Ben, attired elaborately in his Clan costume, sits astride his horse and looks from side to side.*

1362. LS: *as in 1358. At the crossroads, several Clansmen ride forward, pause, and gallop in a cloud of dust out to the right.*

1363. *Fade in.* LS: *as in 1360. In the background, a group of Clansmen rides in from the right and joins the assembly. Ben salutes them.*

1364. ELS: *silhouetted against the sky, Clansmen ride from left to right along the ridge of a hill.*

1365. MLS: *two Clansmen gallop forward along a road between a stream and a cornfield.*

1366. *Fade in/dissolve.* MLS: *the two Clansmen ride forward, one of them holding aloft a fiery cross, as the camera tracks back with them.*

1367. MS: *as in 1359. Lynch continues to hover close to Elsie, as she sinks momentarily into a chair, then rises and turns to go to the rear of the room. He grabs her as she tries to push past him.*

1368. MLS, SAV: *a carriage carrying Stoneman comes forward and goes out left. A group of blacks runs after the carriage and two men on horseback follow a few yards behind.*

1369. MS: *as in 1367. Flinging up her arms, Elsie falls back in a faint and Lynch supports her.*

1370. MLS: *the carriage comes to a stop and a servant alights as Stoneman stands in the carriage and acknowledges the cheers of the crowd.*

1371. MS: *as in 1369. Lynch has Elsie in his arms and is leaning over her, when he hears the commotion outside heralding Stoneman's arrival. He looks to the right.*

1372. MS: *Stoneman is helped from the carriage by the servant as the crowd waves and cheers.*

1373. MLS: *as in 1370. Stoneman enters Lynch's house on the left and the servant gets back into the carriage.*

1374. MS: *as in 1371. Lynch draws the unconscious Elsie closer to him.*

1375. MS: *as in 1296. Stoneman goes left to the door of Lynch's office and knocks with his cane.*

1376. MS: *as in 1374. Lynch hears the knock at the door, looks right, and turns back to look at the woman in his arms.*

1377. MS: *as in 1375. Stoneman questions the sentry standing at the door, and the sentry shakes his head. Stoneman knocks again, impatiently.*

1378. MS: *as in 1376. Lynch reluctantly pulls his gaze away from Elsie and listens to the knocking at the door.*

1379. MS: *as in 1377. Stoneman calls to Lynch through the closed door and pounds his cane on the floor. He turns to the guard, who again shakes his head.*

1380. MS: *as in 1378. Lynch looks right as he strokes Elsie's brow, then moves out left, dragging Elsie with him.*

1381. MS: *as in 1349. Lynch carries Elsie into the inner room and props her up in a chair, as the two servants look on. He instructs the maid to watch her.*

1382. MS: *as in 1379. Stoneman angrily turns to leave.*

1383. MS: *as in 1381. Lynch goes to the rear of the inner room and opens the door to his office.*

1384. MS: *as in 1380. Lynch enters right, groping in his pocket for the key. He goes to the double doors in the rear of his office and unlocks them.*

1385. MS: *as in 1382. Stoneman, hearing the key in the lock, turns and goes back to the door. The door opens, and he enters left.*

1386. MS: *as in 1384. Stoneman comes forward quickly, with a paper in his hand, and Lynch follows him closely.*

1387. LS: *as in 1363. The Clansmen continue to assemble in the field, and Ben salutes the new arrivals.*

1388. M S : *as in 1386. As Stoneman concludes his instructions and is turning to leave, Lynch detains him and speaks.*

1389. T I T L E : ¶"I want to marry a white woman."

1390. M S : *as in 1388. Stoneman smiles and congratulates him with a hearty slap on the shoulder and a handshake.*

1391. T I T L E : ¶The Clans being assembled in full strength, ride off on their appointed mission.

1392. *Fade in.* L S : *as in 1387. A group of assembling Clansmen rides forward to Ben, who salutes them* and leads the army of Clansmen out right.*

1393. T I T L E : ¶And meanwhile, other fates—

1394. M S : *inside the cabin, over the head of the little girl, Phil pleads with Margaret, who remains cool toward him.*

1395. M S : *as in 1390. As Stoneman turns to leave, Lynch speaks and gestures to the right, where Elsie is in the next room.*

1396. *Fade in.* M C U : *behind the unconscious Elsie, the servant holds up a goblet to the maid and taps it with his forefinger, indicating that Elsie has been drugged. Fade out.*

1397. M S : *as in 1395. Lynch points to himself and explains to Stoneman.*

1398. T I T L E : ¶"The lady I want to marry is your daughter."

1399. M S : *as in 1397. Stoneman responds angrily and clenches his fist as if to strike Lynch. As Stoneman turns to leave, Lynch grabs his arm.*

1400. T I T L E : ¶The town given over to crazed negroes brought in by Lynch and Stoneman to overawe the whites.

1401. L S : *left side masked. The square is filled with blacks in a state of agitation and excitement.*

1402. M S : *as in 1399. Lynch becomes angry and calls in a guard. As the guard enters, Stoneman realizes Elsie is in the next room, and he points to the left.*

1403. L S : *a column of Clansmen on horseback rides forward down a straight road and out to the left.*

1404. M S : *as in 1381. Elsie regains consciousness as the maid leads the servant out to the rear right. The servant is stopped by a guard at the door, but makes his way past, as Elsie rises and flings herself at the window on the right.*

1405. T I T L E : ¶White spies disguised.

1406. M S : *two men on horseback are looking about, when their attention is attracted by something out to the left.*

1407. M C U : *Elsie screams from behind the closed window.*

1408. M C U : *Elsie picks up a bottle and raises it to smash the window.*

---

*In the Museum of Modern Art print, this shot (1392) has been edited into three shots, with the title (shot 1391) intervening between Ben's salute and his order to march out to the right.

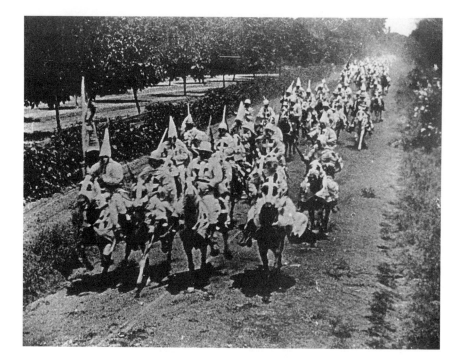

1409. MCU: *as in 1407. The window is smashed, and Elsie rushes forward and begins to scream for help as the maid comes up behind her and attempts to restrain her.*

1410. MLS: *the two spies turn and start to make their way down the street.*

1411. MCU: *as in 1409. Elsie screams frantically as the maid struggles with her.*

1412. MLS: *as in 1408. The maid pulls Elsie away from the window.*

1413. MS: *as in 1402. Stoneman hears his daughter's screams and attempts to go to her, but Lynch overpowers him and shoves him violently into a chair.*

1414. MS: *as in 1404. As Elsie and the maid struggle, the servant rushes forward from the rear right.*

1415. MLS: *as in 1410. As the spies ride away down the street and out to the right, a guard standing at Lynch's door looks after them with suspicion.*

1416. MS: *as in 1414. Elsie faints and is pulled back into the chair by the servants.*

1417. MS: *as in 1413. Lynch holds Stoneman down with one hand as he angrily pounds his chest and points to the inner room. Stoneman dazedly but firmly shakes his head.*

1418. MLS: *as in 1295. The two horsemen have brought a squad to see the broken wagon. They pause for a moment, looking at the wagon, and follow the squad leader out to the right.*

1419. MLS: *in the cabin, Dr. and Mrs. Cameron sit by the fire with the two veterans, and Margaret sits in a chair on the right, with the little girl on her knee. Phil opens the door and goes out right.*

1420. MLS: *Phil enters the outer room through the door on the left and goes over to the window on the right. The wagoner, Jake, and Mammy are sleeping.*

1421. MCU: *Margaret looks away from the door and turns to stare out left.*

1422. CU, CV: *Margaret stares sadly.*

1423. MCU: *as in 1421. The little girl touches a tear on Margaret's cheek, and Margaret draws the child to her.*

1424. LS: *soldiers come in from the left and make their way across the open ground toward the cabin.*

1425. MLS: *as in 1420. Phil closes the door on the right, and the wagoner rises from his chair.*

1426. LS: *a shot is fired from the cabin, and the soldiers drop to the ground. They return the fire.*

1427. MLS: *as in 1425. The veteran rushes in from the left and goes over to Phil, who has a gun in his hand. They come forward together, and Phil points to the left.*

1428. MLS: *as in 1419. Dr. Cameron opens the door on the right and goes through, as Mrs. Cameron and Margaret huddle at the center of the room with the little girl.*

1429. MLS: *as in 1427. Dr. Cameron comes in from the right and joins Phil and the veteran, who try to persuade him to return to the inner room.*

1430. LS: *as in 1426. Under continuing fire from the cabin, the soldiers rise and start to retreat.*

1431. MLS: *as in 1429. The veteran roughly leads a protesting Dr. Cameron to the left.*

1432. TITLE: ¶The Union veterans refuse to allow Dr. Cameron to give himself up.

1433. MS: *the veteran brings Dr. Cameron into the inner room through the door on the right, and explains the old man's intention to his partner. The partner shouts, "No!" and raises his gun to show their commitment to the Camerons' defense. As the partner goes to the rear and starts shooting through the window, the veteran and Dr. Cameron embrace. Dr. Cameron smiles to himself and pushes up his sleeves in excitement, as the veteran runs to the rear and picks up a rifle behind the door. Dr. Cameron turns in circles, looking for a gun, as his wife cowers in fright.*

1434. LS: *as in 1430. The soldiers crouch on the ground at a safer distance from the cabin, as more soldiers enter rear left and approach the cabin from the other side, through the smoke.*

1435. LS: *the column of hooded horsemen gallops forward down a road and out left.*

1436. M S : *as in 1416. As the maid struggles with the gagged Elsie, the servant standing behind the chair looks up in response to noise from the street.*

1437. L S : *as in 1401. Left side masked. Confusion reigns in the crowded street.*

1438. C U : *Elsie, exhausted and with a gag in her mouth, flutters and closes her eyes. The servant's clenched fist is a few inches from her cheek.*

1439. T I T L E : ¶While helpless whites look on.

1440. *Fade in.* M S : *a woman seated in the foreground prays over a Bible. A younger woman kneels at her side. Behind them, a father and daughter, arm in arm, look out the window. Fade out.*

1441. L S : *as in 1437. Left side masked. A white man is pushed to the ground and the mob clamors around him as he is beaten.*

1442. M S : *another white family is gathered in their parlor. Two members stand to one side of the window, looking out.*

1443. L S : *as in 1441. Left side masked. The riotous mob becomes more unruly as the white man is thrown onto his back and beaten with a rifle by a black soldier.*

1444. M S : *in another house, a man with a wooden leg stares out the window. His daughter has her arm around his neck, and his wife, seated nearby, holds a baby.*

1445. T I T L E : ¶Ku Klux sympathizers victims of the black mobs.

1446. L S : *in the middle of a packed crowd on the street in front of Cameron Hall, a man is bounced up and down on a board until he falls forward. In the foreground on the left, a tarred and feathered man is jostled by the crowd.*

1447. M C U : *the tarred and feathered man is pushed around violently by the crowd. The man being bounced on the board is visible at the upper right.*

1448. L S : *as in 1446. The crowd continues to push and shove around the man being bounced up and down and around the tarred and feathered man on the left.*

1449. M S : *the father of another white family looks through the window as his wife lies on her sickbed in the foreground and his two children sit arm in arm in a chair.*

1450. L S : *as in 1443. A fight breaks out among black soldiers in the foreground of the rioting crowd.*

1451. M L S : *as two white men are carried from the jail on the right and taken into the crowd, they are beaten with sticks.*

1452. *Fade in.* M S : *in the jailhouse, the jailers stand helplessly in front of an open cell, as one of the men paces about anxiously and looks to the left.*

1453. M L S : *as in 1451. The frenzy continues outside the jailhouse as another white man is carried into the crowd.*

1454. M S : *as in 1452. The jailers listen to the commotion somewhere off to the left. Fade out.*

1455. M L S : *as in 1453. The crowd presses against the jailhouse door, beating it with clubs and rifles.*

1456. E L S , A V : *in the distance, the column of galloping Clansmen moves down the road from the left and out on the right.*

1457. L S : *as in 1450. In the foreground, soldiers in the crowd jostle a young black woman and start tearing at her clothes.*

1458. L S : *the two white spies stop the column of advancing Clansmen and give their report, and the column rides forward and out lower right.*

1459. M L S : *as in 1455. The mob, growing even more violent, fiercely batters the jailhouse door.*

1460. M C U : *the Clansmen gallop forward, the camera tracking back with them. Ben, at the head of the column, lowers his hood.*

1461. L S : *the Clansmen enter the town from the rear left and come forward down the street. The leader, waving a pistol in the air, brings the column to a halt.*

1462. L S : *iris widens. As the Clansmen enter the square from the left and right rear, black soldiers at the edge of the crowd fire at the horsemen.*

1463. L S : *the horsemen ride forward down the street and out to the left, firing their guns.*

1464. L S : *as in 1462. Clansmen ride from left to right in the rear, as black soldiers, forming a ring around the agitated crowd, fire.*

1465. L S : *the mob in front of Cameron Hall moves to the rear, to follow the black troops moving from left to right down the street.*

1466. M S : *black soldiers lined up by a wall fire out to the left.*

1467. M S : *as in 1417. Lynch in his office hears the commotion and goes left to the window. Stoneman sits dazed and nodding in a chair.*

1468. L S : *Clansmen gallop forward and out left. One horseman is shot and falls to the ground.*

1469. M L S : *as the black riflemen along the wall fire, one is hit and falls forward.*

1470. L S : *as in 1463. A riderless horse comes forward through the smoke, and another Clansman is shot and falls from his mount. In the rear, a group of Clansmen stops and turns.*

1471. M S : *as in 1467. Lynch orders the guard at the door to watch Stoneman, then he exits left.*

1472. M S : *as in 1466. The black soldiers at the brick wall fire.*

1473. L S : *as in 1470. Clansmen gallop down the street out left. A horse and rider fall to the ground.*

1474. M S : *as in 1472. The soldiers fire from their position at the brick wall.*

1475. L S : *as in 1473. A Clansman is shot and falls from his horse, and the horse goes out left.*

1476. L S : *as in 1434. Soldiers lay siege to the isolated cabin from all sides.*

1477. MLS: *as in 1431. In the cabin, Phil fires out the window on the right, while Mammy huddles on the floor and the wagoner ducks below the window in the rear.*

1478. LS: *as in 1476. The soldiers advance slowly, firing at the cabin.*

1479. MLS: *as in 1428. In the inner room of the cabin, the veterans fire out the window, while Mrs. Cameron, Margaret, and the child huddle near the fireplace.*

1480. MCU: *Mrs. Cameron, sobbing with fright, holds the child tightly, and Margaret puts her arms around her mother.*

1481. LS: *as in 1464. The excited mob is gathered in the foreground as Clansmen ride from left to right in the rear and black soldiers fire at them.*

1482. MS: *Lynch emerges from his house amid the fighting, and goes out right.*

1483. MLS: *as in 1477. In the cabin, the wagoner ducks again.*

1484. LS: *Clansmen enter upper right and gallop across the fields toward the cabin.*

1485. MLS: *the four Clansmen fire pistols out to the left as they ride forward.*

1486. LS: *as in 1484. As the Clansmen approach, the soldiers fire at them.*

1487. MLS: *as in 1485. Two of the hooded horsemen turn and ride off to the right. The other two are shot, and one falls with his horse.*

1488. MLS: *as in 1479. Inside the cabin, Dr. Cameron pushes aside the veteran and looks out the window.*

1489. MLS: *as in 1487. The second of the two Clansmen shot also falls to the ground with his horse.*

1490. MLS: *as in 1486. Soldiers move across the fields through the thick smoke.*

1491. MLS: *as in 1488. Dr. Cameron leaves the window and hurries forward and to the left. The camera pans slightly to the left.*

1492. MLS: *as in 1489. Soldiers approach the fallen Clansmen with raised bayonets.*

1493. MLS: *as in 1491. Dr. Cameron tries to reassure his wife for a moment and then moves back to the rear.*

1494. LS: *the two Clansmen who were not hit by the soldiers besieging the cabin come through the gate from the field and onto the road. They gallop off left.*

1495. *Fade in.* LS: *as in 1481. The crowd in the square is gathered behind a line of black soldiers, who fire at a group of mounted Clansmen in the rear.*

1496. MLS: *the black rifleman fire. Two are hit by Clansmen's bullets, and they fall.*

1497. LS: *as in 1495. The Clansmen ride toward the crowd and the line of riflemen protecting them. The panicked crowd scatters.*

1498. MS, CV: *the Clansmen gallop forward, firing pistols. The camera tracks back with them.*

1499. MLS: *as in 1496. The riflemen step back and start to retreat out to the right.*
1500. LS: *as in 1497. The mob flees and the black soldiers move out of the way of the advancing Clansmen.*
1501. MS: *as in 1474. The riflemen at the brick wall retreat.*
1502. CU: *as in 1438. Elsie, gagged and held down in the chair, rolls her eyes deliriously.*
1503. MS: *as in 1471. Stoneman attempts to rise, but the guard pushes him back into the chair with his bayonet.*
1504. MLS: *the mob and the black soldiers run forward across the square as the camera tracks back with them.*
1505. LS: *as in 1500. A group of the mounted Clansmen gallops forward across the square littered with bodies and exits left and right. A larger group of Clansmen remains in the rear.*
1506. MS: *as in 1482. As fleeing soldiers dash from right to left past his front door, Lynch comes in from the right, glances back, and quickly goes in.*
1507. LS: *as in 1465. The crowd, pursued by Clansmen, comes swarming forward down the street in front of Cameron Hall.*
1508. LS: *the crowd runs down the street toward the rear.*
1509. LS: *as in 1507. The black riflemen bring up the rear, running forward down the street.*

1510. LS: *as in 1508. Clansmen enter from right and left, firing at the fleeing crowd.*

1511. MS: *as in 1436. As Lynch's servants run in fright to the rear and exit right, Elsie removes the gag and screams. As she rises from the chair, Lynch grabs her and carries her through the rear door.*

1512. MLS: *Lynch enters left carrying Elsie. Stoneman rises and tries to stop him, but Lynch pushes him down, and several guards burst into the room through the double doors in the rear.*

1513. LS: *as in 1509. Clansmen ride down the street past Cameron Hall.*

1514. LS: *Clansmen enter rear left and foreground right and stop in front of Lynch's house. They dismount and quickly go in.*

1515. MLS: *as in 1512. As the Clansmen burst into Lynch's office, Elsie pulls herself away from Lynch and goes to her father. A shot is fired, and the guard at left falls. A Clansman pushes Lynch violently, and he falls into a chair, where two Clansmen hold him down. The leader turns to Elsie.*

1516. MCU: *the leader puts an arm around Elsie and lifts his hood, and she sees that it is Ben.*

1517. MLS: *as in 1515. Elsie clings to Ben, as the Clansmen hold down Lynch.*

1518. MLS: *as in 1493. In the cabin, the two veterans and Dr. Cameron crouch on either side of and beneath the window in the rear of the inner room. Mrs. Cameron, Margaret, and the child still huddle near the fireplace on the left.*

1519. MCU: *the veteran shoots out the window with his rifle, and his partner does the same with his pistol. Dr. Cameron turns to each and grins with excitement.*

1520. TITLE: ¶News of the danger to the little party in the besieged cabin.

1521. LS: *two mounted Clansmen enter left and gallop down the street toward Lynch's house.*

1522. LS: *the two horsemen enter right and report to the Clansmen assembled in front of Lynch's house.*

1523. MLS: *as in 1517. A Clansman enters Lynch's office from the rear and makes his way through the group to Ben. He excitedly reports the news to his leader, and Ben follows him out. Elsie turns and throws herself into her father's arms, and as Lynch is led out, all but one of the Clansmen exit to the rear. Fade out.*

1524. MLS: *a Clansman leaps onto his horse from the porch railing on the left, and the Clansmen follow him out on the right.*

1525. LS: *Ben leads the Clansmen forward past his house and out left.*

1526. LS, CV: *as in 1478. The besiegers crowd around the cabin.*

1527. MS: *inside the cabin, Dr. Cameron comforts his wife, as Margaret, clutching his elbow, turns away from her father and holds out her arms to the right.*

1528. MS: *Phil fires a rifle out the window on the right and smiles to himself.*

1529. MS: *as in 1527. Margaret leaves her frightened parents and goes out the door on the right.*

1530. MLS: *as in 1483. Margaret enters the outer room on the left and runs over to Phil. They embrace, and Jake urges them to get down.*

1531. MS: *blacks with large sticks and soldiers with rifles batter at the door to the cabin.*

1532. MCU: *as in 1528. Margaret throws her arms around Phil, and at the very moment they embrace, the window on the right is smashed off its hinges and an arm gropes toward them. Phil swiftly turns and raises his pistol.*

1533. MS: *as in 1531. The besiegers continue to clamor at the front door of the cabin.*

1534. MS: *as in 1532. A man starts to climb through the window on the right, and Phil beats him on the head with his pistol. The man withdraws.*

1535. MS: *as in 1533. The soldiers beat at the front door with the butts of their rifles.*

1536. MCU: *Mammy stands by an open window, poised with a club in her hands. When a soldier appears at the window, she hits him on the head with the club, and he falls back.*

1537. LS: *a large number of Clansmen gallop down a road from the right and out on the left.*

1538. MCU: *as in 1536. Again, Mammy hits a soldier on the head as he attempts to enter through the window.*

1539. MS: *as in 1535. The commotion at the front door continues.*

1540. MS: *as in 1518. As the veteran tries to comfort the child crouched down by the bed, Dr. Cameron points to the door, and the veteran dashes out to the right.*

1541. MLS: *as in 1530. The veteran enters left and rushes over to Margaret and Phil. As a soldier succeeds in pushing his rifle through the window, the veteran quickly leads Margaret back to the inner room.*

1542. MS: *as in 1540. Margaret and Phil rush into the inner room, and Mammy and the veteran follow, closing the door quickly behind them.*

1543. MS: *the besiegers succeed in beating down the door of the cabin and two of them enter.*

1544. MLS: *as in 1541. A group of soldiers bursts in and forces Jake and the wagoner back. When the wagoner resists, he is hit on the head.*

1545. MS: *as in 1542. A soldier pushes open the door to the inner room. Phil knocks the intruder on the head with his pistol, and with the veteran, pushes the door shut. Mammy comes over and adds her weight. In the rear, the veteran's partner fires through the window.*

1546. MLS: *as in 1544. A soldier aims his bayonet at the wagoner's chest as Jake is beaten.*

1547. MS: *as in 1545. Dr. Cameron tries to comfort his terrified wife while the veteran leans on the door to keep it closed. Mammy stands in readiness with a soup ladle in her hand.*

1548. MLS: *as in 1546. The wagoner is shot and falls. Near him, a soldier whom Phil has hit also falls.*

1549. MLS: *Dr. Cameron and the veteran turn a table on its side and wedge it against the door, while Phil and Margaret try to keep the door on the left closed.*

1550. MS: *as soldiers beat on the door to the inner room with sticks and rifles, "white-arm" Joe rams the door with his body.*

1551. MLS: *as in 1549. The besieged party struggles to keep the doors closed.*

1552. LS: *the column of Clansmen gallops forward down the road and out left.*

1553. MLS: *as in 1548. As two soldiers and "white-arm" Joe continue to batter the door to the inner room, a soldier picks up a white handkerchief from the floor.*

1554. MLS: *as in 1551. In the inner room, the struggle to hold the doors continues.*

1555. MS: *using their rifles as battering rams, soldiers force the back door.*

1556. MS: *Phil falls back as the back door is pushed open by the attackers. Margaret swipes at a soldier with a bottle.*

1557. MLS: *the Clansmen ride forward as the camera tracks back with them.*

1558. MS: *as in 1556. As a soldier grabs Margaret, Dr. Cameron comes forward and pulls his daughter away from the attacker, and Phil pushes the door shut. Margaret falls at her father's feet, and he holds a gun above her.*

1559. MLS: *the Clansmen continue to gallop forward at full speed as the camera tracks back with them.*

1560. MLS: *as in 1553. The soldier with the handkerchief shows his find to those battering the door.*

1561. MS: *the veteran struggles with one hand to shut the straining door. In his other hand, he holds a rifle above his daughter's head.*

1562. MCU: *the little girl holds Mrs. Cameron in a tight embrace, as the rifle hovers above their heads.*

1563. CU: *tears roll down the terrified child's cheeks.*

1564. MS: *as in 1555. Exulting in their imminent triumph, one of the soldiers smiles as he rams the back door with his rifle.*

1565. MS: *as in 1558. Phil leans despairingly against the door as Dr. Cameron holds a pistol above his unconscious daughter's head.*

1566. *Iris in.* LS: *as in 1526. As Clansmen enter upper left, the besiegers start to flee across the open ground away from the cabin.*

1567. MS: *as in 1564. The soldiers battering at the door freeze in terror and run out left.*

1568. MS: *as in 1565. Phil grabs Dr. Cameron's arm and they look at each other in disbelief.*

1569. MLS: *as in 1560. In the outer room, the attackers are frozen in mid-gesture. They start to move out right.*

1570. MS: *as in 1561. The door against which the veteran has been pushing suddenly swings shut. He opens it and looks out.*

1571. LS: *as in 1566. The Clansmen enter right and the attackers run for their lives across the open ground outside the cabin.*

1572. MLS: *Clansmen enter right and left and dismount in front of the cabin.*

1573. MLS: *as in 1569. Inside the cabin, "white-arm" Joe fires a shot toward the door but is himself hit a moment later when Clansmen burst in. He falls, and a Clansman shoots at a soldier on the right, who also falls.*

1574. MLS: *as in 1551. In the inner room, Dr. Cameron, Margaret, and Phil embrace. As Mammy removes the upturned table, the veteran looks through the door and then turns to the little girl.*

1575. MLS: *as in 1573. The Clansmen in the outer room turn to enter the inner room on the left.*

1576. MS: *as in 1574. As Margaret assists her father in helping Mrs. Cameron into a chair, a Clansman pulls Margaret aside and whispers his identity to her. She embraces him and excitedly indicates to her parents who he is.*

1577. LS: *the mounted Clansmen ride forward, away from the cabin, and out to the right.*

1578. TITLE: ¶Disarming the blacks.

1579. LS: *a group of black soldiers, surrounded on two sides by Clansmen aiming their guns at them, drop their firearms and run out to the right.*

1580. TITLE: ¶Parade of the Clansmen.*

1581. LS: *led by Elsie, Margaret, and Ben, the parade of the Clansmen comes forward through the square filled with cheering townsfolk.*

1582. MS: *as the camera tracks back, the parade moves forward, with Margaret, Elsie, and Ben in the lead. Behind them, surrounded by Clansmen, ride Dr. and Mrs. Cameron and Phil.*

1583. MLS: *a crowd of blacks stares in fear.*

1584. LS: *as in 1581. As the parade makes its way across the square and goes out right, the Klan banner held by the standard-bearer at the head of the parade passes from left to right, close to the camera.*

1585. MLS: *as in 1583. The blacks run to the rear and out left to their quarters.*

1586. LS: *the townsfolk cheer and wave white handkerchiefs as Elsie and Margaret, leading the parade, pull up outside Cameron Hall.*

---

*This title (1580), which appears in the 35mm tinted nitrate print in the Library of Congress, is missing from the Museum of Modern Art print.

1587. MS: *inside a house, a white man excitedly points out the window, and the women rise.*

1588. MLS: *Ben brings his horse up beside Margaret's, leans over and says something to Elsie and his sister, and leads the parade out to the left.*

1589. MS: *as in 1587. The man and the three women stand at the window and wave excitedly.*

1590. MCU: *another group of people standing at their window celebrates the parade with cheers and embraces. A woman brings her fist to her heart and closes her eyes in silent thanks. Fade out.*

1591. *Fade in.* MS: *the man with the wooden leg looks out his window, as his daughter and wife holding a baby wave at the parade.*

1592. MS: *the man with the invalid wife embraces his two children.*

1593. MLS: *as in 1588. The parade continues past Cameron Hall out left. Fade out.*

1594. TITLE: ¶The next election.

1595. *Fade in.* LS: *in the black quarter, mounted Clansmen are lined up on the right as blacks come in on the left.*

1596. MS: *three blacks lean forward in discussion. They look right.*

1597. *Iris in.* MLS, CV: *the Clansmen have their guns drawn.*

1598. MS: *as in 1596. The three blacks, wary of the Clansmen, turn and exit left.*

1599. LS: *as in 1595. The Clansmen remain standing. Fade out.*

1600. TITLE: ¶The aftermath.
¶At the sea's edge, the double honeymoon.

1601. MLS: *on the left, Margaret and Phil are seated on a couch in an interior space. Behind them in back projection is a seascape at sunset.*

1602. *Fade in.* MS: *Ben and Elsie are seated on a bluff overlooking the sea. He turns to her.*

1603. TITLE: ¶Dare we dream of a golden day when the bestial War shall rule no more.
¶But instead—the gentle Prince in the Hall of Brotherly Love in the City of Peace.

1604. LS: *the God of War, projected in the background, is mounted on a horse and with both hands is swinging his sword above his head. On the right, in front of him, lies a huge heap of dead bodies, and on the left a crowd writhes and pleads with him. The image of the God of War fades out.*

1605. LS: *the figure of Christ, projected in the background, holds out his arms above a crowd of dancing and promenading people dressed in heavenly garments. The image of the crowd fades, and the Christ figure remains with his arms outstretched. The scene of the happy, talking throng fades in again, and the Christ figure fades away.*

1606. *Fade in.* MS: *as in 1602. Ben and Elsie look out to sea, as the breeze blows against their faces.*

1607. L S : *the Heavenly throng continues to walk about and dance. Projected in a space in the background, a celestial city can be seen. Fade out.*

1608. M S : *split frame. On the right, Ben and Elsie hold hands and look at each other lovingly. They turn and look left, to the vision of the celestial city on a hill.*

1609. *Fade in.* T I T L E : ¶"Liberty and union, one and inseparable, now and forever!" *Fade out.*

1610. *Fade in.* T I T L E : ¶THE BIRTH OF A NATION or "The Clansman"
        ¶THE END
        Copyright 1915   David W. Griffith Corporation

Contexts, Reviews, and Commentaries

Contexts

The storm of response that *The Birth of a Nation* provoked was phenomenal. Not only was the film the most extraordinary achievement of the cinema, it was, for many, a powerful ideological statement that at least one commentator described as "spiritual assassination." Everyone, it seems, had something to say about the *The Birth of a Nation* in 1915, including the famous and respected social worker, Jane Addams, whose long interview with the *New York Evening Post* on March 13 (not reprinted here), in which she forcefully condemned the film's "pernicious caricature of the Negro race," became a high-water mark in contemporary criticism of *Birth*. "You can use history to demonstrate anything when you take certain of its facts and emphasize them to the exclusion of others," she said.

The National Association for the Advancement of Colored People (NAACP) sought to prevent the film from being screened in Los Angeles, and a few days after its opening in New York, the newly formed organization announced its opposition to the film. (See Thomas Cripps, "The Reaction of the Negro to the Motion Picture *Birth of a Nation*," for a detailed account of the response in Boston, where opposition to the film was most intense.)

Francis Hackett, writing in the March 20, 1915, issue of *The New Republic*, attacked *The Birth of a Nation* as a "vicious and defamatory" film that reflects Dixon's "malignity." Griffith's name appears nowhere in the article, as Hackett blames the film's excesses on Dixon, whose "perversions are cunningly calculated to flatter the white man and provoke hatred and contempt for the Negro."

Dixon and Griffith attempted to answer their detractors in a number of letters and interviews. Griffith was taken aback by the negative reactions to the film, and seemed unable to comprehend them. As he wrote in a new prefatory title for the film on March 12, "We do not fear censorship, for we have no wish to offend with improprieties or obscenities, but we do demand, as a right, the liberty to show

the dark side of wrong, that we may illuminate the bright side of virtue."
Dixon campaigned for the film with
the "frantic intensity" that Francis
Hackett identified as one of the defining features of the clergyman's
temperament.

Brotherly Love

Francis Hackett

I f history bore no relation to life, this motion-picture drama could well be reviewed and applauded as a spectacle. As a spectacle it is stupendous. It lasts three hours, represents a staggering investment of time and money, reproduces entire battle scenes and complex historic events, amazes even when it wearies by its attempt to encompass the Civil War. But since history does bear on social behavior, *The Birth of a Nation* cannot be reviewed simply as a spectacle. It is more than a spectacle. It is an interpretation, the Rev. Thomas Dixon's interpretation, of the relations of the North and South and their bearing on the Negro.

Were the Rev. Thomas Dixon a representative white Southerner, no one could criticize him for giving his own version of the Civil War and the Reconstruction period that followed. If he possessed the typical Southern attitude, the paternalistic, it would be futile to read a lecture on it. Seen from afar, such an attitude might be deemed reactionary, but at any rate it is usually genial and humane and protective, and because it has experience back of it, it has to be met with some respect. But the attitude which Mr. Dixon possesses and the one for which he forges corroboration in history is a perversion due largely to his personal temperament. So far as I can judge from this film, as well as from my recollection of Mr. Dixon's books, his is the sort of disposition that foments a great deal of the trouble in civilization. Sometimes in the clinical laboratory the doctors are reputed to perform an operation on a dog so that he loses the power to restrain certain motor activities. If he is started running in a cage, the legend goes, he keeps on running incessantly, and nothing can stop him but to hit him on the head with a club. There is a quality about everything Mr. Dixon has done that reminds me of this abnormal dog. At a remote period of his existence it is possible that he possessed a rudimentary faculty of self-analysis. But before that faculty developed he crystallized in his prejudices, and forever it was stunted. Since that time, whenever he has been stimulated by any of the ordinary emotions, by religion or by patriotism or by sex, he has reponded with a frantic intensity. Energetic by nature, the forces that impel him are doubly violent because of this lack of inhibition. Aware as a clergyman that such violence is excessive, he has learned in all his melodramas to give them a highly moral twang. If one of his heroes is about to do something peculiarly loathsome, Mr. Dixon thrusts a crucifix in his hand and has him roll his eyes to heaven. In this way the very basest impulses are given the sanction of godliness, and Mr. Dixon preserves his own respect and the respect of such people as go by the label and not by the rot-gut they consume.

From *The New Republic* 7 (March 20, 1915): 185.

In *The Birth of a Nation* Mr. Dixon protests sanctimoniously that his drama "is not meant to reflect in any way on any race or people of today." And then he proceeds to give to the Negro a kind of malignity that is really a revelation of his own malignity.

Passing over the initial gibe at the Negro's smell, we early come to a negrophile senator whose mistress is a mulatto. As conceived by Mr. Dixon and as acted in the film, this mulatto is not only a minister to the senator's lust but a woman of inordinate passion, pride, and savagery. Gloating as she does over the promise of "Negro equality," she is soon partnered by a male mulatto of similar brute characteristics. Having established this triple alliance between the "uncrowned king," his diabolic colored mistress, and his diabolic colored ally, Mr. Dixon shows the revolting processes by which the white South is crushed "under the heel of the black South." "Sowing the wind," he calls it. On the one hand we have "the poor bruised heart" of the white South, on the other "the new citizens inflamed by the growing sense of power." We see Negroes shoving white men off the sidewalk, Negroes quitting work to dance, Negroes beating a crippled old white patriarch, Negroes slinging up "faithful colored servants" and flogging them till they drop, Negro courtesans guzzling champagne with the would-be head of the Black Empire, Negroes "drunk with wine and power," Negroes mocking their white master in chains, Negroes "crazy with joy" and terrorizing all the whites in South Carolina. We see the blacks flaunting placards demanding "equal marriage." We see the black leader demanding a "forced marriage" with an imprisoned and gagged white girl. And we see continually in the background the white Southerner in "agony of soul over the degradation and ruin of his people."

Encouraged by the black leader, we see Gus the renegade hover about another young white girl's home. To hoochy-coochy music we see the long pursuit of the innocent white girl by this lust-maddened Negro, and we see her fling herself to death from a precipice, carrying her honor through "the opal gates of death."

Having painted this insanely apprehensive picture of an unbridled, bestial, horrible race, relieved only by a few touches of low comedy, "the grim reaping begins." We see the operations of the Ku Klux Klan, "the organization that saved the South from the anarchy of black rule." We see Federals and Confederates uniting in a Holy War "in defence of their Aryan birthright," whatever that is. We see the Negroes driven back, beaten, killed. The drama winds up with a suggestion of "Lincoln's solution"—back to Liberia—and then, if you please, with a film representing Jesus Christ in "the halls of brotherly love."

My objection to this drama is based partly on the tendency of the pictures but mainly on the animus of the printed lines I have quoted. The effect of these lines, reinforced by adroit quotations from Woodrow Wilson and repeated assurances of impartiality and good will, is to arouse in the audience a strong sense of the evil possibilities of the Negro and the extreme propriety and godliness of the Ku Klux Klan. So strong is this impression that the audience invariably applauds the refusal of the white hero to shake hands with a Negro, and under the circumstances it cannot be blamed. Mr. Dixon has identified the Negro with cruelty, superstition, insolence, and lust.

We know what a yellow journalist is. He is not yellow because he reports crimes of violence. He is yellow because he distorts them. In the region of history the Rev. Thomas Dixon corresponds to the yellow journalist. He is a clergyman, but he is a yellow clergyman. He is yellow because he recklessly distorts Negro crimes, gives them a disproportionate place in life, and colors them dishonestly to inflame the ignorant and the credulous. And he is especially yellow, and quite disgustingly and contemptibly yellow, because his perversions are cunningly calculated to flatter the white man and provoke hatred and contempt for the Negro.

Whatever happened during Reconstruction, this film is aggressively vicious and defamatory. It is spiritual assassination. It degrades the censors that passed it and the white race that endures it.

Capitalizing Race Hatred

In view of the splendors of national reunion what should be the attitude of every right-minded person toward attempts to revive the passions of the Civil War period, relight the fires of sectionalism, and intensify race prejudices that are unhappily still much alive? The questions sufficiently answer themselves, and when they are answered there is no reason to ask the further question of whether it is desirable, for purely sordid reasons, to exhibit such a moving-picture film as the so-called *The Birth of a Nation*.

Few of us are competent to pass judgment with respect to the tangled facts of the Reconstruction period. A fair and impartial narrative has never been written and probably never will be. But certain big facts shine out in the confusion. One is that never in human history did a victor show more consideration for the defeated. Men but lately in arms were restored to full citizenship, states in rebellion were received back in the sisterhood of the states. Let us rejoice that the Stonemans of Washington were magnanimous, but let us not dishonor ourselves by calling in question their great merit by presenting them as the paramours of quadroon mistresses, moved by petty spite. It is insulting to every man of Southern birth to assume that he is pleased by misrepresentation so colossal.

Another big fact of the Reconstruction period is that the 4,000,000 former slaves, suddenly emancipated but with no way of earning their livelihood except by working at small wages for their former masters, displayed, all things considered, the most exemplary patience. They had protected the women and children on the plantations while the struggle went on which was to decide whether they were to become men or to remain as chattels, and the great body of them continued to exhibit, under the most trying circumstances, docility and kindliness. To present the members of the race as women-chasers and foul fiends is a cruel distortion of history. Bad things occurred, but what man will say that the outrages of black on white equalled in number the outrages of white on black? Which race even to the present day has the better right to complain of the unfairness and brutality of the other?

The very name of *The Birth of a Nation* is an insult to Washington, who believed that a nation, not merely a congeries of independent states, was born during the common struggles of the Revolutionary War, and devoted himself to cementing the union. It is an insult to Lincoln and the great motives inspiring him when he was called on to resist the attempt to denationalize a nation. This nation of ours was not born between 1861 and 1865, and no one will profit from trying to pervert history.

From the *New York Globe*, April 6, 1915.

White men in this country have never been just to black men. We tore them from Africa and brought them over as slaves. For generations they toiled without recompense that their white owners might have unearned wealth and ape the ways of aristocracy. The nation finally freed them, but has but slightly protected them in the enjoyment of the legitimate fruits of their freedom. We nominally gave them the vote, but looked on inactive when the right was invaded. We do not, in any state of the Union, grant to the Negro economic and political equality. No white man of proper feeling can be proud of the record. The wonder is that the Negro is as good as he is. Then to the injury is added slander. To make a few dirty dollars men are willing to pander to depraved tastes and to foment a race antipathy that is the most sinister and dangerous feature of American life.

Reply to the *New York Globe*
Thomas Dixon

Editor of the *Globe,* Sir—As a reader of your paper may I claim the courtesy of a reply to your editorial attack of yesterday on *The Birth of a Nation?*

As author of the book and play on which the larger film drama is based I accept the full moral responsibility for its purpose and its effects on an audience.

We have submitted *The Birth of a Nation* to a jury of three representative clergymen of New York—the Rev. Thomas B. Gregory, Universalist; the Rev. Charles H. Parkhurst, D.D., Presbyterian, and the Rev. John Talbot Smith, D.D., Roman Catholic, editor of *The Columbian,* organ of the Knights of Columbus.

They did not suggest a single change or cut, but fully agreed with the high praise given by the dramatic critic of the *Globe.*

They declare in substance that the play in its final impression on the audience does six things: (1) It reunites in common sympathy and love all sections of our country. (2) It teaches our boys the history of our nation in a way that makes them know the priceless inheritance our fathers gave us through the sacrifice of civil war and reconstruction. (3) It tends to prevent the lowering of the standard of our citizenship by its mixture with Negro blood. (4) It shows the horror and futility of war as a method of settling civic principles. (5) It reaffirms Lincoln's solution of the Negro problem as a possible guide to our future and glorifies his character as the noblest example of American democracy. (6) It gives to Daniel Webster for the first time his true place in American history as the inspiring creator of the modern nation we know today.

The most important point on which I take issue with your editorial is found in the sentence: "Let us rejoice that the Stonemans of Washington were magnanimous, but let us not dishonor ourselves by calling in question their great merit by presenting them as the paramours of quadroon mistresses, moved by petty spite."

Who has ever dared to declare that Thaddeus Stevens, B. F. Butler, and Benjamin Wade, the leaders of Congress during this reign of terror, were magnanimous?

Abraham Lincoln was magnanimous, and his mighty spirit brooded over the Capitol after his death pleading for generous treatment of the South.

The magnanimity extended was in spite of Stevens and his associates, not through them.

The established facts are that Stevens, who lived and died a bachelor, separated a quadroon Negress from her husband of her youth and kept her in his house for

From the *New York Globe,* April 10, 1915.

thirty-six years. For this woman he became a social outcast in Washington and at the last moment lost his place in Lincoln's cabinet, the appointment suddenly going to Simon Cameron, his rival.

He left this woman, Lydia Brown, an annuity in his will and was buried in a Negro cemetery in Lancaster, Pa., that he might sleep beside her in death.

Do you question these facts? If so, I will submit them to a jury of three historians of established character, and if they decide against me I will agree to withdraw *The Birth of a Nation* from the stage.

Was Mr. Stevens magnanimous even when the shadow of death was upon him in the last year of his life?

Read his famous bill to confiscate the remaining property of the stricken, starving South and give it to the Negroes, two years after Lee's surrender!

If you still doubt that he was ungenerous, read his awful speech in the *Congressional Record* pressing this pet measure, House Bill No. 29, to a vote. Nothing so fierce, cruel, and vindictive was ever uttered on the floor of the House of Representatives in our history, before or since.

The stricken South was only saved from this act of brutal vengeance by Mr. Stevens's death. No other man had the ability to pass such a measure.

I am not attacking the Negro of today. I am recording faithfully the history of fifty years ago. I portray three Negroes faithful unto death to every want and two vicious Negroes, misled by white scoundrels. Is it a crime to present a bad black man, seeing we have so many bad white ones?

Reply to the *New York Globe*
D. W. Griffith

ditor of the Globe, Sir—In an editorial in your issue of April 6, 1915, under the heading: "Capitalizing Race Hatred," you undertake to label our picture *The Birth of a Nation* with alleged feelings of sectional difference between the North and South. You ask yourself questions and proceed to answer them in the same old way that the same things have been gone over and over again. Where I must take issue with you is that you intimate that these old differences have been raised and exhibited "for purely sordid reasons," to quote your own words.

In presenting this motion-picture story before the intelligent theater-goers of New York City, in a regular theater, which has been well advertised, I thought the moving drama told its own story. My associates have maintained a dignified silence in the face of an organized attack of letter writers, publicity seekers, and fanatics against our work. We have traced this attack to its source, and know the reasons for it. Without wishing to tell any newspaper its business, permit me to suggest that a cub reporter in one hour could find out that this attack is an organized effort to suppress a production which was brought forth to reveal the beautiful possibilities of the art of motion pictures and to tell a story which is based upon truth in every vital detail. Our story states, as plainly as the English language can express a fact, the reasons for this presentation. In our captions we reiterate that the events depicted upon the screen are not meant as a reflection upon any race or people of today.

I demand to know the authority upon which you base your intimation that this work of art has been exhibited "for purely sordid reasons." I further demand that failing to establish this authority you retract your statement in as prominent and direct a manner as you have given publicity to the opinions of the writer of your editorial.

Our picture tells its own story and we are willing to stand upon the verdict of the New York public as to the fitness of this work of art to be judged as a drama of action based upon the authenticated history of the period covering the action of our plot.

The succeeding paragraphs of your editorial are political generalities which have nothing in common with the truths and purposes of the motion picture *The Birth of a Nation*. Our picture does show historic events which you undertake to use for an entirely different argument. We have contrasted the bad with the good and following the formula of the best dramas of the world we establish our ideals by revealing the victory of right over wrong.

From the *New York Globe*, April 10, 1915.

I do not agree with your statements regarding the history of slavery and the Reconstruction period of this nation, but that is not a matter of importance in this connection. Most well-informed men know now that slavery was an economic mistake. The treatment of the Negroes during the days of Reconstruction is shown effectually and graphically in our picture. We show many phases of the question and we do pay particular attention to those faithful Negroes who stayed with their former masters and were ready to give up their lives to protect their white friends. No characters in the story are applauded with greater fervor than the good Negroes whose devotion is so clearly shown. If prejudiced witnesses do not see the message in this portion of the entire drama we are not to blame.

Your editorial is an insult to the intelligence and the human kindness of nearly 100,000 of the best people in New York City, who have viewed this picture from artistic interests and not through any depraved taste such as you try to indicate. Among those you have insulted are your contemporaries on the newspapers of New York, whose expert reviewers were unanimous in their praise of this work as an artistic achievement. Included in this list is your own able critic, Mr. Louis Sherwin, of the *Globe.*

We have received letters of the heartiest commendation from statesmen, writers, clergymen, artists, educators, and laymen. I have in my possession applications for reservations from the principals of ten schools, who having seen the picture, are desirous of bringing their pupils to view it for its historic truths.

The Rev. Dr. Charles H. Parkhurst, the Rev. Father John Talbot Smith, and the Rev. Thomas B. Gregory are among the clergy who have given us permission to use their names in approval of this picture in its entirety. Parents have asked us to make reservation for them that they may bring their children to see it. In every walk of life there are men and women of this city who have expressed their appreciation of this picture. Do you dare to intimate that these voluntary expressions of approval were voiced "for purely sordid reasons"?

The attack of the organized opponents to this picture is centered upon that feature of it which they deem might become an influence against the intermarriage of blacks and whites. The organizing opponents are white leaders of the National Association for the Advancement of the Colored People, including Oswald Garrison Villard and J. E. Spingarn, who hold official positions in this prointermarriage organization.

May I inquire if you desire to espouse the cause of a society which openly boasts in its official organ, *The Crisis,* that it has been able to throttle "anti-intermarriage legislation" in over ten states? Do you know what this society means by "anti-intermarriage legislation"? It means that they successfully opposed bills which were framed to prohibit the marriage of Negroes to whites.

Do you know that in their official organ, *The Crisis,* for March 1915, they brand 238 members of the Sixty-third Congress as "Negro baiters" because these Representatives voted to prohibit the marriage of Negroes to whites in the District of Columbia?

You close your editorial, in which by innuendo you link our picture to your own assertions, with this sentence:

"To make a few dirty dollars, men are willing to pander to depraved tastes and to foment a race antipathy that is the most sinister and dangerous feature of American life."

That statement is obviously a generality, but it is printed at the end of an editorial which is a covert attack upon our picture, *The Birth of a Nation.* As the producer of that picture, I wish to say if the man who wrote it meant one iota of the sentence just quoted to apply to our picture he is a liar and a coward.

Whether this was the intent of the sentence quoted it could not fail to create an impression in the minds of your readers, damaging my reputation as a producer. Therefore, as a matter of justice, I ask that you publish my statement of the facts.

Reviews

The *Birth of a Nation* became a *succès d' estime* and a *succès de scandale* immediately upon its release. As Mark Vance noted in *Variety* a month after the film opened in Los Angeles and nine days after its premiere in New York, "the daily newspaper reviewers pronounced it as the last word in picturemaking." Vance then goes on to do much the same; but the small handful of reviews selected for inclusion here were chosen because they are more detailed and perceptive, or attempt to be more considered, than most of the daily papers were or could be.

While Mark Vance and W. Stephen Bush are perhaps typical of those who tried to contextualize the film for their readers, they are still reviewers (for example, Vance describes the extended sequence of Gus's pursuit of Flora and her subsequent leap from a high cliff as "nicely cameraed"). Their racism—evident in remarks like, "Griffith struck it right when he adapted the Dixon story for the film. He knew the South and he knew what kind of a picture would please all white classes. Some places the censors are going to find fault. That's a persistent way some censors have" (Vance)—is also perhaps typical of reviewers who were aware of the film's troubled ideology (or "controversial spirit," as Bush describes it), but who hoped it could be safely ignored. Bush gives some indication of being more perturbed by the film's racism than Vance, but concludes with the assessment that "it is altogether probable that [the film's] many fine points will outweigh its disadvantages."

Ward Greene, whose review appeared in *The Atlanta Journal* on December 7, 1915, is blatantly a Southern partisan. "Race prejudice? Injustice? Suppression?" he asks with rhetorical incredulity: "You would not think of those things had you seen *The Birth of a Nation*. For none but a man with a spirit too picayunish and warped for words would pick such flaws in a spectacle so great and whole-hearted as this."

Ned McIntosh's review also appeared on December 7, in *The Atlanta*

Constitution. He gives all the praise to Griffith, who "takes Dixon's teapot-tempest and builds a tornado." He believes that the film "is not designed to arouse your prejudice, and if you are fair-minded and not predisposed, it will not do so." McIntosh makes special mention of the part music plays in the film's effects, and seems conscious of the enormous significance of *Birth* as a moment in the history of representation when he observes that "the great novel of the Civil War has at last arrived—and when it got here it was a moving picture and not a book!"

Harlow Hare, writing in the *Boston American* on July 18, 1915, devotes his entire review to the music of the film, and like McIntosh, marvels at "this . . . marriage of music and spectacle."

Variety
Mark Vance

T*he Birth of a Nation* is the main title David Wark Griffith, the director-in-chief of the Mutual Film Corporation, gave to his picturized version of Thomas Dixon's story of the South, *The Clansman.* It received its first New York public presentation in the Liberty Theatre, New York, March 3. The daily newspaper reviewers pronounced it as the last word in picturemaking. That its enormity and elaborateness made such an impression naturally resulted in the press comparing it with that Italian massive film production, *Cabiria,* and saying without hesitancy that *The Birth of a Nation* overshadowed the foreign film spectacle. In the picturization of *The Clansman* Mr. Griffith has set such a pace it will take a long time before one will come along that can top it in point of production, acting, photography, and direction. Every bit of the film was laid, played, and made in America. One may find some flaws in the general running of the picture, but they are so small and insignificant that the bigness and greatness of the entire film production itself completely crowds out any little defects that might be singled out. The story of the Dixon novel, *The Clansman,* is pretty well known. The Camerons of the South and the Stonemans of the North and Silas Lynch, the mulatto lieutenant-governor, the Civil War, the opening and finish of the Civil War, the scenes attendant upon the assassination of Abraham Lincoln, the period of carpetbagging days and Union Reconstruction following Lee's surrender, the terrorizing of the Southern whites by the newly freed blacks, and the rise of the Ku Klux Klan that later overpowers the Negroes and gives the white men the authority rightfully theirs, all these, including some wonderfully well-staged battle scenes taken at night, are realistically, graphically, and most superbly depicted by the camera. Griffith knows the value of striking, gripping, and melo-dramatic anticlimaxes and also is fully cognizant of the importance of having several big "punches" instead of one for camera visualization. Building up photo-play action and "posing" a picture which would look well reproduced in colors is a natural instinct with Griffith and he's one director who knows how to get action typified intensely. In *The Birth of a Nation* Griffith took his time and thereby builded well. Thousands of feet of celluloid were used and some six months or so he and his codirectors worked day and night to shape the story into a thrilling, dramatic, wordless play that would not pass out overnight in the minds of the millions who are bound to see this picture before it has been laid away to rest. The battle scenes are wonderfully conceived and show two armies in such natural fighting array it is almost unbelievable that one is looking at a picture, staged by

From *Variety,* March 12, 1915.

one whose only purpose was to make it get away from the usual stagey phoniness so apparent in numerous picture battle plays. And the departure of the soldiers was splendidly arranged. Then the death of the famous martyred president was so deftly and ably handled no one can find any fault. Of course there are many who will aver that Griffith should have shown the subsequent death of the assassin, John Wilkes Booth, but as he had an archvillain in the shape of the renegade, Gus, later to deal with severely it was best he stick closer to the story at hand. This same Gus, fiendish and with the lust of the beast in his eye, gives mad chase to the pet sister of "Little Colonel" Ben Cameron and she jumps to her death from a high cliff rather than permit herself be touched alive by that brute in human form. This was also nicely cameraed. Then comes the Reconstruction period following a camera scene of Grant and Lee ending the war at Appomattox. Harassing scenes showing the persecution of the whites with the Camerons more than getting their share and with Ben Cameron organizing the white-robed Ku Klux Klan, which later gives the picture one of the biggest moments of its entire version when it rides down the blacks and later saves a small band of whites about to be massacred alive. Here the renegade Gus is killed. Griffith picturized an allegorical conception at the end showing what universal peace meant to the nation. Some may not care for it, but in the church neighborhoods and where the staunchest of the peace advocates live it will go with a hurrah. There are something like 12,000 feet of film, but the program says it's all there in two acts. There is an intermission just preceding the stirring days of the carpetbaggery action. Griffith struck it right when he adapted the Dixon story for the film. He knew the South and he knew just what kind of a picture would please all white classes. Some places the censors are going to find fault. That's a persistent way some censors have. That scene of the lashing on the back of the old negro will undoubtedly come in for a full share of criticism. The scene of the "black congress" and the negro removing his shoe may be censured, but it's drawn from reported facts. But no matter what the censors censor there will be plenty of film action and interest left to make it the biggest-demanded film production of the present century. It's worth seeing anywhere. Many will see it twice, yea thrice and still obtain much satisfaction and entertainment. It's there with a multiple of thrills. Of the acting company, Henry Walthall made a manly, straightforward character of the "Little Colonel" and handled his big scenes most effectively. Mae Marsh as the pet sister did some remarkable work as the little girl who loved the South and loved her brother. In fact her work was little short of a revelation to many. Ralph Lewis was splendid as the leader of the House who helped Silas Lynch rise to power. George Siegmann got all there could be gotten out of this despicable character of Lynch. Walter Long made Gus, the renegade negro, a hated, much-despised type, his acting and makeup being complete. Mary Alden, Lillian Gish, Robert Harron, Jennie Lee, and Miriam Cooper deserve mention for their excellent work. The other minor characters were satisfactorily portrayed. Donald Crisp had a good makeup as Grant, while Joseph Henabery "posed" most acceptably as Lincoln. It may not be amiss to pass away from critical comment for the moment to say that as D. W. Griffith, the world's best film director, is and has been responsible for so many of the innovations in picturemaking, doing more to make filming an art than any one person, so D. W. Griffith has been the first to bring a "$2 picture" to the box office of a "$2 theater." When it was first reported about this "Griffith feature" would retail to the public at a $2 scale, the picture people shrugged their shoulders, said "50 cents at the most," and let it go at that. But as so many opinions of pictures and their possibilities have gone wrong, so, it appears, is the belief that there can not be a $2 picture as erroneous as many of the others. But it is fitting that Mr. Griffith should have so far progressed and advanced in the art he did so much to foster and improve until he became the first director of a successful film that can compete in $2 theaters with $2 stage productions. That is the concise picture record of a few years, within ten at the most, and for feature pictures, even less. *Cabiria* was an admittedly big film production, a spectacle or series of spectacles that held no general interest through the fault of the maker or director. It drew in certain territory and even then in a desultory manner. But *A Birth of a Nation* [*sic*] has universal appeal to America at least, and the superbness of this production will gain recognition anywhere, with the story carrying, though perhaps to lesser human-interest extent in foreign lands than at home, where the subject is more thoroughly understood. *A Birth of a Nation* [*sic*] is said to have cost $300,000. This is rather a high estimate, but other than the money the film represents, its returns are going to be certain. Not alone is this film playing at a $2 scale in a theater where an orchestra and operator besides the house staff are the principal necessary force, as against a stage production that might have a salary list of from $4,000 to $8,500 weekly, according to the piece, but *A Birth of a Nation* [*sic*] can give as many performances a week as the house wishes it to, and in this particular instance will not give less than fourteen, two shows daily. The stage production in a $2 theater would give eight performances as a rule, perhaps nine and, with a holiday intervening, ten. While the Liberty is advertising the Griffith film up to one dollar "with loge seats $2," the scale is practically a $2 one, made so by the demand for seats. *A Birth of a Nation* [*sic*] is a great epoch in picturemaking; it's great for pictures and it's great for the name and fame of David Wark Griffith. When a man like Griffith in´a new field can do what he has done, he may as well be hailed while he is living.

The Moving Picture World
W. Stephen Bush

The two outstanding features of Griffith's remarkable production, *The Birth of a Nation,* are its controversial spirit (especially obvious in the titles), and the splendor and magnificence of its spectacles. Based in the main on *The Clansman,* it breathes the spirit of that well-known book. *The Clansman* was a special plea for the South in the forum of history. The screen-adaptation has made the plea far more passionate and I might say partisan than the book or the play. It is impossible to give the reader a good idea of this production without sketching at least briefly the views and sentiments expressed and sharply emphasized and reiterated by the distinguished author. The very introduction tells us that the South never had a fair record made of its trials in the Reconstruction period. We are told both in pictures and in titles that African slaves were brought to this country by Northern traders who sold them to the South. Puritan divines blessed the traffic, but when slave trading was no longer profitable to the North the "traders of the seventeenth century became the abolitionists of the nineteenth century."

We next see a typical Northern congregation assembled to hear a sermon. About the platform from which the preacher addresses his audience stands a group of colored children. The preacher takes a young colored boy and passes with him through the congregation. A motherly looking old lady stretches out her arms in sympathy toward the child of the black race, but immediately repulses him with every manifestation of disgust caused by the odor which we must assume the boy carries around with him. Much is then said in titles about "state sovereignty" and we are reminded of what we read in school of Southern statesmen like Calhoun and Toombs and Northern statesmen like Vallandigham.

Mr. Griffith then unfolds a picture of conditions in the South before the Civil War, showing both in titles and pictures that the slaves had easy hours, plenty of time for recreation, comfortable quarters, and kind masters. Here a strange and puzzling character is introduced in the person of a man said "to have risen to great prominence in the House of Representatives in 1860." This man, who plays a very prominent part all through the production, is called "Austin Stoneman." The titles make it plain that this is a fictitious name. Stoneman has a daughter who is never allowed to enter his library. The reason for this must be found in the illicit relations between Stoneman and a mulatto woman. The latter is "insulted" by Charles Sumner. She works herself into a fury of passion. Stoneman enters to find her with part of her upper body exposed. The scene ends with Stoneman kissing the mulatto

From *The Moving Picture World* 23 (March 13, 1915): 1586–87.

and with this title: "Thus the fatal weakness of one man blights the nation."[1] The man called Stoneman bears a striking facial and physical resemblance to the man who succeeded Lincoln in the presidential chair. The description of him in the titles forbids the belief that he is identical with President Andrew Johnson. He is an altogether mystical and apocryphal personage whose identity remains veiled until the very end. . . . The march of Sherman from Atlanta to the sea made the audience gasp with wonder and admiration. Nothing more impressive has ever been seen on the screen and I have to refer to *Cabiria* for a standard of comparison. Nor are the war spectacles the only impressive spectacular features. Two of the most wonderful pictures ever seen on the screen are Lincoln, signing the first call for volunteers, and the surrender of Lee to Grant at Appomattox. It may be said in passing that a finer impersonation of Lincoln has never been witnessed on any screen or on any stage. The audience was deeply stirred by the inspired portrayal of Lincoln and when it became known that the artist who had given the portrayal was present the audience gave him an impromptu ovation between the first and second parts. He lived up to the best of Lincoln traditions both in appearance and in action. The assassination of the martyred president is shown in full detail on the screen. It was a task full of difficulties and one misstep might have proved fatal. The great tragedy is "acted o'er" in the most irreproachable and touching manner.

It must be mentioned too that Mr. Griffith has again shown himself a master in creating and prolonging suspense to the agonizing point. His favorite method of chasing pursued and pursuer through one room after another is still effective and always has the desired effect on the audience. When speaking of the spectacular features of *The Birth of a Nation,* I must not forget his treatment of the Ku Klux Klan. The weird and mystical garb of these defenders of "Aryan race supremacy" has given the director splendid opportunities which he utilized to the fullest. When these "crusaders of the South" are seen mounted on superb horses, dashing furiously through field and forest and river to rescue innocent maidens from brutal assault or to punish "wicked Africans," the audience never fails to respond, but applauds while the spectacle lasts.

It is scarcely necessary to say that the photography is exceptionally fine in a production to which Griffith lends his name. He shows a good deal of his renowned skill in working "close-ups," creating many tense and thrilling situations.

The acting is such as might have been expected with a director of the type and power of Griffith. He has the art of bending his instruments to his uses. They work in strictest obedience to his orders and as a result the Griffith idea is always transferred to the screen with a negligible loss of power and directness. Mr. Walthall's performance was particularly fine. This gifted artist invariably succeeds

---

1. [Editor's note: The correct title is: "The great leader's weakness that is to blight a nation."]

in merging his personality into his part. He might at times have shown a little trace of the grime and the hardship of soldiering. It seemed somewhat improbable that a soldier could look so trim and spick-and-span after what the "Little Colonel" passed through. The parts of Stoneman and Silas Lynch were well taken care of, the old "southron" was a piece of very clever character acting. Not enough praise can be given to the settings, both exterior and interior. Mr. Griffith is justly famous for his ability in these things.

The audience which saw the play at the private exhibition in the Liberty Theater was a most friendly one. It was significant that on more than one occasion during the showing of the films, there were hisses mingled with the applause. These hisses were not, of course, directed against the artistic quality of the film. They were evoked by the undisguised appeal to race prejudices. The tendency of the second part is to inflame race hatred. The negroes are shown as horrible brutes, given over to beastly excesses, defiant and criminal in their attitude toward the whites, and lusting after white women. Some of the details are plainly morbid and repulsive. The film having roused the disgust and hatred of the white against the black to the highest pitch, suggests as a remedy of the racial question the transportation of the negroes to Liberia, which Mr. Griffith assures us was Lincoln's idea.

Whatever fault might be found with the argumentative spirit found in both the titles and the pictures there can be no question that the appeal to the imagination will carry the picture a good way toward popular success. In the South of course, where memories of Reconstruction horrors are still vivid, the picture will have an immense vogue. It is altogether probable that its many fine points will outweigh its disadvantages in every other section of the country.

The Atlanta Journal

Ward Greene

T he story of the Creation was told in eight words, but should the pen of another Moses be raised today he would need ten times that number of pages to do credit to *The Birth of a Nation.*

There has been nothing to equal it—nothing. Not as a motion picture, nor a play, nor a book does it come to you; but as the soul and spirit and flesh of the heart of your country's history, ripped from the past and brought quivering with all human emotions before your eyes.

It swept the audience at the Atlanta Theater Monday night like a tidal wave. A youth in the gallery leaped to his feet and yelled and yelled. A little boy downstairs pounded the man's back in front of him and shrieked. The man did not know it. He was a middle-aged, hard-lipped citizen; but his face twitched and his throat gulped up and down. Here a young girl kept dabbing and dabbing at her eyes and there an old lady just sat and let the tears stream down her face unchecked.

Awakens Many Feelings

For *The Birth of a Nation* is the awakener of every feeling. Your heart pulses with patriotism when those boys in grey march to battle with banners whipping and the band playing "Dixie"; you are wrung with compassion for the mother and her girls desolate at home; you are shocked by the clamor of mighty armies flung hell-bent into conflict; your throat chokes for a boy who dies with a smile on his face beside the body of his chum, the enemy. Then "the South's best friend" crumples under the assassin's bullet and the land of the lost cause lies like a ragged wound under a black poison that pours out upon it. Loathing, disgust, hate envelop you, hot blood cries for vengeance. Until out of the night blazes the fiery cross that once burned high above old Scotland's hills and the legions of the Invisible Empire roar down to rescue, and that's when you are lifted by the hair and go crazy.

Race prejudice? Injustice? Suppression? You would not think of those things had you seen *The Birth of a Nation.* For none but a man with a spirit too picayunish and warped for words would pick such flaws in a spectacle so great and whole-hearted as this. In the first place, the picture does every credit to the negro race, lauds those faithful old black people whose fealty to their masters led them to dare the anger of mistaken fanatics, shows the true progress they have since made in industry and education. This picture is too big a thing to be bothered by such a gnat's sting of criticism.

From *The Atlanta Journal*, December 7, 1915.

Technically Perfect

Technically, *The Birth of a Nation* is perfect. Its stage settings, the acting of the principals, its faithfulness to historic fact, its every intimate detail, its photography, and its skillful blending of scenes laughable and pathetic—all are so well done that you don't even think about them during the picture.

Yet in retrospect they loom big. There is the scene which gives you the flash of a desolate family huddled on a hilltop and far below Sherman's invaders putting the city to the torch and raiding onward to where the sea laps the sand at Savannah.

There is the old Southern home in the very first part of the picture, when the orchestra plays "Sewanee Ribber." An old man sits there and by his side a cat and a puppy mawl each other. The cat claws viciously, you can almost hear the puppy whimper. And you laugh out loud at the joy of it.

They Go to War

When they go to war, your breast swells at the sight of the flower of the Confederacy tripping away to the strains of "The Bonnie Blue Flag." But you smile sympathetically, too, at the darky buck-dancing on the corner and the little pickaninnies rolling funnily in the dust.

You marvel again at the rolling smoke and flash of shell and canister across a far-flung battle line, but you feel as much the pathos when the boy of the North pauses with uplifted bayonet above the body of his chum of the South, until he jerks back from the bullet and wavers down across that body and before he dies smiles that roguish lad's smile and steals his arm across the other's face before he, too, lets his curly head fall in the shadows of the other's shoulder blades.

There is the scene where the "Little Colonel" comes home after the war, wasted, wan, hopeless, pausing, uncertain outside the old mansion where the shattered gate hangs broken on the hinges. And his little sister comes to greet him. She flies out of the house and stops at the threshold and smiles at him. They do not fall into each other's arms, but stand there and try to joke a little to hide the pity in each other's eyes. He fingers the "Southern ermine" on her dress and it ravels away, just like the raw cotton she had bravely donned in honor of his homecoming. And then she cleaves to him with both arms around his neck. And when the picture fades away as he is drawn inside the door, the last thing you feel is the spasm of pain in his face, the last thing you see are twin hands clutched convulsively across his shoulders.

Wonderful Little Sister

That little sister—she is wonderful. Mae Marsh is the girl who plays the role, plays it with an abandon and sincerity that is not acting but living. There, at the last, when she goes to the dark spring for water, you see her smile gayly at a squirrel on a limb; you see the bright-eyed little animal swallow a nut. You follow her mad race through the woods from the black crazed by power. You are with her when she pauses on the precipice and when she plunges downward and rolls over and over at the bottom to writhe for a moment, crushed and broken, before her head snaps back.

She is but one of the stars. That gives you an idea of the lavishness of the picture. Wallace Reid, who is featured in other films as the whole show, is in this picture in but one scene. Yet he is worth it, for his battle with ten negroes in the ginshop of "White-armed Joe" thrills you to the core. He uppercuts one and hurls another across the room, brains a third with a chair, pitches a fourth out of the window, beats them back until a shot spurts grey smoke and he totters into the street and drops forward in a heap.

Ku Klux to Rescue

Then the Ku Klux Klan gathers. The scenes which follow defy description. In the little town of Piedmont the blacks are celebrating, far away across the hills the Klan assembles. Back and forth the scene changes—one moment a street in Piedmont swirling with mad negroes, the next a bugle blast from the orchestra and out of the distance the riders of the Klan sweeping on and on. Back to the street and a house where a white girl trembles in fear before the black horde without, back with the bugle blast to the onrush of the Klan. They are coming, they are coming!

Gallery Goes Wild

You know it and your spine prickles and in the gallery the yells cut loose with every bugle note. The negro mob grows wilder and wilder, the white-shrouded riders are tearing nearer and nearer. Then, with a last mighty blast from the bugle, they sweep into the town and with a shattering volley hammer into the crowd. They fire back, they break, they flee. The Klan beats on them and over them, here a rider knocked off his horse and there another whizzing clean out of the window to the back of his steed—on them and over them to rescue and retribution and final triumph.

And after it's all over, you are not raging nor shot with hatred, but mellowed into a deeper and purer understanding of the fires through which your forefathers battled to make this South of yours a nation reborn!

Don't Miss It

That's why they sold standing room only Monday night and why every matinee at 2:30 and every night performance at 8:30 this week will be packed.

"I wouldn't pay $2 to see any movie in the world," scoffed one man Monday.

A friend took him Monday night. Tuesday he spent $10 to take himself again, his wife, his two children, and his maiden aunt.

And if you haven't seen it, spend the money, borrow it, beg it, get it any old way. But see *The Birth of a Nation*.

The Atlanta Constitution
Ned McIntosh

Ancient Greece had her Homer. Modern America has her David W. Griffith. It was for Homer to show the glory and the grandeur and the heroics of war. It is for Griffith to show the horrors and hideousness and hell of it. So moves the world on apace!

Griffith's *The Birth of a Nation* opened at the Atlanta Theater last night and was seen by one of the largest audiences that ever crowded through the doors of the Atlanta Theater. Never before, perhaps, has an Atlanta audience so freely given vent to its emotions and appreciation as last night. Spasmodic at first, the plaudits of the great spectacle at length became altogether unrestrained. The clapping of hands was not sufficient, and cheer after cheer burst forth. He who gets standing room at *The Birth of a Nation* during the remainder of this week which the picture plays here will be lucky.

It makes you laugh and moves you to hot tears unashamed. It makes you love and hate. It makes you forget decorum and forces a cry into your throat. It thrills you with horror and moves you to marvel at vast spectacles. It makes you actually live through the greatest period of suffering and trial that this country has ever known.

To say that *The Birth of a Nation* is based on *The Clansman* is correct as far as it goes, but it doesn't go far enough. Griffith takes Dixon's teapot-tempest and builds a tornado.

The . . . conception of the man is wonderful.

With such scenes as a kitten and a puppy playing together, Griffith, in the beginning, relaxes the imagination and makes the mind forgetful of any preconceived idea or prejudice concerning the picture.

From this mental attitude, almost of dalliance, Griffith awakens the memories of childhood; warms the heart with romance; quickens the pulse with patriotism; forces the exultant cheer from the lips in the midst of great battles; turns the heart sick with scenes of bloodshed; dims the eyes with tears for woman's sufferings; relieves the tension of emotions with a timely humorous incident; makes you tremble for the peril of a mother passing through the lines to reach a wounded son; interests you with a faithful reproduction of Ford's Theater and the assassination of Lincoln—and when Griffith has done all these things he has just begun!

You are ushered into an antechamber in Washington where a misguided man is plotting a black regime among white people—where a mulatto woman dreams of empire. You live through a period of ruin and destruction in the country where you

From *The Atlanta Constitution,* December 7, 1915.

were born. You see the plot executed and that same country humiliated and crushed under a black heel. Former happiness is shattered by the arrogance of ignorance. You sicken at the sight of an attempt to enforce marital racial equality. Again and again the unbearable hideousness of the days of Reconstruction is borne in upon you. History repeats itself upon the screen with a realism that is maddening. You could shriek for a depiction of relief and—yes, retribution. Thus, over and over, does the picture grind and pound and pulverize your emotions.

But the end is not yet.

The insufferable reason for the Ku Klux Klan has been shown. Next, with a wealth of detail and an intimate knowledge that is astonishing, Griffith brings the spectral army into being before your eyes.

Omit these details of dangerous and mysterious night meetings of men, and of the perils of women secretly making strange white garments with crosses emblazoned upon them.

Comes then an appointed night when two men—men and horses garbed in white from head to hoof—ride out from behind an ordinary country barn that you have seen a hundred times, and canter off down the road. At the top of a hill they stop. One holds high a cross of fire. Upon a distant hill other figures catch the signal. Now a group of white-clad horsemen has foregathered. The scene shifts to a great open field at night. There is a blood-curdling trumpet blast from the orchestra pit, pitched in a minor key. A troop of white figures upon spirited horses dashes at breakneck speed into the picture and wheels into position. There is a cheer from the audience. Comes another blood-curdling trumpet call and another troop, and then another and another and another. Men grimly determined upon a last desperate chance to rescue women and homes and civilization from an unspeakable curse are gathering for the work at hand. At last as far as the camera's scope can gather is assembled a vast, grim host in white. One more troop—they are a little late; you think they have come a long distance—wheels into place, right in the camera's very eye!

The "Little Colonel," hero of the story, and such a hero!—takes his place at the head of the white multitude. Again the trumpet blast. The "Little Colonel" rises in his stirrups and holds aloft a cross of fire. The host moves forward.

The awful restraint of the audience is thrown to the winds. Many rise from their seats. With the roar of thunder a shout goes up. Freedom is here! Justice is at hand! Retribution has arrived!

The scene is indescribable.

The Birth of a Nation is built to arouse your emotions, and it does it. It is designed to educate you, and it does so more than many hours of studying books. It is not designed to arouse your prejudices, and if you are fair-minded and not predisposed, it will not do so.

Any mention of *The Birth of a Nation,* however, is not complete with comment on the picture alone. The picture is not all. There is with the picture an orchestra of a score or more pieces and it is a good orchestra. The music is wonderfully adapted to the picture. The score of an opera could not more perfectly express the sense of the lines than does this music interpret the situations, thought, and spirit of *The Birth of a Nation*. When the theme is love the music breathes romance. From a lullaby, the music surges upward to the crashing crescendo of battle in the next scene. Comes now the wild, barbaric strain of half-breed lust and unjustified ambition. When you would resist the tears of the picture, the orchestra will not let you. When you would be silent under the tremendous strain of the situation on the scene, the orchestra wrests a cry from your throat.

The Birth of a Nation has been criticized and attempts have been made to suppress it. If history should be suppressed in schools for children, *The Birth of a Nation* should be suppressed in a theater of thinking people. The picture is vindicated by historical facts, and does not attempt to misinterpret or warp these facts for the purpose of dragging from their graves prejudices that have been dead long since.

The world has long waited for the American Hugo who could write the *Les Miserables* of the War between the States. Many writers have tried and failed. But the great novel of the Civil War has at last arrived—and when it got here it was a moving picture and not a book!

Boston American
Harlow Hare

One of the most effective features of *The Birth of a Nation* production is its really brilliant musical setting. During the two hours and a half which the big film requires, the orchestra plays an arrangement which perfectly fits the unfolding story and which includes many of the finest bits of melody extant. The library of the old masters and the collections of songs and ballads of the 60's have alike been rifled to make up the score of *The Birth of a Nation*.

When the beaux and belles of '61 danced the small hours away, they did not have the hesitation, the tango or the fox trot, but a waltz or polka tune, a schottische or a lancers, or perhaps the Virginia reel put rhythm in the feet and the tingle in the blood. So David W. Griffith, in his marvelous reproduction of the Piedmont ball in *The Birth of a Nation,* has the young people dancing to the strains of "Comin' Thro' the Rye" changed to waltz time.

On this lovely, almost sensuously intoxicating scene is brought the tattered flag that had been through the first Battle of Bull Run when the Confederates drove the Federals headlong before them and baptized the Stars and Bars in glory.

How the Johnny Rebs exult and how the women cheer as the flag is displayed and one hears the strains of the "Bonnie Blue Flag" succeeding the waltz music! But soon comes the news that the young officers at the ball must go to the front. A scene of wild confusion follows upon the joyous, orderly dance, and at daybreak, when everyone is racing about the streets, the chaos and alarm approaching strife are reflected by the strains of Suppe's "Light Cavalry Overture." The little town of Piedmont has its early share of the horrors of war. Weber's "Freischutz Overture" reproduces them to the ear as the pictures on the screen reproduce to the eye.

Music and Spectacle

A wonderful art, this, the marriage of music and spectacle, and one wonderfully achieved by Mr. Griffith and the man who put together the score, a composite of great themes suitable to Griffith's great ideas rather than an original work. It is, however, comparable to the way European composers like Liszt, Chopin, and Dvorak take the melodies of the common people, the folk music, so to speak, and combine and elaborate them with more erudite themes.

Thus the big moments of the early part of *The Birth of a Nation,* laid in the Southland, revert to "Dixie," "My Maryland," "Marching through Georgia,"

From the *Boston American,* July 18, 1915.

"Tramp, Tramp, Tramp! the Boys are Marching," "Kingdom Coming," "Girl I Left Behind Me," and "Home, Sweet Home." To what other tune should the Southerners bound for war march than to the ever familiar "Dixie"? What more splendidly typifies the rescue of the Piedmonters from the guerrilla troops by their own men than the glorious "Maryland, My Maryland"?

Of course, "Marching Thro' Georgia" sets the pace for the extraordinarily vivid depiction of Sherman's March, but it is a "Marching Through Georgia" with a sad antiphony—wails of the victims in minor keys answering the marching song of the conqueror. "Taps" for the deep tragedy of war's peace; "The Star Spangled Banner" to mark the grand victory of the North, and the inspiring strains of "America" for reunion of North and South in a greater nation when Grant and Lee clasped hands at Appomattox—such is the appropriate, if somewhat obvious, instrumentation of patriotic scenes.

Elsie's Melody

When piquant little *Elsie Stoneman* decides to become a nurse and solace gallant wounded youths back to health, even as Cabinet officers' daughters have done in the present war [World War I] her goings and comings are accompanied by a most adorable little air which she is supposed not only to sing but also to pick on the banjo. In the close-ups you can see the dainty lips fashioning the words of the song and in the full figure you can see her working the banjo a little over time, while the handsome sufferer on the pillow manages to turn his head about three-quarters in order to get a look at her. Many persons have asked what this tune is. It is Henry E. Work's "Kingdom Coming," otherwise known as "Massa's Jubilee," one of the most fetching ditties that was ever picked out of banjo or guitar.

To return to the great war scenes. There is a magnitude about Griffith's representation of war and battle that demands the most elaborate effects. The scenes themselves are enormous, panoramic; the action is both marvelously complex and marvelously vivid; the music must reproduce this immensity, complexity and thrill at once. Thus one is not surprised that Grieg's "Peer Gynt" suite, "In the Hall of the Mountain King," is used for the terrific pictures of "the torch against the breast of Atlanta"; that Wagnerian operatic crashes accompany the cannonading and infantry charging at Petersburg; and that even when a national army tune like "Tramp, Tramp, Tramp" is used, it is elaborate and built up into a great, overwhelming symphonic movement. So, too, in the scene of Lincoln's assassination in Ford's Theatre, Washington, April 14, 1865. The appearance of the emancipator is greeted, as it was greeted on that occasion, by the well-known strains of "Hail to the Chief." But the fatal crisis of that hour can only be rendered by classical music of enormous complexity and power such as Bellini's "Norma Overture," which is the work selected.

Tender Love Motif

Three distinctive strains or motifs run through the second half of the picture, emphasizing by contrast the three elements of which it is composed. For the loves of *Ben Cameron,* the little Confederate colonel, and *Elsie Stoneman,* the dainty Northern heroine, we have Breil's "Perfect Song," an original composition for this play and now published in sheet form. It is one of the most beautiful love themes that has ever been invented. It returns and returns with peculiar increasing effectiveness, but perhaps it is sweetest in the outdoor scene when *Elsie* kisses the dove and *Ben* repeatedly tries to steal a few for himself while she is doing so.

Then there is the wild, chaotic-seeming tune that marks the entry of the negro carpet-bagger mobs and the racket of the rioters. Perhaps Mr. Griffith got this out of the semi-musical cries of the negro dancers on the old plantation in Kentucky when he was a boy. It is certainly original so far as can be learned. It does not represent the negro of today by any means. For the last negro motif in the play is Hermann's beautifully liquid, enticing "Cocoanut Dance" to the strains of which the Hampton Institute films are shown.

But above all and everything else, the biggest thing in the second part of *The Birth of a Nation* and indeed of the whole play is the welcome Ku-Klux-Klan Call, the signal that the Fiery Cross of St. Andrew has been borne from South to North Carolina and back again and that the little band of oppressed whites, including the hero and heroine of the story, are to be saved by these Highlanders from the fury of the riotous elements unloosed upon them. The call makes the welkin ring at the opening of each part of the film. It strikes across the moments of agony, horror and suspense like a clarion note of rescue from another world. The call is not original, but an adaptation of the famous call in Wagner's "Die Walküre."

Stirring Ku-Klux Call

Just a flash of the ghostly horsemen, the big Ku-Klux call, and the spectators become almost frenzied in their applause. Often the call has a weird effect, as when the thin-voiced oboe plays it alone. Often it comes stridently powerful against entirely different notes.

The final Piedmont scenes of *The Birth of a Nation* are very strenuous. It seems almost impossible to conceive how Griffith could have got action of such lightning-like speed, involving such enormous numbers of people and carried on with such apparent defiance of the rules of order yet with a strange logic of its own. While these big flights, riots, and rescues are going on we have the appropriately big music of Tschaikowsky's "1812 Overture," Wagner's "Rienzi Overture," the "Zampa Overture," the Fire Music from "Die Walküre" and "The Ride of the Valkyries." It all ends up, as good adventure stories should, with the triumph of the heroic characters and thus naturally with the parade of the returning clansmen for which of course "Dixie" is the tune. Then after the scenes depicting negro progress above referred to, which are enlivened by the "Cocoanut Dance," the double honeymoon by the sea is shown and the strains of "In the Gloaming" are followed by Breil's "Perfect Song."

Remarkable Finale

The finale of the picture is Griffith's remarkable conception on the one hand of the "human salad" of War with the blond brute on a horse in the background striking at his helpless victims, and, on the other hand, of a Utopian brotherhood of love and peace, with some of the folks like Koreans and others like early Romans, and the figure of the Saviour blessing the glad assembly.

These fine bits of allegory are accompanied by the "Gloria" from Haydn's Mass in C, and as the last Utopian scene fades out and the immortal words of Daniel Webster on Liberty and Union appear on the screen, "The Star Spangled Banner" rings out in all its splendor, and the scenes that have made *The Birth of a Nation* are done.

Commentaries

Although scholarship on Griffith is burgeoning, and there has recently been a renewed interest in his place in the development of the American narrative cinema and his ambivalent relation to the emergence of the classical paradigm, there remains surprisingly little critical work on *The Birth of a Nation* itself. The following four essays, however, admirably provide a context for the controversy surrounding the film's ideology, and have been chosen to represent approaches to *The Birth of a Nation* that complement the discussion of the film in the Introduction.

In her examination of the status of history in *Birth* and the film's status as a historical text, Mimi White reveals the way in which Griffith uses history as a "pretext" for his interest in "the family drama, traditional and normative sexuality, and the assertion of a conventional family structure." From the interplay of "personal" and "public" events depicted in the film emerges the "image of an ideal family unit as the locus of transhistorical forces, an anchor of stability in the eternal scheme of the world," as the Civil War and Reconstruction era are "subsumed under and transcended by divine, ahistorical ideals."

Janet Staiger, in her reconsideration of the reception of *The Birth of a Nation,* offers the thesis that the film is "encrusted with a history of responses and debates which make it a symbol of more than racist propaganda." While reactions to the film in 1915 ranged from liberal to radically conservative, and there were fierce debates about the film's potential effects on spectators, there was general agreement that the film's subject matter could be judged separately from its aesthetic and cinematographic achievements. In the late 1930s, however, the race issue was reconfigured by American leftist radicals concerned about the political crisis in Europe. The film became "not only a litmus test of one's attitudes or beliefs about races, censorship, and aesthetics but also about the international political scene," as Communists attacked the film for its complicity with capitalism's exploitation of workers and blacks, and anti-Stalinists accused the film's critics of being "totalitarians." Staiger outlines the forty-year history that followed of *The Birth of a Nation*'s being used by progressive radicals "as a nodal point for their argument that connections exist between racism and class exploitation and that the representations of films matter to social spectators." Staiger concludes that *The Birth of a Nation,* as an obvious case, indicates some of the difficulties and complexities that currently face film scholars in evaluating movies.

James Chandler's essay sketches a literary genealogy of Griffith's historicism in an effort to reclaim the connections that exist between the modern film epic, launched by Griffith, and the nineteenth-century romantic historical novel, pioneered by Walter Scott. In the series of immensely popular works of fiction that came to be called the Waverly Novels, Scott "changed the course of all kinds of writing about the past," and "eventually became, without question, the most widely influential of all British authors except for Shakespeare."

Chandler refers to the late eighteenth-century context from which Scott emerged with his "sense of a historically specific culture," and describes the features of the new literary form Scott developed that "provided a way of representing large historical events as felt in the popular experience." In a discussion of *The Clansman,* Chandler indicates the extent to which Griffith— "guided by purposes and principles themselves indebted to Scott's example"—transformed, rather than adapted, Dixon's novel.

Like Scott, Griffith recognized "how a historically specific culture sets conditions upon the characters or the plots in question." Chandler notes that Griffith's attention to manners, for example, is "more patient and elaborate than the kind of shortcut Dixon takes," and he establishes an image of the Southern household in order "to make it the site where historical action leaves its mark on everyday life."

In his long and wide-ranging essay, Michael Rogin begins by situating *Birth* "at the juncture of three converging histories, the political history of postbellum America, the social history of movies, and the history of Griffith's early films." He traces the way in which Griffith, Dixon, and Woodrow Wilson, while not holding "identical views of the meaning either of *Birth* or of the history to which it called attention," offered the film "as the screen memory, in both meanings of that term, through which Americans were to understand their collective past and enact their future."

In a discussion of *Judith of Bethulia* (1913) and *The Avenging Conscience* (1914), the two most important longer films Griffith made before *Birth,* Rogin identifies "the demons that were taking over [Griffith's] screen"—demons that recurred as themes in the Biograph films that make up the prehistory of *Birth:* "the presence of weak or repressive fathers, associated with provincialism and tradition; the emergence of female sexuality, imaged in the phallic woman, associated with modernity, and represented by the actress Blanche Sweet; the presentation of domestic, interior space as claustrophobic, imprisoning, and vulnerable to invasion; and the use of rides to the rescue."

Rogin offers an interpretation of the way in which the Southern race war depicted in *Birth* "was not simply about itself." In addition to being "a stand-in for sectional, ethnic, and class conflicts," it was a stand-in for "the conflicts between tradition and modernity and between men and women." When Griffith replaced Blanche Sweet with Lillian Gish in the role of Elsie Stoneman, "he was shifting sexuality from the white woman to the black man. The regression to the presexual virgin and the invention of the black demon went hand in hand," as part of a strategy "to reempower white men."

Griffith made *The Birth of a Nation* to honor his father, and his need to redeem the powerful meanings he associates with his father's sword—one of the director's earliest memories—leads him to appropriate history in his epic film, and the film became, thereby, "a historical force."

The Birth of a Nation: Reconsidering Its Reception
Janet Staiger

In August 1978, the Ku Klux Klan of Oxnard, California, exhibited *The Birth of a Nation* as a fund-raiser and membership promotion. A militant communist splinter group, the Progressive Labor party, counterdemonstrated. And local Mexican-American and black associations protested against both camps. Tempers were hot and eventually violence broke out.[1] Once again, sixty-three years after its first turbulent showings, the 1915 film *The Birth of a Nation* had precipitated a ferocity and wrath sufficient to provoke men and women into a physical response.

One of my questions about the reception of *The Birth of a Nation* is why this film continues to outrage individuals. While the subject matter itself is probably sufficient as a solution to this problem. I would offer the thesis that *The Birth of a Nation* is encrusted with a history of responses and debates which make it a symbol of more than racist propaganda. At least for two decades, diatribes against it and defenses of its director play out major political battles in leftist politics as well as important debates in the history of film scholarship. Consequently, the continuing history of the reception of *The Birth of a Nation* can be considered as a nodal point for analyzing conditions of reception as they relate to evaluating subject matter and narrational techniques, positing effects of movies, and, ultimately, revealing racial attitudes and political positions of a film's opponents and defenders.

Specifically, although the 1915 reception of *The Birth of a Nation* can be organized around interpretations related to the question of racism—in which one can construct a complex continuum of reactions labeled by Joel Williamson as liberal to radical conservatism,[2] in the late 1930s, another continuum transforms the conditions for the film's subsequent reception. This second continuum can be associated with the contemporary political crisis of the European war for leftist radicals. Here the dynamics shift from, on the one hand, according to Communist party members, accusations of the film's complicity with capitalism's exploitation of workers and blacks to, on the other hand, defenses of the film by some leftists breaking from the party line. These defenses include attacking the film's critics as "totalitarians." Consequently, the race issue per se is reconfigured, intersecting

---

1. Gladwin Hill, "Polyglot City Is in Shock after a Melee," *New York Times,* 3 August 1978, A-14.
2. Joel Williamson, *The Crucible of Race: Black-White Relations in the American South since Emancipation* (New York: Oxford University Press, 1984).

From *Interpreting Films: Studies in the Historical Reception of American Cinema* (Princeton, N.J.: Princeton University Press, 1992).

with debates over the political economy and arguments about evaluating films and other cultural products of that political economy. . . . The popular representation of the reception of a film becomes one of the conditions for its subsequent reception. First, a bit of context before I move to an analysis of the history of the film's reception.

The Historical Setting

Most film scholars are somewhat familiar with events surrounding the initial distribution of *The Birth of a Nation*. Thomas Cripps notes that the film appeared as conditions for African Americans were deteriorating. Despite its progressivism in some areas of social action, Woodrow Wilson's presidency was perceived by blacks as a resurgence of "Southern ideals"; black people were denied the ballot box; Jim Crow laws were expanding; and between 1898 and 1908, race riots occurred in Wilmington (North Carolina), New York City, New Orleans, Atlanta, and Springfield (Illinois). However, African-American leadership and consciousness had also "sharpened."[3] Although from the mid-1890s, Booker T. Washington was assumed by many to represent the voice of African Americans, extensive violence by white racist extremists during the same time provoked alternative strategies. W.E.B. Du Bois specifically began to stand out after 1903, with his published attack on Washington's leadership. In 1905, Du Bois organized the Niagara Falls Conference, assaulting accommodationism and promoting a nascent "black is beautiful" campaign. In 1909, the Niagara movement and northern white liberals formed the National Association for the Advancement of Colored People (NAACP), which by 1914 had six thousand members in various cities.[4]

African Americans on the west coast began to protest against *The Birth of a Nation* once they were aware that the film was to be based on Thomas Dixon's

---

3. Thomas Cripps, *Slow Fade to Black: The Negro in American Film, 1900–1942* (London: Oxford University Press, 1977), pp. 41–43; Thomas R. Cripps, "The Reaction of the Negro to the Motion Picture 'Birth of a Nation'" (1963), rpt. in *Focus on "The Birth of a Nation,"* ed. Fred Silva (Englewood Cliffs, N.J.: Prentice-Hall, 1971), p. 111 (hereafter *Focus*). Thomas F. Gossett describes how Wilson contributed to reasserting segregation; *Race: The History of an Idea in America* (Dallas: Southern Methodist University Press, 1963), p. 279.

4. James M. McPherson, "The Antislavery Legacy: From Reconstruction to the NAACP," in *Towards a New Past: Dissenting Essays in American History,* ed. J. Barton Bernstein (New York: Random House, 1967), pp. 126–57; Williamson, *The Crucible of Race,* pp. 70–78. Williamson's thesis for the deepening of antagonisms between whites and blacks extends C. Vann Woodward's economic and political determinations proposed in Woodward's *The Strange Career of Jim Crow* (1955) to include psychological and cultural factors. The deteriorating situation of the blacks was not isolated; racism extended to Jews and Asians as well, with segregation and discrimination particularly overt. The Anti-Defamation League of B'nai B'rith formed in 1913. See Oscar Handlin, ed., *Immigration as a Factor in American History* (Englewood Cliffs, N.J.: Prentice-Hall, 1959), pp. 171–82. Also see John Higham, *Strangers in the Land* (New Brunswick, N.J.: Rutgers University Press, 1988).

play, *The Clansman.*[5] In 1905, Dixon combined two of his novels, *The Leopard's Spots* (1902) and *The Clansman* (1905), into dramatic form and began a theatrical road tour. At that time, however, Dixon's extreme racism was not widely acceptable, even in the South. Joel Williamson in *The Crucible of Race* argues that the recent race riots produced repercussions. For various reasons, including public safety, after 1906 few individuals encouraged representing blacks as beasts and advocating their deportation in order to achieve national unity and security—two extremely radical-conservative positions taken by Dixon.[6] Williamson argues that from 1880 through 1920, three "mentalities" exist in southern thinking about people of color. The "liberal" believed in the black's possibilities. Perhaps the oldest, the "conservative," presumed inferiority but was willing to permit these people in their "place." The "radical conservative" (which Williamson argues emerges in 1889 and appears through 1915 and in which category Williamson places Dixon) thought that the "'new' negro" was regressing into savagery. For this mentality, the paranoia over interracial sex (through rape or marriage) was a fear of the possible "perverted" offspring. As Thomas Gossett expresses it, "If a black has white intermixture, he is especially dangerous. White intermixture, Dixon thought, improved the intellect of blacks without changing their morals."[7] Dixon was not, however, unique in his opinions (and many may have held them more quietly). For example, in 1907, Benjamin R. Tillman, a U.S. senator from South Carolina, defended the South's repression of blacks by arguing that the evils of the Reconstruction era proved the inability of people of color to assume public roles, that they were inherently inferior, and that southern men needed to protect their women. Tillman claimed that black militiamen were overheard to say: "The President is our friend. The North is with us. We intend to kill all the white men, take the land, marry the white women, and then these white children will wait on us."[8] Nor was radical-conservative racism confined to the South. In 1916, New York City anthropologist Madison Grant in *The Passing of the Great Race* claimed that racial "hybrids" were suicidal for the American.[9] Dixon's two novels and play dramatized these beliefs. In 1906 in Philadelphia, blacks rioted over the play, with

5. Cripps, *Slow Fade*, pp. 52–64; "NAACP v. 'The Birth of a Nation': The Story of a 50-Year Fight," *The Crisis* 72, no. 2 (February 1965): 96.

6. Williamson, *The Crucible of Race*, pp. 140–95.

7. Ibid., pp. 4–6. All of Williamson's "mentalities" are categorized from the position's view of the evolutionary potential of people of color, most likely a sensible system given the impact of social Darwinism on discourses of the period. Thomas Gossett, *Uncle Tom's Cabin and American Culture* (Dallas: Southern Methodist University Press, 1985), p. 346.

8. Quoted in Benjamin R. Tillman, *Congressional Record*, 59th Cong., 2d Sess. (21 January 1907): pp. 1140–44, rpt. in *Civil Rights and the American Negro: A Documentary History,* ed. Albert P. Blaustein and Robert L. Zangrando (New York: Washington Square Press, 1968), p. 319.

9. Grant worked at the American Museum of Natural History. His popular book counted as threatening Eastern and Southern Europeans as well as other groups of people. Handlin, *Immigration,* pp. 183–85.

the effect that public safety claims were used to block some openings.[10] *The Clansman,* however, did continue to tour through the end of the decade.

One month prior to *The Birth of a Nation*'s opening in New York City, the NAACP chose the strategy of a nationwide protest against the film, hoping to prevent its exhibition on similar grounds of threat to the peace. This tactical choice produced conflicts among the NAACP's suporters since many of the association's white backers also tended to oppose censorship.[11] Furthermore, the film's technical virtuosity became a compensating feature to rationalize exhibiting the movie. Thus, any individual (then or now) might have conflicting or overdetermined views about *The Birth of a Nation* depending on that person's attitudes toward and judgments of its representation, its technical presentation, and censorship.

The NAACP did manage to delay several showings of the film, and some film review boards required changes. Although violence—such as throwing eggs at the screen—occurred,[12] public safety alarmists were disarmed by the protesters' recognizing the long-term disadvantage of violent tactics. In an effort to "soften" the content, the film was edited, several intertitles were added, and the short-lived Hampton Institute epilogue was tacked on. Aggressive defenses by Dixon and D. W. Griffith also blocked opponents.[13] I will return to these arguments momentarily.

10. Williamson, *The Crucible of Race,* pp. 140–48, 173–75; Gossett, *Uncle Tom's Cabin and American Culture,* p. 346; Cripps, *Slow Fade,* pp. 52–64.

11. "The Clansman" *The Crisis* 10, no. (May 1915): 33; "Fighting Race Calumny," *The Crisis* 10, no. 1 (May 1915): 40–42, 87–88, rpt. in *Focus,* pp. 66–73. Later historical surveys of the events during this period include: "NAACP v. 'The Birth of a Nation,'" p. 96; Cripps, "Reaction," pp. 112–18; Goodwin Berquist and James Greenwood, "Protest against Racism: 'The Birth of a Nation' in Ohio," *Journal of the University Film Association* 26, no. 3 (1974): 39–44; Cripps, *Slow Fade,* pp. 52–64; Nickieann Fleener-Marzec, *D. W. Griffith's "The Birth of a Nation": Controversy, Suppression, and the First Amendment as It Applies to Filmic Expression, 1915–1973* (New York: Arno Press, 1980), pp. 392–424; Richard Schickel, *D. W. Griffith: An American Life* (New York: Simon and Schuster, 1984), pp. 212–302.

12. In New York, the person who threw two eggs during the scene of "Little Sister" jumping off the cliff was a white, Howard Schaeffle. "Egg Negro Scenes in Liberty Film Play," *New York Times,* 15 April 1915, n.p.

13. For details on the alterations, besides the historical surveys (above), see "Films and Births and Censorship," *Survey,* 3 April 1915, 4–5; Seymour Stern, "The Birth of a Nation" *Cinemages,* special issue no. 1 (1955): 9. As Stern describes, among Griffith's deletions were some of the shots of blacks running through the streets of Piedmont, "flashes of screaming white girls being whisked by Negro rapists into doorways in back-alleys of the town," an epilogue "featuring, first Lincoln's forgotten letter to Staunton [*sic*], wherein Lincoln affirms that he does not believe in the equality of the black race with the white, and, finally, full-scale images of the deportation of masses of Negroes from New York harbor to the (filmed) jungles of Liberia as a 'peaceable solution' for American and the Negroes." *Survey* (in 1915) describes an important insertion required by the National Board of Censorship in late March: "These [changes] are said to have been chiefly a substantial reduction in the details of the chase of the white girl by the renegade Negro, which in the original is said to have been the most dreadful portrayal of rape ever offered for public view; the insertion of various soothing captions, such as 'I won't hurt you, little Missy'; the entire excision of a lynching; and a toning down of the scene in which the mulatto all but marries a white girl by force" ("Films and Births and Censorship," p. 4). "'Wid'" in

Between 1915 and 1973 the right to screen *The Birth of a Nation* "was challenged at least 120 times."[14] Indeed, the strategy of the NAACP was to continue its opposition to the film anytime someone tried to revive it. In 1921 the NAACP petitioned the Boston mayor not to show it "because it is a malicious misrepresentation of the colored people, depicting them as moral perverts," while five people were arrested for picketing and protesting in New York City.[15] When *The Birth of a Nation* was to be rereleased with a sound track in 1930, the NAACP and others appealed to Will Hays and the Motion Picture Producers and Distributors Association to censor it, as they controlled sexual and criminal content, but no equivalency for racism was made.[16]

A reinforcement to protesters was apparent proof from social scientists that the film created attitudinal changes. When one of the 1933 Payne Fund studies screened *The Birth of a Nation* to 434 middle and high school students in a predominantly white Illinois town, the researchers determined the "largest effect found in any of the experiments we conducted."[17] The children's "favorable" opinion of African Americans dropped from a mean of 7.46 on a scale of 11 to 0 to 5.93, down 1.48 points. Testing five months later suggested only a partial return to the original views.

But it was later in that decade when a radical transformation in the implications of the film's interpretation and evaluation occurred among a political subculture in the United States. One's view of *The Birth of a Nation* became not only a litmus test of one's attitudes or beliefs about races, censorship, and aesthetics but also about the contemporary international political scene. The film became encrusted with debates and accusations exchanged between party-line Communists and anti-Stalinists.

The Initial Reception of *The Birth of a Nation*

To clarify the complexities and ironies of positions that were to be taken in the late 1930s, when Communists appropriated the film as a symptom of fascist and

"Films and Film Folk" (ca. 13 July 1915), *D. W. Griffith Papers, 1897–1954* (Frederick, Md.: University Publications of America, microfilm) describes the Hampton Institute epilogue as a "shock," coming after *The Birth of a Nation*. Details on its production are in Nickie Fleener, "Answering Film with Film: The Hampton Epilogue, a Positive Alternative to the Negative Stereotypes Presented in *The Birth of a Nation*," *Journal of Popular Film and Television* 7, no. 4 (1980): 400–425.

14. Fleener-Marzec, *D. W. Griffith's "The Birth of a Nation*," p. 483.

15. "NAACP v. 'The Birth of a Nation,'" p. 97; "Negroes Oppose Film," *New York Times,* 7 May 1921.

16. "Movies Turn Deaf Ear to Colored Plea," *Christian Century* 47, no. 2 (24 September 1930): 1140–41.

17. Ruth C. Peterson and L. L. Thurstone, *Motion Pictures and the Social Attitudes of Children* (New York: Macmillan, 1933), p. 38.

monopoly capitalist ideologies, I want to summarize the debates of the midteens since they reappear in the later discussions.[18] The comparison between these

18. Although Cripps, Berquist and Greenwood, Fleener-Marzec, and Schickel provide accounts of the reception of *The Birth of a Nation,* three other studies deserve special note. In 1961, Charles L. Hutchins surveyed much of the critical discussion to date in his master's thesis, "A Critical Evaluation of the Controversies Engendered by D. W. Griffith's *The Birth of a Nation*" (Master's thesis, University of Iowa). Hutchins's purpose was to outline and evaluate "major controversial issues which have grown up around *The Birth of a Nation*" (p. 3). Two stand out for him: Griffith's "treatment of the Negro" and the historical documentation regarding the "treatment of Thaddeus Stevens," the "role of the Negro in the Reconstructed South," and the "causes for the rise of the Ku Klux Klan" (p. 25). Hutchins's thesis is well-organized and useful (despite his evaluation procedures), but since he treats all responses as of the same time, determining patterns that might be considered historical is not possible. John Hammond Moore provides excellent information about the South Carolina press's negative reaction to Dixon's 1905 play but generally approving response for the 1915 film: "South Carolina's Reaction to the Photoplay *The Birth of a Nation,*" *The Proceedings of the South Carolina Historical Association* (1963): 30–40. Russell Merritt studied the Boston events of April 1915, claiming that "most of the audience that came out of the Tremont theatre that night in 1915, for instance, believed Griffith's story was historically true, that *The Birth of a Nation* was a nostalgic, but essentially accurate description of the Civil War years and their aftermath" (p. 26). The evidence for this, however, is uncertain since certainly some Bostonians vehemently protested the film. (See below.) Merritt continues his essay, arguing that in comparison with Dixon, Griffith's representation of blacks is toned down. This approach to the film repeats one associated since 1915 with defenders of the film. "Dixon, Griffith, and the Southern Legend," *Cinema Journal* 12, no. 1 (Fall 1972): 26–45.

In chronological order, the period articles and reviews that I studied are: D. W. Griffith, "The Motion Picture and Witch Burners," n.d. (numerous papers in "Flickerings from Film Land by Kitty Kell" column), rpt. in *Focus,* pp. 16–99; D. W. Griffith, "The Future of the Two-Dollar Movie," n.d. (numerous papers), rpt. in *Focus,* pp. 99–101; Rev. Dr. Charles H. Parkhurst, "'The Birth of a Nation,'" n.d. (review in numerous papers), rpt. in *Focus,* pp. 102–3; "'The Birth of a Nation,'" *New York Times,* 4 March 1915, 9; Hector Turnbull, "A Stirring Drama Shown," *New York Tribune,* 4 March 1915, 9; "Negroes Object to Film," *New York Times,* 7 March 1915, n.p.; "W," "The Birth of a Nation," *The New York Dramatic Mirror* 73, no. 1890 (10 March 1915): 28; Mark Vance, "The Birth of a Nation," *Variety,* 12 March 1915, rpt. in *Focus,* pp. 22–25; George D. Proctor, "The Birth of a Nation," *Motion Picture News* 11, no. 10 (13 March 1915): 40–50; W. Stephen Bush, "The Birth of a Nation," *Moving Picture World* 23 (13 March 1915): 1586–87, rpt. in *Focus,* pp. 25–28; Francis Hackett, "Brotherly Love," *The New Republic* 2, no. 20 (20 March 1915): 185–86, rpt. in *Focus,* pp. 84–86; "A Reconstruction Story," *New York Times,* 21 March 1915, n.p.; "Moving Picture Justly Denounced by Jane Adams [*sic*]," *New York Evening Post,* 25 March 1915, n.p. (in D. W. Griffith Papers); "Protests on Photo Play," *New York Times,* 31 March 1915, n.p.; "Promise to Tone Down Two Scenes of Vicious Photo Play," *New York Age,* 1 April 1915, 1; James W. Johnson, "Views and Reviews," *New York Age,* 1 April 1915, 4; "Films and Births and Censorship," *Survey,* 3 April 1915, 4–5; "Capitalizing Race Hatred," *New York Globe,* 6 April 1915, n.p., rpt. in *Focus,* pp. 73–75; Thomas Dixon, "Reply to the New York Globe," *New York Globe,* 10 April 1915, n.p., rpt. in *Focus,* pp. 75–77; D. W. Griffith, "Reply to the *New York Globe,*" *New York Globe,* 10 April 1915, n.p., rpt. in *Focus,* pp. 77–79; "Dixon on His Motive" (editorial), *New York Globe,* 8 April 1915 (in D. W. Griffith Papers); "What Some Globe Readers Have to Say," *New York Globe,* 9 April 1915 (in D. W. Griffith Papers); National Board of Review, "Censoring Motion Pictures," *The New Republic* 2, no. 23 (10 April 1915): 262–63; "'The Birth of a Nation,'" *Outlook,* 14 April 1915, 854; "Egg Negro Scenes in Liberty Film Play," *New York Times,* 15 April 1915, n.p.; "Negroes Mob Photo Play," *New York Times,* 18 April 1915, n.p.; "Mass.

periods valuably illuminates the complexities and contradictions that this transformation produces.

When *The Birth of a Nation* was originally exhibited, reviewers uniformly praised the presentation of the subject matter, separating off the narrational techniques (i.e., style) from what was being represented. (This "form/content" split is typical of reviewing of the period and is due most immediately to nineteenth-century aesthetics.) The writers then varied: some thought the representations were accurate; others were neutral; some ignored the issue; and the rest regretted or challenged what they saw. Numerous attacks on the subject matter were marshaled, but for the sake of brevity, five may be delineated as major themes. The most obvious indignity was that the film distorted and consequently falsified the history of the Reconstruction era. Within this theme were subroutines: the facts were inaccurate or the examples were not representative of the whole history. Second, and related to the fabrication of history attack, was the assertion that the film misrepresented the character of blacks both as individual people and as a

Protests Vicious Movie," *New York Age,* 22 April 1915, 1; W. James Johnson; "Views and Reviews," *New York Age,* 22 April 1915, 4; "Censorship: The Curse of a Nation," *Boston Evening Transcript,* 23 April 1915, n.p., rpt. in *Focus,* pp. 87–88; Thomas Dixon, "Fair Play for *The Birth of a Nation,*" *Boston Journal,* 26 April 1915, n.p., rpt. in *Focus,* pp. 90–95; D. W. Griffith, "Defense of *The Birth of a Nation* and Attack on the Sullivan Bill," *Boston Journal,* 26 April 1915, n.p., rpt. in *Focus,* pp. 88–90; "Tom Dixon's 'Clansman,'" *The Crisis* 10, no. 1 (May 1915): 19–20; "The Clansman," *The Crisis* 10, no. 1 (May 1915): 33, rpt. as "'The Birth of a Nation': An Editorial," in *Focus,* pp. 64–66; "Fighting Race Calumny," *The Crisis* 10, no. 1 (May-June 1915): 40–42, 87–88, rpt. in *Focus,* pp. 66–73; "Chicago Prepares to Forestall 'Birth of a Nation,'" *Chicago Defender,* 1 May 1915, 3; "The Death of a Movie," *Chicago Defender,* 1 May 1915, 8; "Regulation of Films," *The Nation* 100, no. 2601 (6 May 1915): 486–87; James W. Johnson, "Views and Reviews," *New York Age,* 6 May 1915, 4; "Mayor Thompson Bars 'Birth of a Nation' from Chicago," *Chicago Defender,* 15 May 1915, 2; Rolfe Cobleigh, ["Why I Oppose *The Birth of a Nation*"], [26 May 1915], rpt. in *Fighting a Vicious Film: Protest against "The Birth of a Nation"* (Boston: Boston Branch of the National Association for the Advancement of Colored People, 1915), rpt. in *Focus,* pp. 80–83; "*Birth of a Nation* Case Dismissed," *New York Age,* 27 May 1915, 4; "'The Birth of a Nation,'" *The Crisis* 10, no. 2 (June 1915): 69–71; Helen Duey (?), *Woman's Home Companion,* 1 June 1915 (D. W. Griffith Papers); Charlotte Rumbold, "Against 'The Birth of a Nation,'" *The New Republic* 3, no. 31 (5 June 1915): 125; "Progressive Protest Against Anti-Negro Film," *Survey,* 5 June 1915, 209–10; "The Dirt of a Nation," *Chicago Defender,* 5 June 1915, 8; Henry MacMahon, "The Art of the Movies," *New York Times,* 6 June 1915, sect. 6, p. 8; "Meetings," *The Crisis* 10, no. 3 (July 1915): 148–49; "Wid," "Films and Film Folk" (ca. 13 July 1915) (D. W. Griffith Papers); Harlow Hare, *Boston American,* 18 July 1915, n.p., rpt. in *Focus,* pp. 36–40; "'The Birth of a Nation,'" *Gazette* (Cleveland, Ohio), 11 September 1915, 2; "'The Birth of a Nation,'" *Gazette,* 2 October 1915, [2]; Ward Greene, *Atlanta Journal,* 7 December 1915, n.p., rpt. in *Focus,* pp. 30–33; Ned McIntosh, *Atlanta Constitution,* 7 December 1915, n.p. rpt. in *Focus,* pp. 33–36; "The Attorney General's Broadside," *Advocate* (Cleveland, Ohio), 2, no. 37 (22 January 1916): [4]; S.E.F. Rose, "The Ku Klux Klan and 'The Birth of a Nation,'" *Confederate Veteran* 24, no. 4 (April 1916): 157–59; Henry Stephen Gordon, "The Story of David Wark Griffith," *Photoplay* 10, no. 5 (October 1916): 90–94; and Vachel Lindsay, *The Art of the Moving Picture* (1915) (1922; rpt., New York: Liveright, 1970), pp. 74–77.

race. In particular, reviewers noted that the only people of color shown were either bestial or subservient to whites. As *The Crisis* put it, "The Negro [is] represented either as an ignorant fool, a vicious rapist, a venal and unscrupulous politician or a faithful but doddering idiot."[19]

A third theme was that the film glorified crime, specifically lynching. Writers pointed out ironies and contradictions following from that: pictures showing murder and robbery were routinely censored. Furthermore, whites were willing to suppress by law boxing pictures in which blacks beat whites, but they would not stop the exhibition of *The Birth of a Nation*. Specifically, the 1912 Sims Act preventing interstate transportation of boxing films was enacted after the heavyweight champion, John Arthur "Jack" Johnson, who was black, kept beating white contenders. In 1910, when Johnson defeated Jim Jeffries, at least eighteen blacks were killed in the fight's aftermath, which reinforced sentiment for the passage of the federal bill.[20]

Fourth, opponents argued that the film incited prejudices against people of color, having an immoral effect or threatening public peace (as its predecessor *The Clansman* had done). Finally, *The Birth of a Nation* taught the doctrine that African Americans should be removed from the United States, a doctrine undemocratic, unchristian, and unlawful.

Defenders of *The Birth of a Nation* did not directly respond to all of the opponents' themes, and they introduced ones of their own. Griffith and Dixon both argued that the historical representation was accurate. Griffith wrote in 1915 that to show the history of the West one would have to "show the atrocities committed by the Indians against the whites."[21] Dixon appealed to the argument that historical accounts are variable since they are based on perspectives. At another point he claimed historical truth based on popular consensus: the film "expresses the passionate faith of the entire white population of the South. If I am wrong, they are wrong. The number of white people in the South who differ from my views of the history of Reconstruction could be housed on a half-acre lot [*sic*]."[22]

Regarding the accusation of a biased representation of blacks, Dixon, Griffith, and others claimed that the film authentically depicted the character of blacks during the Reconstruction era, if not now. Furthermore, the film not only portrayed bad people of color but also praised good ones who protected their former masters. Thus, the representation was balanced.

---

19. The more irate reviewers already recognized the racism of "uncle Tom" and "Sambo" characters. "'The Clansman,'" *The Crisis* 10, no. 1 (May 1915): 65.
20. "The Dirt of a Nation," *Chicago Defender,* 5 June 1915, 8; Dan Streible, "A History of the Boxing Film, 1894–1915: Social Reform and Social Control in the Progressive Era" (Unpublished seminar paper, University of Texas at Austin, Spring 1989), pp. 13–22.
21. Griffith, "The Motion Picture and Witch Burners" (1915), rpt. in *Focus,* pp. 96–99.
22. Dixon, "Fair Play for *The Birth of a Nation*," *Boston Journal,* 26 April 1915, n.p., rpt. in *Focus,* pp. 90–95.

Defenders attacked their opponents in three ways. They argued that artistic and dramatic merit justified the film's exhibition, that their opposition was stifling free speech, and that those who wanted the film banned supported interracial marriages. This last theme was particularly promoted by Dixon, but even Griffith writes, "The attack of the organized opponents to this picture is centered upon that feature of it which they deem might become an influence against the intermarriage of blacks and whites."[23]

Among the approximately sixty reviews and articles studied, no extrinsic reasons for alignment with one position or another were discernible; for example, there were no consistencies from a regional perspective. Although Russell Merritt writes, "Most of the audience that came out of the [Boston] Tremont theatre that night in 1915 . . . believed Griffith's story was historically true,"[24] other northerners were not of that opinion, with many of them leading the attack on the film. Dixon claimed he presented "the passionate faith of the entire white population of the South."[25] This view is somewhat supported by John Hammond Moore's survey of South Carolina's reviews. Moore found that the state's papers about-faced from their 1905 denunciation of Dixon's *The Clansman*. When the play toured, reviewers took issue with the historical accuracy of the thesis, chastised the Ku Klux Klan for getting out of hand, and opposed the themes of blacks as beasts and the need to transport them out of the United States. *The Birth of a Nation* received no similar objections, with "almost unanimous approval" of the film.[26] However, the white arrested for throwing eggs at the New York Liberty Theater presentation claimed, "I am a Southerner and a libertarian, and I believe in the education and uplifting of the negro. It made my blood boil to see the play and I threw the eggs at the screen."[27]

The lack of a coherent regional response is scarcely surprising since racism occurs throughout the United States. While a more systematic analysis of opinions might reveal patterns associated with sectors of the nation, Williamson's observation of at least three southern "mentalities" (liberal, conservative, and radical-conservative) during the 1880–1920s seems reconfirmed by this study although these mentalities may be more national than regional. Furthermore, from today's perspective, even the 1880–1920s liberal mentality is scarcely a nonracist attitude.

For these 1915 spectators of *The Birth of a Nation*, besides the questions of causes or types of racism, it is important to consider the complications of assumptions about the possible effects of watching movies and social responses to that

23. Griffith, "Reply to the *New York Globe*" (10 April 1915), rpt. in *Focus*, p. 79.

24. Merritt, "Dixon, Griffith, and the Southern Legend," p. 26.

25. Dixon, "Fair Play for *The Birth of a Nation*" (26 April 1915), pp. 90–95.

26. Moore, "South Carolina's Reaction," p. 40. Williamson argues in *The Crucible of Race* that the radical-conservative attribution of bestial qualities shifted from blacks to other minorities after 1906. Moore's information suggests otherwise.

27. "Egg Negro Scenes in Liberty Film Play," *New York Times*, 15 April 1915.

possibility. While turn-of-the-century reformers operated on the assumption that a scientific study of society and humans provided the basis for policy-making, many also steered away from overt censorship. The National Board of Review, the film industry's voluntary self-regulation system, merely advised film companies about subject matter (although local boards with legal powers could require changes). Confronted by this film, many opponents argued that portions of the film could have real behavioral effects, stimulating or changing preexistent attitudes in directions unfavorable to social harmony. On the basis of actual experiences following theatrical productions, they tried to argue that *The Birth of a Nation* was a threat to public peace. While defenders did not disagree with the position that films could be causal forces, they stressed First Amendment rights of free speech—a widely accepted discourse considered an idea fundamental to the preservation of the United States. As a constructed characteristic of the identity of "American," "free speech" serves as a center-ing notion against which non-American positions are positioned as dangerous. Opponents to *The Birth of a Nation* could only argue, not that the defenders were wrong, but that the film threatened public peace, which might be more important than free speech. This prediction of danger, however, was a hard claim to prove since violence was very local and sporadic.

Placing positions of free speech versus public safety in a continuum of political persuasions (liberal to conservative) is impossible, given the historical variations on this debate. Witness, for example, the 1989 U.S. Supreme Court decision that burning the American flag is acceptable as a form of political expression. Judges labeled in 1989 as "liberal" and "conservative" show up on both sides of the judgment, as do individuals in the subsequent furor over amending the Constitu-tion to prohibit such an act. For the analysis of *The Birth of a Nation,* however, the implications of the differing positions need to be stressed, if not labeled. Everyone agreed that films had some type of effect, but not everyone concurred as to the relative merits of solutions in balance with possible compensating values (e.g., free speech and a widely accepted aesthetic quality). Legal actions related to society's needs were in conflict, but everyone recognized that this film pushed the question to a certain limit. That racist (from today's perspective) material was eventually tolerated is not indicative of a social decision that free speech overrides filmic effects. After all, legal and semilegal apparatus (mainstream industry agree-ments not to compete in subject areas that might provoke the retaliation of pressure groups) did censor subject matter related to certain types of criminal behavior and sexuality. Thus, one conclusion is that either racism was perceived as less menacing than that other subject matter, or it was in the interest of those in positions of authority to permit an amount of racist representation up to the borderline of the tolerable (relative to the counterthreat of suppression of opinion). However you understand these conditions, a significant factor in the reception of *The Birth of a Nation* in 1915 is the political and racist underpinnings of social policy in relation to the film's representation and effectivity.

Thus, the initial reception of *The Birth of a Nation* constitutes what might be called a generic reaction quite understandable within the contradictions of the period's social formation. While I might draw out numerous other discursive strands within the individual essays relating them to their historical contexts, the dominant points involve an agreement that subject matter and narrational procedures could be judged separately, but differences existed over evaluating subject matter and its potential effects on spectators. Here tacit race attitudes intersect with other beliefs—ones about what constitutes acceptable historiography; whether a film should be judged on the content or effects of its subject matter, narrational procedures, or some combination of them; and whether censorship of certain representations is more important than free speech. All three of these issues still concern scholars and citizens today, making these aspects of the reception of *The Birth of a Nation* constant across a stretch of seventy-five years.

A Transformation of the Reception of *The Birth of a Nation*

In the late 1930s, themes from the 1915 period would reoccur, but other revisions are indications of how historical change and political perspectives influence argumentation about films. As events in Europe and the Soviet Union altered the political strategies and alliances of the American radical Left, *The Birth of a Nation* continued to be an exemplary case in film studies for issues of socially acceptable representations of U.S. racial minorities, procedures of response against some subject matter, and systems of evaluating narrational procedures and possible audience effects.

In 1936 Richard Watts published in the leftist journal *New Theatre and Film* a commentary on Griffith that criticized *The Birth of a Nation*'s "cruel unfairness to the Negro." Three years later, Lewis Jacobs published his history *The Rise of the American Film,* concluding that "the film was a passionate and persuasive avowal of the inferiority of the Negro. In viewpoint it was, surely, narrow and prejudiced." But in December 1939, David Platt went further. Writing for the Communist party newspaper, the *Daily Worker,* Platt argued that *The Birth of a Nation,* "by creating racial prejudice, helped create the basis for war [World War I] propaganda." Furthermore, the resurrection of the Ku Klux Klan, aided by the film, worked to harass African Americans to participate in the First World War effort.[28]

---

28. Richard Watts, Jr., "D. W. Griffith," *New Theater and Film* (November 1936), rpt. in *New Theater and Film, 1934 to 1937,* ed. Herbert Kline (San Diego, Calif.: Harcourt-Brace-Jovanovich, 1985), p. 238; Lewis Jacobs, "D. W. Griffith: *The Birth of a Nation*" (1939, from *The Rise of the American Film*), rpt. in *Focus,* p. 159; editor's note for David Platt, "Fanning the Flames of the War," *Daily Worker* (New York City), 20 December 1939, 7. This was one of four articles on prowar filmmaking in 1914–1918 published 18–21 December 1939. Films Platt considered possibly progressive were *Juarez* and *Mr. Smith Goes to Washington;* David Platt, "Will Film World Cave In as It Did in '14?" *Daily Worker,* 21 December 1939, 7.

Now, this argument may need some context. From the early 1930s, but particularly from 1939 until the end of the Hitler-Stalin pact, the *Daily Worker* took an antiwar stance. Part of that project was an appeal to individuals such as blacks to see the European events not from a nationalist perspective but from one of class. This was not their fight since it was not that of any member of the working class; neither capitalists in the United States nor fascists in Germany were the blacks' friends. In early 1940, the *Daily Worker* and its supporters participated with blacks in picketing theaters reviving *The Birth of a Nation*.[29]

Platt's act had a tradition in Marxist aesthetic criticism: demonstrating the complicity of a film or literary text with capitalist goals was a well-established approach to art evaluation and the activation of political sensibilities. Furthermore, after 1915 *The Birth of a Nation* had been continually criticized for its racism by individuals not all of whom were particularly aligned with radical-Left politics. For instance, in 1938 in *Current History,* V. F. Calverton published an outstanding analysis of the historiographical problems of the film, pointing out "its inaccuracies, exaggerations, and historical indecencies and distortions."[30]

29. A socialist newspaper, the *New Leader,* implied in 1940 that the Communist party chose particularly to "court" blacks because of defections due to the Hitler-Stalin pact. While the pact had serious repercussions in the party, direct approaches to blacks were at least a decade old. Ted Poston, "CP Purges Ford as Scapegoat for Failure among Negroes," *New Leader,* 30 March 1940, 4; Philip Taft, "Party Organizer (New York, 1927–1938)," in *The American Radical Press, 1880–1960,* vol. 1, ed. Joseph R. Conlin (Westport, Conn.: Greenwood Press, 1974), p. 262; Cripps, *Slow Fade,* p. 68. Eugene Gordon, "'Yes, I Mean You Guys,' Barks Mr. Paglia," *Daily Worker* ca. 4 January 1940, n.p.; Seymour Stern, "Suppression of Showing Marks 25th Year of 'Birth of a Nation,'" *New Leader,* 16 March 1940, 3.

30. Daniel Aaron, *Writers on the Left* (New York: Harcourt, 1961); Richard H. Pells, *Radical Visions and American Dreams: Culture and Social Thought in the Depression Years* (Middletown, Conn.: Wesleyan University Press, 1973). Additional criticisms and defenses of *The Birth of a Nation* through the 1930s include (in chronological order): Thomas Dixon, "Civil War Truth," *New York Times,* 8 May 1921; "[Griffith] Defends Film Production," *New York Times,* 9 May 1921; "Foes of Klan Fight 'Birth of a Nation,'" *New York Times,* 3 December 1922, 5; "Movies Turn Deaf Ear to Colored Plea," *Christian Century* 47, no. 2 (24 September 1930): 1140–41; Barnet G. Braver-mann, "Griffith: The Pioneer," *Theatre Guild Magazine* 8 (February 1931): 28–31, 60–61 (Braver-mann would soon be an editor of *Experimental Cinema;* he writes: "It is thus clear that Griffith's background did not help him to develop a penetrative social outlook"); Seymour Stern, "Hollywood and Montage," *Experimental Cinema* 4 (1932): 47–52; Peterson and Thurstone, *Motion Pictures and the Social Attitudes of Children,* pp. 35–38, 60–61; Harry Alan Potamkin, *The Eyes of the Movie,* International Pamphlets, no. 38 (n.p., 1934); Seymour Stern, "Birthday of a Classic," *New York Times,* 25 March 1935; Seymour Stern, "'The Birth of a Nation': In Retrospect," *International Photographer* 7 (April 1935): 4–5, 23–24; Richard Watts, Jr., "D. W. Griffith," *New Theater and Film* (November 1936), rpt. in *New Theater and Film,* ed. Klein, pp. 237–40; Archer Winsten, "'The Birth of a Nation' Surprises Old Admirer," *New York Post,* 5 October 1937; Milton MacKaye, *"The Birth of a Nation,"* *Scribner's Magazine* 102, no. 5 (November 1937): 40–46, 69; V. F. Calverton, "Cultural Barometer," *Current History* 49, no. 1 (September 1938): 45–47; Lewis Jacobs, "D. W. Griffith: *The Birth of a Nation*" (1939), rpt. in *Focus,* pp. 154–68.

In February 1940, Platt continued his assault, printing a series of seven articles reviewing the representation of blacks in Hollywood and painstakingly developing the thesis that Hollywood, in cooperation with capitalist interests, "deliberately and carefully fostered" prejudice "to divide Negro and white and rule both." Citing the 1933 Payne Fund Studies and evidence of an increase in lynching in 1915, Platt implied that the film was directly responsible for changes in attitude and behavior.[31]

Whether because of a personal change in politics, a response to Platt's articles, or another cause, Seymour Stern took up in 1940 the defense of the film. Stern was to claim later that articles he wrote in 1940 "provoked a bitter reaction": "former friends and acquaintances ceased to be such." Writing for the socialist and, in his words, "anti-Stalinist" *New Leader,* Stern accused "Negro leaders and left-wing liberals" of attacking Griffith as being "anti-Negro." He went on to claim that after Platt's February *Daily Worker* articles, growing evidence indicated "a well-organized, underground boycott campaign against 'The Birth of a Nation,'" a "campaign of boycott and terrorism." "Several days [after Platt's articles], Communist Party agents and stooges from innocent-front organizations, who had gotten wind of the proposed revival [of *The Birth of a Nation*], visited the manager of the theatre and proceeded to terrorize him in much the same manner as the alleged clansmen in the picture terrorized Negroes."[32] The *New Leader*'s editorial note accompanying Stern's essay said that the article was

> the first of a short series on Communist activity in the movie business, [which] shows how, in accordance with the new Stalinite [*sic*] line on the Negroes, the caviar comrades are trying to suppress the showing of "The Birth of a Nation." . . . The next articles by Seymour Stern, who has spent more than a decade in Hollywood writing motion picture scenarios, will reveal the Communist ramifications in the Museum of Modern Art Film Library and in the documentary [filmmaking] field.[33]

31. David Platt, "Negroes Barred from Hollywood Jobs, Slandered in Its Films," *Daily Worker,* 20 February 1940, 7. This is the second of the series that ran from 19 to 28 February 1940. On the 1933 Payne Fund studies, see Peterson and Thurstone, *Motion Pictures and the Social Attitudes of Children.*

32. Seymour Stern, "Griffith: I. *The Birth of a Nation,*" *Film Culture* 36 (Spring-Summer 1965): 36–37; Seymour Stern, "Suppression of Showing Marks 25th Year of 'Birth of a Nation,'" *New Leader,* 6 March 1940, 3. Stern's reference in 1965 is to his articles in the *New Leader* and *New York Times.* However, the latter essay seems moderately harmless, with another essay in the *New York Herald Tribune* of possibly greater provocation. More likely, Stern's alienation from his colleagues develops from his second article in the *New Leader* in which he attacks Jay Leyda (see below). Seymour Stern, "'The Birth of a Nation' Marked an Industry's Coming of Age," *New York Herald Tribune,* 16 June 1940; Seymour Stern, "Pioneer of the Film Art," *New York Times Magazine,* 10 November 1940, 16–17.

33. "No Show," *New Leader,* 16 March 1940, 3. The following week Stern accused Jay Leyda, assistant curator at the Museum of Modern Art, of "depart[ing] from accepted canons of cinematic criticism, and substitut[ing] outright political propaganda" in Leyda's film notes for a retrospective of Soviet cinema. Seymour Stern, "Film Library Notes Build 'CP Liberators' Myth," *New Leader,* 23 March 1940, 3. Many people believe this article contributed to events that led to the request for Leyda's resignation from the museum.

The Dies Committee was already investigating Hollywood for communists when this invective appeared.

What is happening becomes, in retrospect, ironic and sad. For Stern and Platt, along with Lewis Jacobs and Harry Alan Potamkin, had started the 1930s on a high and cooperative note. In 1930, these four individuals were cofounders and editors of *Experimental Cinema,* an early progressive film journal.[34] However, several factors during the decade were to split these people and their associates into bitter factions.

Among the most significant of these factors were debates by leftists over the connections between literature and social or political policy, the appropriate roles of artists concerning approved party aesthetic policies, and the analysis of subject matter and narrational procedures. The vicissitudes of radical progressive thought in the 1930s about these concerns are extensive and complex. In only the most general terms, in the 1920s, Marxists equated "good art with successful propaganda" but considered aesthetic experimentation permissible. Liberals such as Stark Young at *The New Republic* or Joseph Wood Krutch at *The Nation* dissented from that view, emphasizing internal structure and personal responses over content. This judgment reversed in the next decade. By the mid-1930s, splits among leftists developed over the artists' responsibilities to people, given the crisis of the depression. Could artists afford to detach themselves or their art from social communication? Richard Pells argues that Edmund Wilson's *Axel's Castle* (1931) participates in laying the groundwork for the need to communicate with people, developing the thesis that the symbolists and avant-gardists unconsciously absorbed the worst features of bourgeois individualism: intense subjectivity was inappropriate. Not all radicals agreed.[35]

Another factor, most important at the end of the decade and interpenetrating with aesthetic and cultural theory, was artists' increasing disenchantment with the Communist party as it changed policies during the 1930s. Daniel Aaron argues that the execution of Nicola Sacco and Bartolomeo Vanzetti in August 1927 mobilized many liberals into more radical politics. Furthermore, the depression deepened individuals' beliefs that capitalism was a bankrupt economic system. But after 1937, Stalinism began to seem as threatening as European fascism. The causes for this shift included the purges, dissatisfaction with party policies during the Spanish Civil War, and the blow of the Hitler-Stalin pact on 23 August 1939, followed by Germany's invasion of Poland a week later. It should not be surpris-

34. The first issue (February 1930) of *Experimental Cinema* lists Platt and Jacobs as coeditors for the Cinema Crafters (Philadelphia), with Hollywood editor Stern and New York editor Potamkin.
35. Pells, *Radical Visions and American Dreams,* p. 34. Also see: Aaron, *Writers on the Left;* Ian H. Birchall, "Marxism and Literature," in *The Sociology of Literature,* ed. Jane Routh and Janet Wolff (Keele, England: University of Keele Press, 1977), pp. 92–108; and George Steiner, "Marxism and the Literary Critic," in *Sociology of Literature and Drama,* ed. Elizabeth and Tom Burns (Harmondsworth, England: Penguin Books, 1973), pp. 159–78.

ing that conservatives and even liberals attacked Bolshevik Marxists at this point, but progressives such as socialists did as well. Max Nomad in the *New Leader* proceeded to redefine allies and enemies: "'The Socialist system of collective ownership is compatible with totalitarianism,'" he wrote in January 1941.[36]

Experimental Cinema started publication in 1930. Its initial and consistent stance in favor of Soviet cinema was, as George Amberg put it, "in 1930, . . . implicitly involved [in] a taking of sides, if not a political commitment. The position adopted and advocated by *Experimental Cinema* was unequivocally socialist."[37] However, in 1934 a "bitter dispute" among the journal's staff and supporters developed. The communist Workers' International Relief commissioned Stern and the editors of *Experimental Cinema* to make a film dealing with exploitation of Mexican migrant workers in Imperial Valley, California. Eighteen thousand feet of film were exposed, which the Workers' International Relief claimed publicly in the *Daily Worker* comprised mostly arty shots of cantaloupes. Stern responded that *Experimental Cinema* wanted an "artistic achievement as well as a piece of agitative propaganda." Furthermore, in the same (and to-be-last) issue of *Experimental Cinema* with Stern's justification appeared a tribute to Potamkin, who had recently died. Samuel Brody, writing in the *Daily Worker,* criticized *Experimental Cinema* for printing the tribute, since *Experimental Cinema* had disagreed with Potamkin's aesthetics. Brody wrote that in the previous three years divergent roads had been taken: "Potamkin Leftwards, E. C. to the Right."[38]

In early 1935, *Experimental Cinema*'s major support, the Workers Film and Photo League, broke up, and members adopted variant positions regarding politics and aesthetics. Jacobs remained independent in the far Left. Platt joined the *Daily Worker* as a staff writer, as well as working for other communist cultural publications. Stern continued on as a filmmaker and writer. His articles reflect his taking

---

36. Aaron, *Writers on the Left,* Pells, *Radical Visions and American Dreams,* pp. 342–46; Max Nomad, "1940 Saw Intellectuals Retreat from Leftist Traditional Orthodoxy," *New Leader,* 4 January 1941, 5. Nomad is citing Lewis Corey, in *The Nation* (1940).

37. George Amberg, "Introduction," *Experimental Cinema,* pp. iii–iv. Potamkin at least was already aligned with U.S. Communists. Furthermore, as of issue number 3 (1931), *Experimental Cinema* was receiving support from the Workers Film and Photo League of America and The American Prolet-Kino. Issue 3 lists three coeditors: Jacobs, Platt, and Stern, with Potamkin dropping out because *Experimental Cinema* printed a criticism written by Samuel Brody of a essay that Potamkin had published in *Close Up.* Issue 4 (1932) has five coeditors: Jacobs, Platt, Stern, Alexander Brailovsky, and Barnet G. Braver-mann. The last issue, number 5 (1934) lists editors Jacobs, Stern, and Braver-mann, but Platt is not among the associate or corresponding editors. Platt is listed as teaching at the Harry Alan Potamkin Film School along with Jacobs, Brody, Ralph Steiner, Irving Lerner, and Leo Seltzer (p. 54).

38. William Alexander, *Film on the Left: American Documentary Film from 1931 to 1942* (Princeton, N.J.: Princeton University Press, 1981), pp. 46–47; Russell Campbell, *Cinema Strikes Back: Radical Filmmaking in the United States, 1930–1942* (Ann Arbor, Mich.: UMI Research Press, 1982), pp. 96, 329n.

the position that judgments about aesthetics and narrational procedures were separable from those about subject matter and representation. Later, Stern became a strong anti-Stalinist while defending Griffith and *The Birth of a Nation*.

Given the political and personal context, Stern's 1940 vituperative response to Platt's strongly worded attack—Platt's charge that *The Birth of a Nation* was reactionary and racist—set off an escalation of charges and countercharges that would continue for the next fifteen years and beyond as Stern took on more critics of Griffith. Somewhere along the line Sergei Eisenstein's name must have been invoked, for in January 1941, Eisenstein telegraphed the *Daily Worker* to deny that he had praised *The Birth of a Nation*. His aesthetic choice was clear: "The disgraceful propaganda of racial hatred toward colored people which permeates this film cannot be redeemed by purely cinematographic effects in this production." Eisenstein also refers to his forthcoming article about "the interrelation between Soviet Cinema and the 'old man' of American films," most likely meaning his "Dickens, Griffith, and the Film Today" (1944). There Eisenstein argues that narrational procedures are isomorphically related to ideological development.[39]

In 1946, Peter Noble published "A Note on an Idol" in *Sight and Sound*. Noble accused Griffith of being "a pioneer of prejudice," albeit he was also a pioneer of technique. Noble's reading of the film is extreme, exceeding any 1915 account that I found. He describes Silas Lynch as attempting to rape Elsie Stoneman, whereas initial spectators saw Lynch as violently forcing her to marry him. Additionally, Noble describes Gus as "frothy-mouthed" in his pursuit of Flora.[40] (Every 1915 review did assume, though, that Gus intended to rape Flora Cameron.)

In the following *Sight and Sound* issue, both Griffith and Stern reply. Griffith writes that "my attitude towards the Negroes has always been one of affection and brotherly feeling. I was partly raised by a lovable old Negress down in old Kentucky." He also claims that the film was historically accurate. Stern begins his response with what can only be considered Redbaiting, given the political climate at that time. He compares Noble's remarks to the pre–World War II "anti-Griffith libel issued periodically, and often in the identical phrases, from certain political publications in the U.S.A. and the U.S.S.R." Stern then proceeds to argue and expand upon many of the themes that appeared in the 1915 defenses. *The Birth of a Nation* is historically accurate. In fact, Stern claims that it is based on Woodrow Wilson's *History of the American People*. He accuses Noble of basing his analysis on Jacobs's history of American film, a book filled with "errors, falsehoods and

---

39. "Eisenstein Attacks 'Birth of a Nation' / Protests Slanderous Use of His Name," *Daily Worker,* 14 January 1941, 7(?). Also see in this period: Paul Goodman, "Film Chronicle: Griffith and the Technical Innovations," *Partisan Review* 8, no. 3 (May-June 1941): 237–40; Barnet G. Braver-mann, "D. W. G., The Creator of Film Form," *Theatre Arts* 29 (April 1945): 240–50.
40. Peter Noble, "A Note on an Idol," *Sight and Sound* 15, no. 59 (Autumn 1946): 81–82.

fanciful misinterpretations of American film in general and Griffith and his work in particular."[41]

The second theme is the representation of blacks. The villains in the movie are not "the uneducated and newly-freed Negroes but the *doctrines* of certain fanatical and vengeful Northern whites, who duped the Negroes with glittering promises of wealth and power."[42] Moreover, the film shows good as well as bad African Americans: "In racial hatred, race is race, black is black, and there can be no exceptions."

Stern makes three additional observations. For one, he compares the South during the Reconstruction era to France and Norway during the Nazi occupation. Resorting to reading by allegory, Stern suggests that the South is rejecting the "totalitarianism" of northern radicals (e.g., Stoneman/Thaddeus Stevens): "*The Birth of a Nation* exposes the ideology and tactics of a revolutionary movement; it dramatises the defeat of this movement by a counter-revolution, the leaders and protagonists of which are the people themselves." By paralleling northern carpetbagger politics to fascist totalitarianism and, eventually, to Stalinism, Stern makes *The Birth of a Nation* express liberal, democratic doctrines.

Additionally, Stern explains that it is Communist propaganda to call Griffith a pioneer of prejudice:

> [Noble] is, of course, merely echoing in strangely familiar accents and phrases the astounding falsehoods and unbelievable nonsense on the subject which already have poured in volume from the presses of the N.Y. "Daily Worker," the "New Masses," the defunct "Friday" and "New Theatre," or from such specious and shockingly misleading politico-economic tracts as "The Rise of the American Film."

In this list, Stern ignores several decades of African-American protests. Finally, Stern counters the leftist claims that films have effects. He writes: "Surely Mr. Noble cannot but know that films do not start attitudes or trends in political or social relations; they merely reflect them."

The debates continued for several issues in *Sight and Sound*. In 1948 Noble published a monograph, *The Negro in Films,* only slightly modifying his stance. And in 1950, V. J. Jerome, considered a mainstream Communist, wrote *The Negro in Hollywood Films*—a sophisticated analysis of the ideology of racism in American films.[43]

---

41. D. W. Griffith, *"The Birth of a Nation," Sight and Sound* 16, no. 61 (Spring 1947): 32; Seymour Stern, "Griffith Not Anti-Negro," *Sight and Sound* 16, no. 61 (Spring 1947): 32–35.

42. Italics in the original. This latter ploy comes from a 1921 defense by Griffith. "Defends Film Production," *New York Times,* 9 May 1921.

43. "Without Comment" (Museum of Modern Art pamphlet, ca. 1946, p. 3), rpt. in *Sight and Sound* 16, no. 61 (Spring 1947): 35; E. L. Cranstone, "'The Birth of a Nation' Controversy," *Sight and Sound* 16, no. 63 (Autumn 1947): 119 (Cranstone writes: "We have have heard it all before and know that

Stern continued his defense of Griffith, admitting that the man's films had some faults but maintaining a spirited attack centered on communism and Stalinism as the source of Griffith's troubles. In 1949, as the U.S. Congress stepped up its repression of left-wing radicals and sent the Hollywood Ten to prison, Stern dates the "'official'" start of the Marxist attack on Griffith as 1940, when "the would-be cultural dictators of the Left—the new generation of Marxist film critics and self-styled film 'historians'" tried to destroy Griffith, who "stands in challenging and diametric opposition to contemporary Marxist-Stalinist ideological values." He expands this theme in 1956, publishing "The Cold War against David Wark Griffith," where he asserts that Communists also manipulate film scholarship: "Since the Communist movement is as much an ideological and cultural conspiracy as it is an economic, military and political one, it is not surprising Communists the world over devote considerable time and energy to influencing, and controlling, film criticism and history." Stern's position mellows somewhat in the 1965 number of *Film Culture,* in which Jonas Mekas gives over the issue to Stern's wealth of material about *The Birth of a Nation.*[44] If the film was not one already appropriated by Communists as a cause célèbre, Stern's attacks gave it to them.

Readings of *The Birth of a Nation*'s reception have traditionally been structured by the axes of region (North versus South) and racial attitude (liberal versus racist). This reconsideration has extended the film's reception into history, refusing to assume that the conditions for reception are restricted to the context of the film's original exhibition. I believe that historicizing the reception of *The Birth of a Nation* transforms the text's polysemy, for the political foundation underlying some of the historical debates becomes more apparent. In the film's later reception, racial attitudes are not autonomous effects; they relate to the political agendas of

red-baiting is a dangerous occupation" [p. 119]—an ironical observation given what was about to happen in the United States); Seymour Stern, "The Griffith Controversy," *Sight and Sound* 17, no. 65 (Spring 1948): 49–50; editor's note, *Sight and Sound* 17, no. 65 (Spring 1948): 50; Peter Noble, "The Negro in *The Birth of a Nation,*" *The Negro in Films* (London: Skelton Robinson, 1948): 33–43, rpt. in *Focus,* pp. 125–32; V. J. Jerome, *The Negro in Hollywood Films* (New York: Masses and Mainstream, 1950). Also see: James Agee, "David Wark Griffith," *The Nation* 167, no. 10 (4 September 1948): 264–65; James Mason Brown, "Wishful Banning," *Saturday Review* 32, no. 11 (12 March 1949): 24–26; Dore Schary, "Censorship and Stereotypes," *Saturday Review* 32, no. 18 (30 April 1949): 9–10; Seymour Stern, "'The Birth of a Nation,'" *Cinemages,* special issue no. 1 (1955).

44. Seymour Stern, "D. W. Griffith and the Movies," *American Mercury* 68, no. 303 (March 1949): 308–19; Seymour Stern, "The Cold War against David Wark Griffith," *Films in Review* 7, no. 2 (February 1956): 49–59; Stern, "Griffith: I. The Birth of a Nation," *Film Culture* 36 (Spring-Summer 1965): 1–210. Also see Seymour Stern, "The Soviet Directors' Debt to D. W. Griffith," *Films in Review* 7, no. 5 (May 1956): 202–9. For evidence that Stern's view has its current adherents, see Herbert C. Roseman, "Why the Wacko-Liberals Hate the Late Seymour Stern: The Most Authoritative of D. W. Griffith Scholars Long Ago Exposed Communists' Filmic Distortions," *Quirk's Reviews* (May 1985): 7 (in New York Public Library Performing Arts clipping file on Seymour Stern).

the debaters, causing strange alliances in which a former progressive defends the film using much of the rhetoric and arguments of 1915 radical conservatives. Additionally, complex theoretical questions such as the relation of subject matter and narrational procedures or possible effects of films and the consequences of those effects for social policy (censorship versus free speech) are lost to name-calling and a hardening of lines among the combatants. Consequently, this "encrustation" of the history of *The Birth of a Nation*'s reception has a double implication. For while the conditions for interpreting the film now include those years of political antagonisms, the "crust" that surrounds that interpretation also prevents a clear perception of what was once, and is still, at stake in the evaluation of the movie.

For *The Birth of a Nation* is not a simple problem. Its racism is obvious; its significance in the development of narrational procedures is also apparent. Following codes (or schemata) developed from the aesthetics of the nineteenth century, if not earlier, film histories have separated subject matter and narrational procedures, "content" and "form"; viewers have too.[45] However, what aesthetic, social, and political theories vie in promoting or refusing to accept this separation? For these aesthetics have been sites of contestation. Additionally, how does social policy connect to this question? What are the merits of free-speech-versus-censorship debates?

Currently, these difficulties still face film scholars. Racism appears in numerous films (for example, the *Indiana Jones* and *Star Wars* series). So do all sorts of abhorrent representations of gender, sexual preference, ethnicity, nationality, and class. But the plea for free speech over censorship, the ambiguities of claims of effect, and the shifting vicissitudes of interpretation in relation to historical political contexts make any final evaluation difficult. Consequently, in any historical instance of the reception of a film, particularly ones not so obvious as *The Birth of a Nation,* some moments of that sequence of determining meaning and significance to an individual may be progressive; others, regressive; some may be subversive; others, reactionary. Labeling any single interpretive response as one thing or the other may be very difficult.

That a splinter group of the Communist party would protest the 1978 Ku Klux Klan screening of *The Birth of a Nation* is due to a forty-year history of progressive radicals' using that film as a nodal point for their argument that connections exist between racism and class exploitation and that the representations of films matter to social spectators. The act of defending the film's showing, however, does not automatically associate the proponent with the racists of 1915 or the Redbaiters of 1946, but defenders ought at least to be aware of that part of the encrustation surrounding *The Birth of a Nation.* Thus, the conditions for the continued reception of *The Birth of a Nation* are now very complicated.

---

45. A recent exception to this pattern of separating form and content when discussing *The Birth of a Nation* is Michael Rogin's essay, "'The Sword Became a Flashing Vision': D. W. Griffith's *The Birth of a Nation,*" *Representations* 9 (Winter 1985): 150–95. [Reprinted in this volume.]

The Birth of a Nation: **History as Pretext**
Mimi White

The Double Narrative of History

DW. Griffith's *The Birth of a Nation* is one of the most well-known, and notorious, historical films. Since its release in 1915 the film has aroused fierce debate which is heavily determined by its insistent historical referentiality. Much of the criticism emphasizes the necessity of setting the record straight—the need for an objective, or at least less biased, version of the Civil War and Reconstruction period.[1] In stressing content and interpretation, such discussion asserts a clear distinction between past and present. With respect to the past the debate presumes that "the facts" exist, and only need to be properly selected and arranged, in the manner of assembling a picture puzzle (a difficult, but unambiguous task). The premise and goal of this conception of historical investigation is an idealized, coherent, and unified image of past events. The corollary of this is that interpretation, distortion, and/or misunderstanding of the "unified past" belongs to the domain of the present, as "the facts" are subjected to the biases and values of the historian. Thus, for example, the southern heritage of D. W. Griffith and Thomas Dixon is taken as an "explanation" of the view of the Civil War and Reconstruction presented in *Birth*.

In relation to this, a reexamination of the status of history in *Birth,* and in turn the film's status as an historical text, can be initiated. In the most general sense, history emerges as the dominant pretext of the film. The Civil War and Reconstruction era serve as the preexistent site within which events unfold; and as an "alibi discourse," the premise or occasion for developing a story whose values and meanings extend beyond the purview of any single social-historical moment.

For purposes of analysis it is necessary to isolate the two dominant lines of narrative development which comprise the film. The film recounts the story of a nation—the United States during and after the Civil War—and the story of two families—the Camerons and the Stonemans. While the stories develop simultaneously, and often overlap or intersect, they are not equivalent or interchangeable. In the film's text, the familial story is privileged, introduced before the account of the national struggle, and extending past the focus on national affairs. At the same time, it is the national story which is directly treated as "historical" by

---

1. Fred Silva, ed., *Focus on The Birth of a Nation* (Englewood Cliffs, N.J.: Prentice-Hall, 1971). In particular see the essays on pp. 64–99, 102–3, and 111–43.

From *Enclitic* 5, no. 2/6, no. 1 (Fall 1981/Spring 1982): 17–24.

the film, with citations of verbal and visual texts as references for its visual and narrative construal of events.

While the moments of intersection between the familial and national stories seem to establish continuity between the two narrative levels, they equally point out the distance which separates them. Conflicting motivations are introduced, and the very narrational gesture of connection indicates a shift in the narrative focus of interest. This movement—a slippage which pervades the film's trajectory—is at times almost literally embodied in the film's representation. Towards the end of Part I, for example, Elsie and Phil Stoneman attend a play at Ford's Theater on the night of President Lincoln's assassination. The title introducing the sequence reads:

A gala performance to celebrate the surrender of Lee, attended by the President and staff. The young Stonemans present.
> AN HISTORICAL FACSIMILE of Ford's theatre as on that night, exact in size and detail, with the recorded incidents, after Nicolay and Hay in "Lincoln, A History."

The following shot is an iris-in on the theater interior, beginning with Elsie and Phil at their seats. In both the title and the image there is a movement from the central narrative situation to a broader historical context involving a traversal of narrative space. In the title the Stonemans' presence at the gala is separated from the citation of the historical source; in the image, the Stonemans are initially isolated by the iris transition.

The family members are present at the "big historical event." It is Elsie Stoneman who first notices John Wilkes Booth in the theater. Her admiring gaze through opera glasses is the mechanism of filmic continuity, motivating his introduction into the space of the narrative. But Elsie and her brother are no more than witnesses. They do not—and cannot—intervene in the historical drama which will inevitably occur. In light of the already-familiar sequence of events— Abraham Lincoln will be shot by Booth at the gala performance—her glances emerge, in all their artificiality, as an effort to place her "in" historical events.

While the two central families in the film are given prominent positions in national affairs—Stoneman is a leader in Congress, the two sons lead troops in the war, the Cameron son is an instigator of and leading figure in the Klan—they are primarily fictional characters. They may be "based on," but do not "represent" historical personages.[2] It is on this basis that different levels of narrative motiva-

---

2. In *The Film and History: Restaging the Past* (New York: Barnes and Noble, 1980). Pierre Sorlin elaborates on similarities between the Stoneman character and Thaddeus Stevens. He argues, on pp. 32–33, that comparisons between historical films and "real" history prove fruitless since they rely on limited, isolated pieces of information and do not account for the structural logic of a film. One might, however, argue that *The Birth of a Nation* effects a displacement of history with respect to the

tion can emerge, corresponding to the "personal" or familial context on the one hand, and the "public" or national sequence of events on the other. The family members, and their fates, are not simply representative of national events, with problems caused and resolved by the national struggle. Similarly, their intervention in national affairs, albeit prominent, is not merely construed as concern for an interest in the fate and stability of the United States. On the contrary, the initial and final stability of the Stoneman and Cameron families is treated by the film apart from the national story. At this level, the family story traces a defined group of characters through a drama in which imbalances in, and threats to the traditional family structure are eliminated, while sons and daughters advance to assume their positions in married couples. (An advance which, needless to say, is part of an ever-repeating cycle.) However, all of this transpires in the context of a particular and well-known period of history.

The Status of the Historical Referential

Throughout the film, the interplay between "personal" and "public" events signals an unstable position for and conception of history. With respect to the national story *Birth* seems fairly self-conscious about its presentation of an important period in United States history. This is most evident in its citation of verbal and visual source documents. Through a process of quotation the film anchors itself in history; prior historical texts (contemporaneous with or chronologically closer to the represented events) are invoked as a term of authority, a basis of credibility.[3] The film thus positions itself as a "new" text in a lineage of material pertaining to the Civil War and Reconstruction era. But the use of citation is neither consistent nor sustained. It is an intermittent practice which the film employs to (re)establish its bearings, but which it dispenses with, once having marked its "authenticity" and "historicity" in such a manner. Moreover, the film draws on the authority of an extra-textual historical tradition only in particular situations.

First of all, source citations tend to precede what might be considered "difficult" representations—scenes involving noted historical figures or events which

Stoneman character similar to that enacted by the narrative as a whole. At first certain character elements are stressed in the narrative which make Stoneman a likely "Stevens figure." In particular his position as a congressional leader and his relationship with a mulatto are important here. But after Lincoln's assassination both of these roles or qualities are "forgotten" by the text. The ailing Stoneman moves to Piedmont; and Lydia, his mulatto maid, seems to reign as queen of Lynch's power domain, no longer affiliated with Stoneman. In other words, Sorlin ignores the textual cues which initially promote parallels between Stoneman and Stevens; and the way in which they are then minimized or dropped as pertinent elements of the narrative as the film progresses.

3. A preliminary, though sketchy discussion of how historical films combine historical and fictional events can be found in Sorlin, *The Film and History*, pp. 20–22. He also develops a typology of the kinds of historical evidence frequently used in historical films, pp. 61–64.

are available through other representations. This occurs, for example, with Lincoln signing the call for volunteers (which is the first representation of Lincoln in the film), and the signing of the Appomattox peace treaty. In both cases the characters present on the screen—Lincoln, Grant, Lee—preexist the film as recognizable figures through paintings, photographs, etc.; because of their prominence and familiarity, these scenes are likely to be recognized as constructions, threatening the film's proper unity. These scenes are marked as reproductions, reconstructions which are "true to life" since (so the intertitles claim) they are modelled on photographs of the "real" event. In such cases, source citation serves as the text's assertion of "authenticity" precisely at moments which stretch the viewer's belief.[4] However, the very gesture to secure the reality of the representation simultaneously points to the impossibility of an unreconstructed, unmediated version of the past. In this way to authorize and justify its own representation, the film must undermine—if only slightly—its self-sufficiency as a text; to define itself as "properly" historical is to construct itself in relation to other texts.

This tendency is carried even further in the second notable use of source citation in the film. At issue here are the titles which provide supplementary historical information or quote directly from history books. Although it is used infrequently in the film, this material is presented in relation to *particular* narrative developments. The very rarity of its occurrence suggests it is significant, fulfilling a specific function. In the introduction to the raid on Piedmont, a sub-note in the title reads "The first Negro regiments of the war were raised in South Carolina." During the subsequent scene, the Cameron house is looted by black soldiers led by a "scalawag white captain." The second part of the film (dealing with the Reconstruction era) opens with lengthy quotations (three title cards) from Woodrow Wilson's *History of the American People,* explaining the rise of the Ku Klux Klan as a necessary action of self-preservation on the part of the white South.

In both cases the invocation of historical authority (in one case a "fact," in the other a prominent text) is set apart from the film's general narrative intertitles; moreover, no other historical event is supplemented in this way. This suggests that certain narrative situations—in particular black soldiers ransacking a southern household during the war and the heroic portrayal of the Klan—require extra narrational authorization. These titles seem to confirm the historical validity of these moments, assuring us they are not mere "invention" (and perhaps fulfill this function in the immediate context). But they emerge in the overall context of the film as peculiarly self-justifying, as if the cinematic presentation, on its own, would not be sufficient. Since the narrative developments in question are particularly open to charges of racial bias, it hardly seems accidental that the film turns to outside historical sources at these moments. Insofar as only certain events

4. The mechanisms of belief at work in historical films is discussed in Jean-Louis Comolli's "Historical Fiction: A Body Too Much," *Screen* 19 (Summer 1978): 41–53.

seem to require mediation through authoritative concurrence, the verbal titles amount to a defensive position.

Supplemental notes also intervene at times to bridge, conflate, or even confuse narrative levels within the film. In these cases, a kind of slippage between the historical information and the film's representation is introduced. For example, after the war, a title introducing the South Carolina legislature reads:

The riot in the Master's Hall.
The negro party in control of the State House of Representatives, 101 blacks against 23 whites, session of 1871.

AN HISTORICAL FACSIMILE of the State House of
Representatives of South Carolina as it was in 1870.
After photograph by "The Columbia State."

This is followed by a fade-in on an empty assembly room which dissolves to a room full of activity. The next title reads, "Historical incidents from the first legislative session under Reconstruction." In the course of the sequence, black legislators in gaudy, shabby attire eat, drink, put their bare feet on desks, and behave in a generally raucous manner. (The first rule instituted by the House speaker is that all members must wear shoes.)

What is curious about the progression of this scene is the use of a source citation which would seem to assure authenticity. A gap between the source and the filmic representation is, however, immediately evident in the title-card itself, which situates events in 1871 and the source in 1870, prior to the depicted scene. This shift is repeated in the following shot, which opens on an empty room as the intratextual "referent" of the citation only to dissolve to the active scene. In other words, the film proceeds by means of a detour which allows it to invoke the authority of a primary historical source even though the source is displaced with respect to the represented event. In this way, there is a "carryover" as the presumed authority of the historical source supports the film's particular representation of decorum in the State House under black majority rule. This implication is carried even further in the second intertitle as a connection is established between the "historical facsimile" (based on a primary source document) and the "historic incidents" subsequently portrayed. In this case the citation confuses the status of the filmic representation, as it presumes to authenticate an image and a series of events which it does not designate.

Finally, the use of source citation as a "bridge" is seen in the Ford's Theater sequence. The two dominant levels of narrative development converge within the diegesis—two of the main characters in the familial drama are present at a major national event—but remain essentially separate with respect to motivation or cause-effect connections. The sequence begins and ends with Elsie and Phil Stoneman; their arrival at and departure from the theater frames the assassination of Lincoln, an event which has nothing to do with their presence. This bracketing of national historic events by the familial drama is a pattern which repeats the structure of the film as a whole. The Stoneman and Cameron families are introduced prior to national upheaval, and are unified at the end of the film after national turmoil has been resolved.

The Priority of the Family

The national and familial stories follow a parallel course of development even as the priority of the family is sustained. The film progresses from pre–Civil War stability through the chaos of war and Reconstruction to final stability when white dominance is reasserted in the South. This progression is in turn subdivided into two narrative "moves" which constitute Parts I and II of the film. In the first, the Civil War is fought and won by the North, presumably bringing peace and stability. However, Lincoln's assassination upsets the possibility for resolution. With respect to the two families, their initial state of comfortable and peaceful friendship is shaken in the course of the war. They are finally reunited at the end of the film—in fact more closely bound as a unit, as the remaining son and daughter in each are married.

With the onset of the Civil War, major national developments are relegated to intertitles, excluded from the filmic representation. Familiar battles and dates may be mentioned (for example, the Battle of Bull Run is announced in a title) but are not subjected to dramatic treatment. The battles and wartime activity depicted in most detail are precisely those which involve the Stoneman and Cameron families. Once the war starts, the filmic sequence of events is as follows: the Stoneman brother depart for war; the Cameron sons go off to fight; Elsie Stoneman tells her father about her brothers' departure.[5] An intertitle then informs us that two and a half years have elapsed; Ben Cameron, in the field, receives a letter from his Pet Sister; and the sister receives a letter in return.

To this point there have been no battle scenes. The first wartime violence involves the Piedmont raid which concentrates on the looting of the Cameron house. (The father is wounded by the Northern troops as he attempts to protect his home.) In the first actual battle scene, the youngest sons of each family die in one another's arms, and the accompanying intertitle explains, "On the battlefield, war claims its bitter, useless sacrifice. True to their promise, the chums meet again." The impact of the war is visually specified as a loss to the two families; and the promise of the youths pierces through the chaos of war, as they find one another in the field. After their deaths, the film presents the reaction of the two families to the boys' deaths.

It is only at this point that the film presents the "spectacle" of war somewhat removed from the personal lives of the two central families, in the relatively long

---

5. The differences between the two departure scenes are discussed at length in Sorlin, *The Film and History*, pp. 90–91.

sequence showing the marching of troops and burning of Atlanta. However, the epic scale of this sequence is tempered by two familial references. In the course of the sequence the second Cameron son dies; even though he is a minor figure in the familial drama (and has hardly been seen until this point) his death is singled out for "close-up" treatment. Moreover the march of the troops is framed with reference to a symbolic familial context. The opening title explains, "While women and children weep, a great conqueror marches to the sea," and the troops are visually framed by a woman and three children overlooking the fields in which the soldiers march. Thus, the major impact and significance of the film is shown to be the disruption of family units.

In the next big battle sequence, Ben Cameron and Phil Stoneman each lead troops and face one another in battle. Here, as with the younger sons, the familial values dominate, more powerful than the values and antagonisms at stake in the war. When Ben goes into the field to offer water to a wounded enemy soldier both sides temporarily cease fire, and his heroic and humane action is cheered by his Northern adversaries. Similarly, when Ben is wounded, Phil takes him off the field to assure he will receive medical attention. It is not simply that the war is depicted with reference to the characters in the familial drama. Rather, in the simultaneous development of the familial and national stories, the personal drama dominates and becomes the center of causal explanation for events as well as the generator of narrative interpretation. The war and national developments in general are minimized in favor of the family members who are motivated by concerns which are not specifically national.

Stoneman, for example, is the primary Northern supporter of the slave cause. As a prominent political figure, he promotes the mulatto Silas Lynch to a position of power after the war. When he is introduced he is shown to have a clubfoot and to wear a wig which he often pushes back to scratch his skull. Thus, he is presented as physically deformed, vain, and uncouth. Moreover, he is sexually attracted to his mulatto maid, an attraction which is described as "The great leader's weakness that is to blight a nation." In the film's early scenes, Stoneman fights with Sumner, a leading [Republican] statesman, who treats the maid with distant formality and is (falsely) accused by her of sexual assault. From the outset, the North–South struggle and Stoneman's allegiances are affiliated with physical deformity and social-sexual "abnormality" (even "perversion"). By the end of the film it is made perfectly clear that Stoneman's avowed egalitarian principles do not have general applicability; he is shocked—even horrified—to learn that his mulatto protege wants to marry his own daughter. In this way, Stoneman's support of a particular cause is construed as a function of his personal deformity.

More generally the impact of the war is primarily defined in relation to the Stoneman and Cameron families. The "raid on Piedmont" is depicted as an attack on the Cameron household specifically. The intertitle "War claims its bitter, useless sacrifice" precedes the death of the two sons of both families. After the Camerons receive news of their son's death, the intertitle "Others also read war's sad page" is specified in the visual representation as Elsie Stoneman and her father learning of the young Stoneman's death. The "others" in question are not the nation at large, but the family whose members we already know; it is a personal tragedy. In every case the generalized implication of the title is dramatically and visually interpreted in terms of the two families at the heart of the personal drama.

In the face of this personal story, the Civil War becomes a secondary issue. The national conflict properly speaking (that is, the conflict between the North and South) is readily suspended or forgotten when human, familial values surface. Thus, both sides cease fire when Ben Cameron, in the midst of battle, provides water for his wounded "enemy." Ben is later saved from execution as a traitor when his mother personally visits President Lincoln to request a pardon. The national drama is progressively submerged beneath and overcome by solidarity which emerges on a higher level. With the family at its center, another range of values and a different sphere of struggle begins to emerge which cuts across, and ultimately displaces the Civil War and the specificity of the national history.

Familial Clans and Universal History

The general structure of the film already suggests such a displacement, insofar as the end of the war per se does not bring peace or national unity. Rather, it results in an intensification of violence; the "reconstruction" era generates new dangers and generalizes the wartime violence. Women are now directly subject to threats and death. The Pet Sister of the Cameron family leaps to her death when pursued by a "renegade" black soldier. Elsie Stoneman is held captive by her father's protege and nearly forced into an undesired marriage with the mulatto leader. In fact both of these incidents demonstrate the danger of Stoneman's personal "blight" spreading through society as a result of the unsatisfactory resolution of the war. In both families, the fathers are humiliated. Cameron is paraded before his former slaves in chains, and Stoneman is overpowered by Lynch and held captive when he objects to the marriage proposal.

The blacks who control the government in South Carolina, and in Piedmont in particular, are shown to be self-interested boors, promoting their own prestige and well-being. The law allowing for interracial marriage is construed as license for black men to force their attentions on unwilling white women. It is in the face of continual harrassment, physical threats, and life danger that the Ku Klux Klan arises. In the context of reigning chaos the Klan emerges as a necessary and heroic force, protecting not only the Stoneman and Cameron families, but the white population at large. As the Klan gathers to combat Silas Lynch and his mob of supporters, the film—in crucial contrast with the representation of the Civil War—shows a series of white families endangered by the riots and assaults of freed blacks. It is here that the "nation," construed as a collectivity of citizens, is most seriously threatened. Within the terms of the filmic representation, the battle to resolve Reconstruction becomes the critical war. The Klan not only rescues the Stonemans, held captive by Lynch, and the Camerons, beseiged by black troops in a cabin, but also the rest of the white families in Piedmont. It is precisely the White Nation as a whole that now demands liberation, needs to reassert dominance, as opposed to the artificial, indeed "unnatural" geographic division of the Civil War. The need for and importance of solidarity among whites as a race is underscored by the former Union soldiers who shelter and join forces with the Camerons in the face of black troops.

In comparison to this final struggle, the Civil War can now be seen as merely a particular moment in human-social history which posed a temporary threat to a more essential and universal order. The "history" enacted by the film, developed with specific reference to the Cameron and Stoneman families, finds its coherence and meaning in relation to general familial and racial groups (or clans). Ultimately what emerges is the image of an ideal family unit as the locus of transhistorical forces, an anchor of stability in the eternal scheme of the world. In this context, the Civil War is an "aberration" (from the point of view of the film's larger narrational frame). However, in relation to the familial trajectory, it does serve as a purification rite, eliminating potential perversions of the "natural" family structure and allowing a stronger, more "ideal" family unit to surface.

At the start of the film there are two sons and one daughter in the Stoneman family, and three sons and two daughters in the Cameron family. From the outset, particular links are established between one son and daughter in each, as well as between the two younger sons. By the end of the film, having withstood the violence of the Civil War and Reconstruction, each family has one son and one daughter, allowing for a symmetrical exchange and union. However, the sons must first prove themselves worthy of taking the daughters away from their respective fathers. In both cases the daughters' loyalty to their fathers temporarily prohibits recognition of their suitors; and affection is transferred only after the fathers, impotent in the face of a threat, are aided or rescued by the sons. Phil Stoneman helps Margaret Cameron's father escape from captivity, killing one of Lynch's soldiers in the process. Ben Cameron leads a Klan force which rescues Lucy Stoneman and her father from Lynch. In the final triumphant march through town. Lucy and Elsie ride in front, symbolic mothers of the New Order.

Prior to this the other family members have been eliminated. However, they are characterized in a manner which suggests they would not be easily assimilated into a new generation of familial union. The second son in the Cameron family holds a position of minimal importance. The younger sons share a playful intimacy, and die on the battlefield in one another's arms. Their youth places them in a "pre-sexual" stage, which is reinforced by the absence of female counterparts for either of them; and the extent of the physical expression of their affection for one another, culminating at the moment of their deaths, implicates homosexuality in their relationship. Both of these dispositions place them outside a normative heterosexuality necessary to maintain the traditional family structure. Similarly, the Cameron Pet Sister is very young, and there are overtones of incest in her relationship with her older brother. She keeps his letters from the war over her breast, and comforts him in Elsie's absence. In this way she poses a threat to the generational renewal of the "ideal" family unit. She is killed off in the film when, chased by Gus, she leaps to her death.

From this point of view, the Civil War and its impact can be conceived as a rite of purgation, eliminating propensities or drives that might upset the symmetry and balance of the traditional family structure.[6] The whole film and the so-called tragedy of war work out to allow for "perfect" mating, as one son and one daughter remain in each family for an equal marriage exchange. In fact the war itself with its misalignments may even be construed as an effect of misplaced and perverse sexual desires. (One might recall here Stoneman's "blight," which is obviously cured when he violently rejects Lynch's proposal to marry Elsie.)

In this light, the "truth" of particular events in and of American history (in the most familiar sense) are hardly at issue. Rather, the family drama, traditional and normative sexuality, and the assertion of a conventional family structure are the center of interest in the film. Crucially, this focus is guaranteed by the vision of the world which encloses the film as a whole in a narrative frame.

The film begins and ends with references to a past, outside the immediate social circumstances of the central story, and to a future beyond the events of the central story. Both periods are depicted as eras of peace, harmony, and order. The film opens with the presentation of a slave auction in the American colonies, preceded by a title which reads, "The bringing of the African to America planted the first seed of disunion." The counterpart of this prologue is a vision of final union as the Prince of Peace, Jesus Christ, hovers over a pastoral scene, foretelling of a generalized, as yet unachieved state of global harmony. The nature of the final images strongly suggests a Paradise lost and regained, Edenic union which can only be restored through divine intervention. This vision, asserted as true and total union, is beyond the struggles of both the nation and the White Clan. It literally comes after the restoration of peace and order by the Ku Klux Klan in the South and the reassertion of white supremacy and dominance. In fact, with respect to the film's diegesis, it is a moment which has not yet arrived. However, the family's position and definition in relation to this universal conception of the world is provided by the dissolves which link the two couples on their honeymoon with this final vision.

In this way a hierarchy is established in which the national story—of the Civil War and its aftermath—is merely a moment (and here, an aberrant one) in the history of the family as a structure which is, at its best, the earthly-social

---

6. Specific scenes in the film emphasize the purgative ritual nature of events. In particular, one of the first Klan attacks is preceded by dipping a flag in the blood of the Pet Cameron sister after her death, evoking a pagan rite. This connection was pointed out to me by David Bordwell.

expression of divine values. The family structure and divine scheme are essentially ahistorical. They both assume an ideal, static state of being rather than movement, change, or contradiction through time.

All of this, finally, comes back to clarify the unstable position and use of
historical texts in the film—the selective assertion of source documents and
factual material. For in the final analysis the historical events properly speaking
are precisely (and only) the occasion for examining universal values gone awry. In
relation to the overriding narrative scheme of the film, these events are only a
moment in a history of far broader scope, as the lineage of world history is
conceived in relation to racial and familial groups. These groups must inevitably
encounter and pass through particular social and national events, at least until the
apocalyptic vision is fulfilled. But their value and meaning are measured against
an absolute standard which is divine in origin and expresses itself outside the
domain of political interests (in the limited sense) or government institutions and
practices. Thus any particular social-historical reality is subsumed under and
transcended by divine, ahistorical ideals, a process and relation which is mirrored
in the structure and trajectory of the film itself.

The Historical Novel Goes to Hollywood:
Scott, Griffith, and Film Epic Today

James Chandler

I suspect that other Americans of the baby-boom generation might share with me a sense that some of their most memorable early experiences of "culture" were at certain kinds of movies in certain kinds of theaters. From about 1956 to 1963, select movie theaters ran such lavish Hollywood epics as *The Ten Commandments, The Bridge on the River Kwai, Ben Hur, Spartacus, Lawrence of Arabia,* and (the beginning of the end) the Taylor-Burton *Cleopatra.* One knew it was culture not so much because of the production extravagances of the films themselves (huge sets, cast of thousands, three-hour format with intermission) as because of the marketing strategies that framed our consumption (advanced booking, expensive seats, long runs, lavish programs). What one did not know then— what I certainly did not know—was that the whole cultural package, marketing strategies and all, had been initially put together by and for D. W. Griffith's *The Birth of a Nation* in 1915, and redeployed for sound-era epics in, for example, David O. Selznick's *Gone With the Wind* (1939), a film based on a novel that had in turn been based on Griffith's masterpiece.

Film historians have by now amply documented the cultural and institutional impact of *The Birth of a Nation,* and have partially substantiated Griffith's right to call his autobiography *The Man Who Invented Hollywood.*[1] They also suggest, in effect, that when Griffith broke off from the Biograph Company to make *The Birth of a Nation,* he was right to call his new company "The Epoch Producing Corporation." By a historiographical logic that Hans Blumenberg has traced, however, to define an epoch, no matter how clearly and distinctly, is inevitably to raise the question of the circumstances of its coming into being—to ask how and out of what it was indeed produced, and thus to compromise its clarity and distinctness.[2] And so one must with the epoch produced in and by Griffith's epic. What shall we say are the preconditions of *The Birth of a Nation?*

The first really strenuous effort to see a history of practice *behind* Griffith— without, however, denying him his due as an innovator—is the landmark 1944 essay by Sergei Eisenstein that is echoed in my subtitle. This essay—"Dickens, Griffith, and the Film Today"—is famous partly for its exposition of Griffith's

---

1. *The Man Who Invented Hollywood: The Autobiography of D. W. Griffith* (Louisville: Touchstone, 1972).
2. Hans Blumenberg, *The Legitimacy of the Modern Age,* trans. Robert M. Wallace (Cambridge, Mass.: MIT Press, 1983), 457–481.

From *The Romantics and Us: Essays on Literature and Culture,* ed. Gene W. Ruoff (New Brunswick, N.J.: Rutgers University Press, 1990).

parallel montage, the cinematic technique, much employed by Eisenstein himself, of cutting back and forth between different lines of action. The essay is also famous for Eisenstein's appreciative commentary on the achievement of D. W. Griffith, whom he regarded not only as a founder of Hollywood movies as we know them, but also as the innovator whose example enabled Soviet directors to surpass his own achievement. The burden of Eisenstein's essay, however, is to show that, just as Griffith's techniques had helped enormously to make Russian film what it had become by the 1940s, so Dickens, whom Eisenstein portrays as the representative Victorian novelist, had contributed enormously to what Griffith had been able to do with his films in the first place. "From Dickens," writes Eisenstein, "from the Victorian novel, stem the first shoots of American film esthetic, forever linked with the name of David Wark Griffith."[3]

Eisenstein prosecutes his case by suggesting that there are two major aspects of Griffith's film style and that they correspond to (or "reflect," as he puts it) the two faces of Griffith's America. The first face is the industrialized world of "speaking automobiles, streamlined trains, racing ticker tape, inexorable conveyor-belts" (198). The second face is the America that we identify with "an abundance of small-town and patriarchal elements in . . . life and manners, morals and philosophy, the ideological horizon and rules of behavior in the middle strata of American culture." The first, "Super-Dynamic America," is "the 'official,' sumptuous Griffith, the Griffith of tempestuous tempi, of dizzying action, of breathtaking chases"; the second, "Small-Town America," is the America of "the traditional, the patriarchal, the provincial" (198). Eisenstein associates each of these Americas with a technique that Griffith developed for the cinema—Small-Town America with the close-up and Super-Dynamic America with the parallel montage—and he argues that both techniques are derived from Dickens's practice in fiction.

I don't mean to contest either of these particular claims. There is evidence, which Eisenstein cites, that Griffith knew Dickens's work well; one of Griffith's earliest films, for example, was based on Dickens's *The Cricket and the Hearth*. And there is also the famous anecdote recorded by Linda Arvidson Griffith, which Eisenstein relates, about the filming of *Enoch Arden*. In planning this 1911 two-reeler, Griffith proposed repeated crosscutting between the seafaring husband shipwrecked on his island and the patient wife awaiting his return on the seashore near their home. Asked by an unnamed executive how he expected audiences to find such a series of images intelligible, Griffith is supposed to have replied: "Well, doesn't Dickens write that way?"[4] This seems to constitute ample warrant for Eisenstein's

3. Sergei Eisenstein, "Dickens, Griffith, and the Film Today," in *Film Form,* trans. Jay Leyda (London: D. Dobson, 1951), 232–233.

4. Ibid., 200–201. See also Griffith's acknowledgment—"I borrowed the 'cutback' from Charles Dickens"—in "What I Demand of Movie Stars," collected in *Focus on D. W. Griffith,* ed. Harry M. Geduld (Englewood Cliffs, N.J.: Prentice-Hall, 1971), 52.

elaboration of how Griffith developed the practice of montage out of Dickens's conspicuous tendency to shift abruptly between his novels' subplots.

In the course of his argument, however, Eisenstein eventually locates his claims about the literary sources of particular film techniques within a larger horizon of argument, as Dickens comes to stand in for the entire literary tradition before film:

> Let Dickens and the whole ancestral array . . . be superfluous reminders that both Griffith and our cinema prove our origins to be not solely as of Edison and his fellow inventors, but as based on an enormous cultured past. . . . Let this past be a reproach to those thoughtless people who have displayed arrogance in reference to literature, which has contributed so much to this apparently unprecedented art and is, in the first and most important place: the art of viewing—not only the *eye,* but *viewing*—both meanings being embraced in this term. (232–233)

This is an eloquent and powerful admonition, and perhaps not heeded as often as it ought to be. But for critics who may be disposed to look at the literary preconditions of the cinema, the emphasis that Eisenstein has placed on Dickens, both as a synecdoche for the literary tradition and as the source of certain film-narrative techniques, can be misleading in the way it obscures another literary genealogy for Griffith's filmmaking, especially in *The Birth of a Nation*. In accepting too entirely Eisenstein's focus on Dickens and on Griffith's "Victorianism," on which so much has been written, we lose sight of connections, on which nothing has been written, between Griffith's seminal film epic and what might be called the *romantic* line in nineteenth-century fiction, the line that follows from Walter Scott.[5] The Dickens line also obscures Griffith's involvement in a program to rewrite history on film, and thus blocks the way to a consideration of Griffith in respect to a crucially understudied issue in current cultural studies: the use of film in the representation of history. In its way of "viewing" history, and indeed of "writing" it, *The Birth of a Nation* marks the intersection of what Raymond Williams would call emergent and residual cultural formations. Given Griffith's explicitly apocalyptic conclusion, one might even be tempted to place the film at the interpenetration of two Yeatsian gyres, one spiraling outward toward its position of dominance in American modernity, the other winding down from its position of dominance in British romanticism.[6]

---

5. But see Philip Rosen's brief but suggestive remarks on Scott, Lukács, and classical cinema in "Securing the Historical: Historiography and the Classical Cinema," in *Cinema Histories, Cinema Practices,* ed. Patricia Mellancamp and Philip Rosen, AFI Monograph Series, vol. 4 (Frederick, Md.: University Publications of America, 1984), 26–28.

6. For more on Dickens and Griffith, see Richard Schickel, *D. W. Griffith* (New York: Simon and

. . . It would have seemed strange to most of their informed contemporaries that Wordsworth, and not Scott, would someday be chosen to epitomize the cultural history of the romantic period. Scott was the dominant poet of the period from the turn of the century until about 1813, when he turned down the poet laureateship. In the field of poetry, Scott's popularity gave way to Lord Byron's, but Scott retreated from poetry only to attack the literary marketplace under a different banner. His second conquest was unprecedented in its success. Keats wrote in 1819 that there had been "three literary kings in our Time—Scott—Byron—and then the scotch nove[ls]."[7] But this was actually a way of saying that there had been only one literary king, for "scotch novels" is a nickname for the extraordinary series of works that Scott published when, after declining the laureateship, he decided to complete a novel that he had begun in 1805 and that appeared in 1814 as *Waverley, or 'Tis Sixty Years Since*. In the two decades until his death in 1834, Scott would produce more than two dozen more works of fiction in the series that came to be called the Waverley Novels.

Most of the best of these were completed by 1819, when Keats made his comment, and by which time Scott had already added to his list such novels as *Guy Mannering, The Antiquary, Rob Roy, The Heart of Mid-Lothian, Old Mortality, The Legend of Montrose, The Bride of Lammermoor*, and *Ivanhoe*. With these books, Scott changed the course of all kinds of writing about the past, left his mark on drama and opera as well, and eventually became, without question, the most widely influential of all British authors except for Shakespeare. Even Scott's most relentless adversary, Mark Twain, seemed to acknowledge this point, negatively, when he said that Scott "did measureless harm, more real and lasting harm, perhaps, than any other individual that ever wrote."[8] To speak only of fiction: if Scott had not lived, the literary oeuvres of Balzac and Hugo in France, Cooper and Hawthorne in America, Manzoni in Italy, and Tolstoy in Russia would all look substantially different. In England, specifically, the same can be said for most of Thackeray, much of George Eliot, and, indeed, some of Dickens's own work, especially *A Tale of Two Cities*— although it is a matter of some moment to us here that, for Dickens, Scott's work figures as an object less of emulation than subversion.

What Scott's successors recognized in his fiction was a new literary form, but different writers seized on different aspects of that form, and it is not monolithic

---

Schuster, 1984), 112–113. On Griffith's "Victorianism," see Lary May, *Screening Out the Past* (Chicago: University of Chicago Press, 1983), 94–97. I have found no discussions of Griffith's relationship to Scott and Scott's historical novel.

7. *The Letters of John Keats,* ed. Hyder E. Rollins, 2 vols (Cambridge: Harvard University Press, 1958), 2:16.

8. Samuel Clemens, *The Writings of Mark Twain,* 37 vols. (New York: G. Wells, 1923), 12:377.

even from Waverley novel to Waverley novel. What is distinctive about the novels as a group is certainly nothing so simple as the location of an action at an earlier period. There had already been ample precedent for that in the eighteenth century's novel-of-the-past, chiefly in the Gothic tradition that peaks in the 1790s with the popular works of Ann Radcliffe and Monk Lewis. The difference is that, in the eighteenth-century cases, a past setting contributes only atmosphere and ornamentation. These works are informed by neither historical knowledge nor historical theory; they are marked by unsignaled anachronism at every level, and by no recognition of how a historically specific culture sets conditions upon the characters or the plots in question. There is no effort to establish historical relation between the past moment and the present because there is so little sense of what it is that makes a past moment different. The conditions for marking out a historically specific culture had not yet emerged with sufficient force to shape, or be shaped in, a new form of fiction.

The place where such conditions were developing during the late eighteenth century was the young Scott's Edinburgh, capital of what is now called the Scottish Enlightenment. Scott attended Edinburgh University in the 1780s, and there he was schooled in the principles of the so-called "philosophical history," as worked out by David Hume, Adam Smith, and some of their less well known contemporaries, Adam Ferguson, William Robertson, and John Millar. One explanation of how philosophical history emerged in Scotland when it did posits a historical self-consciousness induced by the country's accelerated development through several economic stages in relatively little time after the Union with England in 1707. Scott himself offered such an account in the Postscript to *Waverley* in 1814, and when he turned to his first English historical novel with *Ivanhoe* (1819), he explained that his choice of period for an English novel had been guided both by the wish to find a stage of civilization in England's history equivalent in primitiveness to, say, early eighteenth-century Scotland and by the sense that, to do so, it was necessary to go all the way back to the English Middle Ages.

Another factor that contributed to Scott's sense of a historically specific culture, although this affected Scott's audience as powerfully as it did him, was the experience of the French Revolution and the Napoleonic Wars. The age defined by 1789 and 1815, the Pan-European dates of the Bastille and Waterloo, was the period that helped to define what the notion of a historical period *was* for nineteenth-century historiography. It can scarcely be an accident that the historical novel sweeps Britain and Europe in the half-decade after Napoleon's final defeat. This was, after all, a defeat that lent at least a temporary sense of closure to the Revolutionary period, and that allowed various nations to take stock of the cultural transformation that had been wrought during the previous quarter-century of tumult and change. In the century that followed, the historical novel helped more than one nation to invent a tradition about its own genesis.[9]

A more thoroughgoing account of the influences on Scott's historicism would include other factors as well—for example, his early exposure to the developing German sense of history in such works as Goethe's *Götz von Berlichingen,* which Scott translated into English. But to speak of a developing awareness of historical change and cultural specificity is not yet to raise the question of a literary form in which this awareness might have been articulated. The new form, as it was developed by Scott and imitated by great nineteenth-century novelists in each of the western nation-states, can be sketched under several primary rubrics. First, under the heading of *subject matter,* Scott normally represented an earlier stage of society as divided against itself, with that past conflict itself typically defined as a struggle between older and newer centers of power, and usually leading to a social resolution, but often at great human cost. The second rubric is *documentation.* Scott was a serious antiquarian long before he took to fiction. He specifically offered his novels as a record of former manners and struggles, and he thus took pains to indicate, in footnotes and multiple prefaces, just what evidence had guided him in representing the past as he had. Third comes the term that Scott used to designate what it was that he was concerned to document in the past culture in question: *manners.* Manners (what the French social commentators called *moeurs*) are, for Scott, what a culture primarily consists in. His prefaces stress that the great challenge facing the historical novelist is to make past manners live for modern readers without either leaving them unintelligible for the sake of fidelity or creating anachronism for the sake of making them intelligible. Fourthly, as for *plot,* Scott's method here would set a local or domestic action, in which the intimate manners of the culture could be displayed, against the background of a larger historical development. This arrangement allows for much negotiation between the strictly factual and the more broadly typical historical representations in the novel—as well as between official or public or political history, on the one hand, and unofficial or private or popular history on the other. As Hugh Trevor-Roper has shown, Scott's accommodation of the political and military chronicle to the materials of domestic history changed the practice not only of novelists but also of nineteenth-century historians.[10]

The fifth and last rubric is *characterization,* for which Scott developed a number of related and influential practices. Virtually all of his novels are populated with actual historical personages whose characteristics and actions he

9. On the imagination of nationalism, see Benedict Anderson, *Imagined Communities* (London: Verso, 1983); on nationalist constructions of heritage, see *The Invention of Tradition,* ed. E. J. Hobsbawm and Terence Ranger (London and New York: Cambridge University Press, 1983); on the role of Scott in both projects see Tom Nairn, *The Break-up of Britain* (London: NLB, 1977), 148–169.

10. Sir Hugh Trevor-Roper, "Sir Walter Scott and History," *The Listener* (19 August 1971), 225ff.

elaborated out of standard biographical materials. These are the kinds of characters whom Hegel called "world historical individuals," and they correspond to the
heroes and protagonists of the classical epic form—Achilles and Odysseus, for
example, who stand not only as the leaders of their societies but also as the
epitomes of their respective unified cultures. However, because Scott tends to
project his incipient nation-states not as culturally unitary, but rather as divided
against themselves, these kinds of figures are not the protagonists of the historical
novel. As Georg Lukács has shown in his great but problematic study of the
historical novel, the world historical individuals become minor characters in
Scott's world, and the protagonist at center stage is a relatively mediocre character
who is caught between the two factions whose conflict at once defines his
character and produces the emergent nation for which he or she comes to stand.[11]

So in *Waverley*, for example, the historical Bonny Prince Charles is a minor
character who represents one side of the Scottish-English conflict of the mid-
eighteenth century. The title character, Edward Waverley, on the other hand, is
Scott's invention and is designed to play the role of someone caught between
sides, whose ordinary and typical character formation is defined precisely by his
having experienced two sides of the conflict. This much becomes clear early on in
the novel when it is explained that his Whig English father elects to share
Waverley's upbringing with a Tory uncle who is a sympathizer in the cause of
Scottish rebellion. In *Ivanhoe*, to take one of the other better-known examples, the
historical Richard the Lion-Hearted and his brother (later King) John are minor
characters who represent aspects of a political conflict in the novel, whereas
Ivanhoe himself is the fictional personage whose character is formed out of the
conflicts that he finally tends to mediate. In respect to the Saxon-Norman conflict,
for example, Ivanhoe is a Saxon who is sympathetic with Richard's (i.e., not
John's) wing of the Norman regime. In the end, he helps to reconcile his recal-
citrant Saxon father, Cedric, to the cause of his cultural father, Richard, and thus
to prefigure the social compromises that, on this account, lay ahead in English
social development.

Taken together, all the features of Scott's form provided a way of representing
large historical events and movements as *felt* in the popular experience. This is the
point emphasized by Lukács, and it was not lost on the nineteenth-century authors
who followed Scott. If space permitted, a story well worth telling here would be
that of the eclipse of the nineteenth-century historical romance in the shadow of
modernism. A high modernist novel such as *To the Lighthouse* (1927), for example, turns the historical novel inside out—not showing domestic action within
a framework of history but, so to speak, history within a framework of domestic

---

11. Georg Lukács, *The Historical Novel*, trans. Hannah and Stanley Mitchell (London: Verso, 1962),
19–47.

action. The first and last of the book's three sections are separated by the interlude section—"Time Passes"—that deals with the period of the Great War. But here, as in David Jones, the war is represented only in parenthesis. Woolf knew Scott's fiction well—her commentary on it is as incisive as any we have—and in *To the Lighthouse* itself she seems to acknowledge the challenge her fiction poses to his tradition when she makes Mrs. Ramsay's extended reflections on her husband's reading of Scott the climactic passage of the book's long opening part. For Mrs. Ramsay is given to understand Mr. Ramsay as contemplating precisely the extinction of his own work in the mirror of the great Scottish author who, by 1927, is no longer read.

The story of Scott's extinction in high modernism is not immediately to the point here, however, since this movement was twice removed from the southern American culture in which Griffith, a Kentuckian, matured. Mark Twain reported on what he saw of this culture in the chapter he devoted to Scott's influence on the South in his 1883 *Life on the Mississippi:*

If one take up a Northern or Southern literary periodical of forty or fifty years ago, he will find it filled with wordy, windy, flowery "eloquence," romanticism, sentimentality—all imitated from Sir Walter, and sufficiently badly done, too—innocent travesties of his style and methods, in fact. This sort of literature being the fashion in both sections of the country, there was opportunity for the fairest competition; and as a consequence, the South was able to show as many well-known literary names, proportioned to population, as the North could.

But a change has come, and . . . the North has thrown out that old inflated style, whereas the Southern writer still clings to it. . . . There is as much literary talent in the South, now, as ever there was, of course; but its work can gain but slight currency under present conditions; the authors write for the past, not the present; they use obsolete forms and a dead language.[12]

Reports of Twain's exaggerations have been greatly exaggerated. In his analysis of Scott's influence, to which we will return, he stands on very solid ground.[13] In 1883, when Twain wrote this, young David Griffith was eight years old, and his father, Roarin' Jake Griffith, was still two years from his death. Friends of the Griffiths in this period report Saturday evening gatherings where, with young David hidden under a table to listen, his father, to whom he said *The Birth of a Nation* was so powerfully indebted, would regale the company with tales of the

---

12. Clemens, *Writings,* 12:376–377.
13. George Dekker's recent *American Historical Romance* (Cambridge: Cambridge University Press, 1987), which reached my hands only after delivering the lecture version of this essay, is the first really full study of Scott's literary influence in America. Dekker devotes a long chapter precisely to the question of Scott's literary influence in the South; see 272–333.

war and readings from Shakespeare, Poe, and Scott, but not Dickens, who was after all, in the eyes of some observers, Scott's Yankee-supported rival.[14]

Nor did the Scott craze—what Twain called "the Sir Walter disease"—die out among Southern writers in the 1880s. The 1906 racist novel by Thomas L. Dixon (a South Carolinian) that caught Griffith's eye and eventually prompted him to undertake his epic film of 1914 is precisely one of the sort that Twain describes as still in the thrall of Scott's literary spell. That much is already indicated in its title, *The Clansman,* spelled in such a way as to emphasize the connection it envisioned between the Ku Klux Klan, whose aims the novel promotes, and the Highland clans that Scott had portrayed in "the scotch novels." The title character, Ben Cameron, comes from a Scottish family whose clan appears in *Waverley.* The archaic manor house on the family plantation is grandly referred to as Cameron Hall. When, late in the novel, young Cameron "summons the clans" for the Klansmen's ride to the rescue in defense of what is called their "Aryan Birthright," he does so under "The Fiery Cross of Old Scotland's Hills," a line used for one of Griffith's insert titles in the corresponding scene from the film. The summoning of the clans with the fiery cross is depicted in chapter eighteen of Scott's 1819 novel, *The Legend of Montrose,* and a long note to Scott's popular poem, *The Lady of the Lake,* discusses the passing of the cross as a logistical mechanism in rounding up dispersed clansmen and the symbol of the cross as an ideological occasion to show unquestioned loyalty to the chieftain.[15]

These are just the superficial indicators. The novel that Griffith chose for his epic venture is subtitled "An Historical Romance," and its subject matter embodies the paradigmatic traits of the form that Scott called by the same name. The subject matter of *The Clansman* is the prehistory of a nation divided against itself. It attempts to document its action by way of historically particularized debates on slavery. It emphasizes differences in "manners" both between the North and South and between nineteenth- and twentieth-century America. It creates a domestic plot, centered around the Southern and Northern families, respectively, of the young lovers, Ben Cameron and Elsie Stoneman, and it sets this plot against the larger national events of the Reconstruction Era. While giving center stage to the

---

14. Mentioned in two of the biographies, apparently on the authority of the Oglesby papers at the Museum of Modern Art in New York: Martin Williams, *Griffith: First Artist of the Movies* (New York and Oxford: Oxford University Press, 1980), 7, and Robert Henderon, *D. W. Griffith: His Life and Work* (New York: Oxford University Press, 1972), 28. Henderson also mentions readings from Goldsmith. Neither biographer makes anything of Griffith's early and powerful exposure to Scott in this way and in the context of his father's reputation as a Confederate-veteran raconteur of the war.

15. Dixon's novel has one major Dickensian moment, taken from *A Tale of Two Cities:* Phil Stoneman, Elsie's brother, sneaks into the prison where Cameron is being held, near the end of the novel, and changes places with him, very much à la Sydney Carton and Charles Darnay. But the framework of the novel remains mainly un-Dickensian.

fictional lovers, it makes its historical personages minor characters who represent polarized ideological positions in the national crisis.

Some of these points can be illustrated from the novel's opening sequence. The novel (unlike the film) begins in a Washington hospital with the meeting of Elsie Stoneman, daughter of Pennsylvania Senator Austin Stoneman (closely modeled on the abolitionist Thaddeus Stevens, also a senator from Pennsylvania during the War and Reconstruction), and Ben Cameron, the wounded Confederate colonel who becomes the Klansman of the title. Elsie is the boundary-crossing character in the novel. She later goes to South Carolina with her abolitionist father, but remains there with Cameron in the end, plighting her troth with the Klansman on its last page. Their meeting in the hospital at the outset takes place on the day of Lee's surrender at Appomattox, which is announced by newsboys outside the hospital windows. This interleaving of domestic-fictional and public historical events is conspicuously insisted upon throughout the opening sequence. It culminates with the evening scene, five days after the surrender, when Elsie and Ben go to Ford's Theater for a production of *Our American Cousin* which the President has announced in advance he will attend. The centerpiece of this opening sequence is a Scottesque episode, between surrender and assassination, in which Cameron's mother, having come from South Carolina to see her wounded son, is accompanied by Elsie to Lincoln's office to sue for a pardon from "the Great Heart." Elsie succeeds where Mrs. Cameron fails, but only after a series of debates between Lincoln and her father (the Stevens character) about larger policy questions of amnesty toward the postwar South.

This sequence depicts Lincoln not only as a Southern sympathizer but actually as a Southerner himself. At their White House interview, Mrs. Cameron and Lincoln hold the following exchange:

> "I must tell you, Mr. President," she said, "how surprised and how pleased I am to find you are a Southern man."
>
> "Why didn't you know that my parents were Virginians, and that I was born in Kentucky?"
>
> "Very few people in the South know it. I am ashamed to say I did not."
>
> "Then, how did you know I am a Southerner?"
>
> "By your looks, your manner of speech, your easy, kindly ways, your tenderness and humour, your firmness in the right as you see it, and, above all, the way you rose and bowed to a woman in an old, faded black dress, whom you knew to be an enemy."[16]

Dixon offers relatively little in the way of set-piece descriptions of "manners," but this shows that the subject has some importance in the novel, even if the concept

---

16. Thomas Dixon, *The Clansman: An Historical Romance of the Ku Klux Klan* (Ridgewood, N.J.: The Gregg Press, 1967), 31.

of manners is beginning to undergo a shift toward its prevalent modern American associations with etiquette. "Easy, kindly ways" should have been enough without the particularization ("above all") of the "way [he] rose and bowed to a woman."

Coming to Dixon's opening sequence from Scott, one will also be quickly reminded of the role of pardons in the thematic structure of the Waverley novels. Pardons provide institutional agency for the work of reconciling opposing sides in a society at war with itself: *Waverley, Ivanhoe,* and *The Bride of Lammermoor* all involve crucial acts of pardon. Indeed, Elsie's appeal to Lincoln probably owes a specific debt to *The Heart of Mid-Lothian,* where, in the context of Scottish insurrection, the fictional Jeannie Deans, having traveled from Edinburgh to London, sues for the pardon of her sister Elsie to the historical Duke of Argyll, with like success, and with similarly large political resonances.[17]

---

17. In the hospital chapter, a Union eyewitness reports to Elsie how it was that Ben Cameron fell in battle and came to be placed in a Northern hospital. It is a scene that Griffith shoots in great detail. Having led one charge against a regiment of Union troops commanded by Phil Stoneman, young Cameron, the Little Colonel,

> " . . . sprang on the breastwork. . . . He was a handsome figure—tall, slender, straight, a gorgeous yellow sash tasselled with gold around his waist, his sword flashing in the sun, his slouch hat cocked on one side and an eagle's feather in it.
>
> "We thought that he was going to lead another charge, but just as the battery was making ready to fire, he deliberately walked down the embankment in a hail of musketry and began to give water to our wounded men.
>
> "Every gun ceased firing, and we watched him. He walked back to the trench, his naked sword flashed suddenly above the eagle's feather, and his grizzled ragamuffins sprang forward and charged us like so many demons. . . , giving that hellish rebel yell at every jump." (8–9)

When Cameron falls during this charge, he is cared for by Phil Stoneman, as Cameron had cared for the Union troops. The whole episode echoes the charge in the central battle scene of *Waverley,* the Battle of Preston. Here the young Englishman, allied through circumstance with the Scots in the Civil War of 1745, helps to lead a charge with the Mac-Ivor clan, alongside the Cameron clan, against his own English countrymen:

> "Down with your plaid, Waverley," cried Fergus, throwing off his own: "we'll win silks for our tartans before the sun is above the sea."
>
> The clansmen on every side stript their plaids, [and] prepared their arms. . . . Waverley felt his heart at that moment throb as it would have burst from his bosom. . . . The sounds around him combined to exalt his enthusiasm; the pipes played on, and the clans rushed forward, each in his own dark column. As they advanced they mended their pace, and the muttering sounds of the men to each other began to swell into a wild cry. . . .
>
> "Forward, sons of Ivor," cried their Chief, "or the Camerons will draw first-blood"—They rushed on with a tremendous yell. (336)

In the course of the ensuing battle, Waverley saves one enemy (i.e., English) officer, and attempts to succor another one as well. When Griffith shoots the episode of the Little Colonel succoring a dying Union soldier, he seems to be following Scott's account even more closely than Dixon:

> Waverley could perceive that [this officer] had already received many wounds, his clothes and saddle being marked with blood. To save this good and brave man [who was actually his former commander], became the instant object of his most anxious exertions. . . . But [the dying warrior]

If Dixon's book suggests the continuing power of Scott in early twentieth-century Southern literary culture, then Griffith's selection of this book may be said to indicate something about his own taste in historical fictions. If Griffith had simply undertaken an unambitiously faithful rendering of Dixon's narrative (i.e., an "adaptation"), not much more could be said of the matter.[18] But what Griffith did, in the event, was to recast much of Dixon's action and to reframe the entire plot. Further, in undertaking this transformation of Dixon he seems to have been guided by purposes and principles themselves indebted to Scott's example. In neither his relation to Dixon nor to Scott, however, is Griffith engaged in a project of adaptation. Griffith reimagines Dixon's project with suggestions from Scott but in so doing he develops his own kind of cinematic "writing," what Truffaut might have called an *écriture cinématique de l'histoire.*

In order to lend the air of documentary authority to his film narrative, as Scott once did for his fictions, Griffith provided still shots of newspaper pages, citations of Woodrow Wilson's *History of the American People,* and various historical statistics. Far more ingenious, however, was what he did with the composition of certain scenes. At a half-dozen points in the film we are given insert titles to announce that the setting for the ensuing scene replicates a Civil War–period photograph or historical painting. The first such setting we are given is the interior of the Lincoln's office in which Elsie and Mrs. Cameron eventually sue for pardon. This interior is first shown in the scene of Lincoln's signing of the proclamation to draft seventy-five thousand Northerners to serve in the Union army: the insert title declares the scene a "historical facsimile" based on a Matthew Brady photograph of the event. The pains taken with the details of the assassination sequence are famous—Griffith researched the line in *Our American Cousin* on which Booth pulled the trigger—and at the beginning of this sequence,

---

felt that death was dealing closely with him, and resigning his purpose, and folding his hands in devotion, he gave up his soul to his Creator. (338)

It is true that the charge of the Scots clansmen here leads to a victory rather than a defeat, but it is also true that overall, like the Confederate cause, theirs is a hopeless and romantic effort, doomed from the start. Further, just as Cameron's helping the Union soldier is returned in kind by Stoneman, thus saving his life, so Waverley's aid to the first fallen Englishman, Colonel Talbot, leads to a later pardon of *his* life.

18. I do not here take up the question of Griffith's relation to the play version of *The Clansman* that achieved some popularity soon after the publication of the novel, though the connection between the play and the film is reinforced by the fact that the first New York run of the film took place at the Liberty Theater where, nine years earlier, the play had briefly run—see Schickel, *D. W. Griffith,* 267. Nor do I take up the important question of the relation of all of these works, Dixon's and Griffith's, to *Uncle Tom's Cabin* and its early nineteenth-century stagings; Leslie Fiedler offers a start on this issue in *The Inadvertent Epic: From Uncle Tom's Cabin to Roots* (New York: Simon and Schuster, 1979), 43–57.

too, we are informed that the setting is based on a historical facsimile of Ford's Theater.[19] These and other such moments in *The Birth of a Nation* create an illusion of what might be called "documentary space" for encounters of fictional characters with historical figures and circumstances. Griffith's deployment of textual sources and his replication of historical settings combine to pioneer the cinematic equivalent of Roland Barthes' "history effect": the "documentary effect."

An even more strenuous effort in Griffith's narrative transformation of *The Clansman* follows from his decision to add an hour's worth of material of his own devising to introduce and contextualize the event with which Dixon's novel begins. The meeting of Elsie Stoneman (Lillian Gish) and Ben Cameron (Henry Walthall) in the Washington hospital on Appomattox Day does not occur until one-third of the way into Griffith's three-hour film. That first hour's footage, then, is the obvious place to look for evidence of how Griffith set about his task to rewrite not only Dixon but American history as well. We can note, for instance, that whereas Dixon's book starts with the end of the war, some of the most memorable action in *The Birth of a Nation* occurs in the battle scenes. In depicting military struggles of the Civil War, Griffith managed to weave fictional elements into the military chronicle as Scott had done in novels like *Waverley* and *Old Mortality* and likewise Tolstoy, in the same tradition, with the celebrated accounts of the Napoleonic Wars in *War and Peace*. The camera locations on hilltops high above charging troops in the battle scenes, or over the serpentine progress of Sherman's march to the sea, give the sense of both wide scope and elevated historical perspective. Both the subject matter and the representational techniques in Griffith's pioneering battle footage lend the Scott-like sense of epic scale to what, in Dixon, had been a more modestly conceived historical representation. Like Scott's depictions of the Battle of Preston, the Porteous Riots, or the Siege of Torquilstone, Griffith's military events unfold in a kind of "epic space." On the one hand, then, Griffith's transformation of Dixon showed his ambition to carry on Scott's project of updating the epic form. In the Dedicatory Epistle to *Ivanhoe* (a copy of which Twain said one could find on every Southern mantelpiece in the 1880s), Scott alludes to the creation of "the modern epopée," the task of modernizing in prose the epic tradition he had received in verse. Griffith further modernized, or better, *re*modernized, the prose epic as it came to him by projecting it into film.[20]

---

19. Schickel comments that Griffith "stress[ed] to the point of exaggeration in his publicity the amount of historical research," but he concedes that that amount was large—*D. W. Griffith*, 237.

20. To "remodernize" in this context is to maintain the sense of the antique-modern distinction which is in fact elided in the movement called modernism, as I have tried to suggest in suggesting Woolf. If the "postmodern" is that which proceeds in the face of the antique-modern distinction (the synecdoche for antiquity in the films of the 1980s is often the 1950s), then Scott is the prototypical postmodern author and modernism in fiction, prepared for by Dickens's successful appropriation of Scott's readership, would be understood as the displacer of postmodernism, rather than the other way around.

In respect to the equally important *domestic* dimension of his project, on the other hand, Griffith also resorted to Scott's example to produce a fuller representation than he found in Dixon of what Scott, in the same Dedicatory Epistle, called "*la vie privée* of our forefathers." In prefixing the hour of new material to Dixon's opening sequence, Griffith's twofold strategy was to preserve the sense of the meeting of Elsie and Ben as a first encounter while simultaneously creating a prehistory for their relationship. His way of handling this balancing act, in a "script" that he apparently kept only in his head as he shot the film, was to develop an expositional sequence around a visit in late 1860 (dated by newspaper reference) of Elsie's brothers from their eastern Pennsylvania home to the Cameron estate in Piedmont, South Carolina. The invitation for this visit, extended from Ben Cameron to Phil Stoneman, obviously presupposes a still prior (but unexplained) friendship between them, perhaps as recent college friends; in Dixon's version, Cameron and Stoneman meet for the first time on the battlefield after Cameron's ill-fated charge. Griffith takes the trouble to motivate and insert the visit sequence because it enables him to offer a study in comparative cultures or systems of manners before the outbreak of the war. This intention is signaled forcefully at the moment when the younger Stoneman brother descends from the carriage outside Cameron Hall and faces the younger Cameron brother for the first time: "Chums—the younger sons," reads the insert title, "North and South." They immediately begin to twit each other about their manners and attire: "Where did you get that hat?" Their friendship, with its Chaplinesque sparring and horseplay, becomes a comic leitmotif through the visit, but is given tragic symbolic authority later in the film when, wearing the more uniform costumes of Union and Confederate soldiers, they meet on the battlefield and die in a mutual embrace.

The narrative device of the visit is supported by the use of parallel cutting that juxtaposes images of domesticity in the North and South. It is made clear even before the visit, for example, that unlike the scene at Cameron Hall, the image of the domicile in the North is dispersed among three different locations. The domestic action of the Stoneman family, who are motherless, occurs partly in a Washington apartment where Elsie lives with her aunt, partly in a Pennsylvania house that offers the support of neither parents nor neighbors, and partly in the Washington office of Senator Stoneman, where Lydia, the mulatto housekeeper, is supposed to have usurped the role and vastly augmented the power of the absent mother.[21] The juxtaposition of each of these domestic settings with the self-consciously full and "organic" culture of the Southern manor, both before and after the visit, suggests invidious conclusions about fragmentation, perversion,

21. For a full account of the role of the absent mother in *Birth* and indeed for a powerful account of various race and gender relations in the film, see Michael Rogin's tour-de-force essay "'The Sword Became a Flashing Vision': D. W. Griffith's *The Birth of a Nation*," *Representations* 9 (Winter 1985): 150–195. [Reprinted in this volume.]

and isolation in the North. One is particularly struck by a series of mirror shots involving the Pennsylvania household of the Stonemans and the Southern culture of Cameron Hall. In the former, the house stands on the left, its curtained doorway facing right, onto a walkway where the three young Stonemans appear alone and consistently parentless in the foreground and where the background is empty except for two laborers, one black and one white, whose work seems unpurposeful and who remain marginal in the life and attention of the Stoneman trio. In the corresponding shots of Cameron Hall, by contrast, the household appears on the *right* of the screen, its porched entranced way facing *left,* onto a street where a community—of which the Camerons old and young are very much a part, including contented-looking black slaves—carries out its affairs in ritualized harmony. To sustain this sort of contrast through the outbreak of the war, Griffith offers parallel scenes of farewell to departing soldiers. The Stoneman brothers exit right from the house to the empty walkway and then through a hedge, in a strangely barren farewell scene, played only with Elsie, who puts up a brave face in front of her brothers and then collapses, distraught, into the arms of an unidentifiable older woman—her aunt, perhaps, or a servant—who emerges suddenly from the doorway in the background. In the mirror scene in front of Cameron Hall, the Cameron brothers exit left, to the crowded village street, with the support of assembled family and friends.

The juxtapositions are so routinely invidious that it is almost misleading to say that two cultures are being compared here.[22] And indeed the visit of the Stoneman brothers to Cameron Hall serves chiefly to introduce Southern culture. It occasions a survey of the system of manners that animates and organizes the domestic Southern "household" (here with the ancient resonances of "economy"), and it therefore enables Griffith to provide a form of attention to manners that is more patient and elaborate than the kind of shortcut Dixon takes, for example, in the dialogue he writes for Lincoln and Mrs. Cameron. Griffith stages scenes first on the porch of Cameron Hall, then in the large foyer, and then in the interior sitting room. Then, with the visitors, we move "over the plantation to the cotton fields" on an excursion in which the young whites loaf and court, and slaves work the fields as part of a "natural" setting. Finally, the young whites visit "in the slave quarters," where, despite the slaves' twelve-hour work day that the insert title acknowledges, there is supposed to be energy at mid-day for music and dancing: performed, in this case, for the entertainment of the white masters.

I mean to stress that, in its exposition of a culture through the manners and customs of a "household" ("economy"), Griffith's film is far more like the model of Scott's fiction, as outlined above, than it is like its immediate source in Dixon's

---

22. The asymmetry of the mirroring can be seen in the detail of the pillars; the four grand ones in the colonial porch of Cameron Hall inadequately answered by the two small and squarish ones in the strangely curtained porch of the Stoneman house.

novel. Indeed, the visit to the household across the cultural boundary of the incipient nation is a narrative strategy powerfully realized by Scott in the beginning of *Waverley* and *Ivanhoe,* and for something like the same purpose: to create a sense of *"la vie privée"* of the forefathers. The strategy is to suggest a deep cultural division within an emerging society and to bring strangers from one side of the cultural division to the other, as guests whose introduction to the objects and habits of the house serve to introduce the reader to those things. The action of Scott's first novel begins with Waverley's crossing of the Scottish border to visit the Baron Bradwardine at his estate, Tully-Veolan, and we follow his journey into the Highlands for another such visit, this time to the castle of Fergus Mac-Ivor. *Ivanhoe* begins with the visit by a hostile Norman pair, Prior Aymer and the Knight Templar, Brian de Bois-Guilbert, to Rotherwood Hall, household of Cedric the Saxon, father of Ivanhoe. In reimagining Dixon with help from Scott, Griffith is not finally "adapting" either author, but is rather developing his own kind of historical writing, an ambition Woodrow Wilson seemed to recognize when he praised the movie after its White House screening as "like writing history with lightning."[23]

One of the uses to which Griffith puts the image of the organically unified Southern household, once he has established it, is to make it the site where historical action leaves its mark on everyday life. The porch, foyer, and interior sitting room of Cameron Hall are the sites that compose what we might call the "domestic space" on which Griffith will inscribe the events of the 1860s, thus bringing them home to the businesses and bosoms of his characters. As the film moves forward from the early 1860 visitation sequence to depict the outbreak of the war, various political struggles, and the famous battle sequences—all still part of his own preface to Dixon's action—he sees to it that these developments are signally registered in Cameron Hall. This effect is achieved in several ways. The most obvious and direct of these is the use of verbal message, either through a messenger or by means of specific documents that usually appear as still shots and are then allowed to occasion responses from the family—what an insert title calls "read[ing] war's sad page." This practice is established early in the film, during the Stoneman visit, when Dr. Cameron, "the kindly master of Cameron Hall," is shown reading a newspaper article of late 1860 that predicts: "If the North Carries the Election, The South Will Secede."

The second way is by depicting the economic effects of the war on the house and its furnishings. The most frequently recurring shot of the interior of the house is that of the grand foyer with the divided stairway ascending both to the upper right and upper left in the background. This space is steadily stripped of its original trappings and appointments as the war progresses. The actual carrying off of furniture and goods is explicitly depicted, and much is made, as again later in *Gone With the Wind,* of the women's efforts to provide makeshift replacements for the wardrobes they no longer

23. Quoted in Schickel, *D. W. Griffith,* 270.

have. The Cameron household is even used to suggest what might have become of the South if Lincoln had lived to implement his policy of postwar leniency toward the South. In the few days between Appomattox and Assassination, Griffith brings Ben Cameron home from Washington to Piedmont and shows the Cameron family already reconstructing their own household: not only by the physical labor of rehabilitation but also by advertising for boarders with a sign hung on the porch.

These first two techniques, showing both the information relay and the impact of the war on the domestic economy, prepare for a third: the use of parallel montage in the mode of sheer tour de force. For Griffith suggests a kind of mental telepathic communication between characters at the Hall and actors in the great events elsewhere. The most obvious example of this sort of telepathic montage occurs during the battle scene when the Little Colonel is shot and wounded; in the course of the charge that the Little Colonel leads against the enemy, Griffith cuts intermittently to the parents and sisters back at Cameron Hall, where they assume a posture of family prayer in the interior sitting room.

Finally, the impingement of the war upon the family is also just dramatized. For instance, when the Cameron sons are seen off to war, the parents and sisters (in a shot that prepares for the later telepathic montage), are shown retreating to the interior setting room to assume intensely self-absorbed postures of contemplation in front of a camera so "candid" that it offers a badly obstructed view of Mrs. Cameron. Contrasted with the pensiveness and subtlety of this dramatization of the war's effect on the family is the long sequence that shows the raid on Cameron Hall by a company of renegade Union troops. In the course of this raid, the Cameron daughters retreat room by room from the invasion of the black Union troops until they reach the innermost sanctuary of the house. Here they remain, while black soldiers plunder the house, until they and the rest of the family are rescued by a company of Confederate soldiers who happen to hear the commotion. The same black Union troops reappear, as it were, in the siege of the small cabin that shelters a group of Northern and Southern whites, represented as the future of the nation, and the same Confederates reappear to rescue them in the costume of the Ku Klux Klan. The difference between the two raids will prove important. At this point I will only add that the episode of the raid on the manor house may—like the woman's plea to the great man for pardon of another, the succoring of the fallen enemy, and the visit to the household of the cultural other—derive specifically from an episode in Scott's fiction: in this case, the raid on Tully-Veolan by the Highland renegades during Waverley's first visit there. The term "raid" itself is a Highland corruption of "road," as in "taking to the road" to plunder goods, and the very availability of the word to Griffith may even have been a function of Scott's influence in popularizing it.[24]

---

24. See Ernest Weekley, "Walter Scott and the English Language," *The Atlantic Monthly* (November 1931): 148:599. I thank Stuart Tave for the reference.

That there are crucial aspects of Griffith's mode of representing history which have little to do with Scott, or which may indeed run counter to salient tendencies in the Waverley novels, is a point too obvious to belabor. Miriam Hansen's important discussion of Griffith in "Myths of Origin in Early American Cinema" argues two claims, for example, that delimit the implication of what I have been trying to establish here. The first is that Griffith was committed to a view of his medium as a potentially transparent mode, a "universal language" or "moving picture Esperanto" that could overcome the Babel of the pre-Hollywood word. Though Scott's fiction has enjoyed global appreciation, his own stress seems to fall on the *un*transparency of his medium, and his frequent resort to writing dialogue in dialect seems a mark of his commitment to the power of the local. Secondly, Hansen shows that Griffith's historiographical ambitions for film participated in a wider contemporary discourse, which preexisted *The Birth of a Nation,* about the capacity of the "new art" to effect "the unlimited reproduction of actual events on the screen."[25] With such limitations understood, however, I would like to consider, in closing, some possible implications of the argument I have been pursuing. What follows from the substitution of Scott's name for Dickens's in Eisenstein's formula?

In the first place, only by seeing how elements of Scott's fiction inhere independently in Dixon's novel and in Griffith's film can we begin to notice how Griffith's Scott differs from Dixon's. In Dixon's novel, the work of the clan produces a reincarnation of the splendor of the Old South, which had been implied but not been previously represented in the narrative. Griffith, by contrast, begins *The Birth of a Nation* with a long exposition of antebellum Southern culture. Although this first hour of the film appears to express an elegiac longing for the Old South, especially in juxtaposition with the North, Griffith is actually providing us with a way of seeing that the feudal aspects of the antebellum Southern culture must change. Griffith's insert titles in the opening visit explicitly introduce us to "the manners of the old school" and "a quaintly way of life that is to be no more." The recurrence of the camera and the narrative to the image of the house in which these qualities are invested permits the viewer to track their destruction. In *Waverley,* Scott had used a similar technique in his set-piece descriptions of Tully-Veolan before, during, and after the '45 Rebellion. When Margaret Mitchell and David O. Selznick combine, in effect, to revise *The Birth of a Nation* as *Gone With the Wind,* they do not move beyond the indulgence of elegiac regret for the destruction of Tara, symbol of what the Old South is supposed to have been.[26] But

25. Miriam Hansen, "Universal Language and Democratic Culture: Myths of Origin in Early American Cinema," in *Myth and Enlightenment in American Literature,* ed. Dieter Meindle and Friedrich Horlacher (Erlangen: Universität Erlangen-Nürnberg, 1985), 321–351.
26. Fiedler does not comment at length on Selznick and Griffith, but his discussion of Mitchell and Dixon is informative. He cites a letter from Mitchell to Dixon in which she says: "I was practically raised on your books and love them very much." *The Inadvertent Epic,* 59.

as the prospective orientation of Griffith's very title means to suggest, the steady stripping away of the trappings of Southern splendor is finally to be viewed as a potentially salutary process, as is the analogous divestiture of the feudal in *Waverley*. The Confederacy's delusion of grandeur is identified in some of the film's significant details. When Cameron returns to Piedmont just days after Appomattox, his "little sister" (Mae Marsh) prepares for his homecoming by ornamenting the best of her ragged dresses with a cotton trim that she has marked here and there with short lines of black soot: "'Southern ermine' from raw cotton for the grand occasion," the insert title explains. The second half of the movie concerns the rise of Silas Lynch, the black man whom Austin Stoneman attempts to make his puppet ruler in reconstructed South Carolina. Once in power, he is identified in an insert title as "the social lion of the new aristocracy," a man who seeks to be "king" of a new "empire" of which his co-conspirator, Lydia—Stoneman's mulatto housekeeper—seeks to be "queen." (Lynch himself seeks Elsie Stoneman for that role.) Black rule thus makes its appearance in Griffith's Reconstruction as the residue of all that was backward or self-deceived in antebellum white society.

The local culture of antebellum Southern society was vital enough, on Griffith's representation, but he insists that its forms of life remained local. It could not, within the prewar social framework, overcome its own class structure nor make the necessary passage from national units (households, clans, states) to united nation. An early insert title for the scene of Lincoln's signing of the conscription act opines that the "power of the sovereign states, established when Lord Cornwallis surrendered to the individual colonies in 1781, is threatened by the new administration." This comment seems defensive about states' rights in behalf of the Confederate position, but this is a viewpoint that the film will move beyond. Its representation of the war and the reconstruction advocates the unity of the racial nation at the expense of the autonomy of the state. This view, which Griffith offers as the longer perspective on current events, must be extended to the global situation, where his idea of the nation can be seen to transcend America itself. Only such an extension of the view can explain the film's ostentatious pacifism in the context of World War I, which Griffith seems to have regarded as benighted fratricide between political states that shared a common national—i.e., Aryan—birthright.

The debilitated Southern culture—both no longer and not yet a nation—whose feudal trappings are stripped away in the divestiture of Cameron Hall is reinvested with power, the film suggests, in the shabby log cabin to which Dr. Cameron, his only surviving daughter, and Phil Stoneman (her lover) take refuge. The resonances of this cabin in the Lincoln hagiography are called up by the bearded Union soldier who offers the group sanctuary—perhaps (as perhaps too with the Lincoln–look-alike Union guard in the Washington hospital scene) one of the thirty-odd actors who auditioned for the Lincoln part but lost out to the multi-talented Joseph Henabery. There are also resonances of Griffith's autobiography which opens with his account of how the "pretentious" antebellum Kentucky "mansion" of his family was destroyed by "guerillas, disguised as Union raiders." So "the second house that father built was quite small. And it was here that I was born."[27] It is in this cabin that, in the film's self-mythology, the promise of a new nation is threatened and redeemed by the timely rescue ride of the Ku Klux Klan. This ending is Griffith's and not Dixon's, and it corresponds to his change of title from *The Clansman* to *The Birth of a Nation*. No more than Dixon can Griffith be excused from the charge of undisguised white supremacism. But Dixon's novel ends, as a late chapter title puts it, with "The Reign of the Clan," while Griffith's ends with the reign of "Liberty and Union"—the union to be born of the concluding double marriage of Stoneman sister and brother from Pennsylvania with Cameron brother and sister from South Carolina.

The shorthand way of putting the difference between Griffith's Scott and Dixon's is to say, roughly, that Dixon's Scott is more like the one that Twain puts down and Griffith's is more like the one that Lukács raises up. For where Lukács's Scott produced a form that is generally in line with an advancing social consciousness, Twain's Scott stood squarely in the way of such advances. Twain's account of Scott's relation to the French Revolution is directly relevant:

> . . . the Revolution broke the chains of the ancien régime and of the Church, and made a nation of abject slaves a nation of freemen; and Bonaparte instituted the setting of merit above birth, and also so completely stripped the divinity from royalty that, . . . they are only men since, . . . and answerable for their acts like common clay. . . .
>
> Then comes Sir Walter Scott with his enchantments, and by his single might checks this wave of progress, and even turns it back; sets the world in love with dreams and phantoms; with decayed and swinish forms of religion; with decayed and degraded systems of government; with the sillinesses and emptinesses, sham grandeurs, sham gauds, and sham chivalries of a brainless and worthless long-vanished society. . . . Most of the world has now outlived a good part of these harms, though by no means all of them; but in our South they flourished pretty forcefully still. . . . There, the genuine and wholesome

---

27. *The Man Who Invented Hollywood: The Autobiography of D. W. Griffith* (Louisville: Touchstone, 1972), 19. Here I quote the passage in full, partly because the Prologue, from which it is taken, begins in a mode resonant of *Waverley*'s preface:

A scant half-century ago Queen Victoria was firmly seated in the throne of Great Britain and the world slid along nicely at three miles an hour.

Down in Old Kentucky, near Louisville, was the house of my father, Colonel Jacob Wark Griffith, a Confederate cavalry officer. . . . Once there had been quite a pretentious place—more or less like the popular conception of Kentucky mansions—with poplar and osage orange groves leading up to its portals. Guerrillas, disguised as Union raiders, burned the house down in the first year of the war. The second house that father built was quite small. And it was here that I was born. Here also was whelped the wolf pup of want and hunger that was to shadow me all my life.

civilization of the nineteenth century is curiously confused and commingled with the Walter Scott Middle-Age sham civilization, and so you have practical common sense, progressive ideas, and progressive works, mixed up with the duel, inflated speech, and the jejune romanticism of an absurd past that is dead, and out of charity ought to be buried. But for the Sir Walter disease, the character of the Southerner—or Southron, according to Sir Walter's starchier way of phrasing it—would be wholly modern, in place of modern and medieval mixed, and the South would be fully a generation further advanced than it is. (12:376–377)

Most modern Scott scholars, even without the help of Lukács's book, would call Twain's account an oversimplification. Twain saw Scott's sympathy for feudal antiquity as unqualified and unbounded, and he wrote *A Connecticut Yankee in King Arthur's Court* to debunk such sentimentalization. Modern defenders of Scott would argue that the representation of chivalric culture in *Ivanhoe* is scarcely the idealization that Twain sees there, and the same could be said for the archaic Highland culture typified by Fergus Mac-Ivor in *Waverley.*

How to find and construe the evidence for Twain's view is best indicated, paradoxically, in his most outlandish claim in Chapter 46 of *Life on the Mississippi:* "Sir Walter had so large a hand in making Southern character, as it existed before the war, that he is in great measure responsible for the war" (377). Even Twain himself acknowledges that this must seem a wild proposition. The way to read it, if also to qualify it, is to recognize that the Scott who made the Southern character what it was—i.e., among other things, a character reckless enough to go to war against the North—is the Scott that the South imagined when it read him: the Scott of the idealized past and the romantic lost cause, the Scott of mythicized Celtic aura and rigid class stratification. To back up Twain's breezy and sarcastic overview of Scott's influence one can consult a more patient analysis of the issue in a book like Rollin Osterweis's *Romanticism and Nationalism in the Old South.* Osterweis shows that the sales of Scott's books in the South were massive. He mentions pilgrimages of Southerners to Scott's medievalized house at Abbotsford and argues that at least two Southern state houses were influenced by Scott's taste in architecture. He cites much evidence of the kind briefly alluded to by Twain that Scott's diction was much adopted in Southern writing and conversation.[28] Grace Landrum's earlier research on the adoption of Scott's names had already turned up a host of "Walter Scotts, Rowenas, Ellen Douglases, Flora MacIvors . . . on family trees" and had discovered that one Richard Ivanhoe Cocke had been commencement orator at William and Mary in the 1830s.[29]

28. Rollin G. Osterweis, *Romanticism and Nationalism in the Old South* (New Haven: Yale University Press, 1949), 41–53. I thank Neil Harris for the reference.
29. Grace Warren Landrum, "Sir Walter Scott and His Literary Rivals in the Old South," *American Literature* (November 1930) 2:256–276.

Twain's extravagant claim about Scott gains particular credibility, I think, when one considers the degree to which, as the author who brings together the crusading medievalism of *Ivanhoe* with the celebration of the Highland clans in the Scottish novels, Scott articulated precisely that cultural conjunction in which the Ku Klux Klan conceived its own group identity. Scott's peculiar conjunction is discernable in the very name of the organization. It is obvious that the latter part of the name derives from the social unit of the Scottish Highlands, and we have already noted that, for example, the Klan's celebrated symbol of the burning cross derives from a Highland custom that was publicized and popularized by Scott in both fiction and poetry. It is less widely recognized, perhaps, that the first part of the organization's name, from the Greek for circle, *kuklos,* has medievalized origins in such antebellum organizations as The Knights of the Golden Circle. This K.G.C., as it was known, was already campaigning in the 1850s for a Southern empire to include what would become the Confederate states as well as most of Texas and Central America in a "slaveocracy," with themselves, as a sort of round table, at its center of power. This earlier organization, in turn, rode the wave of a Scott-inspired medieval revival of earlier decades, a revival that included renewed duelling and mock-medieval tournaments. When the Confederacy was formed, it identified itself powerfully with an archaic chivalric code obviously associated with Scott. As if to confirm this association, Confederate military men composed Scottesque and Scottish-sounding ballads about how "Like heroes and princes they lived for a time."

> Chivalrous, chivalrous people are!
> In C.S.A.! In C.S.A.!
> Aye, in chivalrous C.S.A.![30]

It would clearly be a mistake to go all the way with Twain's assumption that one writer, no matter how powerful his influence, can be called the cause of such large cultural tendencies. But the really disturbing point about those Klansman on parade in their Crusader costumes at the end of *The Birth of a Nation* is that their resemblance to the knights at Scott's Ashby-de-la-Zouche is not just a function of Griffith's or Dixon's knowledge of *Ivanhoe*—not just an issue at the level of treatment, so to speak—but goes back to white supremacist groups before the war who emulated what they thought they read in Scott to constitute themselves a Southern knighthood.

There is certainly a residue of this Southern Scott in *The Birth of a Nation.* Griffith did, after all, shoot much of Dixon's story as it was. He said that *The Birth of a Nation* owed more to his father than to himself, and his autobiography opens with a raft of idealized stories of Roarin' Jake:

---

30. Osterweis, *Romanticism and Nationalism,* 46.

Suffering from a festering shoulder wound, he was about to lead a charge at the Battle of Corinth in Tennessee when he received a Minié ball through his hip. Unable to mount a horse, he turned the charge over to a subordinate. But when he saw his troops preparing to go into the fray without him, the fires of battle flamed high in the Old War Horse. Commandeering a horse and buggy, he rushed to the front of the long curved line of sabers sweeping down the field, leading the charge in person. This was a moving picture indeed . . . a hatless middle-aged man, his long beard flying in the wind; around him the roar of battle; behind him his charging troops . . . while he, in a careening buggy, rockets into the jaws of death, his great voice calling down the wrath of God and Lee upon the enemy. (25)

The implication is clearly that they don't make men like that anymore, except in movies. But Griffith protests in the same pages that he "hold[s] no nostalgic grief for the past" and embraces "Edison, Ford, and Marconi." The protest, too, must be taken seriously. Dixon looks back to a time of looking backward, but it is characteristic of Griffith's peculiar nostalgia that he looks back to a time of looking forward. Much more like Scott than Dixon in this respect, Griffith's work is at once modernizing and archaic. This was one of the truths about Griffith captured in Eisenstein's analysis of the two faces of Griffith's America, and it is uncannily close in kind to the truth that Virginia Woolf captured about Scott in "Gas at Abbotsford," the essay that begins from the puzzle that Scott built himself a medieval mansion in the 1810s, but at the same time made it the first private residence in Britain to be fitted for the use of gas.[31]

Finally, I hope that attention to ways of reproducing the historical novel in the cinema may prove helpful in discriminating among various examples of the modern film epic. It may help to tell those epics which are great-man styled historical biographies—Abel Gance's *Napoleon,* and later *Spartacus, Lawrence of Arabia,* and *Gandhi*—from those which tend to employ some version of the mediocre fictional hero caught in the middle of a conflict—as with the Al Pacino character, a disinterested trapper drawn into the struggle for American War of Independence, in *Revolution.* The lavish film epic that swept the Oscars (fifties-style) in 1988 was *The Last Emperor,* an interesting case to consider in these terms. At first it appears to be the glamorous film biography of a great man who changed history. This would have been a strong departure from the Bertolucci of *1900,* in which the depiction of Italian political struggles at the turn of the century is handled more along the lines suggested in Lukács's analysis of Scott. But the imperial splendor of *The Last Emperor* is jarring not only in the context of Bertolucci's prior work, but also in the face of the film's apparent endorsement of

31. Virginia Woolf, "Sir Walter Scott," in *The Moment and Other Essays* (London: Hogarth Press, 1947), 50–59.

the 1947 revolution in China. The film ultimately enacts the undoing of the typical course of the great-man–centered film epic. For instead of presenting the great man's rise to greatness through his education toward certain monumental traits of character, *The Last Emperor* circumscribes the young emperor's education into the powers and pleasures of emperorship in the Eternal City within the context of his socialist reeducation into the responsibilities of ordinary life. The film gives us a complex culture in which the would-be great man is remade for the purpose of popular citizenship.

I have offered these last suggestions only to indicate possibilities of application. Fully recognizing the residual forms of nineteenth-century historical fiction in twentieth-century historical cinema will involve a far more complicated analysis than I have produced here, but it is a task that needs to be carried out. Most "modern cultures" find themselves depending more and more on the film medium in establishing the antiquity against which they define themselves. We tend to rely on distinctions far too simple between, on the one hand, documentary films and, on the other, history films that have, as we say, gone Hollywood.[32] The French once developed a term for license-taking in historical representation that is a very close equivalent to what we mean when we speak of history gone Hollywood: they called it *histoire Walter Scottée*. I have tried to suggest that the connection between these two terms is more than happenstance or casual analogy. They are both aimed invidiously at forms that claim to represent the past in a way that rivals the work of antiquarians and professional historians.

Since both the historical novel and the Hollywood history are clearly epic forms, they aspire, as epics have always done, to shape the culture they represent. The "reconstruction" with which *The Birth of a Nation* is ultimately concerned is the reconstruction of America in 1915; in the end, Griffith imagines *himself* to be riding to the nation's rescue.[33] When, breaking off from the Biograph Company, Griffith started his own operation for the purpose of making *The Birth of a Nation,* he called the new entity "The Epoch Producing Corporation." Given his ambi-

---

32. As this essay was going to press, the journal of the American Historical Association published an excellent forum, centering on just these kinds of issues, around an essay by historian and historical filmmaker (*Reds, The Good Fight*) Robert Rosenstone, "History in Images / History in Words: Reflections on the Possibilities of Really Putting History onto Film," *American Historical Review* (December 1988): 1173–1227. Rosenstone makes both of these points—that we are increasingly dependent upon film for our sense of the past and that the documentary / dramatic distinction is far more problematic than we tend to assume—and both are picked up by other contributors. See especially Hayden White's contribution to the forum: "Historiography and Historiophoty," 1193–1199.
33. I am indebted to Linda Williams's excellent discussion of this point in a public lecture series on Griffith at the Film Center of the Art Institute of Chicago in Autumn 1987. Her comments on and technical help with this essay have been invaluable to me. I also wish to acknowledge the technical help of Paul Buchbinder and Peter Ferry, the comments of Corey Creekmur, Arthur Knight, and Robert Streeter, and the wisdom of the late Gerald Mast, who steered the essay into a much better course than I had once intended for it.

tions, the pun in the title has to be intended, and such ambition demands our most vigorous critical attention. Developing the connection between the romantic historical novel and modern film epic ought to be illuminating for both forms of epoch production. Without such illumination, our modern cultures will appear to us, in the darkened seats, with the inexorability of circling clouds in an evening sky.

"The Sword Became a Flashing Vision": D. W. Griffith's *The Birth of a Nation*

Michael Rogin

"He achieved what no other known man has ever achieved," wrote James Agee. "To watch his work is like being witness to the beginning of melody, or the first conscious use of the lever or the wheel; the emergence, coordination, and first eloquence of language; the birth of an art; and to realize that this is all the work of one man." The man was D. W. Griffith. The work climaxed in a single movie, *The Birth of a Nation,* "the first, the most stunning and durably audacious of all American film masterpieces," wrote Arlene Croce, "and the most wonderful movie ever made." *Birth* joined aesthetic invention to mass appeal. Nothing like it had ever been seen before, and it was seen by millions more people than had ever seen any other movie, more than would see any other movie for half a century. A *Variety* poll of two hundred film critics voted *The Birth of a Nation* the greatest motion picture in the first fifty years of the industry.[1]

Griffith's inspiration was *The Clansman,* a best-selling novel by Thomas Dixon and the second volume in a trilogy about the Reconstruction South. When his assistant Frank Woods brought him *The Clansman,* as Griffith told the story, he "skipped quickly through the book until I got to the part about the Klansmen, who according to no less than Woodrow Wilson, ran to the rescue of the downtrodden South after the Civil War. I could just see these Klansmen in a movie with their white robes flying. . . . We had had all sorts of runs-to-the-rescue in pictures and horse operas. . . . Now I could see a chance to do this ride-to-the-rescue on a grand scale. Instead of saving one little Nell of the Plains, this ride would be to save a nation."[2]

I have borrowed insights from Ann Banfield, Kim Chernin, and Catherine Gallagher throughout this essay and benefited from their responses to an earlier version. Elizabeth Abel and Jim Breslin also supplied valuable readings, and I am grateful for the contributions of Joel Fineman, Kathleen Moran, Carolyn Porter, and Paul Thomas. Nancy Goldman of the Pacific Film Archive, University of California Art Museum, helped obtain films and arrange screenings. She and the archive provided indispensable support for this project. I want also to acknowledge the help of participants in the Christian Gauss seminar at Princeton, before whom this material was originally presented.

1. James Agee, *Agee on Film* (Boston, 1958), 313; Arlene Croce, quoted in Martin Williams, *Griffith, First Artist of the Movies* (New York, 1980), 77; Roy E. Aitken, *The Birth of a Nation Story* (Middleburg, Va., 1965), 4.
2. James Hart, ed., *The Man Who Invented Hollywood: The Autobiography of D. W. Griffith* (Louisville, Ky., 1972), 28–29.

From *Ronald Reagan, The Movie and Other Episodes in Political Demonology* (Berkeley and Los Angeles: University of California Press, 1987).

American movies were born, then, in a racist epic. "The film that started it all"[3] builds to its sustained climax from two attempted rapes of white women by black men. It depicts, after the triumph of death in the Civil War and in Lincoln's assassination, a nation reborn from the ride of the white-robed Knights of Christ against black political and sexual revolution.

Celebrants of *Birth*'s formal achievement, with few exceptions, either minimize the film's racialist content or separate its aesthetic power from its negrophobia. Against the evidence before their eyes, they split Griffith's "gift for making powerful emotional connections" from "Thomas Dixon's racial message." They imitate Griffith's split between good and evil, white and black, by blaming Dixon for the perversions in Griffith's movie. Griffith and his audience, in that view, did not share Dixon's propagandistic purposes; they were the victims of "unconscious racism."[4] That unconscious is visible on the screen in *Birth,* and it invites us not to avert our eyes from the movie's racism but to investigate its meaning. Instead of rescuing Griffith's form from his content, we will examine the relationship between the two by situating *Birth* at the juncture of three converging histories, the political history of postbellum America, the social history of movies, and the history of Griffith's early films. By placing the film in history before looking directly at it, we can grasp the multiple rescue operations performed by the ride of the Klan.

Birth brought together three Southerners who moved north at the end of the nineteenth century, Griffith, Dixon, and Thomas Woodrow Wilson. Dixon and Wilson got to know each other as Johns Hopkins graduate students. After Dixon became a minister and Wilson a professor, Dixon nominated Wilson to receive an honorary degree at his own undergraduate alma mater, Wake Forest. "He is the type of man we need as President of the United States," Dixon wrote the board of trustees. Dixon resigned his pulpit to write novels and plays; Griffith, before he turned to movies, acted his first important role in one of Dixon's touring companies. Griffith used *The Clansman,* Wilson's *History of the American People,* and other materials provided by Dixon as sources for *Birth,* and he and Dixon worked together in making and promoting the movie. Dixon appealed to Wilson to see *Birth.* The President, who was not appearing in public because his wife had recently died, invited Dixon to show the film at the White House. This first movie screened at the White House swept Wilson off his feet. "It is like writing history with lightning," as Dixon reported the President's words, "and my only regret is that it is all so terribly true." When the new National Association for

---

3. Herman G. Weinberg, quoted in Harry M. Geduld, ed., *Focus on D. W. Griffith* (Englewood Cliffs, N.J., 1971), 8.

4. Quotes are from Richard Schickel, *D. W. Griffith: An American Life* (New York, 1984), 299, 279. See also pp. 29, 213, 232–237. I have learned a lot from this detailed, sensitive biograhy, but Schickel minimizes and apologizes for Griffith's racism.

the Advancement of Colored People (NAACP) and humanitarian social reformers tried to have *Birth* banned, Dixon used Wilson's endorsement to promote the film for months, before political pressures finally forced the President publicly to separate himself from the movie. The three Southerners did not hold identical views of the meaning either of *Birth* or of the history to which it called attention. But they shared a common project. They offered *The Birth of a Nation* as the screen memory, in both meanings of that term, through which Americans were to understand their collective past and enact their future.[5]

I

Asked why he called his movie *The Birth of a Nation,* Griffith replied, "Because it is. . . . The Civil War was fought fifty years ago. But the real nation has only existed in the last fifteen or twenty years. . . . The birth of a nation began . . . with the Ku Klux Klans, and we have shown that."[6]

Griffith appeared to be following Woodrow Wilson and Thomas Dixon and claiming that the Klan reunited America. But the Klan of Wilson's *History* and Griffith's movie flourished and died in the late 1860s. Griffith's "real nation," as he labeled it in 1915, "only existed in the last fifteen or twenty years." Dixon traced a line from the Klan to twentieth-century Progressivism, and Griffith may seem to be endorsing that view. But the floating "it" of Griffith's response made claims beyond those of Wilson and Dixon. "It" located the birth of the nation not in political events but in the movie. In Griffith's syntax the "it" that gave birth to the nation was *The Birth of a Nation* itself. Let us understand, in turn, each of these three linked attributions of national paternity, to the historic Klan, to Progressivism, and to the moving picture.

Among the freed Negroes of the postbellum South, wrote Woodrow Wilson, "some stayed very quietly by their old masters and gave no trouble; but most yielded, as was to have been expected, to the novel impulse and excitement of freedom. . . . The country was filled with vagrants looking for pleasure and gratuitous fortune. . . . The tasks of ordinary life stood untouched; the idlers grew insolent, dangerous; nights went anxiously by, for fear of riot and incendiary fire." There was, Wilson continued, a "veritable apotheosis of the negro" among North-

5. Cf. Raymond Allen Cook, *Fire from the Flint: The Amazing Career of Thomas Dixon* (Winston-Salem, N.C., 1968), 51–52, 72, 163–173; Edward D. C. Campbell, Jr., *The Celluloid South* (Knoxville, Tenn., 1981), 47; Seymour Stern, "Griffith: The Birth of a Nation, Part I," *Film Culture* 36 (Spring–Summer 1965): 34–36; Arthur S. Link, *Wilson: The New Freedom* (Princeton, 1956), 253; Thomas Cripps, *Slow Fade to Black* (New York, 1977), 62; Russell Merritt, "D. W. Griffith Directs the Great War: The Making of *Hearts of the World," Quarterly Review of Film Studies* 6 (Winter 1981), 47; John Hope Franklin, "*Birth of a Nation*—Propaganda as History," *The Massachusetts Review* 20 (Autumn 1979): 417–433.

6. *New York American,* 28 February 1915, in Geduld, *Focus on D. W. Griffith,* 28.

erners. They saw him "as the innocent victim of circumstances, a creature who needed only liberty to make him a man." Embracing Thaddeus Stevens's "policy of rule or ruin," the North determined to "put the white South under the heel of the black South."[7]

Stevens's policies, Wilson went on, caused "the veritable overthrow of civilization in the South." Forced "by the mere instinct of self-preservation" to take the law into their own hands, white Southern men made "the delightful discovery of the thrill of awesome fear which their sheeted, hooded figures sent among their former slaves." "It threw the Negroes into a very ecstasy of panic to see these sheeted 'Ku Klux' move near them in the shrouded night," wrote Wilson, "until at last there had sprung into existence a great Ku Klux Klan, an Invisible Empire of the South."[8]

Griffith filmed *The Birth of a Nation* during Wilson's presidency. He used some of the words I have quoted for the intertitles that introduce Part Two of the film. He put on the screen the images—faithful blacks and rioting incendiaries, Negroes frightened by white sheets, Northern illusions about black liberty contrasted with black dangers to white civilization—in Wilson's prose. But the very first shot after the intermission, the title "The agony which the South endured that a nation might be born," was taken not from Wilson's *History* but from Dixon's fiction. *Birth* followed Wilson in its sympathy for Lincoln's aborted dream of reunion; like Wilson, it justified the Klan as a response to Lincoln's assassination. But after Wilson's Klan suppressed black independence, a suppression necessary for the South to prosper, it grew lawless and was itself suppressed.[9] Wilson's Klan signified the continuing conflict between North and South. Dixon and Griffith's Klan gave birth to a united nation. Griffith was telescoping developments that came to fruition in the history not that Professor Wilson wrote but that President Wilson helped to make.

The plantation myth of postbellum America was as much a product of Northern needs as Southern ones. The rapid social transformation of the North after the Civil War, from predominantly rural and native-born to visibly immigrant and industrial, generated compensatory celebrations of the antebellum plantation South. At the same time, the massive influx of immigrants from southern and eastern Europe—"men out of whose ranks there was neither skill nor energy nor any initiative of quick intelligence," as Wilson described them, "as if the countries of the south of Europe were disburdening themselves of the more sordid and hapless elements of their population"—created Northern sympathy for Southern efforts to control an indispensable but racially inferior labor force. Imperialism reinforced this mixture of class and racial antagonism. The Spanish-American War and the suppression of the Philippine

7. Woodrow Wilson, *A History of the American People*, vol. 5, *Reunion and Nationalization* (New York, 1901), 19–20, 49–50.

8. Ibid., 49–50, 60.

9. Ibid., 62–64, 75–78.

independence movement gave the nation its own colonial people of color, and the need for racial tutelage abroad merged with fears of racial uprisings at home.[10]

The Reverend Thomas Dixon (who had the largest Protestant congregation in New York City) resigned his pulpit after the Spanish-American War to lead a crusade against the "black peril." Dixon's evangelical sermons, which emphasized personal sin and social conduct, had been more concerned with immigrant mobs than with Negroes. The subjugation of the Philippines reconnected this transplanted Southerner to his past. Wilson also defended the war against the Philippines. Imperialists like Wilson and Dixon tied the racial question at home to America's world mission abroad. Dixon subtitled *The Leopard's Spots,* the first volume in his Klan trilogy, *A Romance of the White Man's Burden.* "Our old men dreamed of local supremacy. We dream of the conquest of the globe," explains the novel's hero, and we must not be "chained to the body of a festering Black Death." The Spanish-American War "reunited the Anglo-Saxon race," wrote Dixon, "and confirmed the Anglo-Saxon in his title to the primacy of racial sway." As Northern capital and xenophobia migrated south, replacing carpetbaggers and Northern egalitarianism, only reluctance to embrace negrophobia, as Dixon saw it, stood in the way of the birth of the nation. "It was seen by thoughtful men that the Negro was an impossibility in the new-born unity of national life," Dixon wrote; he titled the chapter with those sentiments "Another Declaration of Independence." The original ending of *Birth,* "Lincoln's solution," showed masses of Negroes being loaded on ships; they are being sent back to Africa.[11]

---

10. Ibid., 212; see also Mary Odem, "Wilson and the Immigrants" (Unpublished seminar paper, University of California, Berkeley, 1984); George M. Frederickson, *White Supremacy* (New York, 1981), 188–191.

11. Maxwell Bloomfield, *"The Leopard's Spots:* A Study in Popular Racism," *American Quarterly* 16 (Fall 1964): 387–392; Cook, *Fire from the Flint,* 79–112; Woodrow Wilson, "The Ideals of America," *Atlantic Monthly,* December 1902, 721–734; Thomas Dixon, *The Leopard's Spots: A Romance of the White Man's Burden* (1902; republished, Ridgewood, N.J., 1967), 334–335, 408, 439. See also Chapter 3, [*Ronald Reagan, The Movie*].

Although critics blame "populism" for Dixon's and Griffith's racism, Southern Populism poses the racial menace in *The Leopard's Spots.* Populism, as Dixon saw it, combined "the two great . . . questions that shadow the future of the American people, the conflict between Labour and Capital and the conflict between the African and the Anglo-Saxon race." Class relations could be humanized, Dixon believed, were it not for the threat of black power. But Populist demagoguery, by mobilizing the class resentments of blacks and poor whites, threatened racial amalgamation. Dixon's hero achieved political power and romantic success by uniting the white South against Populism. Walter Hines Page, the anti-Populist apostle of the new, industrial South, got Doubleday to publish *The Leopard's Spots.* Secretary of State John Hay read proof for and endorsed the second novel in Dixon's trilogy, *The Clansman.* Hay had been Lincoln's private secretary as a young man; he wrote the antilabor novel *The Breadwinners* and was the architect of America's imperial vision. Dixon's attack on Populism and the endorsement of his vision by Page and Hay further illuminate the intertwined racial, class, and imperial histories that lie behind *Birth.* Cf. Schickel, *Griffith,* 29, 76–78; Dixon, *Leopard's Spots,* 244–245; Fred A. Silva, *Focus on "The Birth of a Nation"* (Englewood Cliffs, N.J., 1971), 94.

Woodrow Wilson also endorsed the war on the Philippines for catapulting America to world power and providing a model for political leadership over immigrants and workers at home.[12] When the Southern race problem became national, the national problem was displaced back onto the South in a way that made the South not a defeated part of the American past but a prophecy of its future. Dixon, Wilson, and Griffith thereby reclaimed Southern loyalties they had left behind in their personal quests for new, national identities.

The reunion between North and South climaxed during Wilson's presidency. The first Southerner elected president since the Civil War, Wilson presided over the celebrations of national reconciliation that marked the war's fiftieth anniversary. Griffith began shooting *Birth* on 4 July 1914; he released the movie fifty years after Appomattox. Wilson was so impressed by *Birth* that he offered to cooperate with more of Griffith's historical projects. "I am deeply interested in what you intimate as to future motion pictures," he wrote the filmmaker, "and if it is possible for me to assist you with an opinion about them at any time, I shall certainly try to do so." Wilson was not the only Washington official who saw and blessed the film. Through his ties to North Carolina Progressive Josephus Daniels, Dixon obtained an interview with Edward White, Chief Justice of the Supreme Court. After the normally forbidding White confided that he had ridden with the Klan in his youth, he arranged a showing of *Birth* before an audience of Supreme Court justices, senators, and congressmen. Some of these men were later embarrassed by their participation in this event, once *Birth* came under widespread attack, but the Washington screenings had singled out *Birth* in an unprecedented way for the stamp of political approval. The North was ready for a film that, although it did not endorse the traditional Southern view of the Civil War, sympathized with the antebellum South and nationalized the Southern view of reconstruction.[13]

The similarities between immigrants and Negroes initiated the reunion between North and South. But as blacks became a sign of the negative American identity, Progressives took immigrants to the national bosom. Antebellum Southerners had identified their oppression by a centralized state with the sufferings of the subject nationalities of the Hapsburg Empire. Dixon turned that decentralist tradition in a nationalist direction and based his Klan trilogy on the trilogy of a Polish patriot. Southern patriotism was beginning to mean not resistance to the Northern state but loyalty to a united nation. "You are American by the accident of birth," the Polish hero of a later Dixon novel tells a native. "We are Americans because we willed to come. . . . We saw the figure of liberty shining here across the seas. . . . It is our country . . . as it can't be yours who do not realize its full meaning."[14]

12. Wilson, "Ideals of America," 721–734.
13. Cripps, *Slow Fade to Black* 26–27; Schickel, *Griffith,* 224; Cook, *Fire from the Flint,* 171–172; Merritt, "Griffith Directs the Great War." 47.
14. Cook, *Fire from the Flint,* 71; F. Garvin Davenport, Jr., "Thomas Dixon's Mythology of Southern History," *Journal of Southern History* 36 (August 1970): 361.

Wilson also shifted his view of immigrants during the Progressive period. South Europeans were no longer a threat to America's historic, Teutonic identity (the view in *History* and other early writings). Now, like Wilson himself, they had given up their inherited, local identities to embody American ideals. Wilson saw that regenerate national identity in Griffith's Klan. Its visionary brotherhood melded diverse individuals into a purposeful union. The fifty years that had elapsed between the Klan Wilson wrote about and the Klan Griffith filmed allowed Wilson to praise Griffith for transforming his *History* into prophecy.[15]

As Wilson embraced immigrants, he segregated government employees. Black officeholders—significant numbers worked in the Post Office and Treasury Department—were separated from their white co-workers. White women had been "forced unnecessarily to sit at desks with colored men," explained Wilson's son-in-law, Secretary of the Treasury William G. McAdoo, and this proximity created "friction." Beginning in the Wilson administration, blacks worked in separate rooms and used separate bathrooms. Black political appointees were fired, and those holding civil service positions were downgraded or dismissed as well. In appealing to immigrants at the expense of blacks, the Democratic party was returning to its antebellum roots. And it was seeking political support from the audience for motion pictures.[16]

The first movies were one-reel immigrant entertainment. They were shown in storefront nickelodeons in working-class neighborhoods for a nickel admission, which anyone could afford. The motion picture was "the first democratic art," said *The Nation,* and movies broke down class and gender divisions. Middle-class youths, wandering into the nickelodeons, were exposed to working-class temptations. "Girls drop in alone," complained Jane Addams, and "the darkness takes away the feeling of responsibility." When men offered girls "certain indignities," Addams warned, the girls found it hard to refuse. Movie houses in "undesirable localities" turned immigrant girls into prostitutes. Vice districts had once been places for men, but movies were threatening that gender distinction.[17]

The content of movies made them even more subversive. Over half the early motion pictures were made in Europe, and few presented such American motifs as the rags-to-riches story or the settlement of the West. They depicted instead, without moral judgment, poverty, premarital sex, adultery, and slapstick violence (often against people in authority). Making "a direct and universal appeal to the

---

15. Odem, "Wilson and the Immigrants," 1–16; Rogin, "The King's Two Bodies," [*Ronald Reagan, The Movie*], pp. 94–99.

16. Link, *Wilson,* 467; Lawrence J. Friedman, *The White Savage* (Englewood Cliffs, N.J., 1970), 157–163.

17. Lary May, *Screening Out the Past: The Birth of Mass Culture and the Motion Picture Industry* (New York, 1965), 19–67; Russell Merritt, "Nickelodeon Theaters, 1905–1914: Building an Audience for the Movies," in Tino Balio, ed., *The American Film Industry* (Madison, Wis., 1976), 57–72; Jane Addams, *The Spirit of Youth and the City Streets* (New York, 1909), 75–103.

elementary emotions," movies appealed to "all nations, all ages, all classes, both sexes." Their stories were permeated, in *The Nation*'s words, "with the very ideas of the crowd in the streets."[18]

Addams and other reformers saw promise as well as danger in the movies. As the *Outlook* put it, "the very potency of the motion picture for degrading taste and morals is the measure of its power for enlightenment and education." Like political progressives, cultural reformers wanted not to exclude immigrants but to enlighten and Americanize them. Seeking to capitalize on the breakdown of class and cultural barriers, reformers sought a mass entertainment of cultural uplift, not one that exploited immigrant frustrations and pulled the middle class into the mores of the ghetto. Because we failed to organize leisure as we organized production, wrote Addams, city youth was exposed to violent temptations. The solution was to reform movies, not abolish them, so that the motion picture could operate like a "grand social worker." Reformers instituted movie censorship, but selective prohibition was not sufficient to turn movies to positive cultural use. Reformers needed an ally behind the camera. Griffith looked like the man.[19]

Griffith had begun making movies because he could not get work on the stage. He shared the reformers' discontent with the film of the present and their high hopes for its future. "Reform was sweeping the country," he later wrote. "Newspapers were laying down a barrage against gambling, rum, light ladies, particularly light ladies. There were complaints against everything, so I decided to reform the motion picture industry." He did so with a film which brought movies out of the nickelodeons and into the two-dollar theaters. *Birth* established film as a legitimate art, one whose appeal cut across class, ethnic, and sectional lines. The opposition between North and South in the film, as well as that between immigrant and native in the history outside it, had been replaced by the opposition between white and black.[20]

That opposition did not pit white bodies against black ones, however, for the same actors who rode under the Klan sheets also put on blackface. The contrasting disguises, which point to the common identity they aim to hide, expose the projective fantasized character of Griffith's blacks. The opposition that engaged Griffith, Wilson, and the mass audience was between represented black chaos on the one hand and a transformed and sanctified white host on the other. *Birth*'s visionary images completed Wilson's *History* by pointing to his future, to his world crusade to end all war. We will analyze those images and conclude with that crusade. To do so we must enter Griffith's world on the screen. The Southern race war depicted in *Birth,* I have been suggesting, was not simply about itself; it was

18. Merritt, "Griffith Directs the Great War," 63–65, 75–79; May, *Screening out the Past,* 36–37; Robert Sklar, *Movie-Made America* (New York, 1975), 105–106.

19. May, *Screening Out the Past,* 52–53, 59; Addams, *Spirit of Youth,* 6, 75–100.

20. May, *Screening Out the Past,* 71. The interpretation in these paragraphs draws heavily from May.

also a stand-in for sectional, ethnic, and class conflicts. It was a stand-in as well, we are about to see, for the conflicts between tradition and modernity and between men and women.

II

To understand Griffith, wrote Sergei Eisenstein, "one must visualize an America made up of more than visions of speeding automobiles, streamlined trains, racing ticker tape, inexorable conveyer-belts. One is obliged to comprehend this second side of America as well—America, the traditional, the patriarchal, the provincial."[21]

D. W. Griffith, as Eisenstein implies, was a child of provincial America. He was born in 1875 on a Kentucky farm; when his father died seven years later, as Griffith told the story, Jake Griffith's faithful ex-slaves were at his bedside. But Griffith's father came to rest at home only in defeat and at the end of his life. He was a wanderer, drinker, gambler, and storyteller, wounded in mythic exploits during the Civil War. Instead of working the family farm, he took out three mortgages on it. After he died the family lost the farm and moved to Louisville. From there David Griffith wandered, alone or with touring acting companies— north to New York; west to Chicago, San Francisco, and points between; and back home to Louisville—before beginning to make movies in New York City.[22] Against stage authorities and theatrical "rules" and in the name of depicting "real life," Griffith invented the techniques of narrative cinema. He fathered the distinctively modern art form.[23]

Griffith's story of paternal failure and modern invention is one strand in the general crisis of patriarchy at the end of the nineteenth century. Traditional paternal authority, which had rigidified and become fragile, was assaulted in two modes, which Henry Adams's famous distinction between the dynamo and the virgin invoked—namely, that of scientific, industrial technology and that of the New Woman. Eisenstein pointed to one form of the crisis, in which mechanization took command. Griffith filmed speeding automobiles and streamlined trains, but he went beyond the motion shown in a scene to the motion that constituted it. Griffith found a formal vocabulary for the pace of modern life. Paralleling the other industrial arts, he broke up traditional sequences into their component parts and reassembled those parts to make something new. Life was "more fragmented and faster-moving than in previous periods," said the French painter Ferdinand Léger in 1913. As the cubists and futurists in different ways put movement on

---

21. Sergei Eisenstein, *Film Form* (New York, 1949), 197.
22. I rely on Schickel for Griffith's biography unless another source is indicated.
23. Robert Welsh, "David Griffith Speaks," *New York Dramatic Mirror,* 14 January 1914, 48–49, 54; Tom Gunning, "Weaving a Narrative: Style and Economic Background in Griffith's Biograph Films," *Quarterly Review of Film Studies* 6 (Winter 1981): 12–25.

canvas, Griffith captured it on film. He invented few technical innovations, but he was the first to put the new film techniques to significant dramatic use.[24]

Griffith understood, like no filmmaker before him, that the unit of film was not the scene but the shot. He was "bitten by the lightning bug," complained the Reverend Dr. Stockton. Stockton counted sixty-eight shots in a single Griffith one-reeler; the average in non-Griffith films was eighteen to thirty. By cutting back and forth, Griffith juxtaposed events separated in time (the flashback) and space (the cutback) and collapsed the distinctions between images in the head and events in the world. By speeding up, reversing, and stopping time, he brought the past into the present (or rather, as Stephen Kern says, controlled what the past would become). By juxtaposing events widely separated in space, he overcame the barriers of distance (barriers overcome in the film plot by the ride to the rescue). Griffith created an art of simultaneities and juxtapositions rather than traditions and continuities.[25]

Griffith also used editing to dynamize action within single scenes. He broke up the homogeneity of physical space through camera angles and closeups. Cutting from medium to long shots and in to closeups and varying the lengths of the shots, he pulled the viewer into the action. He broke down the barriers not just of time and space and inside and outside but of audience and film. By establishing a camera-eye point of view, Griffith gave significance to objects, body parts, and faces. The symbolic meanings of these part-objects augmented or displaced traditional narrative conventions. Griffith made images the medium of film.

Griffith justified his movie method in the name of realism. "The motion picture," he said, "approaches more closely real life" than does the stage. "The motion picture is what technique really means, a faithful picture of life." "The Biograph camera doesn't lie," proclaimed advertisements for Griffith's one-reelers. Formal conventions, Griffith believed, separated the theater from reality. At the same time that paternal moral principles were giving way to politics (a subject of Adams's *Education*) and their intellectual formulas were being overthrown in the new social sciences, movie realism, too, was revolting against the formalism of the fathers.[26]

The realist movie required its own forms, however. Tom Gunning has recently argued that Griffith developed the narrative techniques of bourgeois realism in the

24. Henry Adams, *The Education of Henry Adams* (Boston, 1973), 379–390, 428–435; Geduld, *Focus on D. W. Griffith*, 1; Stephen Kern, *The Culture of Time and Space, 1880–1920* (Cambridge, Mass., 1983), 11. For general discussions of Griffith's cinematic contributions, cf. Williams, *Griffith*, 34–44; Louis Jacobs, *The Rise of American Film* (New York, 1967), 98–110; Sklar, *Movie-Made America*, 48–54.

25. Jacobs, *Rise of American Film*, 98; George C. Pratt, "In the Nick of Time: D. W. Griffith and the 'Last-Minute Rescue,'" in Marshall Deutelbaum, ed., *"Image" on the Art and Evolution of the Film* (New York, 1979), 74–75; Kern, *Culture of Time and Space*, 29–30, 38–39; Welsh, "Griffith Speaks," 49, 54.

26. Jacobs, *Rise of American Film*, 14, 118–119; Welsh, "Griffith Speaks," 49, 54; May, *Screening Out the Past*, 73; Morton White, *Social Thought in America: The Revolt Against Formalism* (Boston, 1957).

Biograph one-reelers. Before Griffith, working-class audiences watched unmotivated characters engage in scenes of antisocial comedy and unmediated violence. These episodes were not made into stories. Griffith organized psychologically motivated social types into narratives of modern life. He wanted, like other middle-class progressives, to get closer to life without falling into chaos. Parallel editing, in which the director cut back and forth between two scenes or components of a single scene, responded to the demands of a complex narrative style.[27] But parallel editing did not simply contribute to storytelling; its juxtapositions, contrasts, dismemberments, and boundary breakdowns endangered narrative control and threatened to create chaos. The source of that chaos visible on screen was the female image.

Traditional patriarchal forms were under siege at the end of the nineteenth century not just from technology but from what was conceived of as nature, from regressive forces as well as progressive ones. The movement forward and outward in external time and space—railroads, clock-time, scientific exploration, and imperialism—entailed at the same time a movement backward and inward in psychological time and space. And women, whether out in the world or confined to the home, stood for that regressive, disorganizing power. Partly, they posed a threat to order in their own right because of their efforts at emancipation. Partly, they stood as a symbol and accessible scapegoat for more distant social and political disruptions. Instead of providing a refuge from modern disorder, the New Woman fueled it.[28]

The New Woman appears everywhere at the end of the nineteenth century, in the work force and reform movements, in literature, art, social thought, and psychology. Existing beneath and within the stereotypical Victorian roles of wife, mother, spinster, and fallen woman, a female presence emerged by the century's end (in the male imagination) as the prepatriarchal, originary source of male identity. As working girl, fashion-conscious wife, or lady of the night, the New Woman represented the modern city. But even where women stood for fecundity and reproduction, like Henry Adams's Diana of the Ephesians or Theodore Roosevelt's maternal ideal, they were a force larger than life. "She was the animated dynamo; she was reproduction," wrote

27. Gunning, "Weaving a Narrative," 12–25.

28. The interpretation of the patriarchal crisis and the male fear of women in this and the following paragraph derives from Nina Auerbach, *Woman and the Demon* (Cambridge, Mass., 1982); Rosalind Coward, *Patriarchal Precedents* (London, 1983); Carl Schorske, *Fin-de-Siècle Vienna, Politics and Culture* (New York, 1980), 208–280; Fred Weinstein and Gerald Platt, *The Wish to Be Free* (Berkeley and Los Angeles, 1969); Arthur Mitzman, *The Iron Cage* (New York, 1970); Michael Rogin, "Max Weber and Woodrow Wilson: The Iron Cage in Germany and America," *Polity* 3 (Summer 1971); 557–575, and "On the Jewish Question," *Democracy,* Spring 1983, 101–114; Martin Green, *The von Richtofen Sisters* (New York, 1974); David M. Kennedy, *Birth Control in America* (New Haven, 1970), 42–52; Adams, *Education of Henry Adams,* 379–390, 427–435, 441–447, 459–461; Debora L. Silverman, "Nature, Nobility, and Neurology: The Ideological Origins of 'Art Nouveau' in France, 1889–1900" (Ph.D. diss., Princeton University, 1983); Eugene W. Holland, "Politics and Psychoanalysis," *Salmagundi,* no. 66 (Winter–Spring 1985): 155–170.

Adams; he was describing a fertility goddess more than a domestic mother. Whatever her social form, the New Woman was imaged as monstrous and chameleonlike. Her permeable boundaries absorbed children and men.

The revolt of the sons against their fathers combined rebellion with sexual freedom, as young men imagined themselves on the side of women against patriarchal authority. But the alliance of youth and women that was intended to liberate the sons threatened to empower the female instead. We normally associate Griffith with victimized women, not powerful ones. But his films before *Birth* suggest that Griffith created women needing rescue in order to rescue himself from their female predecessors on his screen. Strong women in Griffith's early movies liberated him from patriarchy and tradition only to subject him to female power. *Birth* was the solution to that problem.

"*The Birth of a Nation* owes more to my father than it does to me," said Griffith,[29] and that movie may seem to retreat from modern realism to pastoralism and provincialism. In fact the film employs tradition to sanctify modern force. It returns neither to paternalism nor to history but replaces them. It celebrates not the restoration of Southern patriarchy but the birth of a new nation. And it locates reality not in the world viewed, either pastoral or modern, but in the cinematic image and the camera eye. Instead of generating the powerful female images that threatened Griffith, *Birth* culminated the filmmaker's appropriation of a power experienced as female.

III

Between 1907 and 1913 Griffith made hundreds of one-reel motion pictures for the Biograph Company. The social exploration and psychological interiorization in these movies, the film cut and the intrusive camera eye, opened a Pandora's box for the filmmaker as his techniques threatened to turn on their inventor. Four recurrent themes in these movies make up the prehistory of *Birth;* the presence of weak or repressive fathers, associated with provincialism and tradition; the emergence of female sexuality, imaged in the phallic woman, associated with modernity, and represented by the actress Blanche Sweet; the presentation of domestic, interior space as claustrophobic, imprisoning, and vulnerable to invasion; and the use of rides to the rescue. These rescues are meant to reassert the contrast between good and evil, the domestic refuge and the menacing invader, male strength and female weakness, but they leave behind traces of a dangerous boundary breakdown. The collapse of gender and social difference that emerged in these films led Griffith to generate a new and deeper system of differences in *Birth*.[30]

29. Hart, *Man Who Invented Hollywood,* 26.

30. On binary oppositions and their breakdown, filmic and social, in a Griffith one-reeler, see Rick Altman, "*The Lonely Villa* and Griffith's Paradigmatic Style," *Quarterly Review of Film Studies* 6 (Spring 1981): 123–134.

There is not space here to trace *Birth*'s genealogy through the Biograph one-reelers. But the troubles taking over Griffith's screen climaxed in the two most important longer films he made between the one-reelers and *Birth*—*Judith of Bethulia* (1913) and *The Avenging Conscience* (1914).

Judith of Bethulia (Blanche Sweet) is a widow dressed in black at the beginning of Griffith's version of the biblical story. Her Jewish town is menaced by the Assyrian general Holofernes. Judith puts on makeup, adorns her head with spiky peacock feathers, and veils her face. By masquerading as a painted lady, a courtesan, Sweet transforms herself from a helpless victim in need of rescue (her role in the one-reeler *The Painted Lady*) to the rescuer of Bethulia. Her depersonalized erotic flowering points to Holofernes's death.

Holofernes (Henry Walthall) is a bearded patriarch. He commands a bacchanal from his couch-throne and seems to have the women around him at his service. But languishing on his couch as he observes his dancing girls, Holofernes is a curiously passive figure. The women move in *Judith;* Holofernes, like the movie audience, is a voyeur. His soldiers worship Holofernes's sword, but it is Judith who will seize it. The scene between Judith and Holofernes, orchestrated for a sexual climax, climaxes when she cuts off his head.

Judith caresses Holofernes as he lies on the couch; she gives him wine, they drink, he passes out. Cut to his head and shoulders, then to her raised arm. Her hand is off camera. Judith stands behind Holofernes; cut to the sword in her hand. Judith holds up the sword; in shape and in location above her head, it has replaced the peacock feathers she no longer wears. Judith in close-up raises the sword. Cut to Holofernes's head rolling from the couch and bouncing on the step below. Cut to his headless body, one arm limply outstretched. The shot, of one arm instead of two, at once calls attention to the single, phallic member and (by way of the missing arm and head) to its metaphoric absence.[31]

In cutting up Judith before she dismembers Holofernes, the camera fetishizes the female body, for it substitutes eroticized body parts for the whole. Such fetishized part objects, argued Freud, assuaged the male viewer's fear of castration. Since the boy child imagines the female as a castrated male, the fetish

---

31. In "The Taboo of Virginity" Freud writes, "Beheading is well-known to us as a symbolic substitute for castration; Judith is accordingly the woman who castrates the man who has deflowered her." Judith links beheading to castration for Freud. But he only makes that connection by doubly disempowering the woman. Insisting that Judith is "using a patriotic motive to mask a sexual one," Freud sunders her act from the political significance of beheading a king. Moreover, by analyzing a German play in which Judith is a virgin and suggesting that the playwright had "divined the primordial theme that had been lost in the tendentious biblical story," Freud turns a widow's power into a virgin's revenge. There is nothing virginal about Griffith's Judith. See Sigmund Freud, "The Taboo of Virginity," in James Strachey, ed., *The Standard Edition of the Complete Psychological Works of Sigmund Freud,* 24 vols. (London, 1955), 11:205–208. I am indebted for this reference to N. Sine, "Cases of Mistaken Identity: Salome and Judith at the Turn of the Century" (Unpublished paper, 1985).

restores her missing male member. But the fetishized body part or object—foot, hand, hat, sword—also stands in for the intact female body. Were that body whole, moreover, it would call attention to the absent phallus. Film cuts that dismember the woman on screen thus doubly disempower her, it is argued, by substituting a (male) fetish for her bodily integrity. At the same time, man looks and woman is looked at. The male gaze inherits the father's phallic power, on this line of thought, as it looks at a passive woman on display. The eye establishes sexual difference by observing what the female lacks.[32]

The erotics of voyeurism and the fetishization of women lie at the origins of cinematic form, and Griffith's films as a whole connect the founding moment in American cinema to a particular political, sexual, and racial content. But *Judith of Bethulia* read by itself assigns power not to the male gaze but to the filmmaker who directs it. Griffith may have cut up Judith to control her, since he was making a woman his parricide. The camera-fetishized Judith turns on the male viewer nonetheless, for she decapitates Holofernes. He is the headless body; she is the woman with the penis. When Holofernes's soldiers see his headless body, they become a disorganized mass. The Jews, who have placed his head on a pole, rout the Assyrians in battle.

Judith of Bethulia was Griffith's first spectacular. He broke Biograph's rules about time and money in making the movie, and the excitement of taking power animated the entire set. Decapitating the patriarch, Griffith freed himself from Biograph's restrictive production rules. Decapitation also freed his camera. Cutting back and forth between opposed forces in the familiar ride to the rescue did not engage Griffith's talents in this film. Instead he invented what Eisenstein (denying Griffith had done it) would call dynamic montage, the creation of a wholly new set of images from the dismembered parts of the quotidian world.

Griffith's commitment to patriarchy and provincialism, Eisenstein argued, blocked his formal progress, allowing him to juxtapose contrasting images but not to constitute fundamentally new ones. In Eisenstein's view the dualism of Griffith's social vision (which Eisenstein attributed to Griffith's inability to transcend class rather than racial and sexual divisions) generated parallel montage; it prevented Griffith from discovering dynamic montage.[33]

Eisenstein grasped the relation between form and content but overlooked Griffith's breakthrough. For the first time on film, in the Assyrian siege of Bethulia, Griffith juxtaposed separate shots to create a single, complete, new mental image. The camera shifts from the beleaguered people behind the walls to the defenders

32. Cf. Sigmund Freud, "Fetishism," in *Standard Edition,* 21:152–157; Laura Mulvey, "Visual Pleasure and Narrative Cinema," in Karyn Kay and Gerald Peary, eds., *Women and the Cinema* (New York, 1977), 412–428; E. Ann Kaplan, *Women and Film* (New York, 1983), 31–52, 202; Stephen Heath, "Difference," *Screen* 19 (Autumn 1978): 51–112.
33. Eisenstein, *Film Form,* 205, 223, 227–230, 234–237, 243–245, 253.

atop them, to the attackers outside, to Judith in her chamber, to Holofernes in his camp. Like a cubist painter, Griffith liberated the eye to roam everywhere. The siege of Bethulia is the first example of dynamic montage on film; Holofernes's beheading is the second.[34]

Griffith freed himself from Biograph by making *Judith;* when Biograph took away his artistic control over future productions because of the length and cost of this film, he left that company and formed one of his own. Its most important production before *Birth* was *The Avenging Conscience.*

Beginning in 1910 and with increasing frequency over the next three years, critics had complained that Griffith's films were becoming morbid. The psychological, expressionist melodramas that troubled the critics featured suicide, neurosis, family estrangement, forbidden temptation, and failed rides to the rescue. *Conscience* is the culmination of these gothic one-reelers. One critic calls it his most important film before *Birth,* a judgment that is justified not cinematically but psychologically. Based on several Edgar Allan Poe stories and intercut with lines from "Annabelle Lee," *The Avenging Conscience* took Griffith further inside the parricidal psyche than he wanted to go. *Birth* took him out again.[35]

Blanche Sweet as Annabel has no sword in *Conscience,* and she is not an active subject like Judith. The primitive, pre-oedipal source of life and death seems to have been replaced by a passive sexual target of oedipal rivalry. But as the subject, object, and eliciter of desire, Sweet as Annabel disempowers both herself and the two male protagonists. Their collective disturbance generates madness and parricide.

Henry Walthall plays an orphan who has been raised by his uncle. This withered old man wears an eye patch, and his dessication contrasts to Sweet's ripeness. She caresses her furry little dog with her foot and lifts the fence for it to crawl under. Cut to her meeting with the nephew. Griffith juxtaposes their erotic encounter to the embittered, isolated uncle. The cut from her sexuality to his single eye, by contrasting her puppy to his missing organ, underscores the uncle's emasculation.[36] "Embittered by youthful happiness" as he sees another young couple

---

34. Cf. Sklar, *Movie-Made America,* 56.

35. Cf. Russell L. Merritt, "Mr. Griffith, *The Painted Lady,* and the Distractive Frame," in Deutelbaum, *"Image,"* 47; Seymour Stern, "Griffith and Poe," *Films in Review* 2 (November 1951): 23.

36. Griffith had used puppies to signify female independence in *The Battle of Elderbush Gulch* (1913). The puppies figure in a mise-en-scène whose plot, actresses (Mae Marsh and Lillian Gish), and family name (the Camerons in both movies) presage *The Birth of a Nation.* Marsh's puppies run off at the beginning of the action, and Marsh recklessly follows them. In *Birth*'s parallel scene, Marsh kills herself to escape a black rapist; in *Elderbush Gulch* Indians kill a puppy instead and are killed in turn, precipitating an Indian attack. Gish's baby crawls into danger during the attack; by rescuing it Marsh atones for her earlier transgression. It is as if, in the repetition and undoing of the earlier scene, Griffith was illustrating Freud's belief that the mature woman replaces her wish for an active sexual organ with a baby.

besides the one played by Sweet and Walthall in love, the uncle forces his nephew to send Annabel away.

The nephew watches a spider devour an ant and determines to murder his uncle. Griffith borrowed Poe's hieroglyphic method, wrote Vachel Lindsay, to replace narrative by symbol.[37] Visual emblems like the fly and the spider pull viewers "into the plan of a fevered brain." As the nephew raises a gun to shoot his sleeping uncle, Griffith cuts to an "Italian" laborer (George Siegmann) with his arm around a girl. The Italian relinquishes the girl; the nephew lowers his gun. After this double anticlimax the Walthall character imitates the spider instead of the masculine laborer and strangles his uncle. He walls the body up in the fireplace and joins Annabel.

A flower that wilted when the uncle separated the lovers comes alive again after the murder. But the detective (Ralph Lewis) plucks another flower for his buttonhole as he comes in the nephew's door. It is a sign that the nephew will not enjoy the fruits of his crime. The Walthall character is also at the mercy of the Italian, who has witnessed the murder and blackmails the murderer. But psychological bond overcomes narrative logic and turns Siegmann into Walthall's assistant. Siegmann serves Walthall, since the Italian stands for the access to women that provoked the nephew's crime. The detective, investigating the crime, represents the uncle's prohibition. Although he finds no evidence of foul play, the detective awakens the nephew's avenging conscience. The uncle's ghost materializes behind the lovers; it appears to the Walthall character as he sleeps. Questioned again by the detective, the nephew stares at the pencil that the detective taps on the table; it mimics the beat of his uncle's heart. The detective has repossessed the pencil-penis as well as the flower. Griffith uses an iris-in (in which an image in the shape of an eye opens up until the whole screen is filled) on one of the detective's eyes to invoke the one-eyed uncle. But the detective's eye, like the camera eye and unlike the uncle's eye patch, can see into the murderer.

"They are neither man nor woman; they are neither brute nor human; they are ghouls, ghouls, ghouls," announces a title; we watch, with the nephew, as human bodies with animal heads dance in the fireplace. The Walthall character's nightmares drive him to an isolated cabin, on which the opposing forces, one led by the detective and the other by the Italian, converge. Trapped in the cabin (the detective had earlier nailed shut its trap door), the nephew prepares to hang himself. Cut to Annabel leaping into the sea. At that moment the Walthall character awakens; his uncle is alive, the flower is wilted, and we realize we have been inside his dream. The uncle blesses the lovers, and the film ends with Walthall and Sweet on a hillside overlooking the water. But that happy ending fails to erase the film. The successful slaying of the patriarch in *Judith* required giving the woman the sword. Taking it from her and making her the object of desire was even more disturbing,

37. Vachel Lindsay, *The Art of the Moving Picture,* rev. ed. (New York, 1970), 152–153.

for it entombed the young man in parricidal, self-destructive guilt. Nonetheless, by intensifying Griffith's nightmare of desire, *Conscience* allowed him to engage in an inspired act of inversion and free himself from the demons that were taking over his screen.

IV

Turned inside out, the characters and images of *The Avenging Conscience* gave birth to *The Birth of a Nation*. The figures from Walthall's fevered brain step out of *Conscience*'s claustrophobic private interior. Walthall awakens from his nightmare into history; more accurately, he enters epic history in the form of Griffith's dream. *The Birth of a Nation* is the dream wish that rescues Walthall from his avenging conscience. The film is divided into two parts. After an initial meeting between the Northern Stoneman boys and their Southern Cameron cousins, Part One is devoted to a display of the Civil War. Part Two chronicles the Cameron-Stoneman romances that were promised in Part One and interrupted by the Civil War. The Ku Klux Klan saves the white South from Northern Reconstruction and black sexual assault.

Ralph Lewis, as the Northern Reconstruction leader Austin Stoneman, orchestrates the white South's punishment out of his passion for a female mulatto. The Little Colonel, played by Henry Walthall, loves Stoneman's daughter, Elsie, and he leads the Klan to rescue her from the blacks whom her father has unleashed. Sexual desire generates violence, in *Birth* as in *Conscience,* but that desire belongs to Lewis as Austin Stoneman, not to Walthall as the Little Colonel. Siegmann, the Italian representative of Walthall's libido in *Conscience,* plays Silas Lynch, the mulatto protégé and extension of Lewis's desire in *Birth*. Spottiswoode Aitken, who played Walthall's uncle in *Conscience,* plays his father in *Birth*. He is still emasculated, but now his helplessness is permission giving for the young man, not life denying. Instead of having to relinquish what Aitken has denied or kill him, the Little Colonel rescues his father. In *Birth*'s climax as in *Conscience*'s, two forces—one good and the other evil—converge on an isolated cabin. But his innocent family has replaced the guilty Walthall inside the cabin, and Walthall leads the ride to their rescue. The psychological pursuit of detective Lewis after criminal Walthall turns into the physical chase of Walthall's Klan after Lewis's Negroes.[38] Griffith has projected Walthall's internal turmoil onto blacks and Klansmen. Blacks save Walthall by appropriating his desire; the Klan acquires his conscience. Since that conscience is now directed at the other rather than the self, Walthall can ride at its head.

The Klansmen "look like a company of avenging spectral crusaders," remarked the *New York Times*. A writer described them in one scene as "vanishing like

---

38. Edward Wagenknecht, *The Movies in the Age of Innocence* (Norman, Okla., 1962), 98–99.

ghouls." "Moving," in Dixon's words, "like figures in a dream," the Klansmen have emerged from Griffith's dream. Making their "spectral dash through the night," they save Walthall from his nightmare.[39]

The mounted Klansmen invert, repeat, and dematerialize Walthall's ghouls. They are the ghouls turned upside down, since instead of animal heads atop human bodies, human heads ride animal bodies. The Klansmen (called cyclopes) are horned, like Walthall's ghouls. But those ghouls, like the uncle's personal ghost, remain grotesquely physical. The white robes that cover horns, riders, and horses transfigure human bodies into an impersonal, anonymous "spectral army," as one reviewer saw it, "a vast grim host in white."[40]

Blanche Sweet's leap to her death in *Conscience* pays for Walthall's murderous desire. Sweet's leap anticipates the little sister's leap to her death to escape a black rapist's murderous desire in *Birth*. Walthall and his lover look down over the water in the happy endings of both movies.[41] Blanche Sweet is not that lover in *Birth,* however, for Griffith excised her from the second film. That single failure of repetition is the key to *Birth*'s inversion of *Conscience*. When Sweet left *Birth,* she took with her the female sexuality that had provoked first the hero's desire and then his avenging conscience. Mae Marsh, who played the little sister in *Birth,* replaced Sweet in the leap to the death; Lillian Gish replaced Sweet as the object of Walthall-Siegmann's desire.

Griffith had planned to cast Sweet as Elsie Stoneman. When she was temporarily unavailable to rehearse the scene in which Siegmann (as Silas Lynch) seizes and forcibly embraces her, Griffith asked Gish to stand in. Gish recalls, "I was very blonde and fragile-looking. The contrast with the dark man evidently pleased Mr. Griffith, for he said in front of everyone, 'Maybe she would be more effective than the mature figure I had in mind.'" The Walthall-Sweet couple was destroying itself in the films before *Birth:* Walthall commits suicide in *Death's Marathon;* Sweet beheads him in *Judith;* she kills herself in the dream that constitutes *The Avenging Conscience*. *Birth* marked Sweet's disappearance from Griffith's screen.

When Griffith replaced Sweet with Gish he was shifting sexuality from the white woman to the black man. The regression to the presexual virgin and the invention of the black demon went hand in hand. White supremacists invented the black rapist to keep white women in their place. That strategy, counterposing the black man to the white woman, hid a deep fear of union. Griffith wanted what one viewer called the "contrast between black villainy and blond innocence" to undo the association of his unconscious, which had merged women and blacks. Critics

---

39. *New York Times,* 4 March 1915, p. 4; Stern, *"Birth of a Nation,* Part I," 123; Thomas Dixon, Jr., *The Clansman* (Lexington, Ky., 1970), 342; James Shelley Hamilton, "Putting a New Move in the Movies," *Everybody's Magazine* 32 (June 1915): 680.
40. *Atlanta Constitution,* 7 December 1915, in Silva, *Focus on "The Birth of a Nation,"* 35.
41. Wagenknecht, *Movies in the Age of Innocence,* 98–99.

who excuse Griffith's "unconscious racism" and separate it from his sexism overlook the link in Griffith's unconscious (as Faulkner's Joe Christmas would run it together): "womenshenegro."[42]

Griffith had romances with his leading actresses. The "mature figure" Sweet developed as she reached adulthood led him to shift his affections first to Marsh and then to Gish. Inverting the oedipal triangle of one woman and two men (depicted, for example, in *Conscience*), Griffith was squiring both Marsh and Gish when he made *Birth*. If Gish emerged from her dressing room after rehearsals dressed for the evening, Marsh would know Griffith was taking the other actress out, and she would make other plans. If Gish left in street clothes, Marsh dressed up.[43] The two women assaulted by blacks on camera were the objects of Griffith's attention offscreen.

Griffith's cinematic mirroring of his offscreen relations to his heroines was duplicated in his use of his villain. As the mulatto Silas Lynch, George Siegmann carried out Austin Stoneman's orders. As the director's chief assistant, he carried out Griffith's orders. Just as Lynch sees to the details of Stoneman's plan to "put the white South under the heel of the black South," so Siegmann passed Griffith's orders on to the cast and oversaw the logistical details of the production. Karl Brown, assistant cameraman on *Birth*, described Siegmann as a "gentle-hearted, soft-spoken human elephant, sensitive to Griffith's every whim, yet powerful enough to bend everyone else to his will."[44] Stoneman bends Lynch to his will only to discover that Lynch's will is for his daughter. Tracing Lynch's actions back to their source—to Griffith behind the camera and Stoneman in front of it—breaks down the divisions Griffith set up between male and female, white and black, the production of the film and its story.

Thomas Jefferson fathered the normal American racial fantasy that freed the fathers from desire. Inverting the social psychology of the slave South, Jefferson located desire in the black man and made the white woman its object.[45] The rapist Gus and Silas Lynch (whose name turns the black victims of lynching into aggressors) are Jefferson's children. Read as the successor to the Blanche Sweet films, *Birth* shifted sexuality from white women to blacks. Stoneman's liaison with his mulatto mistress, moreover, allowed Griffith to retain the sexual woman by making her black; Lydia's arm-waving gestures recall Judith's simulation of passion.

42. Lillian Gish, *The Movies, Mr. Griffith, and Me* (Englewood Cliffs, N.J., 1969), 133; Jacqueline Dowd Hall, "The Mind That Burns in Each Body: Women, Rape, and Racial Violence," in Ann Snitow et al., eds., *Powers of Desire* (New York, 1983), 331–333, 337; Milton Mackaye, "*The Birth of a Nation*," *Scribner's*, November 1937, 45–46; Schickel, *Griffith*, 233–234, 578; William Faulkner, *Light in August* (New York, 1968), 147. Cf. Frederickson, *White Supremacy*, 104.
43. Schickel, *Griffith*, 217–219.
44. Ibid., 220; Karl Brown, *Adventures with D. W. Griffith* (New York, 1973), 57.
45. Thomas Jefferson, *Notes on Virginia*, in Adrienne Koch and William Peden, eds., *The Life and Selected Writings of Thomas Jefferson* (New York, 1944), 256–262; Winthrop D. Jordan, *White over Black* (Baltimore, 1969), 429–481.

At the same time *Birth* registered, in however distorted a way, the origin of desire that Jefferson denied. Stoneman's liaison called attention to the mulatto (Lynch as well as Lydia), and the mulatto in American history signified the white man's desire for the black woman. Tracing that desire back to its paternal origin, Griffith made Stoneman's passion for Lydia the source of the South's oppression. Griffith wanted to demonize blacks and keep them under control at the same time. It was already provocative to depict black revolutionaries on-screen; no one had done it before and no one would do it again for half a century.[46] To give the black man a will of his own, in addition, violated the constraints of the political unconscious. Depriving these id figures of their reason kept them politically dependent and retained them as projections of white desire. If blacks were not to have minds of their own, however, the film required a bad white father.

Griffith employed two reversals to distinguish Stoneman from the actual patriarchs who controlled black slaves. He made Stoneman subservient to Lydia, and he moved the interracial union from the South to the North. Stoneman, as audiences were intended to know, was modeled on Thaddeus Stevens. Stevens had a mulatto house-keeper, and she was probably his mistress.[47] Fidelity to historical detail allowed historical distortion, since this interracial constellation typified the antebellum South, not the North.

Griffith borrowed the details of his Stevens caricature—massive brown wig, club-foot—from hostile Southern descriptions of the Pennsylvania congressman. Stevens was a "horrible old man," as one biographer of Andrew Johnson put it, "craftily preparing to strangle the bleeding, broken body of the South." He wanted to watch "the white men, especially the white women of the south, writhing under Negro domination." Both Dixon and Griffith focused on Stoneman's clubfoot—"the left leg ended in a mere bunch of flesh"—as a distended, sexualized, aggressive weapon. But in two seemingly contradictory ways, Griffith departed from the Southern caricature. Stevens was an ascetic-looking, cadaverous, "pale, emaciated, death-like" old man during the Civil War and Reconstruction. Griffith's wife described Griffith, too, as a "cadaverous-looking young man," and Dixon was also "weirdly gaunt" and "almost cadaverous." But unlike Stevens and Dixon, Griffith has a sensual face; he gave that sensuality to Stoneman. Stoneman is the most negroid looking of all the major characters in *Birth*, blacks as well as whites. By making Stoneman Northern and negroid, Griffith wanted to distance him from the Southern white man, who was actually the male bearer of historically significant interracial sexuality. That splitting allowed Griffith to depict monstrous paternal desire.[48]

46. Donald Bogle, *Toms, Coons, Mulattoes, Mammies, and Bucks* (New York, 1973), 16.
47. Fawn M. Brodie, *Thaddeus Stevens, Scourge of the South* (New York, 1959), 86–91.
48. Ibid., 369–70, 386; Mrs. D. W. Griffith (Linda Arvidson), *When the Movies Were Young* (New York, 1925), 47; Cook, *Fire from the Flint*, 78; Dixon, *Clansman*, 39, 132, 143. Kim Barton has influenced my understanding of Stoneman.

At the same time, Griffith gave Stoneman children, although Stevens had none, and made him a loving father. The conscious intention was to make Stoneman's love for his daughter a counterweight to his love of blacks. The unconscious intention was to confuse the two desires, for Stoneman's sensuality first emerges in seductive contact not with his mulatto mistress but with his daughter.

After beginning with the slave trade, which sowed "the seeds of disunion," *Birth* shows the divided Stoneman family. Elsie fondles her father and adjusts his wig. The scene shifts to Stoneman and Lydia in a house from which his children are excluded. Lydia's embrace of Stoneman parallels Elsie's. That juxtaposition of white family and black will break down after the Civil War. In Part Two of the movie, shots 626–693, Lynch appears for the first time. Stoneman is shown with his mulatto mistress and mulatto protégé, as if they constituted a family. He tells Lynch not to scrape, that he is the equal of any white man. Elsie replaces Lydia in the next scene. Lynch stares at her and, after he leaves, she caresses her father. The sequence establishes a circuit of desire initiated by Lydia that runs from Lynch to Elsie to Stoneman. The camera also sets up the formula that Stoneman is to Lydia as Lynch wishes to be to Elsie. Drop out the two middle (shadow) terms, and Stoneman's wish is for his daughter. The blacks have been invented as a defense against what their invention allows to return, father-daughter incest.

Stoneman, like the father in Freud's primal horde, monopolizes his women and directs the mob of (black) men. There is no Stoneman mother, and her absence suggests a family triangle too explosive to be more explicit. Were Elsie's mother present, she would either separate Elsie from Lydia or else be the mulatto herself. The one alternative is insufficiently charged, the other forbidden. Having moved Southern racial and sexual entanglements north, Griffith can give the Southern family a mother. Whatever the ages and genders of the antebellum Southern blacks, they are all asexual children.

The missing Stoneman mother at the film's opening establishes the racial division within the Stoneman family as the central division in the movie. The film's second opposition, between North and South, supersedes the racial contrast in Part One in order to give way to it in Part Two. The visit of the Stoneman boys to the Cameron plantation, home of Ben Cameron, the Little Colonel, promises to override the sectional division, and the Civil War does not frustrate that promise but realizes it.

Griffith's battle scenes twin North and South in two ways, one private and sentimental, the other epic and impersonal. Two sets of Camerons and Stonemans meeting in battle constitute the first mode. One younger brother is about to stab the other when, at the moment of recognition, he is fatally shot. The two die embracing. The older Cameron, Ben, leads a charge against Phil Stoneman's lines, is wounded but survives. Like the family interactions earlier in the movie, these scenes are emotionally overwrought. On the other hand, the panoramic battle scenes are distant, beautiful, and otherworldly; they are a cinematic triumph.

An iris-in opens up from a woman and her children onto the first panorama, Sherman's march to the sea. The camera takes the woman's position, and we look down on a slow, curved, marching line. Griffith cuts back and forth from the still observers to tiny soldiers silhouetted against a red flame, as if "The torch of war against the breast of Atlanta" were the family's dream. The receptive camera displays an eerily pastoral landscape. Cut to a close-up of starved soldiers eating corn before Petersburg. The scenes of this battle compose an ecstasy of pain. Panoramic shots of curved lines of battle alternate with closeups of the charge. Tiny transparent soldiers move across the screen as hand-tinted red flames light up the sky; it is impossible to tell one side from the other. Union soldiers enter the screen from the right, Confederate from the left; otherwise the two sides are indistinguishable.[49] Clumps of trees on the battlefield and a hill in the background accentuate the roundness and passivity of the scene. "War's peace," a close-up of dead bodies, is reconstructed from a Mathew Brady photograph. The camera's passivity has obliterated the differences between North and South.

Griffith censored out the greatest destruction at Petersburg, the one suffered by black troops sent into the crater opened up by Northern mining under Southern lines. He sentimentalized battle scenes like the Little Colonel's charge by per-sonalizing them. But that charge is mock-heroic and fails. It does not spoil what Agee rightly labeled Griffith's unforgettable images of the war. The Southern director left a record of war as the triumph of death.[50]

Southern extras who played both Union and Confederate soldiers objected to putting on Northern uniforms. "My daddy rode with Jeb Stuart. I ain't no god damn Yankee," one protested.[51] Griffith's father rode with Joe Wheeler; the son shot, directed, and merged both sides. The South is the ultimate victim of Griffith's war, to be sure. But he used Lincoln to nationalize victimization. Stoneman and his blacks, not the North as a whole, torture the bleeding body of the South. A triptych of victimization linking North and South, which concludes Part One, justifies the reversal of Part Two.

Lincoln and Stoneman meet in the central scene of that triptych. Stoneman, hobbling up to Lincoln, demands vengeance against the South; Lincoln refuses, and Stoneman hobbles away. This contrast, between the vengeful tyrant and the benevolent patriarch, actually feminizes Lincoln. A stooped, warm, androgynous figure, called "the great heart," Lincoln has responded to the pleas of Elsie and Ma Cameron at the end of the war and pardoned the Little Colonel. "I shall deal with them as if they'd never been away," he tells Stoneman of the Confederate states. The maternal image of Lincoln was a common one, promoted by Lincoln himself. It drained the President of war's ferocity and anticipated his martyrdom.

The assassination, the triptych's final scene, follows Lincoln's meeting with Stoneman. Lincoln draws his shawl around him in a feminine gesture that

49. Gish, *Movies, Mr. Griffith, and Me*, 140.
50. Richard Slotkin, *The Crater* (New York, 1980); Agee, *Agee on Film*, 313.
51. Schickel, *Griffith*, 227.

anticipates both his danger and his helplessness. The president's martyrdom twins him with the defeated South. Booth limps from the stage onto which he has jumped after the shooting; the limp twins him with Stoneman. Lydia's embrace of Stoneman when they learn of the assassination brings Part One to an end.

Ben Cameron's return home, the first panel of the triptych, sets the tone for the two Lincoln scenes. After a title, "The homecoming," we see the Cameron street and front yard; everything is in need of repair. Ben enters the picture and limps slowly toward home. The defeated, limping colonel climbs the stairs of his porch in the longest single shot in all of Part One (fifty-seven feet) and is greeted by his little sister. (Only two single shots in Part Two are longer: Ben shows little sister his Klan costume in one; in the other he holds her as she dies.) Female arms reach out from the door and draw Ben in.[52]

Cameron's limp foreshadows Stoneman's and Booth's in the next two scenes. The intent of the repetition is to contrast the devastation that makes cripples to the devastation wrought by them. The limping Stoneman walks away from Lincoln, who has promised to bring the South home; the limping Ben is welcomed home by a woman. But Stoneman's "weakness which will blight a nation" (a conflation of his passion for the mulatto with his clubfoot) shades into the Little Colonel's weakness. Lydia's arm around Stoneman repeats the arms around Ben. The contrast collapses between mulatto and the white female, sex and family, for both villain and hero are placed intolerably under the power of a woman.

Eisenstein contrasted Griffith's invocations of patriarchal calmness to his displays of modern speed. Part One ends in stillness, not motion; that stillness, however, a landscape after battle, registers not the triumph of patriarchy and tradition but their defeat. The father-daughter incest that, in the Stoneman family, is displaced onto the mulatto returns to its maternal source in Ben's homecoming. Fathers were once sons, and the father's desire for the daughter, the homecoming suggests, defends against being drawn back into the power of the mother. The bifurcation between mulatto and mother, a second defense besides father-daughter incest against the mother-son bond, breaks down at the end of Part One. Mother and mulatto threaten to unite, not to dismember the father by using the sword as Judith had but rather to emasculate the son by confining him in the home. Griffith takes the sword from Judith in Part Two, runs it through black aggression, and puts it into the hands of the Klan. The blacks who take over Piedmont's streets and invade the Cameron home, by intensifying the Little Colonel's claustrophobic familial confinement, give him the opportunity to bring it to an end. The Klan's ride to the rescue that saves a nation from black rule saved Griffith from (and

52. The arms belong, on close inspection, to little sister, but they are easily mistaken for the mother's. Gilbert Seldes, for example, wrote, "From behind the door, as the soldier enters, comes the arm of his mother drawing in her son" (quoted in Richard Griffith et al., *The Movies,* rev. ed. [New York, 1981], 32). Shot lengths are in Theodore Huff, *The Birth of a Nation Shot Analysis* (New York, 1961).

thereby allowed him to make) *The Birth of a Nation,* Part One. Griffith could register war's devastation and Southern defeat because he was also filming the triumph of the Klan. Critics who want to rescue *Birth*'s greatness by excising Part Two of the film fail to see the dependence of each part on the other.[53] Overriding the binary oppositions in the film between North and South, black and white, male and female, is the opposition between Parts One and Two.

V

Griffith displaces sexuality from white men to women to blacks in order, by the subjugation and dismemberment of blacks, to reempower white men. The project of disempowering women that culminates in Part Two of *Birth* emerges from the pre-*Birth* history of Griffith's movies. It also emerges from his source. The Elsie of Thomas Dixon's *Clansman* is a New Woman, a believer in female equality. "I deny your heaven-born male kingship," she tells Ben. "I don't care to be absorbed by a mere man. . . . My ideal is an intellectual companion." Ben, by contrast, is a Southern cavalier indifferent to politics. The black threat politicizes Ben, and Elsie adopts his point of view. Repudiating her previous identity as "a vain, self-willed, pert little thing," she tells him, "in what I have lived through you I have grown into an impassioned, serious, self-disciplined woman."[54]

Charles Gaston, the hero of *The Leopard's Spots,* Part Two, also wins his bride by leading a negrophobic crusade. "You will share with me all the honors and responsibilities of public life," he tells Sallie Worth. She responds, in the novel's last words, "No, my love, I do not desire any part in public life except through you. You are my world." Gaston's triumph marks the defeat of Sallie's father. General Worth opposed their marriage; he is "beaten," he tells Gaston, by the force of the hero's negrophobia.[55]

Stoneman is also beaten at the end of *Birth.* These defeats may seem to represent the transfer of women from fathers to husbands, the reinscription and transmission of patriarchy. Gaston does promise "to eliminate the negro from our life and reestablish for all time the government of our fathers." But Gaston repudiates the paternalist stance that made the Negro "the ward of the republic." He wants blacks subject to the law not of paternalist planters but "of the survival of the fittest."[56] *Birth,* Part Two, also restores male dominance, but the instrument of that restoration is not the traditional father but the warrior brothers. Unlike such

53. Cf. Arlene Croce, quoted in Williams, *Griffith,* 74; and Jay Leyda, "The Art and Death of D. W. Griffith," in Geduld, *Focus on D. W. Griffith,* 161–167. Leyda offers, nonetheless, the best analysis I have seen of the differences between the two halves of the film.

54. Dixon, *Clansman,* 127, 149, 163–164, 333.

55. Dixon, *Leopard's Spots,* 468, 447.

56. Ibid., 418, 420.

nostalgic pastorals as *True Heart Susie* (1919) and *Way Down East* (1920), Part Two invokes traditional values in the service of modern force.

"*The Birth of a Nation,*" Griffith wrote in his autobiography, "owes more to my father than it does to me." Yet Griffith shot the war in which his father was shot, the war that registered his father's defeat. The movie dwells on defeated fathers. Dr. Cameron, the sympathetic paternal figure, is thrown to the ground and paraded in chains before his former slaves. Helpless to resist the raiders who invade his home during the war, he cannot keep black troops out of it after the war is over. Griffith's father, to be sure, is the model for the Little Colonel, not the doctor. Griffith remembered hearing stories of his father's exploits in the war and of his mother staying up nights sewing Klan robes. He made *Birth,* he said, from those stories. "Underneath the robes and costumes of the actors playing the soldiers and night riders, rode my father." But Griffith's father never rode in the Klan. He drank, told stories, did no work, and lived in the past in the years before he died. When Griffith recalled thread in connection with his father, it was not the thread that sewed Klan robes but the thread that sewed up his father's war-torn stomach. That thread was rotten, Griffith claimed, because the Northern blockade prevented good surgical thread from reaching the South. The rotten thread broke, as Griffith told the story, his father's stomach burst, and he died. Griffith did not mention that his father was swilling bourbon and eating pickles when he got his fatal attack. Griffith's father was a cavalry officer, but the horse charges that dominate *Birth* are those of the Klan. In the memories transmuted into film, Griffith's mother sewed the sheeted shroud from which his father's failed body was reborn. Roaring Jake Griffith rode through—in Wilson's words—"the shrouded night," a member of a "spectral army, . . . a vast grim host in white." "The ghostlike shadowy columns," as Dixon called the Klan, were led by the father's shade. Haunted by Griffith's father, *Birth* celebrates not his living body but his ghost.[57]

Patriarchal weakness raised the specters of black and female power in the movie Griffith made to honor his father. These specters are not laid to rest by the restoration of traditional patriarchy in the form of either the gentlemanly Dr. Cameron or the primal Austin Stoneman. Defeated as a black mob, the primal horde is reborn as a white mass. Split in two, it slays the father. Griffith put on the screen Rev. 19:14–15: "And the armies *which* were in heaven followed him upon white horses, clothed in fine linen, white and clean. And out of his mouth goeth a sharp sword, that with it he should smite the nations."

---

57. Hart, *Man Who Invented Hollywood,* 26–28; Schickel, *Griffith,* 30–31; Wilson, *Reunion,* 60; Silva, *Focus on "The Birth of a Nation,"* 35; Dixon, *Clansman,* 39. Klansmen liked to be called, and to convince blacks they were, the "ghosts of the Confederate dead." See Gladys-Marie Fry, *Night Riders in Black Folk History* (Knoxville, Tenn., 1975), 112, 136. Paul Thomas first showed me that the Klan sheets were shrouds.

"About the first thing I remember was my father's sword," Griffith told an interviewer after *Birth* was released. That sword inspired *Birth,* Griffith explained, "As I started the book [*The Clansman*], stronger and stronger came to my mind the traditions I had learned as a child, all that my father had told me. The sword I told you about became a flashing vision. Gradually came back to my memory the stories a cousin, one Thurston Griffith, had told me of the Ku Klux Klan." "The sword remains the first memory I have of existence," Griffith repeated in 1930. In the trailer to the sound version of *Birth,* released that year, Walter Huston presents Griffith with a cavalry sword like the one his father carried in the war.[58]

Griffith first used that sword in *His Trust* and *His Trust Fulfilled* (1910) to symbolize a dead master's power. Consciously or unconsciously, in *His Trust* he filmed the opening scene of *The Leopard's Spots.* The widow of a soldier killed in the war, wrote Dixon, "took the sword of her dead lover husband in her lap, and looked long and tenderly at it. On the hilt she pressed her lips in a lingering kiss." Then she hung the sword on the wall.[59] In the film as in the book, a slave has brought the sword home. He refuses to leave his mistress after emancipation and devotes himself to his dead master's child (Charles Gaston, who will grow up to be the hero of *The Leopard's Spots,* Part Two). Griffith's black hangs the sword in his own cabin after the big house burns down. For him and for the widow, it signifies devotion to the dead master. The associations of sword, child, Negro devotion, and the dead father's power that Griffith found in *The Leopard's Spots* awakened a childhood memory.

> About the first thing I remember was my father's sword; he would put it on to amuse me. The first time I saw that sword was when my father played a joke on an old Negro, once his slave but who with the heads of four other families refused to leave the plantation; those four families were four important factors in keeping the Griffith family poor.
>
> Down South the men usually wore their hair rather long; this Negro, who in our better days had been the plantation barber, had been taken to Louisville, . . . and had seen Northern men with their close-cropped hair; when he came back he got hold of my brother and cut his hair close, Northern-style.
>
> When father saw this he pretended to be enraged; he went into the house, donned his old uniform, buckled on this sword. . . .
>
> Then, drawing his sword, he went through the technical cuts and thrusts and slashes, threatening the darkey all the time with being cut up into mincemeat.
>
> The old Uncle was scared pale, and I took it seriously myself until a wink and a smile from father enlightened me.[60]

58. D. W. Griffith, "My Early Life," *Photoplay* (1916), in Geduld, *Focus on D. W. Griffith,* 13–14, 39–40; Schickel, *Griffith,* 15, 555.

59. Dixon, *Leopard's Spots,* 9–13.

60. Geduld, *Focus on D. W. Griffith,* 13–14.

Griffith had been unconsciously preparing to make *Birth* since age five, he said, which would have been his age in this scene. He recalled the barber story at the height of his powers, just after he filmed *Birth*. Fifteen years later, when he was no longer able to make movies, the darker side of the sword memory took over. "The only person I ever really loved was my father," Griffith confessed, but he doubted that his father loved him, and as his first memory he replaced the story of the sword and the Negro with a tale of a dog and a gun.[61]

His favorite sheepdog, as Griffith remembered it, fell in helpless, forbidden love with the sheep. In its passion, the dog bit them to death. Griffith's father tied the dog to a tree to shoot it and young David fled the scene, "but I couldn't run fast enough to get away from the report of the gun." The boy identified in both memories with victims of his father's violence. He was saved from the terror of sharing the black's fate by the discovery that his father was playacting, but he could not escape participating in the fate of the dog. In the sword memory, the boy shifted, by way of theatricality, to the side of his father; in the gun memory, as a violently hungry self, he remained his father's victim. It was a black, Griffith remembered, who told him to go on the stage, and an actor called Gloomy Gus (Griffith gave the name Gus to *Birth*'s rapist) who told him to try Biograph. Both the sword and the gun were screen memories, but only one led Griffith to the screen. The other returned only after the screen was lost.[62]

One child who worshiped his father's sword (in *The Leopard's Spots*) grew up to lead a negrophobic crusade. Another child who worshiped his father's sword grew up to film one. But the sword, so prominent in Griffith's accounts of the sources of *Birth,* is not prominent in the film we see. The Little Colonel, as he leads his failed charge, waves the Civil War sword of defeat. "The sword [that] . . . became a flashing vision" originally formed *Birth*'s climax. But that sword, which castrated the black rapist, has been cut out of the film.

Birth realized progressive hopes for an uplifting cinema with mass appeal, a cinema with American themes. But the realization of those dreams, as Lary May has written, looked very different from what humanitarian reformers had imagined. Cultural guardians had always favored film censorship. Movies of the first black heavyweight champion, Jack Johnson, knocking out a white contender had been banned in the name of racial peace. Now white humanitarians like Jane Addams joined with black activists to support banning *Birth* as well.[63]

61. Williams, *Griffith,* 4; May, *Screening Out the Past,* 68.

62. Schickel, *Griffith,* 15; Hart, *Man Who Invented Hollywood,* 73; Robert M. Henderson, *D. W. Griffith: His Life and Work* (Oxford, 1972), 54. In "Screen Memories," Freud wrote, "Our childhood memories show us our earliest memories not as they were but as they appeared at the later periods when the memories were revived. . . . And a number of motives, which had no concern with historical accuracy, had their part in thus forming them" (*Standard Edition* 3:322).

63. May, *Screening Out the Past,* 80–86; Cripps, *Slow Fade to Black,* 56–62; Bogle, *Toms, Coons, Mulattoes,* 7; Francis Hackett, "Brotherly Love," *New Republic,* 20 March 1915, 185.

Birth showed white victory, not black, however, and the two were hardly reversible. The National Board of Review (set up by the industry to pass on motion pictures) applauded *Birth,* not on free-speech grounds but because of its historical accuracy and educational value. Most members of the cultural elite agreed, in Dorothea Dix's words, that the movie was "history vitalized." "Go see it," she urged her readers, "for it will make a better American of you."[64]

There were moments in the film, however, that the censors agreed to sacrifice. They cut out a quote from Lincoln opposing racial equality, although Lincoln had actually spoken the offending words. They censored "Lincoln's solution" at the end of the film, which showed blacks deported to Africa, although Lincoln favored emigration. They eliminated some graphic black sexual assaults on white women. And they cut out Gus's castration. Censors found truthful and educational the suggestions of black sexual violence (so long as they were implied rather than stated), but they wanted to bury the (more accurate) representations of white racist speech and action. The missing footage of castration, seen by Los Angeles audiences for weeks after *Birth*'s release and in the South for half a decade, takes us to the heart of Griffith's project.[65]

Viewers now watch Gus foam at the mouth as he lopes after little sister. In the original version he probably raped her, as he does in *The Clansman;*[66] now she leaps to her death to escape him. Gus flees; he is captured and brought before a conclave of the Klan. As Gus lies passive and helpless, the Little Colonel takes off his hood. Walthall, who played a character exposed as a parricide in *Conscience,* now unmasks himself as the innocent avenging conscience. Gus is "Guilty" (a title announces) and about to be killed.

The Southern plantation novelist Thomas Nelson Page, who was the most popular novelist in early twentieth-century America and Woodrow Wilson's ambassador to Italy, blamed lynching on the preaching of racial equality by some whites and "the determination [of others] to put an end to the ravishing of their women by an inferior race." Page invoked "the ravishing and tearing to pieces of white women and children" to excuse the murder and dismemberment of black men. Early twentieth-century audiences knew Southern blacks accused of sexual crimes were often lynched and castrated. The headline in a 1934 Alabama newspaper, for example, making history as well as reporting it, proclaimed, "Florida to Burn Negro at Stake: Sex Criminal Seized from Jail Will Be Mutilated, Set Afire, in Extra-Legal Vengeance for Deed." Reports of early viewings of Gus's

---

64. Stern, *"Birth of a Nation,* Part 1," 170; Silva, *Focus on "The Birth of a Nation,"* 102; Schickel, *Griffith,* 277; Russell Merritt, "Dixon, Griffith, and the Southern Legend," *Cinema Journal* 3 (1972): 28.

65. Stern, *"Birth of a Nation,* Part 1," 66, 123, 164. [Ed. note: There is no evidence for these speculations. See note 26 to my Introduction.]

66. Ibid., 66; "Films and Births and Censorships," *The Survey,* 3 April 1915, 4.

punishment also referred to his "mutilation." That footage is now lost or unavailable, but Seymour Stern left a detailed record of it. (There is, regrettably for those who want to blame *Birth*'s racism on Dixon, no castration scene in *The Clansman*.)[67]

First a masked Klansman steps forward. (The picture of him towering over Gus was used in billboards and other advertisements for the film.) Then the Little Colonel performs a mystic ceremony with his sister's blood. (This ceremony now appears in the film after Gus's execution and will be described in a moment.) Cut to the Klansman. He raises his arm, with his back to the camera, and holds up a small sword. Against the background of the storm music from Beethoven's *Pastoral Symphony,* he plunges the sword down. He repeats this "ritualistic and totemic gesture," as Stern calls it, to the crash of Beethoven's storm. Cut to a closeup of Gus's face, his mouth flowing blood and his eyes rolling in agony. Griffith synchronizes his cutting to the cutting of the sword. "In flash-cuts, the Klansman's hand now plunges and rises, plunges and rises, again, again, and still again, on each down-beat of the timpani, all within a few frames of film. On the final thunder-crash of the series, there is a final flash of the castrated Negro's pain-racked face and body. Gus is dead."[68] The father's threat to make mincemeat of a black, which frightened the son, turned out to be play. The grown son, through his film cuts in a play, made that threat real. "My father's sword . . . became a flashing vision" to castrate Gus.

But the sword that castrates Gus has also been severed from the father's body. The father who wielded the sword in Griffith's memory, as Griffith went on to say, was "all shot to pieces," was mincemeat himself inside.[69] Griffith sensed the connection between violence and internal patriarchal weakness: a damaged body makes vindictive Walthall's uncle in *Conscience* and Stoneman in *Birth*. *Birth*'s aim, however, was to rescue the father, not expose him, to insulate the father from his violence, not to eliminate it entirely. To guarantee the sword's invulnerability, it had to be protected from the father's "shot to pieces" body (which ruptured soon after the sword memory) and from the threats that the father's weakness opened up. These dangers, which were at once displacements of the feared father and alternatives to him, were the threats of women and blacks. Griffith rescued the paternal sword by detaching it from the father's body and putting it into the hands of the father's specter. He not only gave the sword to the mystic body but also removed the hat (which was menacing on Judith since it prefigured her sword) from the woman's head to the massed horned Klansmen. Griffith paid homage to his father by turning the penis into a phallus. He sacrificed the member's vulnerable bodily connection and raised it to a weapon of vengeance.

67. Friedman, *White Savage,* 57–68; Thomas Nelson Page, "The Lynching of Negroes—Its Cause and Prevention," *North American Review* 178 (1904): 36–39, 45; Hall, "Mind That Burns," 329; Stern, "*Birth of a Nation,* Part I," 123.
68. Stern, "*Birth of a Nation,* Part I," 123–124.
69. Griffith, in Geduld, *Focus on D. W. Griffith,* 15.

The liberty blacks wanted, Dixon and Griffith insisted, was sexual. "Equality. Equal rights. Equal politics. Equal marriage" reads a placard in the black-dominated South Carolina legislature. Griffith and Dixon accused *Birth's* opponents of promoting miscegenation. Dixon called the NAACP the Negro Intermarriage Society and claimed it "hates *The Birth of a Nation* for one reason only—it opposes the marriage of blacks to whites." One purpose of *Birth,* Dixon boasted, "was to create a feeling of abhorrence in white people, especially white women, against colored men." Griffith and Dixon imagined a monstrous America of the future, peopled by mulattoes. Stopping black men from penetrating white women gave birth to a redeemed nation. The nation was born in Gus's castration, from the wound that signified the white man's power to stop the black seed.[70]

Mixture of blood from "the surviving polygamous and lawless instincts of the white male," Dixon wrote in *The Leopard's Spots,* had "no social significance": the offspring of black mothers were black. But give Negro men access to white women, and they will destroy "the foundation of racial life and of civilization. The South must guard with flaming sword every avenue of approach to this holy of holies."[71] The sword guards the female genitalia not only to protect the white woman from the black phallus but also to keep her from acquiring a phallus of her own. The sword that passed from Griffith's father to Judith is put into the Klansman's hands; the sexuality displaced from the white male to the white female is cut off by that sword.

Castration protected white women, in the film's ideology. "The southern woman with her helpless little children in a solitary farm house no longer sleeps secure," warned the president of the University of North Carolina in 1901. "The black brute is lurking in the dark, a monstrous beast, crazed with lust. His ferocity is almost demonical." Beneath that public justification for dismembering the black beast lay an anxiety about the freedom not simply of blacks but of women. The scene at *Birth's* final climax in which Lynch assaults Elsie (also not in Dixon's novel) is intended to repeat, invert, and justify Gus's castration. But the blacks whom Lynch orders to gag Elsie are doing the white man's work. When Stoneman's instruments break free from his control and assault and silence his daughter on screen, they reveal Griffith's desire behind the camera. "It may be no accident," writes Jacqueline Dowd Hall, "that the vision of the black man as a threatening beast flourished during the first phase of the southern woman's rights movement, a fantasy of aggression against boundary-transgressing women as well as a weapon of terror against blacks. Certainly the rebelliousness of that

70. Dixon, in Silva, *Focus on "The Birth of a Nation,"* 79, 94–95; NAACP, Boston Branch, "Fighting a Vicious Film," in Geduld, *Focus on D. W. Griffith,* 94. Ann Banfield, in her interpretation of Artemesia Gentileschi's painting of Judith beheading Holofernes, first suggested to me the connection between castration and birth.
71. Dixon, *Leopard's Spots,* 336.

feminine generation was circumscribed by the feeling that women were hedged about by a 'nameless horror.'"[72]

Women and slaves resemble one another at the opening of *Birth*. Both move with short, jerky, childlike motions. The hidden danger is that women will mature; the filmed danger is that blacks will. The woman cannot have a penis, for that would be a sign of her power. But the woman without a penis is a sign of what can happen to the man. Having turned women into blacks to keep women childlike, Griffith castrates the black rapist to make him female. The passivity forced upon the defeated South is now enforced on Gus. It is not the white man who is in danger of becoming a woman, without a penis, says the castration, but the black. Blacks must either embrace the sword, as the loyal Negro does at the end of *His Trust Fulfilled* (miming his mistress's action at the opening of *His Trust*), or be castrated by it. Anticipating Joe Christmas's fantasy of "womanshenegro" when he created the black rapist, Griffith anticipated Percy Grimm's fantasy when, just as Percy castrated Joe Christmas, Griffith castrated Gus.[73]

Judith climaxes as a severed head issues forth from the wound in Holofernes's trunk; the image merges castration and birth. *The Avenging Conscience* begins with a woman (Walthall's mother) dying in childbirth. The associations of castration, birth, and death, disturbing in those films, are redemptive in *Birth*. *Birth* entails, however, not just the sacrifice of the black male but of Ben's little sister as well. The camera that lingers on Ben and little sister in the three longest shots of the film, the overwrought scenes between the two siblings, and the confusion between Ben and Phil Stoneman (in the novel they look "as much alike as twins"), all locate fraternal desire in the incestuous subtext of the film. Just as Lynch is the dark side of Stoneman's desire for his daughter, so Gus mediates between the Little Colonel and his little sister. These forms of incest defend against the deeper, incestuous desire generated from the birth of the son. The homecoming to mother paralyzes Ben. Paternal and fraternal desire is displaced onto the blacks who are punished for it. The displacement and punishment of that desire gives birth to the new nation.[74]

The birth of a nation required Flora's blood as well as Gus's and the original scene sequence, which joined the two rituals, came perilously close to mixing their blood together. In the present version we see four cyclops dump Gus's body on Lynch's porch. After the title "The Klan prepares for action," audiences watch Ben Cameron soak a flag in a chalice. He speaks: "Brethren, this flag bears the red

72. Hall, "Mind That Burns," 347n., 337.

73. Cf. Neil Hertz, "Medusa's Head: Male Hysteria under Political Pressure," and Catherine Gallagher, "More about 'Medusa's Head,'" *Representations* 4 (Fall 1983): 27–57; Faulkner, *Light in August,* 437–440.

74. Dixon, *Clansman,* 20. *Light in August* is Faulkner's text for the castration, *Absalom, Absalom* for the brother-sister incest, and *Go Down Moses* for the displacement of mother-son by father-daughter incest.

stain of the life of a Southern woman, a priceless sacrifice on the altar of an outraged civilization." Ben raises a small fiery cross and intones, "I quench its flames in the sweetest blood that ever stained the sands of Time." That bloody cross summons the Klan. The Little Colonel quenches the fiery cross in his sister's blood to bind the sheeted white males to hunt the black beast.[75]

The castration scene clarifies Griffith's intentions, which is why the censors took it out. But the cinematic transformation following that scene is manifest even in its absence. To the music of Klan clarion calls and the cheers of movie audiences, the Klansmen assemble. The ride of the Klan reenacts and reverses Civil War battles. Northern soldiers were indistinguishable from their Southern brothers; the massed, white-robed men on horseback contrast to the chaotic black mob. Blue and gray intermingled in Civil War charges; the Klan stands out against and routs the blacks. Hand-to-hand slaughter marked Civil War battles. Klansmen on horseback tower over black men on foot. Civil War close-ups showed suffering; Klan close-ups show movement and power. Ben led Southern stragglers in his quixotic charge, and he alone reached Northern lines. Now he stands before a massed, invincible Klan.

Klansmen ride with or into the camera; their power contrasts to the futility of Civil War charges. A distant camera filmed passive, curved Civil War battle lines. The Klan rides forcefully in close-ups and straight lines. When the Klan is filmed in a curve, riding around a bend, its power contrasts with the stillness of Sherman's curved march. The confusions of night Civil War battles contrast to a breathtaking single line of Klansmen silhouetted in a long shot at night. The tiny transparent Civil War soldiers were shades; Klan shrouds incarnate large forceful presences. Panoramic Civil War battle scenes, with remarkable depth of field, dwarfed the human participants. The Klan fuses humans into an animal, mechanical, sacred power. The dead soldiers on the Civil War battlefields rise up, an "Invisible Empire," and ride to regenerative victory.

Virtuoso parallel editing climaxes the movie, but the aesthetic force of the climax is inseparable from its political message. Griffith moves among Lynch's assault on Elsie ("Lynch, drunk with wine and power, orders his henchmen to hurry preparations for a forced marriage"), the Negroes' assault on the Union veterans' cabin in which the Camerons have taken refuge, and the Klan rides to the rescue. He cuts in this montage from the Lincoln log cabin refuge ("The former enemies of North and South reunited again in defense of their Aryan birthright") to Elsie's fluttering, helpless motions (as Lynch seizes her and kisses her white garment) to Klansmen moving forcefully through the water. The Klan ride to rescue Elsie doubles the black assault on the cabin. Griffith's parallel cross-cutting, his failure to transcend dualistic oppositions, marks no victory of patriarchy

75. This scene inverts Ahab's black mass on the *Pequod.* See Herman Melville, *Moby Dick* (New York, 1956), 140–141.

and provincialism over modern speed. The moving picture camera and the moving Klan, welding white individuals into a mystic union, embody Griffith's prophetic vision. Upon the collapsed distinction between the mechanical North and the traditional South, he erected an apocalyptic division between black and white.

The formal advances in Griffith's earlier films also juxtaposed opposites. But these contrasts—between what happened in one time or place and what happened in another; between self and other, inside and outside, fantasy and reality; between public and private, rich and poor, good woman and bad—instead of reinforcing traditional distinctions threatened to break them down. In social terms modern technique seemed to augur the triumph of mass society, in psychological language it foretold a regression to dual unity with the primal mother. America would not be a democracy, said the young Woodrow Wilson in an unguarded moment, until there were a black woman in the White House.[76] *Birth* responded to that fear. It erected a system of differences—between male and female, white and black, good and evil—whose purpose was to withstand its own collapse and so defend against the breakdown of all difference.

The violent sacrifice of a monstrous double, in René Girard's terms, gives birth to a regenerate order. Ritual murder averts a sacrificial crisis of indiscriminate violence. It ushers in the distinction between culture and nature, a system of differences and a system without them. Griffith's system without differences is black, female, and democratic, the differentiated system is white, male, and hierarchic. But motion, speed, and the breakdown of difference constitute the new culture as well. In Girard's words about the "enemy brothers" who have slain the primal father, "We are left with a group of people all bearing the same name, all identically dressed. . . . Their resemblance is such that they do not possess identities of their own." The Klan not only brings about national unity; it also submerges human divisions in a merged, sacred brotherly horde.[77]

One image in this climax, however, unsettles the entire film. Two horsemen in blackface survey the Piedmont streets. Identified as "White spies disguised," they turn toward the room in which Elsie is imprisoned when they hear her cries for help. But the Negroes who bind and gag her when she screams for help are also whites in blackface. So is the "black spy" who sees a Cameron sister with that other disguise, the Klan robe. The "white spies" cannot be told from other Negroes in the film not because their paint covers their whiteness but because the other's paint does not. Masks transform some white bodies into a white host and other white bodies into a black mob. Whites in white sheets defeat whites in blackface. The climax of *Birth* does not pit whites against blacks, but some white actors against others.

76. Friedman, *White Savage,* 155; Henry W. Bragdon, *Woodrow Wilson: The Academic Years* (Cambridge, Mass., 1967), 231.

77. René Girard, *Violence and the Sacred* (Baltimore, 1978), 4–22, 48–49, 56–64, 79–83, 203, 236, 307.

Sometimes they were the same white actors. White extras switched back and forth from playing Klansmen to playing blacks, just as Griffith cut back and forth from one scene to another. Elmo Lincoln, first seen as the slave auctioneer at the opening of the film, played both a Klansman and the black owner of the gin mill in which Gus hid. Bobby Harron, killed as Elsie Stoneman's younger brother, was resurrected as a free Negro. Joseph Henabery, assassinated as Lincoln, played thirteen bit parts in Part Two. He recalled, "In one sequence I played in a group of renegade colored people, being pursued by white people—and I was in both groups, chasing myself through the whole sequence." Griffith had split the fraternal primal horde into black desire and white punishment; blackface enabled whites to "impersonate" (Griffith's word for playing a role) both sides.[78]

Dixon and Griffith, one opponent of the film pointed out, "ought to realize that if the Negro was as bad as they paint him in these films he was what the South made him; he was the shadow of her own substance."[79] Historically and cinematically, that concessive "if" gives too much away. Griffith's Negroes were as bad as he painted them because he painted whites black. The obviousness of blackface, which fails to disguise, reveals that the Klansmen were chasing their own negative identities, their own shadow sides.

Griffith did use hundreds of black extras throughout the film. He gave several blacks small bits of business to do (an old black man dances the buck-and-wing early in the film), and one black woman has a small individuated role. Neither she nor any other black actors appear in the list of credits, however, and no blacks were given major parts. Griffith explained, "On careful weighing of every detail concerned, the decision was made to have no black blood among the principals."[80]

Blacks were barred from the theater stage; there were none in Griffith's company, and the scarcity of established black actors may have influenced Griffith's decision. But he preferred creating his own leading players to using established ones, and he wanted to invent his own blacks as well. He was following the tradition of blackface minstrelsy, the first form (before movies) of American mass culture, which appropriated black masks for white actors. Minstrels mimed blacks, but the referent was not allowed to possess his representation. A few black troupes did appear after the Civil War, however. When one played Louisville, where young Griffith was living, a local reporter commented, "The success of the troupe goes to disprove the saying that a negro cannot act the nigger."[81]

---

78. Stern, *"Birth of a Nation,* Part I," 3–4; Gish, *Movies, Mr. Griffith, and Me,* 139; Kevin Brownlow, *The Parade's Gone By* (New York, 1968), 54.

79. NAACP, Boston Branch, "Fighting a Vicious Film" 1 (Boston, 1915), 19.

80. Stern, *"Birth of a Nation,* Part I," 5, 14; Griffith, in Geduld, *Focus on D. W. Griffith,* 41.

81. Robert Toll, *Blacking Up: The Minstrel Show in Nineteenth-Century America* (New York, 1974), 3–57, 202; Mackaye, *"The Birth of a Nation,"* 45–46.

Griffith allowed a few blacks to act the nigger. But he did not want to let the representation of blackness go. On the one hand, Gus, Lynch, and Lydia were so menacing that only whites could safely play them. The contrast of "black villainy and blond innocence"[82] when Lynch seized Elsie had to remain metaphorical. The conventions of representation (that this was only a scene in a movie) broke down in the face of blackness, since no black could be allowed to manhandle Lillian Gish. On the other hand, whites in blackface allowed Griffith to inhabit the fantasies he imposed on blacks, to keep those fantasies his own. Griffith represented blackness without having it take him over. But his fear of giving blacks autonomy traces his blacks back to him.

Disguise is not only the method of *Birth* but (with the racial opposition that it seems to undermine) the movie's major theme. Austin Stoneman's wig, which Elsie adjusts at the film's opening, is a sign of his hidden bad motives. It marks him as a hypocrite. The first page of Griffith's pamphlet attacking film censorship shows a dark, devilish figure putting on the mask of reform. Hiding under the disguise of virtue, "the malignant pygmy has matured into a caliban."[83] The contrast between a whiteness that protects the growth of blackness and a blackface that hides whiteness may appear unstable; blackface may seem to expose Griffith's resemblance to Stoneman, using "paint and powder" to deceive (as the later Griffith heroine, True Heart Susie, will refuse to do). The Little Colonel also employed disguise, however, masking his identity under Klan robes. On one level Griffith is contrasting masks of pretended with masks of genuine virtue, deception with regeneration, hypocrisy with masks of genuine virtue, deception with regeneration, hypocrisy with grace. He is celebrating the role of costume and ceremony in personal transformation. (Griffith once attributed his virtues to the fact that as an actor he had "impersonated" Lincoln.) But to celebrate impersonation does not oppose the Klansman to the white in blackface. It joins them together, for the movie puts both disguises to regenerative use. White sheets and black masks establish a fixed opposition that real bodies resist. Sheets and masks enable rebirth without the mediation of female sexuality. Klan robes dress the warrior band in drag. They break down individual difference without obliterating the male self in merger with the female body. The deeper opposite of the white in blackface, indeed, of the system of represented binary oppositions itself, is the white with black blood, the mulatto.[84]

"Its purpose was to bring order out of chaos," Dixon wrote of the Klan in *The Leopard's Spots*. "Henceforth there could be but one issue—are you a White Man or a Negro?" If order depended on distinguishing white from black, however,

---

82. Mackaye, *"The Birth of a Nation,"* 45–46.
83. D. W. Griffith, *The Rise and Fall of Free Speech in America* (Los Angeles, 1916), 1, 5.
84. Wagenknecht, *Movies in the Age of Innocence*, 78–79. The Sambo mask put on by blacks kept black feelings hidden from whites. Both blackface minstrelsy and Klan robes, as Gladys-Marie Fry pointed out, borrow the mask to use against its originators. See Fry, *Night Riders*, 6. For seeing the Klan as men in drag, I am indebted to Uli Knopfelmacher.

Dixon's very next words threatened chaos. "There was but one question to be settled: 'Shall the future American be an Anglo-Saxon or a Mulatto?'" In shifting from black to mulatto Dixon acknowledged the mixture he was trying to prevent. He reestablished the boundary by making mulattoes into blacks: "One drop of Negro blood makes a Negro. It kinks the hair, flattens the nose, thickens the lip, puts out the light of intellect, and lights the fire of brutal passions. The beginning of Negro equality as a vital fact is the beginning of the end of this nation's life. There is enough negro blood here to make mulatto the whole Republic."[85]

The spread of blackness through interracial sex (Ike McCaslin's nightmare at the end of *Go Down Moses*) was one form of national rebirth; blackface was its alternative. Mulattoes with "black blood" were stuck in their blackness. Dressed in blackface (or watching others so dressed), whites played with blackness as part of their self-fashioning. Griffith took an interest in clothes as a young man, he later wrote, because he could not change his body.[86] Griffith discovered in *Birth* that changing clothes allowed him to leave the body behind.

Griffith wanted to assume negative identities if he could discard them, but he also required stable nurture and recognition from others. Self-abnegating blacks and women like the hero of *Trust* and the heroine of *True Heart Susie* supplied, in Erikson's terms, basic trust. The dependence on blacks and women, in Griffith's depiction, allowed white men to be free. But that dependence also rooted the mobile, self-making identity in its opposite. Boundary division was built on boundary breakdown, selfhood in one on its absence in the other. Griffith, who needed both dependence and autonomy, feared that the one wiped out the other; he sacrificed the autonomy of women and blacks. But the wish for basic trust that obliterates the autonomy of the other brings with it anxiety over vengeance. Given the primitive sources of the need for basic trust in infantile dependence and attachment, the women and blacks from whom support was demanded became repositories for the panic against which trust defends, of violence, loss, and mobile desire.

Blackface played with boundary breakdown, retaining control over it, and Griffith returned to blackface in the 1920s. He planned to star Al Jolson in a film called *Black and White*. Jolson would play a detective who puts on blackface to investigate a crime and saves a falsely accused man from being executed. Since both the suspect and the detective are innocent underneath their guilty appearances, *Black and White* took as its explicit theme the difference between blackface and blackness. When Jolson backed out of the movie, another actor and another director in Griffith's company made it. A few years later Jolson starred in the first talkie. Like *Black and White,* it moved blackface from method to subject. Blackface frees the character Jolson plays in *The Jazz Singer* from his inherited, Jewish immigrant identity. Jolson becomes a jazz

---

85. Dixon, *Leopard's Spots,* 152, 161, 244.
86. Hart, *Man Who Invented Hollywood,* 33.

singer over his father's objections; "Mammy," sung in blackface after he has become a star, expresses his gratitude to his mother. But self-consciousness about the method undercut blackface. *The Jazz Singer*'s homage to the technique that had founded American mass entertainment, first in minstrelsy and then (through *Birth*) in movies, brought blackface to an end.[87]

The Jazz Singer did not do away, however, with the principle for which black-face stands; it rather exhausted blackface as a way of standing for that principle. Blackface was a synechdoche for the freedom provided by representation. It pointed to Griffith's effort, thematized by white sheets in *Birth*'s plot and by blackface in its production, to replace history by image.

VI

The emphasis on impersonation may seem to contradict Griffith's belief in the historical accuracy of film. The director went to enormous trouble to reconstruct historical vignettes accurately in *Birth,* for he wanted to acquire the aura of history for film. The actors on stage at his Ford's Theater read the play that was performed the night Lincoln was shot; Griffith shot Booth shooting Lincoln at the same moment in the play. Critics praised the historical accuracy of *Birth.* The vice crusader Charles Parkhurst, who had tried to close the New York nickelodeons, insisted, "A boy can learn more pure history and get more atmosphere of the period by sitting down three hours before the films that Griffith has produced with such artistic skill than by weeks or months of study in the classroom."[88]

Griffith agreed. He imagined that in the public library of the future, instead of reading about history and "ending bewildered without a clear idea of exactly what did happen, and confused at every point by conflicting interpretations . . . you will merely . . . press the button and actually see what happened. There will be no opinions expressed. You will merely be present at the making of history."[89]

Accuracy, however, required impersonation. Joseph Henabery was not Lincoln any more than he was black. Henabery impersonated Lincoln by getting as close to the details of his beard, posture, and clothing as he could. Historical authenticity entailed disguise. Griffith and Dixon offered to pay ten thousand dollars to Moorfield Storey, president of the NAACP, if he found a single historical in-accuracy in *Birth.* The pretense may seem absurd; Thaddeus Stevens, for starters, had no children. But Ralph Lewis played Stoneman, not Stevens. He impersonated a

87. Schickel, *Griffith,* 483; Bogle, *Toms, Coons, Mulattoes,* 26; May, *Screening Out the Past,* 218. On dependence and autonomy see Hanna Fenichel Pitkin, *Fortune Is a Woman: Gender and Politics in the Thought of Niccolo Machiavelli* (Berkeley and Los Angeles, 1984).
88. Williams, *Griffith,* 62; May, *Screening Out the Past,* 61.
89. D. W. Griffith, "Five-Dollar 'Movies' Prophesied," *The Editor,* 24 April 1915, in Geduld, *Focus on D. W. Griffith,* 25.

historical type just as (in Vachel Lindsay's account of the gathering of the Klan) "the white leader, Colonel Ben Cameron (impersonated by Henry B. Walthall) enters not as an individual, but as representing the white Anglo-Saxon Niagara."[90]

When Storey asked Griffith what mulatto lieutenant governor had bound and gagged a young white woman to force marriage on her, Griffith avoided answering and tried to shake Storey's hand. Storey refused. By imitating the Little Colonel, who had refused (to Atlanta audience cheers) to shake Lynch's hand, Storey had gotten Griffith to play the lieutenant governor. But even if Griffith found himself on the wrong side of that reenactment, it testified to film's power. *Birth* used impersonation in the service of a vision that by tapping collective fantasies created a conviction of truth beyond history. Contingencies and conflicting interpretations constitute history. Griffith's aim was to abolish interpretation; that project made representation not an avenue to history but its replacement.[91]

Griffith claimed to be filming history in *Birth,* just as he said he was filming his father, but he also claimed to be bringing a new history into being. "We've gone beyond Babel, beyond words," he said in 1914. "We've found a universal language—a power that can make men brothers and end war forever."[92] That preverbal universal language did not simply create a historical eschatology, a move from the traditional to the sacred. It replaced history by film. Presented as a transparent representation of history (more transparent than language could ever be), movies actually aimed to emancipate the representation from its referent and draw the viewer out of history into film.

Movie images seen from afar allowed audiences to keep their distance, to be voyeurs instead of participants. But that protection, as in dreams, broke down defenses and opened a road to the unconscious. The size of the image and its reproducibility, the closeup and film cut, the magical transformations on-screen and film's documentary pretense—all these, Griffith sensed, dissolved the boundaries that separated audiences in darkened theaters from the screen. The silent-film epic, moreover, accentuated movies' visionary aura. "Words, after all, are a clumsy method of conveying thought. They close expression in so many ways," said Griffith. *Birth* used titles, to be sure, but it stood closer to music than to words. Not only were its filmic rhythms musical, but Griffith also used an orchestra to reinforce the beats and themes on screen. To watch and hear *Birth* as it was originally shown was to enter an immediate, prelogical universe of the primary processes.[93]

90. Brownlow, *Parade's Gone,* 50–53; Schickel, *Griffith,* 294; Lindsay, *Art of the Moving Picture,* 74.
91. Schickel, *Griffith,* 294; *New York Sun,* 4 March 1915, in Geduld, *Focus on D. W. Griffith,* 86. Cf. Catherine Gallagher, "The Politics of Culture and the Debate over Representation," *Representations* 5 (Winter 1984): 115–147.
92. May, *Screening Out the Past,* 60.
93. Schickel, *Griffith,* 290; Stern, *"Birth of a Nation,* Part I," 103–118.

Griffith founded a preverbal art. It pulled viewers back to the condition, before language, of illusory unity with the originary source of being. Film, in Griffith's imagination, evoked and made itself the substitute for an ominous, preverbal, maternal power. *Birth* replaced birth.

"I have even heard it said that if it hadn't been for the transfusion of your blood into it the motion picture would have died," a reporter commented to Griffith after *Birth* opened. "I believe in the motion picture not only as a means of amusement, but as a moral and educational force," Griffith replied. "Man is a moving animal. It isn't so with woman. Their natures are different." Griffith was describing women as the victims of male mobility, victims whom the movie would rescue. "Do you know that there has been less drinking in the past five years, and that it is because of motion pictures?" asked Griffith. Men who once frequented the saloon went to the motion picture theater. Because they watched movement on the screen instead of moving themselves, Griffith concluded, "the domestic unities are preserved." Movies preserved traditional values by replacing modern life, by moving for modern men.[94]

The motion picture protected women from men, Griffith claimed. But in response to the reporter's metaphor, which broke down the boundary between body and film, he invoked the stereotypical gender division. Griffith's blood transfusion protected women by appropriating them. *Birth* transubstantiated Griffith's blood into celluloid so that he and his audiences could live inside film.

As film replaced the female body, it also ingested history. Plays, explained Griffith, were "the art of interpretation glorified." Movies were superior to plays because playgoers were aware of the artificial, representational effects. "Concealment [was] one of the rarest attributes of true art," wrote Griffith, and silent film concealed "the brain behind this art" as words could never do. Griffith's distinction went beyond the interpretation that points to itself and the one that, rendering itself invisible, "impersonates" reality. Silent film, like the "hand of God," lifted people from their "commonplace existence" into a "sphere of poetic simulations." It did not render reality. It was the Real. To be "present at the making of history" was to be present at the viewing of film.[95]

VII

The Birth of a Nation, by appropriating history, itself became a historical force. It not only showed millions of viewers how to see and enact domestic conflicts but also pointed toward the Great War. But Griffith's reentry into history through American entry into World War I initiated the process by which he fell out of film.

94. *New York American,* 28 February 1915, in Geduld, *Focus on D. W. Griffith,* 28–29.
95. D. W. Griffith, "The Future of the Two-Dollar Movie," in Silva, *Focus on "The Birth of a Nation,"* 100; Schickel, *Griffith,* 301; Brownlow, *Parade's Gone,* 628–629; May, *Screening Out the Past,* 73.

Birth, like Wilson, claimed to be against war. "Dare we dream of a day when bestial war shall rule no more?" asks the penultimate title, and a bestial war god (of the sort Africans worshipped) is succeeded on the screen by a white-robed Christ. But the white Knights of Christ who erased the Civil War were not pacifists. Like America in World War I, they were fighting a war to end war.

Karl Brown, the assistant cameraman on *Birth* and *Intolerance,* also connected Griffith's movies to American entry into World War I. He wrote, "Here was *his* story, the story he had used so effectively time and time again, played right before his eyes: his famous run to the rescue. Only this time it was not a handful of desperate people but a typical Griffith production on the most gigantic scale: all Europe under the iron heel of a monstrous enemy, with the rescue now coming from the massed might of America."[96]

That was Wilson's vision as well. Griffith put on the screen Wilson's "ghostly visitors," whose "invisible Empire" saved a nation. Now, [. . .] Wilson borrowed Griffith's images to celebrate the Americans who rescued Europe. "What we had to have," wrote George Creel, who headed Wilson's Committee on Public Information, "was no mere surface unity, but a passionate belief in the justice of the American cause that would weld the people of the United States into one white hot mass instinct with fraternity, devotion, courage, and deathless determination." "Those dear ghosts that still deploy upon the fields of France"—as Wilson evoked them after the Armistice—were the ghosts of Griffith's Klan.[97]

Dixon and Griffith also saw the connection between *The Birth of a Nation* and World War I. Dixon agitated in print and film for American entry into the war; he called his novel and movie *The Fall of a Nation.* "What we film tomorrow will strike the hearts of the world," Griffith had declared in 1914, "and end war forever." After *Intolerance* (1916), Griffith began *Hearts of the World* to bring America into the war to end war. Griffith began *Hearts* at Lloyd George's urging, to create sympathy for the Allied cause. He reported to Wilson during the production of the film and screened it at the White House.[98]

Hearts (1918) was the most popular war movie of its time, but the cross-purposes at work in the film fatally compromised it. On the one hand, *Hearts* was a remake of *Birth.* It contained, observed William Everson, "the same family structure, the same separations and reunions, the same editing patterns." A romance is set against the background of war, in which Germany and France replace the North and the South. George Siegmann plays the German officer von Strohm

96. Brown, *Adventures with Griffith,* 177–178.
97. Michael O'Malley, "With a Thousand Eyes: Movies and the American Public, 1908–1918" (Unpublished seminar paper, Berkeley, Cal., 1985), 20. O'Malley quote is from George Creel, *How We Advertised America* (New York, 1920), xv, 5.
98. Davenport, "Dixon's Mythology," 341; Cook, *Fire from the Flint,* 184–185; May, *Screening Out the Past,* 60; Merritt, "Griffith Directs the Great War," 47–57.

instead of the mulatto lieutenant governor Silas Lynch; once again he chases, seizes, and mauls Lillian Gish. Scenes of German officers ravishing French girls, omitted from the film when it played after the Armistice, parallel the scenes of black sexual violence censored from *Birth*. Tramping Americans coming to rescue Europe fill the screen in the film's final image. They reincarnate the ride of the Klan. Griffith dedicated *Hearts* to President Wilson.[99]

Hearts could not simply repeat *Birth*, however, for the Germans had to stand simultaneously for the North of Part One and the blacks of Part Two. If American entry were to save Europe from World War I, then the American ride to the rescue would transform the Great War as American Civil War (*The Birth of a Nation*, Part One) into the Great War as Klan triumph (*Birth of a Nation*, Part Two). But had *Hearts* simply repeated Part One, it would have had to merge the Germans with the French. That would not justify an American ride to the rescue, so Griffith had to collapse Part One into Part Two. *Birth* made equivalent the two sides in the Civil War; *Hearts* distinguished the noble French from the bestial Germans. Neither of the two lovers in *Hearts* could be German, so their rescue could not reunite Europe. The French troops are sufficiently dirtied by the war, moreover, to fail to rise to the role of the Klan. Although they also ride to rescue Lillian Gish, they are too disorganized and battle-weary to replicate the Klan's transcendent order. Their ride to the rescue substitutes interminable length for visionary power.

Bobby Harron, who plays the Henry Walthall role, does not lead the ride to rescue Gish. Trapped together in the familiarly claustrophobic room (after she, not he, stabs a German soldier), Gish and Harron are both menaced by George Siegmann as von Strohm. They make a suicide pact in case the Germans break down the door. Griffith succumbed to more than propaganda exigencies when he merged Harron and Gish as victims. *Hearts* marks Griffith's fall into masochistic nostalgia.

Although that shift in Griffith's movies derived in part from his private history, his confidence, like that of Euro-American culture as a whole, was also shattered by World War I. In order to film a war that distinguished the French from the Germans, Griffith had to avoid the greater horrors of trench warfare, even in scenes where *Hearts* imitated *Birth*'s Civil War battles. Generally Griffith's battle scenes lacked the nonjudgmental implacability that marked his refusal to take sides in *Birth*. In personalizing the conflict and in showing troop breakthroughs, Griffith made meaning where no meaning resided. The war Griffith directed, said Richard Schickel, with its sweeping movements and decisive victories, was the war that generals on both sides were fantasizing. It was not the soldier's war.[100]

Griffith sensed the inadequacy of *Hearts* as a depiction of World War I. "Viewed as a drama," he said, "the war is in some ways disappointing. . . . I found

99. Schickel, *Griffith*, 353; May, *Screening Out the Past*, 92.
100. Schickel, *Griffith*, 353–354; Merritt, "Griffith Directs the Great War," 51, 58–59.

myself saying . . . Why this is old stuff. I have put that stuff on myself so many times." Griffith's feeling that he had already staged World War I did not empower him, however. Instead it opened a gap between theatricality and the void underneath. "A modern war is neither romantic nor picturesque," Griffith continued. "Everyone is hidden away in ditches. As you look out across No Man's Land there is literally nothing that meets the eye but an aching desolation of nothingness. . . . It is too colossal to be dramatic. No one can describe it. You might as well describe the ocean or the Milky Way." Faced with world war, Griffith could not give dramatic form to the forces of history. Instead of appropriating reality, theater pointed to an emptiness it could not express. Europeans, Griffith explained, "become great actors. They talk and laugh and act much like the people over here, but it is acting, for the Great Fear is over everybody and everything." "After the war is over," as Griffith put it in another interview, "the farmer boy['s] . . . saber may flash as of old, but it will never be the same. Under the shining armor he will in imagination feel the crawling vermin of the trenches." Because Griffith sensed the failure of his filmed war to overcome the real one, *Hearts* lacks *Birth's* conviction.[101]

Woodrow Wilson presided over a Red Scare during and after World War I in which thousands of Americans were jailed or deported. As if he wanted to avert his eyes from the persecution his nationalism had unleashed, Wilson condemned *Hearts* for stirring up hatred by its depiction of German bestiality. *Birth* forged a bond between the President and the filmmaker; *Hearts* severed it.[102]

The League of Nations would have redeemed the horrors of war for Wilson and protected him from its actual character. But Wilson collapsed in the struggle for the league. His new wife ran the White House for months after the President was incapacitated, and although Wilson lived out his life for four more years, he was out of touch with postwar America. A culture of consumption at odds with Wilson's messianic dreams flourished in life and on film. But the Progressive vision that Wilson and Griffith shared also had its legacy—100 percent Americanism and a revived Ku Klux Klan. The new Klan, organized in 1915 in response to *Birth*'s popularity, screened the movie in the 1920s to help build a membership in the millions. But the new Klan's targets, immigrant Catholics and Jews rather than blacks, signaled the disintegration of the Progressives' melting-pot dream. Wilson's son-in-law, William G. McAdoo (he had presided over the segregation of the Treasury Department during Wilson's presidency and then become general counsel for Griffith's company, United Artists), received Klan

101. Schickel, *Griffith,* 354–355; Henry C. Carr, "Griffith, Maker of Battle Scenes, Sees Real War," *Photoplay* 13 (March 1918): 23; "War, Shorn of Romance, Is Sounding Its Own Knell," *Current Opinion* 64 (April 1918): 258. (I am indebted to Michael O'Malley for this reference.)
102. Merritt, "Griffith Directs the Great War," 57.

support and a plurality of delegate votes for more than fifty ballots at the 1924 Democratic presidential nominating convention.[103]

Dixon attacked Bolshevism and the New Woman in his novels of the 1920s and 1930s; he also attacked the revived Klan, since it was anti-Catholic rather than anti-Negro. In Dixon's final novel, *The Flaming Sword* (1939), Negro Communists take over America. Dixon shared the fantasy of that danger with Martin Dies's House Un-American Activities Committee, with Mississippi's representatives Theodore Bilbo and John Rankin. But Dixon's obsessions had lost their national resonance. Although he saw *The Flaming Sword* as a sequel to *The Birth of a Nation,* it was a commercial failure.[104]

Griffith, like Wilson and Dixon, never recovered from World War I. "Are we not making the world safe for democracy, American Democracy, through motion pictures?" he asked.[105] But his own contribution to that project was coming to an end. Griffith continued to make significant movies after *Hearts,* but they lacked either the power of *Birth* and *Intolerance* or the freshness of the Biograph one-reelers. Retreating to an elegiac mode of pastoralism and tradition, Griffith embraced an aesthetic of victimization. His films did not celebrate patriarchy, but they were paralyzed by their failure to challenge it. In *Broken Blossoms* (1919) Lillian Gish plays a daughter whose father (Donald Crisp) beats her to death. In *True Heart Susie* (1919) Gish plays a virtuous country girl whose self-abnegation finally wins back her wayward childhood sweetheart. In *Way Down East* (1919) Gish is seduced and abandoned, loses her baby, and, cast out in a snowstorm, nearly drowns in an icy river. And in *Orphans of the Storm* (1924) Gish's head is beneath the guillotine for the prolonged climax of the movie. The guillotine is known as the black widow, recalling Judith; it is as if, in his last successful film, Griffith was finally taking back *Judith* by reversing the sexual politics of decapitation.

Audiences flocked to Griffith's movies for a few years after the war, until his financial difficulties cost him first his artistic independence and then his ability to make films. These troubles were not caused, Richard Schickel has recently shown, by production costs or box office failures. Griffith sabotaged himself with the enormous expense of building and operating his studio-estate in Mamaroneck, New York. There was no compelling artistic reason for that studio. But Griffith wanted a plantation, a patriarchal pastoral retreat. This flight from modernity, onscreen and off, could not sustain the filmmaker. Griffith had credited movies with reducing the consumption of liquor when he made *Birth.* As his movies declined in the 1920s, his drinking increased. His final film, *The Struggle* (1931),

103. G. Charles Neimeyer, "David Wark Griffith: In Retrospect, 1965," in Geduld, *Focus on D. W. Griffith,* 129; Stern, *"Birth of a Nation,* Part I," 67, 79–80; Link, *Wilson,* 246–247; Schickel, *Griffith,* 400–403.
104. Bloomfield, *The Leopard's Spots,* 395–396; Cook, *Fire from the Flint,* 196, 216–223.
105. May, *Screening Out the Past,* 60–61.

began as an attack on Prohibition. But the fall of Griffith's alcoholic protagonist turned the movie into an exposé of drink. When audiences and reviewers laughed at the film's excesses, Griffith retired to his hotel room and drank for weeks. He never made another movie.[106]

Interviewed on film for the sound rerelease of *Birth* in 1930, Griffith recalled the stories of his father's heroic suffering during the Civil War and of his mother's sewing Klan robes afterward. When Walter Huston asked him whether the history recounted in *Birth* was true, Griffith replied, "You can't hear" such stories "and not feel it is true. . . . I think it's true, but as Pontius Pilate asked, 'What is Truth?'" Losing confidence in film's ability to transubstantiate childhood screen memories into reality, Griffith was sensing the violence of *Birth*'s project and identifying not with the white-robed Knights of Christ but with Christ's crucifier.[107]

Griffith lived sixteen more years after *The Struggle;* he was neither poverty-stricken nor friendless during most of that time. But two episodes, one at the beginning of his forced retirement and the other at the end, exhibit the consequences for Griffith of falling out of film. In 1932 an English producer invited him to direct a remake of *Broken Blossoms.* To convince the producer to replace the actress he had chosen for the Gish role with one Griffith preferred, as Gish had once replaced Blanche Sweet, Griffith himself played the scene in which Battling Burrows beats his daughter. He seemed to lose control and actually become Battling Burrows, and the terrified producer had to pull him off the girl. That night a drunken Griffith called Gish in New York and pleaded with her to come to England and rescue him.[108]

Fifteen years later a reporter who wanted to interview Griffith convinced a young woman (who had never heard of the once-legendary director) to call him on the phone. Griffith invited her to his hotel room, and although he tried to shut the door behind her, the reporter forced his way in. Griffith lunged for the girl a few times in front of the reporter, just as Siegmann ("drunk with wine and power") went after Gish in *Birth*'s forced marriage scene. After she eluded him, Griffith refilled his glass and answered the reporter's questions.[109]

No longer able to direct Donald Crisp and George Siegmann, Griffith was playing them. Six months later his body, weakened by drink like his father's, ruptured from within like his father's. Stripped of the shroud that had memorialized a mythic patriarch, Griffith had entered his father's dead body.

106. Schickel, *Griffith,* 416–419, 560–564.
107. Silva, *Focus on "The Birth of a Nation,"* 9.
108. Henderson, *Griffith,* 280–284.
109. Ezra Goodman, *The Fifty-Year Decline and Fall of Hollywood* (New York, 1961), 4–5.

Filmography and Bibliography

Griffith Filmography, 1908–1931

The most complete listing of Griffith's Biograph work is to be found in the appendices to Robert M. Henderson's *D. W. Griffith: The Years at Biograph* and in *D. W. Griffith and the Biograph Company* by Cooper C. Graham, Steven Higgins, Elaine Mancini, and João Luis Vieira (Metuchen, N.J.: Scarecrow, 1985). Richard Schickel provides useful, brief annotations to his checklist of Griffith's Biograph films in *D. W. Griffith: An American Life*. Full filmographies of Griffith's feature films are included in Iris Barry and Eileen Bowser's *D. W. Griffith: American Film Master* and in Edward Wagenknecht and Anthony Slide's *The Films of D. W. Griffith*. Biograph films are listed below under the year of their production, while the longer films (from 1914 onwards) are listed under the year of their release.

1908 *The Adventures of Dollie*
The Redman and the Child
The Tavern Keeper's Daughter
A Calamitous Elopement
The Greaser's Gauntlet
The Man and the Woman
For Love of Gold
The Fatal Hour
For a Wife's Honor
Balked at the Altar
The Girl and the Outlaw
The Red Girl
Betrayed by a Hand Print
Monday Morning in a Coney Island Police Court
Behind the Scenes
The Heart of O'yama
Where the Breakers Roar

The Stolen Jewels
A Smoked Husband
The Zulu's Heart
The Vaquero's Vow
Father Gets in the Game
The Barbarian, Ingomar
The Planter's Wife
The Devil
The Romance of a Jewess
The Call of the Wild
After Many Years
Mr. Jones at the Ball
Concealing a Burglar
The Taming of the Shrew
The Ingrate
A Woman's Way
The Pirate's Gold
The Guerilla

The Curtain Pole
The Song of the Shirt
The Clubman and the Tramp
Money Mad
Mrs. Jones Entertains
The Feud and the Turkey
The Test of Friendship
The Reckoning
One Touch of Nature
An Awful Moment
The Helping Hand
The Maniac Cook
The Christmas Burglars
A Wreath in Time
The Honor of Thieves
The Criminal Hypnotist
The Sacrifice
The Welcome Burglar
A Rural Elopement
Mrs. Jones Has a Card Party
The Hindoo Dagger
The Salvation Army Lass
Love Finds a Way
Tragic Love
The Girls and Daddy

1909   *Those Boys*
The Cord of Life
Trying to Get Arrested
The Fascinating Mrs. Frances
Those Awful Hats
Jones and the Lady Book Agent
The Drive for Life
The Brahma Diamond
The Politician's Love Story
The Joneses Have Amateur Theatricals
Edgar Allan Poe
The Roué's Heart
His Wife's Mother
The Golden Louis
His Ward's Love
At the Altar
The Prussian Spy

The Medicine Bottle
The Deception
The Lure of the Gown
Lady Helen's Escapade
A Fool's Revenge
The Wooden Leg
I Did It, Mama
A Burglar's Mistake
The Voice of the Violin
And a Little Child Shall Lead Them
The French Duel
Jones and His New Neighbors
A Drunkard's Reformation
The Winning Coat
A Rude Hostess
The Road to the Heart
The Eavesdropper
Schneider's Anti-Noise Crusade
Twin Brothers
Confidence
The Note in the Shoe
Lucky Jim
A Sound Sleeper
A Troublesome Satchel
'Tis an Ill Wind That Blows No Good
The Suicide Club
Resurrection
One Busy Hour
A Baby's Shoe
Eloping with Auntie
The Cricket on the Hearth
The Jilt
Eradicating Auntie
What Drink Did
Her First Biscuits
The Violin Maker of Cremona
Two Memories
The Lonely Villa
The Peach Basket Hat
The Son's Return
His Duty
A New Trick
The Necklace

The Way of Man
The Faded Lilies
The Message
The Friend of the Family
Was Justice Served?
Mrs. Jones' Lover, or I Want My Hat!
The Mexican Sweethearts
The Country Doctor
Jealousy and the Man
The Renunciation
The Cardinal's Conspiracy
The Seventh Day
Tender Hearts
A Convict's Sacrifice
A Strange Meeting
Sweet and Twenty
The Slave
They Would Elope
Mr. Jones' Burglar
The Mended Lute
The Indian Runner's Romance
With Her Card
The Better Way
His Wife's Visitor
The Mills of the Gods
Pranks
Oh, Uncle
The Sealed Room
1766, or The Hessian Renegades
The Little Darling
In Old Kentucky
The Children's Friend
Comata, the Sioux
Getting Even
The Broken Locket
A Fair Exchange
The Awakening
Pippa Passes
Leather Stockings
Fools of Fate
Wanted, a Child
The Little Teacher
A Change of Heart

His Lost Love
Lines of White on the Sullen Sea
The Gibson Goddess
In the Watches of the Night
The Expiation
What's Your Hurry
The Restoration
Nursing a Viper
Two Women and a Man
The Light That Came
A Midnight Adventure
The Open Gate
Sweet Revenge
The Mountaineer's Honor
In the Window Recess
The Trick That Failed
The Death Disc
Through the Breakers
In a Hempen Bag
A Corner in Wheat
The Redman's View
The Test
A Trap for Santa Claus
In Little Italy
To Save Her Soul
Choosing a Husband
The Rocky Road
The Dancing Girl of Butte
Her Terrible Ordeal
The Call
The Honor of His Family
On the Reef
The Last Deal
One Night and Then—
The Cloister's Touch
The Woman from Mellon's
The Duke's Plan
The Englishman and the Girl

1910   The Final Settlement
His Last Burglary
Taming a Husband
The Newlyweds

The Thread of Destiny
In Old California
The Man
The Converts
Faithful
The Twisted Trail
Gold Is Not All
As It Is in Life
A Rich Revenge
A Romance of the Western Hills
Thou Shalt Not
The Way of the World
The Unchanging Sea
The Gold Seekers
Love Among the Roses
The Two Brothers
Unexpected Help
An Affair of Hearts
Ramona
Over Silent Paths
The Implement
In the Season of Buds
A Child of the Ghetto
In the Border States
A Victim of Jealousy
The Face at the Window
The Marked Time-Table
A Child's Impulse
Muggsy's First Sweetheart
The Purgation
A Midnight Cupid
What the Daisy Said
A Child's Faith
The Call to Arms
Serious Sixteen
A Flash of Light
As the Bells Rang Out
An Arcadian Maid
The House with the Closed Shutters
Her Father's Pride
A Salutory Lesson
The Usurer
The Sorrows of the Unfaithful

In Life's Cycle
Wilful Peggy
A Summer Idyll
The Modern Prodigal
Rose o' Salem Town
Little Angels of Luck
A Mohawk's Way
The Oath and the Man
The Iconoclast
Examination Day at School
That Chink at Golden Gulch
The Broken Doll
The Banker's Daughters
The Message of the Violin
Two Little Waifs
Waiter No. 5
The Fugitive
Simple Charity
The Song of the Wildwood Flute
A Child's Stratagem
Sunshine Sue
A Plain Song
His Sister-in-Law
The Golden Supper
The Lesson
When a Man Loves
Winning Back His Love
His Trust
His Trust Fulfilled
A Wreath of Orange Blossoms
The Italian Barber
The Two Paths
Conscience
Three Sisters
A Decree of Destiny
Fate's Turning
What Shall We Do with Our Old?
The Diamond Star
The Lily of the Tenements
Heart Beats of Long Ago

1911   *Fisher Folks*
His Daughter

The Lonedale Operator
Was He a Coward?
Teaching Dad to Like Her
The Spanish Gypsy
The Broken Cross
The Chief's Daughter
A Knight of the Road
Madame Rex
His Mother's Scarf
How She Triumphed
In the Days of '49
The Two Sides
The New Dress
Enoch Arden, Part I
Enoch Arden, Part II
The White Rose of the Wilds
The Crooked Road
A Romany Tragedy
A Smile of a Child
The Primal Call
The Jealous Husband
The Indian Brothers
The Thief and the Girl
Her Sacrifice
The Blind Princess and the Poet
Fighting Blood
The Last Drop of Water
Robby the Coward
A Country Cupid
The Ruling Passion
The Rose of Kentucky
The Sorrowful Example
Swords and Hearts
The Stuff Heroes Are Made Of
The Old Confectioner's Mistake
The Unveiling
The Eternal Mother
Dan the Dandy
The Revenue Man and the Girl
The Squaw's Love
Italian Blood
The Making of a Man
Her Awakening

The Adventures of Billy
The Long Road
The Battle
Love in the Hills
The Trail of the Books
Through Darkened Vales
Saved from Himself
A Woman Scorned
The Miser's Heart
The Failure
Sunshine Through the Dark
As in a Looking Glass
A Terrible Discovery
A Tale of the Wilderness
The Voice of the Child
The Baby and the Stork
The Old Bookkeeper
A Sister's Love
For His Son
The Transformation of Mike
A Blot on the 'Scutcheon
Billy's Stratagem
The Sunbeam
A String of Pearls
The Root of Evil

1912   *The Mender of the Nets*
Under Burning Skies
A Siren of Impulse
Iola's Promise
The Goddess of Sagebrush Gulch
The Girl and Her Trust
The Punishment
Fate's Interception
The Female of the Species
Just Like a Woman
One Is Business, the Other Crime
The Lesser Evil
The Old Actor
A Lodging for the Night
His Lesson
When Kings Were the Law
A Beast at Bay

An Outcast Among Outcasts
Home Folks
A Temporary Truce
The Spirit Awakened
Lena and the Geese
An Indian Summer
The Schoolteacher and the Waif
Man's Lust for Gold
Man's Genesis
Heaven Avenges
A Pueblo Legend
The Sands of Dee
Black Sheep
The Narrow Road
A Child's Remorse
The Inner Circle
A Change of Spirit
An Unseen Enemy
Two Daughters of Eve
Friends
So Near, Yet So Far
A Feud in the Kentucky Hills
In the Aisles of the Wild
The One She Loved
The Painted Lady
The Musketeers of Pig Alley
Heredity
Gold and Glitter
My Baby
The Informer
The Unwelcome Guest
Pirate Gold
Brutality
The New York Hat
The Massacre
My Hero
Oil and Water
The Burglar's Dilemma
A Cry for Help
The God Within
Three Friends
The Telephone Girl and the Lady
Fate

An Adventure in the Autumn Woods
A Chance Deception
The Tender-Hearted Boy
A Misappropriated Turkey
Brothers
Drink's Lure
Love in an Apartment Hotel

1913   *Broken Ways*
A Girl's Stratagem
Near to Earth
A Welcome Intruder
The Sheriff's Baby
The Hero of Little Italy
The Perfidy of Mary
A Misunderstood Boy
The Little Tease
The Lady and the Mouse
The Wanderer
The House of Darkness
Olaf—An Atom
Just Gold
His Mother's Son
The Yaqui Cur
The Ranchero's Revenge
A Timely Interception
Death's Marathon
The Sorrowful Shore
The Mistake
The Mothering Heart
Her Mother's Oath
During the Round-up
The Coming of Angelo
The Indian's Loyalty
Two Men of the Desert
*The Reformers, or The Lost Art of
    Minding One's Business*
The Battle of Elderbush Gulch
Brute Force (also known as *Wars of
    the Primal Tribes*)
Judith of Bethulia

1914   *The Battle of the Sexes.* Scenario by Griffith, based on the novel by Daniel Carson Goodman.

The Escape. Scenario by Griffith, based on the play of the same title by Paul Armstrong.

Home, Sweet Home. Scenario by Griffith.

The Avenging Conscience. Scenario by Griffith, suggested by Edgar Allan Poe's "The Telltale Heart" and other works by Poe.

1915   *The Birth of a Nation.* Scenario by Griffith and Frank Woods, based on the novel and the play *The Clansman,* by Thomas Dixon, with additional material from Dixon's *The Leopard's Spots.*

1916   *Intolerance.* Scenario by Griffith.

1918   *Hearts of the World.* Scenario by Griffith, writing under two pseudonyms.

The Great Love. Scenario by Griffith and Stanner E. V. Taylor, under a pseudonym.

The Greatest Thing in Life. Scenario by Griffith and Stanner E. V. Taylor, under a pseudonym.

1919   *A Romance of Happy Valley.* Scenario by Griffith, under a pseudonym.

The Girl Who Stayed at Home. Scenario by Stanner E. V. Taylor.

Broken Blossoms. Scenario by Griffith, based on "The Chink and the Child," by Thomas Burke.

True Heart Susie. Scenario by Marion Fremont.

Scarlet Days. Scenario by Stanner E. V. Taylor.

The Greatest Question. Scenario by Stanner E. V. Taylor, based on a story by William Hale.

1920   *The Idol Dancer.* Scenario by Stanner E. V. Taylor, based on the story "Blood of the Covenanters," by Gordon Ray Young.

The Love Flower. Scenario by Griffith, based on the story "The Black Beach," by Ralph Stock.

Way Down East. Scenario by Anthony Paul Kelly and Griffith, based on the play by Lottie Blair Parker, Joseph R. Grismer, and William Brady.

1921   *Dream Street.* Scenario by Griffith, under a pseudonym, based on two stories, "Gina of the Chinatown" and "The Sign of the Lamp," by Thomas Burke.

Orphans of the Storm. Scenario by Griffith, under a pseudonym, based on the play *The Two Orphans,* by Adolph d'Ennery and Eugene Cormon.

1922   *One Exciting Night.* Scenario by Griffith, based on his own pseudonymous story.

1923   *The White Rose.* Scenario by Griffith under a pseudonym.

1924   *America.* Scenario by Robert W. Chambers, based in part on his novel *The Reckoning.*

Isn't Life Wonderful. Scenario by Griffith, based on the short story by Maj. Geoffrey Moss.

1925   *Sally of the Sawdust.* Scenario by Forrest Halsey, based on the musical play *Poppy,* by Dorothy Donnelly.

That Royle Girl. Scenario by Paul Schofield, based on the novel by Edwin Balmer.

1926   *The Sorrows of Satan.* Scenario by Forrest Halsey, adaptation by John Russell and George Hull, based on the novel by Marie Corelli.

1928   *Drums of Love.* Scenario by Gerrit J. Lloyd.

The Battle of the Sexes. Scenario by Gerrit J. Lloyd, based on the novel *The Single Standard,* by Daniel Carson Goodman.

1929   *Lady of the Pavements.* Scenario by Sam Taylor, based on a story by Karl Volmoeller.

1930   *Abraham Lincoln.* Screenplay by Stephen Vincent Benét and Gerrit J. Lloyd.

1931   *The Struggle.* Screenplay by Anita Loos and John Emerson.

Selected Bibliography

For citations of contemporary responses to *The Birth of a Nation*, see Janet Staiger, "*The Birth of a Nation:* Reconsidering Its Reception" (reprinted in this volume), note 18; for criticisms and defenses of the film through the 1930s, see note 30; and through the 1940s, see notes 39–43.

Agee, James. "David Wark Griffith." *The Nation,* September 4, 1948. Reprinted in *Agee on Film,* vol. 1. New York: Putnam, 1983.

Aitken, Roy E., as told to Al P. Nelson. *The Birth of a Nation Story.* Middleburg, Va.: William W. Denlinger, 1965.

Altman, Rick (guest editor). *Quarterly Review of Film Studies* 6, no. 1 (Winter 1981). Special Griffith issue.

Armour, Robert A. "History Written in Jagged Lightning: Realistic South vs. Romantic South in *The Birth of a Nation.*" In *The South and Film,* edited by Warren French. Jackson: University Press of Mississippi, 1981.

Arvidson, Linda (Mrs. D. W. Griffith). *When the Movies Were Young.* New York: E. P. Dutton, 1925. Reprint, Benjamin Blom, 1968; Dover paperback, 1969.

L'Avant-Scène du Cinéma 193/194 (October 1977). Special issue on *The Birth of a Nation.*

Baldwin, James. *The Devil Finds Work.* New York: The Dial Press, 1976.

Barry, Iris. *D. W. Griffith: American Film Master.* Revised by Eileen Bowser. New York: The Museum of Modern Art/Doubleday, 1965.

Belton, John. "Classical Style, Melodrama, and the Cinema of Excess: Griffith and Borzage." In *Cinema Stylists.* Metuchen, N.J.: The Scarecrow Press, 1983.

———. "*The Birth of a Nation.*" *Sight & Sound* 45, no. 2 (Spring 1976): 85–86.

Berquist, Goodwin, and James Greenwood. "Protest Against Racism: *The Birth of a Nation* in Ohio." *Journal of the University Film Association* 26, no. 3 (1974): 39–44.

Beylie, Claude. *"Naissance d' une Nation:* La Piste du géant." *Cinéma 71* 154 (March 1971): 135–138.

Bitzer, G. W. *Billy Bitzer: His Story.* New York: Farrar, Straus, Giroux, 1973.

Bravermann, Barnet. "David Wark Griffith: Creator of Film Form." *Theater Arts* 29 (April 1945): 240–250.

Brown, Karl. *Adventures with D. W. Griffith.* 2nd ed. New York: Da Capo Press, 1976.

Brownlow, Kevin. *The Parade's Gone By.* New York: Alfred A. Knopf, Inc., 1968.

Cadbury, William. "Theme, Felt Life, and the Last-Minute Rescue in Griffith after *Intolerance.*" *Film Quarterly* 28, no. 1 (1974): 39–49.

Calverton, V. F. "Cultural Barometer." *Current History* 49, no. 1 (September 1938): 45–47.

Carter, Everett. "Cultural History Written with Lightning: The Significance of *The Birth of a Nation.*" *American Quarterly* 12 (Fall 1960): 347–357. Reprinted in Silva, ed., *Focus on "Birth,"* 133–143.

Casty, Alan. "The Films of D. W. Griffith: A Style for the Times." *Journal of Popular Film* 1 (Spring 1972): 67–69.

Chandler, James. "The Historical Novel Goes to Hollywood: Scott, Griffith, and Film Epic Today." In *The Romantics and Us: Essays on Literature and Culture,* edited by Gene W. Ruoff. New Brunswick, N.J.: Rutgers University Press, 1990.

Cook, Raymond, A. "The Man Behind *The Birth of a Nation*" [on Thomas Dixon, Jr.]. *The North Carolina Historical Review* 29 (1962): 519–540.

Cooper, Miriam (with Bonnie Herndon). *Dark Lady of the Silents: My Life in Early Hollywood.* Indianapolis: Bobbs-Merrill, 1973.

———. "NAACP v. *The Birth of a Nation:* The Story of a 50-Year Fight." *The Crisis* 72, no. 2 (February 1965): 96.

Cripps, Thomas. "The Reaction of the Negro to the Motion Picture *Birth of a Nation.*" *The Historian* 25 (May 1963): 344–362.

———. "The Year of *The Birth of a Nation.*" In *Slow Fade to Black: The Negro in American Film, 1906– 1942.* New York: Oxford University Press, 1977.

Crowther, Bosley. *The Great Films: Fifty Golden Years of Motion Pictures.* New York: G. P. Putnam's Sons, 1967.

Cuniberti, John. *"The Birth of a Nation"*: A Formal Shot-by-Shot Analysis Together with Microfiche. Woodbridge, Conn.: Research Publications, 1979.

Dixon, Thomas, Jr. "The Story of the Ku Klux Klan." *The Metropolitan Magazine* 22 (September 1905): 657–669.

Dorr, John. "The Griffith Tradition." *Film Comment* 10 (March–April 1974): 48–54.

Eisenstein, Sergei. "Dickens, Griffith, and the Film Today." In *Film Form,* edited and translated by Jay Leyda. New York: Harcourt Brace, 1949.

Everson, William K. *American Silent Film.* New York: Oxford University Press, 1978.

———. "The Films of D. W. Griffith, 1907–1939." *Screen Facts* 3 (May– June 1963): 1–27.

————. "Griffith and Realism: A propos de *The Birth of a Nation*." *Cinemages* 5 (1955).

"The Film Artistry of D. W. Griffith and Billy Bitzer." *The American Cinematographer* 50, no. 1 (January 1969): 86–91, 148–153, 172–173.

Fleener, Nickie. "Answering Film with Film: The Hampton Epilogue, a Positive Alternative to the Negative Black Stereotypes Presented in *The Birth of a Nation*." *Journal of Popular Film and Television* 7, no. 4 (1980): 400–425.

Fleener-Marzec, Nickieann. *D. W. Griffith's "The Birth of a Nation": Controversy, Suppression, and the First Amendment as It Applies to Filmic Expression, 1915–1973*. New York: Arno Press, 1980.

Franklin, John Hope. "*Birth of a Nation*—Propaganda as History." *The Massachusetts Review* 20 (Autumn 1979): 417–434.

Geduld, Harry M., ed. *Focus on D. W. Griffith*. Englewood Cliffs, N.J.: Prentice-Hall, 1971.

Gish, Lillian, with Ann Pinchot. *Lillian Gish: The Movies, Mr. Griffith, and Me*. Englewood Cliffs, N.J.: Prentice-Hall, 1969.

Goodman, Paul, "Film Chronicle: Griffith and the Technical Innovations." *Partisan Review* 8, no. 3 (May–June 1941): 237–240.

Griffith, D. W. "*The Birth of a Nation*." *Sight and Sound* 16, no. 61 (Spring 1947): 32.

————. *The Man Who Invented Hollywood: The Autobiography of D. W. Griffith*. Louisville: Touchstone, 1972.

————. *The Rise and Fall of Free Speech in America*. Los Angeles: n.p., 1916.

Hackett, Francis. "Brotherly Love." *The New Republic*, March 20, 1915. Review of *The Birth of a Nation*. Reprinted in MacCann, *The First Film Makers*, 160–163.

Hansen, Miriam. "The Hieroglyph and the Whore: D. W. Griffith's *Intolerance*." *South Atlantic Quarterly* 88, no. 2 (Spring 1989): 361–392.

Henderson, Robert. *D. W. Griffith: His Life and Work*. New York: Oxford University Press, 1972.

Huff, Theodore. *A Shot Analysis of D. W. Griffith's "The Birth of a Nation."* New York: The Museum of Modern Art, 1961.

Hutchins, Charles L. "A Critical Evaluation of the Controversies Engendered by D. W. Griffith's *The Birth of a Nation*." Master's thesis, University of Iowa, 1961.

Inscoe, John C. "*The Clansman* on Stage and Screen: North Carolina Reacts." *The North Carolina Historical Review* 64, no. 2 (April 1987): 139–161.

Jacobs, Lewis. "D. W. Griffith: *The Birth of a Nation*." In *The Rise of the American Film: A Critical History*. New York: Teachers College Press, 1939.

Lang, Robert. "D. W. Griffith." In *American Film Melodrama: Griffith, Vidor, Minnelli*. Princeton, N.J.: Princeton University Press, 1989.

Lawson, John Howard. "Film as History—D. W. Griffith." In *Film: The Creative Process*. 2nd ed. New York: Hill & Wang, Inc., 1967.

Leab, Daniel J. *"The Birth of a Nation."* In *From Sambo to Superspade: The Black Experience in Motion Pictures.* Boston: Houghton Mifflin, 1975.

Leblanc, Gérard. "L'art de raconter et de persuader: *La naissance d'une nation." CinémAction* 54 (January 1990): 58–63.

Lennig, Arthur. *The Silent Voice: A Text.* Troy, N.Y.: Walter Snyder, 1969.

Leyda, Jay. "Film Chronicle: The Art and Death of D. W. Griffith." *The Sewanee Review* 57 (Fall 1949): 350–56. Reprinted in Geduld, *Focus on Griffith,* 161–167.

Lindsay, Vachel. "The Picture of Crowd Splendour." *The Art of the Moving Picture.* New York: The Macmillan Company, 1915. Reprint, New York: Liverwright, 1970.

MacCann, Richard Dyer, ed. *The First Film Makers.* Metuchen, N.J.: The Scarecrow Press, Inc., 1989.

Marks, Martin. "Joseph Carl Breil's Score for *The Birth of a Nation."* In "Film Music of the Silent Period, 1895–1924." Ph.D. dissertation, Harvard University, 1989.

Martin, Marcel. "Pas d'accord! De quoi broyer du noir." *Cinéma 71* 154 (March 1971): 139–140. [A response to *"Naissance d'une Nation:* La Piste du géant." See Beylie.]

May, Lary. "Apocalyptic Cinema: D. W. Griffith and the Aesthetics of Reform." In *Screening Out the Past: The Birth of Mass Culture and the Motion Picture Industry.* New York: Oxford University Press, 1980.

Merritt, Russell. "Dixon, Griffith, and the Southern Legend: A Cultural Analysis of *The Birth of a Nation." Cinema Journal* 12, no. 1 (Fall 1972): 26–45. Reprinted in *Cinema Examined,* edited by Richard Dyer MacCann and Jack C. Ellis. New York: E. P. Dutton, 1982.

———. "D. W. Griffith's *The Birth of a Nation:* Going After Little Sister." In *Close Viewings: An Anthology of New Film Criticism,* edited by Peter Lehman. Tallahassee: The Florida State University Press, 1990.

———. "The Impact of D. W. Griffith's Motion Pictures from 1908 to 1914 on Contemporary American Culture." Ph.D. dissertation, Harvard University, 1970.

Messel, Rudolph. "D. W. Griffith." In *This Film Business.* London: Ernest Benn, Ltd., 1928.

Meyer, Richard J. "The Films of David Wark Griffith: The Development of Themes and Techniques in Forty-two of His Films." *Film Comment* 4 (Fall–Winter 1967): 92–104.

Moore, Douglas Cameron. *A Study of the Influence of the Film, "The Birth of a Nation," on Attitudes of Selected High School White Students Toward Negroes.* Urbana, Ill., n.p., 1971.

Moore, John Hammond. "South Carolina's Reaction to the Photoplay *The Birth of a Nation." The Proceedings of the South Carolina Historical Association* (1963): 30–40.

Mottet, Jean. "D. W. Griffith: Des débuts à *The Birth of a Nation."* Doctorat de troisième cycle, Université Paul Valéry, Montpellier, 1974.

Mottet, Jean, ed. *D. W. Griffith: Colloque international.* Paris: Publications de la Sorbonne/Editions L'Harmattan, 1984.

Neale, Steve. "The Same Old Story: Stereotypes and Difference." *Screen Education* 32–33 (1979–80): 33–37.

———. *The Negro in Films* [1948]. New York: Arno Press, 1970.

Noble, Peter. "A Note on an Idol." *Sight and Sound* 15, no. 59 (Autumn 1946): 81–82.

O'Dell, Paul. *Griffith and the Rise of Hollywood.* New York: A. S. Barnes, 1970.

Oms, Marcel. *"La Naissance d'une Nation,* oeuvre maçonnique." *Les Cahiers de la Cinémathèque* 17 (Christmas 1975): 99–106.

———. "De quelques thèmes maçonnique dans l'oeuvre de D. W. Griffith." In Mottet, ed., *D. W. Griffith: Colloque international,* 221–229.

Petric, Vlada. "David Wark Griffith." In *Cinema: A Critical Dictionary,* edited by Richard Roud. New York: Viking, 1980.

Platt, David D. "The Negro in Hollywood." *Daily Worker,* February 19–28, 1940.

Positif. Dossier on D. W. Griffith in nos. 262 (1982), 264 (1983), 265 (1983), and 266 (1983).

Ramsaye, Terry. *"The Birth of a Nation."* In *A Million and One Nights: A History of the Motion Picture Through 1925* [1926]. New York: Simon and Schuster, 1986.

Rebhorn, Marlette. *"The Birth of a Nation:* Prejudice Triumphant." In *Screening America: Using Hollywood Films to Teach History.* New York: Peter Lang, 1988.

Rogin, Michael. "The Great Mother Domesticated: Sexual Difference and Sexual Indifference in D. W. Griffith's *Intolerance." Critical Inquiry* 15, no. 3 (Spring 1989): 510–555.

———. "'The Sword Became a Flashing Vision': D. W. Griffith's *The Birth of a Nation." Representations* 9 (Winter 1985): 150–195. Reprinted in *Ronald Reagan, The Movie and Other Episodes in Political Demonology.* Berkeley and Los Angeles: University of California Press, 1987.

Schickel, Richard. *D. W. Griffith: An American Life.* New York: Simon and Schuster, 1984.

Silva, Fred, ed. *Focus on "The Birth of a Nation."* Englewood Cliffs, N.J.: Prentice-Hall, 1971.

Silverman, Joan L. *"The Birth of a Nation:* Prohibition Propaganda." *The Southern Quarterly* 19, nos. 3–4 (Spring–Summer 1981): 14–21.

Simcovitch, Maxim. "The Impact of Griffith's *Birth of a Nation* on the Modern Ku Klux Klan." *Journal of Popular Film* (Winter 1972): 45–54.

Sorlin, Pierre. "The American Civil War" [*The Birth of a Nation*]. In *The Film in History: Restaging the Past.* Totowa, N.J.: Barnes and Noble Books, 1980.

———. *"La Naissance d'une nation* ou la reconstruction de la famille." *L'Avant-Scène du Cinéma* 193–194 (October 1977): 4–13.

Spears, Jack. "Milestone and Masterpiece: *The Birth of a Nation."* In *The Civil War on the Screen, and*

Other Essays. Cranbury, N.J.: A. S. Barnes, 1977.

Staiger, Janet. *"The Birth of a Nation:* Reconsidering Its Reception." In *Interpreting Films: Studies in the Historical Reception of American Cinema.* Princeton, N.J.: Princeton University Press, 1992.

Stern, Seymour. *"The Birth of a Nation." Cinemages* 1 (1955): 9.

———. "Griffith: I—*The Birth of a Nation." Film Culture* 36, Special Griffith Issue (Spring–Summer 1965).

———. "Griffith Not Anti-Negro." *Sight and Sound* 16, no. 61 (Spring 1947): 32–35.

———. "Suppression of Showing Marks 25th Year of *Birth of a Nation." New Leader,* March 16, 1940, 3.

Taylor, Clyde. "The Re-birth of the Aesthetic in Cinema." *Wide Angle* 13, nos. 3–4 (July–October 1991): 12–30.

Tyler, Bruce M. "Racist Art and Politics at the Turn of the Century." *The Journal of Ethnic Studies* 15, no. 4 (Winter 1988): 85–103.

Vardac, A. Nicholas. *Stage to Screen: Theatrical Origins of Early Film: David Garrick to D. W. Griffith* [1949]. New York: Da Capo Press, 1987.

Wagenknecht, Edward, and Anthony Slide. *The Films of D. W. Griffith.* New York: Crown Publishers, 1975.

Watts, Richard, Jr. "D. W. Griffith." *New Theater and Film* (November 1936). Reprinted in *New Theater and Film, 1934 to 1937,* edited by Herbert Kline. San Diego: Harcourt Brace Jovanovich, 1985.

White, Mimi. *"The Birth of a Nation:* History as Pretext." *Enclitic* 5, no. 2/6, no. 1 (Fall 1981/Spring 1982): 17–24.

Williams, Martin. *Griffith: First Artist of the Movies.* New York: Oxford University Press, 1980.

Wood, Gerald. "From *The Clansman* and *The Birth of a Nation* to *Gone With the Wind:* The Loss of American Innocence." In *Recasting: Gone With the Wind in American Culture,* edited by Darden Asbury Pyron. Miami: University Presses of Florida, 1983.